CW01261015

Reading Gladstone

Reading Gladstone

Ruth Clayton Windscheffel
St Hilda's College, Oxford

palgrave
macmillan

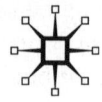

© Ruth Clayton Windscheffel 2008

All rights reserved. No reproduction, copy or transmission of this publication may be made without written permission.

No portion of this publication may be reproduced, copied or transmitted save with written permission or in accordance with the provisions of the Copyright, Designs and Patents Act 1988, or under the terms of any licence permitting limited copying issued by the Copyright Licensing Agency, Saffron House, 6-10 Kirby Street, London EC1N 8TS.

Any person who does any unauthorised act in relation to this publication may be liable to criminal prosecution and civil claims for damages.

The author has asserted his right to be identified as the author of this work in accordance with the Copyright, Designs and Patents Act 1988.

First published 2008 by
PALGRAVE MACMILLAN

Palgrave Macmillan in the UK is an imprint of Macmillan Publishers Limited, registered in England, company number 785998, of Houndmills, Basingstoke, Hampshire RG21 6XS.

Palgrave Macmillan in the US is a division of St Martin's Press LLC, 175 Fifth Avenue, New York, NY 10010.

Palgrave Macmillan is the global academic imprint of the above companies and has companies and representatives throughout the world.

Palgrave® and Macmillan® are registered trademarks in the United States, the United Kingdom, Europe and other countries.

ISBN-13: 978-0-230-00765-9   hardback
ISBN-10: 0-230-00765-1   hardback

This book is printed on paper suitable for recycling and made from fully managed and sustained forest sources. Logging, pulping and manufacturing processes are expected to conform to the environmental regulations of the country of origin.

A catalogue record for this book is available from the British Library.

A catalog record for this book is available from the Library of Congress.

10 9 8 7 6 5 4 3 2 1
17 16 15 14 13 12 11 10 09 08

Printed and bound in Great Britain by
CPI Antony Rowe, Chippenham and Eastbourne

To my family and the staff of St Deiniol's Library

Turning now to the title of this paper, I remind the reader that the history of which it speaks is not the limited and fragmentary record commonly known under that name, but is nothing less than the sum total of human life and human experience, as lived and as gathered on the surface of the globe, within the lines already laid down. And here arises my concluding question. If in history, thus understood, there is an unity, should there not be a reflection of that unity in study? ... Each writer is bettering (if he be not worsening) the thought, the frame, or the experience of man, upon the subject on which he writes, works, or teaches; he is enlarging the text; he is extending the bounds of the common inheritance.

William Ewart Gladstone[1]

Statues more or less representative of him have been reared here and there, but the books of St Deiniol's tell more of the kind of man William Ewart Gladstone was than could any sculpted marble or storied brass.

James Capes Story[2]

Contents

List of Figures	viii
Acknowledgements	xiii
List of Abbreviations	xvi
Introduction	1

Part I Reading the Reader

1 *Sacred Dramas*: The History of a Collection, 1815–96	23
2 Rhythms of Reading	44

Part II Making the Reader

3 The Gentleman's Inheritance, 1809–36	81
4 A Place of Deceptive Tranquillity: Gladstone's Temple of Peace	101

Part III St Deiniol's Library

5 Humanity: Libraries, Literature, and Liberalism	131
6 Divinity: Gladstone, Oxford, and *Lux Mundi*	159

Part IV Transforming the Reader

7 Political Lotus-Eater to Grand Old Bookman: Re-presenting Gladstone the Reader	193
Conclusion	234
Notes	240
Bibliography	296
Index	319

Figures

Figure 0.1　John Tenniel, 'Critics', *Punch, or the London Charivari*, 14 May 1870. St Deiniol's Library Collection　9
Figure 1.1　'The Study, Hawarden Castle', G. B. Smith, *The Life of the Right Honourable William Ewart Gladstone* (London, Paris and New York, n.d.), vol. II, p. 257. St Deiniol's Library Collection　32
Figure 1.2　The Exterior of the 'Tin Tabernacle' (1890). Flintshire Record Office Photographic Collection　39
Figure 1.3　The Interior of the 'Tin Tabernacle' (Divinity Room) (n.d.) Flintshire Record Office Photographic Collection　39
Figure 3.1　Thomas Hargreaves, *William and Helen Gladstone* (c. 1816). C. A. Gladstone　82
Figure 3.2　Alexander Munro, 'Sketch for John and Anne Gladstone's Memorial, Fasque', May 1854, GG MS 450. C. A. Gladstone　98
Figure 3.3　Alexander Munro, 'Sketch for John and Anne Gladstone's Memorial, Fasque', June 1854, GG MS 450. C. A. Gladstone　99
Figure 3.4　Alexander Munro, *The Gladstone Memorial, Fasque* (1854). C. A. Gladstone　100
Figure 4.1　*Temple of Peace, Hawarden Castle* (c. 1880). Flintshire Record Office Photographic Collection　103
Figure 4.2　*The Library at Fasque* (2002). C. A. Gladstone. Photograph: the author　105
Figure 4.3　*The Hawarden Castle Library* (n.d.). Flintshire Record Office Photographic Collection　106
Figure 4.4　Alexander Munro, *Paolo and Francesca* (1853). Birmingham Museums and Art Gallery　118
Figure 4.5　William Dyce, *Beatrice*, or, *Lady with Coronet of Jasmine* (1859). Aberdeen Art Gallery　122

Figure 6.1	'St Deiniol's Library: the Warden's room', H. Friederichs, *In the Evening of his Days* (London, 1896), p. 122. St Deiniol's Library Collection	179
Figure 6.2	'St Deiniol's Hostel: the prayer room', H. Friederichs, *In the Evening of his Days* (London, 1896), p. 141. St Deiniol's Library Collection	180
Figure 6.3	'The Aged Reader', *William Ewart Gladstone* (Bristol, 1898). St Deiniol's Library Collection	187
Figure 7.1	William Bradley, *William Ewart Gladstone* (1839). C. A. Gladstone	195
Figure 7.2	'H.B'. [John Doyle], *The New Christmas Pantomime* (1845). University of Manchester	196
Figure 7.3	William Bradley, *William Ewart Gladstone* (1841). Provost and Fellows of Eton College. Photograph: the Courtauld Institute	197
Figure 7.4	John Lucas, *William Ewart Gladstone* (1843). Glenalmond College	202
Figure 7.5	'Holiday Occupations of the Gladstone Ministry', *Penny Illustrated Paper*, 9 August 1873, GG MSS. C. A. Gladstone	208
Figure 7.6	'Far from the Madding Crowd', *Judy*, 27 January 1875. St Deiniol's Library Collection	210
Figure 7.7	William Currey, *William Ewart Gladstone and William Henry Gladstone* (1877). Flintshire Record Office Photographic Collection	216
Figure 7.8	William Currey, *William Ewart Gladstone* (1877). Flintshire Record Office Photographic Collection	217
Figure 7.9	*Gladstone and Family Woodcutting* (n.d.) Flintshire Record Office Photographic Collection	218
Figure 7.10	Sydney Prior Hall, *Gladstone Reading the Lesson in Hawarden Church* (1892). National Portrait Gallery, London	219
Figure 7.11	Sydney Prior Hall, *Gladstone Reading in the Temple of Peace* (n.d.). National Portrait Gallery, London	220
Figure 7.12	Sydney Prior Hall, *Gladstone Reading in the Temple of Peace* (Watercolour Study) (n.d.). National Portrait Gallery, London	221

x *Figures*

Figure 7.13	John McLure Hamilton, *William Ewart Gladstone sitting at his literary desk in the Temple of Peace* (*c.* 1896). C.A. Gladstone	222
Figure 7.14	*Gladstone in the Temple of Peace* (*c.* 1885). Flintshire Record Office Photographic Collection	225
Figure 7.15	J. H. Spencer, *Gladstone lying in state in the Temple of Peace* (1898). National Archives, London	230
Figure 7.16	J. H. Spencer, *Gladstone lying in state in the Temple of Peace* (1898). National Archives, London	230

Published with the generous support of the
Isobel Thornley Bequest, University of London

Acknowledgements

In January 1999, I left Oxford and work on one venerable legacy of the Victorian age – the Oxford English Dictionary – for North Wales and life in another nineteenth-century cultural institution – St Deiniol's Library. I spent four years in Hawarden studying the reading habits, book collecting, and surviving library of four-times British prime minister William Gladstone, generously supported by scholarships from the University of Chester and the Library's Warden and Trustees. This research underpinned my doctoral thesis (awarded by the University of Liverpool in 2003) and several articles, and firmly undergirds the present study. My endeavours were encouraged and inspired by two dedicated PhD supervisors – Dr Jon Lawrence and Professor Roger Swift. Their professionalism, scholarliness, and lightness of touch all combined to make my experience of graduate life both enjoyable and challenging, and their continued support continues to elicit my deepest gratitude.

In St Deiniol's Library I discovered not only a remarkable archive, but also a second home. The professional and personal debts which I owe to all the staff of this unique institution are very great. Above all I must record my heartfelt thanks to Peter and Helen Francis, Gregory Morris, Karen Parry, and Patsy Williams – all of whom have become dear friends as well as having been congenial colleagues. The interdisciplinary ethos and refreshingly non-hierarchical atmosphere of St Deiniol's make it a particularly conducive atmosphere in which to study. My work owes much to the many residents at, and friends of, St Deiniol's with whom I have discussed Gladstone over the years. I would like, in particular, to thank Ian Bradley, Colin Cruise, Malcolm Hicks, Bill Pritchard, Lionel Madden, and Michael Wheeler for many stimulating discussions. I also owe a significant debt to that dedicated and eclectic band of Gladstone scholars and enthusiasts who have sheltered under the 'Gladstone Umbrella' at St Deiniol's since 1999. This annual colloquium has been a great source of inspiration to me, and the friendships which have been forged under its auspices are highly prized. In this context I express my gratitude for the guidance and rigour of David Bebbington; the comradeship of Mark Nixon; the insight, humour, and wise counsel of Roland Quinault; and the support and encouragement of Jenny West.

Apart from St Deiniol's, two academic institutions in particular have contributed significantly to the production of this book. During the academic year 2003–4 I held an academic tutorship at the University of Strathclyde in Glasgow. The challenging task of transforming thesis to book began there and was greatly facilitated by the supportiveness of my colleagues, particularly David Brown, Richard Finlay, Conan Fischer, Jim Mills, Rogelia Pastor-Castro, John Young, and Bill Wurthmann.

To St Hilda's College, Oxford, I also owe a substantial debt. My four-year research fellowship here has not only enabled me to finish this project and begin new work, it has also provided me with a congenial and tranquil academic base. I have particular thanks to offer to Judith English (Principal 2001–7) and the College's Governing Body for affording me this unique opportunity; to my fellow historians – Anna Bayman, Janet Howarth, Hannah Smith, and Jenny Wormald – for their friendship and advice; and to all my students. I would also like to thank Alexandra Wilson, not only for our invaluable discussions of Victoriana, but also for our friendship, which began at St Hilda's.

Although so much of my research was undertaken at St Deiniol's, a number of other libraries, archives, museums and galleries and their staff require my thanks: Flintshire Record Office; the Bodleian Library, Oxford; Pusey House, Oxford; the Heinz Library and Archive, National Portrait Gallery; the British Library; the Department of Prints and Drawings, the British Museum; and Audrey Linkman and the Manchester Photography Archive. My profound thanks also go to Sir William Gladstone for his sustained interest in this project, for allowing me access to the Temple of Peace in Hawarden Castle, and for assisting me to obtain illustrations for this book. My thanks also go to my Palgrave editors: Michael Strang, Ruth Ireland, and Sailendra Dewan. Needless to say, the responsibility for any remaining errors is entirely mine.

For formal permissions to reproduce material in this volume – both text and visual – I wish to thank and acknowledge Mr Charles Gladstone; the BBC; Stephen Knowles; Flintshire Record Office; Aberdeen Art Gallery; Birmingham Museums and Art Gallery; Eton College; the Courtauld Institute; the University of Manchester; Glenalmond College, Perthshire; the National Archives, London; Special Collections of the Honnold / Mudd Library for the Claremont Colleges, Claremont, California; and the Warden and Trustees of St Deiniol's Library, Hawarden. Every effort has been made to trace rights holders, but if any have been inadvertently overlooked the author and publishers would be pleased to make the necessary arrangements at the first opportunity.

This book would not have been written without the affection, humour, and loyalty of a great many friends, all of whom have contributed in a number of diverse, but equally important, ways to my completion of what follows. In particular I would like to thank Rob Berry; Mike Davis; Matthew Grimley and Catherine Holmes; Zoltán Hesley; Alison and Mark Hornsey; Juliet and Marty Jopson; Sheila and George Kerr; David Lambert and Carolyn Andrews; John-Paul McCarthy; Simon Morgan; Natalia Nowakowska and Nick Kerigan; Rowan O'Neill; Abbie and Steve Palmer; Jonathan and Nicola Phillips; and Alan and Katy Robinson.

My parents, Graham and Brenda Clayton, have inspired and supported me in all my endeavours for 35 years; my brother Adam and sister-in-law Pippa have been unstinting, unconditional, and irreplaceable in their love and encouragement. For these reasons, as well as much else, *Reading Gladstone* is dedicated to them. I would also like to thank my parents-in-law, Malcolm and Susan, and brother-in-law Philip for their warm and generous support. Monty has been an invaluable companion, especially by insisting that I take regular breaks from writing for restorative walks in the park.

My last and most important thanks are reserved for my husband, Alex. I am very grateful that despite having first heard me speak about the Grand Old Man in 2004, he has continued to listen patiently ever since. I find it almost impossible to do justice to how fundamentally his love, friendship, humour, and perspicacity have contributed, not only to what follows, but to all I have accomplished over the last three years. Quite simply, without Alex, neither this book nor my life would be complete.

RCW
Oxford, Christmas 2007

Abbreviations

AMG	Anne Mackenzie Gladstone, sister
ARG	Anne Robertson Gladstone, mother
BL GP	British Library, The Gladstone Papers [Additional Manuscripts 44086–44835]
CG	Catherine Gladstone, wife
EST	Edward Stuart Talbot, warden of Keble College, Oxford and nephew by marriage
FRO	Flintshire Record Office, Hawarden
GD	M. R. D. Foot and H. C. G. Matthew, eds, *The Gladstone Diaries: with prime ministerial correspondence*, 14 vols (Oxford, 1968–96)
GG	The Glynne-Gladstone Manuscripts
HJG	Helen Jane Gladstone, sister
HNG	Henry Neville Gladstone, son
JG	Sir John Gladstone, father
NPG	National Portrait Gallery
ODNB	*Oxford Dictionary of National Biography* (2004)
PMP	J. Brooke and M Sorensen, eds, *The Prime Minister's Papers: W. E. Gladstone*, 4 vols (London, 1971)
RG	Robertson Gladstone, brother
SDL	St Deiniol's Library
SEG	Stephen Edward Gladstone, son
TG	Thomas Gladstone, brother
WEG	William Ewart Gladstone

Introduction

'An omnivorous reader, a constant purchaser, and the recipient of many gifts from authors, Mr. Gladstone has been accumulating books all his life.' So *Harper's New Monthly Magazine* described Gladstone the reader in 1882.[1] One of a burgeoning number of publications noticing and discoursing – more or less accurately – on the statesman's reading, *Harper's* did not underestimate the length, the nature, or the seriousness of Gladstone's bibliographical habits. When he died in 1898, Gladstone had read, according to his diary, approximately 20,000 titles (including periodical articles), written by over 4500 authors.[2] He had also accumulated a sizeable library of more than 30,000 items. There is no doubt that Gladstone's books held a position of central importance to his life: he spent a goodly proportion of it reading in his library, and the collection provided him with an invaluable resource for both his professional and personal endeavours. Furthermore, Gladstone's principal retirement project during the 1880s and 90s was the foundation of a library, constructed in galvanized iron and named after the Welsh saint Deiniol, which received the majority of his books. What is more, this foundation was chosen to serve as Gladstone's national memorial following his death – the books being re-housed in a suitably grand gothic edifice – in an act which situated his identity as a reader, as well as his books themselves, at the very centre of his official legacy.

In many ways this decision accurately reflected the high levels of contemporary public interest in Gladstone's reading and library at his death. A report published in *The Library* in 1898, observed of Gladstone that nothing was 'so engaging the attention of his biographers in the daily and weekly press as his love of his library, his power of absorbing himself in his books whether in or out of office and often under the most engrossing aspect of public affairs'.[3] This was no understatement: whole pieces were devoted to Gladstone's bibliographical interests. Nor was this interest purely generated by the death itself: in 1890, for example, Gladstone had been featured as one of the *Bookworm's* series of 'Bookworms of Yesterday and To-day',[4] and, in 1896, the *Westminster Gazette* had published Hulda Friederichs's *In the Evening of his Days: a study of Mr. Gladstone in retirement, with some account of St Deiniol's Library and Hostel*.[5] As well as press interest, many contemporary popular biographies contained chapters devoted to Gladstone's home life, library, and amazing reading habits. Moreover, the inclusion of such material was regarded as essential to the audience's understanding of Gladstone. As Arthur John Butler observed in 1899 of Gladstone's scholarly and literary interests: 'Any account of Mr. Gladstone's career which should fail to consider this side of his activity would indeed be hopelessly incomplete.'[6]

The constancy of Gladstone's reading – running like an uninterrupted skein throughout his periods of office as well as through his interludes of retirement, and strongly reinforced by the memorial library's institution – ensured that biographers and commentators continued to feel Gladstone's relationship with books to be an important factor when weighing his significance. All the full-scale biographies subsequent to John Morley's 1903 three-volume official portrait pay some attention to Gladstone as a reader and annotator, as a collector of books, and as the founder of St Deiniol's Library. However, while instinctive expressions of astonishment at the scale and breadth of his reading have been constant, less interest has been shown in why and how he read, how he collected and used his library, and in how reading functioned as part of those tense negotiations which took place between his public and private roles. What investigations of these topics there have been have remained, for many years, both small scale and low key. Likewise, the St Deiniol's foundation itself has featured consistently, but not significantly, in Gladstone biography since the 1950s. The tenor of the majority of descriptions is descriptive: when and how Gladstone founded the library and how he funded and organized it, with very little being essayed on the question of why Gladstone founded St Deiniol's.

Reading Gladstone

These largely unexplored questions are the ones which animate this monograph. The reading Gladstone of the title signifies, in the first instance, a particular persona. Reading Gladstone refers to Gladstone's persona when he was engaging with texts, a persona this study seeks to explore by examining how his reading functioned as an expression of self: as a personal habit, a regulator of individual existence, or, in other words, a measure of time. Whether as a diversion or a studious, educative practice, reading and working with books contributed significantly, not only to Gladstone's quotidian experiences, but also to his remembrance of the past – his own, his family's, and that of his religion, his nation, and its culture – as well as his projections for the future, as demonstrated, for example, by his ambitious reading timetables and authorial projects. What kind of person, then, was Gladstone the reader? Where did this compulsion to read and collect books come from? What led him to the books he bought and read? What was it about him – his personality, aspirations, and anxieties – that made him read? What did he hope to gain from his hours of concentrated study, or his few stolen minutes with a book? What did he think the consequences of his reading might be? Did Gladstone the reader change over time, and if so, why and how? Moreover, what influence did external factors have? How much impact did his family, upbringing and education, friends and faith, position and profession have on making him the voracious reader that he was? Did it make a difference where he did his reading?

In turn, what effect did the routines, patterns, as well as habits of mind engendered by Gladstone's reading have on those who surrounded him? Encounters with Gladstone the reader were commonplace, whether one was a member of his family and household, friend or professional acquaintance, an object of philanthropic endeavour, a fellow traveller, or one constituent in a teeming crowd. To whom did Gladstone wish to talk or ask about books and why? What was the origin of this compulsion to transmit book knowledge to others, and in what frames of reference did it operate?

Reading Gladstone therefore also connotes the endeavours of others to decode and deal with this somewhat irrepressible figure. How was Gladstone the reader and scholar regarded by his contemporaries? As simply representative of a familiar class of privileged, well-educated men, with both the wealth and leisure to afford to indulge in the wide reading and scholarly reflections apparently demanded by the altruistic imperatives of 'public life'? Or was he seen as out of the ordinary – extreme, odd, and uncharacteristically, if not dangerously, bookish? This book also seeks to uncover how contemporaries sought to read Gladstone and what they really thought of him, not just in the hagiographical period following his death but also while he was alive and reading. Evidence of reception and reader-response is notoriously fugitive, especially when we are seeking it in popular or ephemeral domains, but the fact that we might not find does not mean that we should not look. We should not expect the reception of Gladstone the reader to be straightforward or unchanging. The processes of re-reading, re-evaluation, and re-assessment were going on here too, and not purely in response to the activities of Gladstone himself.

Reading Gladstone also alludes to our attempts to read him as an historical figure. This is the Gladstone we construct through reading and analysing his own surviving diaries, letters, speeches, articles, as well as by weighing contemporary opinion and accumulated scholarship. This reading Gladstone has not, so far, been regularly equated in the historiography with the ones discussed above. It is argued here that, firstly, a more focused and secure correlation is required, and, secondly, that an approach to understanding Gladstone, which is rooted in the contingencies and ephemeralities of reading practice has much to recommend it, freighted as it is with myriad implications for our reading and understanding of Gladstone in a variety of public and private spheres. This is, firstly, because reading Gladstone acknowledges that, by studying Gladstone, we are reading a text – in fact a series of them – all constructed, and often mediated, accessorized, and sometimes polished products aimed at particular audiences. When contemporary biographers, such as David Williamson and John G. Smith, purposefully set out to write 'non-political' biographies of 'Gladstone the man', they tacitly recognized the extent to which Gladstone's public image was both a creation and a filtered façade, while attempting themselves to go beyond it.[7] And, as John Gardiner has noted, Gladstone has, since his death, continued to be constantly reinterpreted and reconfigured – wittingly or not – according to changing needs and priorities.[8] It is argued here that, partly because of the persistence of a number of long-established historiographical paradigms and also because of the type of sources used, many of these transmogrifications have succeeded in shoring up, rather than challenging, old orthodoxies. Conversely, the Gladstone who reread, re-annotated, and re-evaluated books was not an individual of easily identifiable fixed convictions, or demonstrably linear mental development, and as such sits uncomfortably and questioningly with many extant Gladstonian personifications. Gladstone's reading – and by this I mean not just the physical record represented by his surviving books, many of them crackling with his terse annotations, but also his hermeneutical reading of what it meant to operate as an intellectual in politics – can help us understand more fully what, for example, motivated and shaped his emergence from scholarly retirement to protest the 'Bulgarian atrocities', draw attention to the plight of Afghanistan's hill villages, and champion the Irish Home Rule cause. This is a work which, I believe, offers us important and previously overlooked insights into Gladstone's complex and enigmatic imaginary. It does so by repeatedly indicating how complicated, unchronological, and imaginative such processes were, challenging many of our longheld assumptions as a result. Furthermore, by so interrogating the workings of a particular category of Gladstonian representations – those generated by and in response to his reading – we are also impelled to try and read his audiences engaged in their own multifarious acts of reading.

The place of reading in Gladstonian scholarship

The publication of the *Gladstone Diaries*, between 1968 and 1996, reaffirmed for modern students of Gladstone the sheer importance of books and reading in his life, and brought the surviving evidence of Gladstone's library and reading to the attention of a larger audience. The remarkable index of Gladstone's reading compiled from Gladstone's daily lists, and Colin Matthew's emphatic endorsement of the diary's importance promised at last to bring Gladstone the reader into the spotlight. Matthew himself drew on his unparalleled knowledge of Gladstone's diary and lists of reading in his definitive biography, which sought to integrate Gladstone's reading into the traditional political narrative. Roy Jenkins, the author of one the most lively retellings of Gladstone's life, remained so fascinated by his subject's reading habits after his book's publication that he spoke about it regularly, speculating excitedly about the psychological significance of Gladstone's 'obsession'.[9] Such an approach was adopted seriously by Travis Crosby, who plausibly suggests that Gladstone's collection and ordering of books was essentially stress-relieving behaviour.[10] However, by far the most important contribution to this field, drawing deeply on the evidence of Gladstone's reading, is David Bebbington's monograph, *The Mind of Gladstone: religion, Homer and politics*, published by Oxford University Press in 2004.[11] This scholarly book is not only one of the most significant recent contributions to Gladstonian studies but also to the wider histories of nineteenth-century liberalism, religion, and intellectual life. Fundamental to the book's achievement is its author's immersion in the statesman's reading. Bebbington points to the necessity of understanding Gladstone's relationship with books in his introduction, and encourages further work, pointing out that his monograph is 'a case-study in the evolution of Gladstone's thinking', not a full intellectual biography.[12] For, although Bebbington comments on many aspects of Gladstone's reading, demonstrates the importance of his private library, draws renewed attention to the books of St Deiniol's as crucial historical sources for the Gladstone scholar, and in many ways implicitly demonstrates the intellectual context for its foundation, he does not seek to provide a fully integrated, cultural history of either Gladstone reading or his library.[13] In an ambitious chapter recently published, William McKelvy offers some stimulating suggestions about how to read Gladstone's reading in the context of a discussion loosely focusing on Gladstone's Homeric studies.[14] Drawing on an earlier encyclopaedia article on Gladstone the reader, McKelvy gives a clear indication of the possibilities offered by the interdisciplinary approach adopted here, although the limited scope of both his source material and his word limit makes it hard for him to demonstrate the truth of many of his conclusions, as does his neglect of St Deiniol's.[15] Essays by Peter J. Jagger, Frederick W. Ratcliffe, and T. W. Pritchard remain the main published sources of information on the latter, and, while they provide valuable, concise narratives, making important use of diary entries, family letters, and uncatalogued documents relating to the library's foundation, they are necessarily limited in scope and analytical intensity.[16] The lack of in-depth interpretations is compounded by the fact that, by and large, those focusing on Gladstone's political life have found his library difficult to explain within their frame of reference. Colin Matthew sees Gladstone's planning of St Deiniol's as evidence of the septuagenarian's optimism, sharing a belief with Jenkins that the practical organization of the library project took the place of tree felling as Gladstone's physical exercise. They also concur in thinking that Gladstone designed the library 'as his memorial',[17] making ultimately unhelpful comparisons with the American presidential practice of instituting memorial libraries. Misleading interpretations such as these remain standing, not only because St Deiniol's has not so far been effectively interrogated by those approaching Gladstone with a primary interest in his intellectual development, but also because more than a little resistance has been offered to such revisionist perspectives. Bebbington's reconfiguring work has, for example, attracted strong criticism from some quarters, questioning the efficacy of placing the study of Gladstone's intellectual life on a level with that of his political existence.[18] Previous essays in the craft were similarly criticized. For example, in 1986, Michael Lynch disparaged

Peter Jagger's attempt to articulate the importance of St Deiniol's as part of Gladstone's life and legacy.[19] This strongly suggests that this long-term sidelining of Gladstone the reader is deeply rooted, firstly, in long established historiographical conceptualizations of Gladstone as a political figure, and, secondly, in the generic nature of the traditional biographical form.

The political animal

Gladstone is still predominantly seen as a political animal. While in theory this is both understandable and justified, the conservative frames of reference which many Gladstonian scholars continue to adopt are not. Recent popular synopses, by Eugenio Biagini and Michael Partridge, largely follow a traditional formula, while the overriding political emphasis of the last Gladstone biography to be published in the grand style, Richard Shannon's exhaustive and intricate two-volume *magnum opus*, is somewhat constraining.[20] As Stefan Collini commented at the time of the latter's publication:

> At times ... the perspective of the biographer as retrospective lobby correspondent can seem a little restricted ... Gladstone's intellectual and literary life occupies very little space indeed in this huge book ... When in 1894 he [Gladstone] does, finally relinquish the premiership, at the age of 85, Shannon deals briskly with his retirement plans.[21]

Shannon is not alone in paying less attention than he might to Gladstone's last years: Philip Magnus, for instance, described Gladstone as 'a retired Titan in impotent old age'.[22] As well as being symptomatic of privileging Gladstone's official, public life, such brevity reflects the selectivity common to, but not always sufficiently recognized or justified by, biographers. On the contrary, it is argued here that we should look again at Gladstone's last years. Gladstone's retirement was a time of major and far-reaching projects, most significantly the development and publicizing of St Deiniol's Library, an endeavour on which he lavished as much commitment and research as he was wont to invest in his political activities. Furthermore, Gladstone's attitude to retirement, which had been seriously occupying him for decades before he did finally withdraw, was complex, and, considering the real shift in cultural attitudes to that period of life occurring in the late-nineteenth century, is worthy of further historical attention.[23]

The stimulating methodologies and insights offered by those interdisciplinary cultural studies which have burgeoned over recent years have had a minimal impact on the methodologies, perspectives, and assumptions which students of Gladstone have habitually employed. Perhaps the most glaring omission is that of a sustained gendered analysis of Gladstone.[24] Furthermore, there remains important work to be done regarding the representation and reception of Gladstone in a variety of spheres. That a figure who was both so personally eclectic and who operated as such a multifaceted cultural icon within his society should not have been reassessed from such perspectives is surprising. In contrast, the historiography of Gladstone's great 'rival', Benjamin Disraeli, has evolved an entirely different set of historical concerns and interests. Disraeli was a successful novelist, celebrated wit, and dandy, as well as accomplished politician, and these aspects of his personality are reflected in recent scholarly treatments of him. These include cross-disciplinary explorations of his romanticism, Orientalism, ethno-cultural and national identities, and of his interpretation of history.[25] This historiographical difference in many ways perpetuates assumptions established when the two men were still alive, as illustrated in the 1870 *Punch* cartoon 'Critics' (Figure 0.1).

Drawn by John Tenniel and captioned 'Mr. G-D-S-T-NE. "Hm! – Flippant!" Mr. D-S-R-LI. "Ha! – Prosy!"', this image not only exhibited Gladstone's reputation for disapproving ponderousness among his contemporaries, here referring directly to his scholarship and literary criticism, but also reinforced the popular notion that an intense, personal rivalry – generated by the polar opposition of their personalities – animated Gladstone and Disraeli's often acrimonious encounters.[26] Despite the efforts of a minority of scholars to undermine this persistent paradigm, Gladstone and Disraeli's relationship continues to be viewed through this restricting lens.[27] Moreover, whereas gendered and culturally alert readings of Disraeli proliferate, Gladstone is still seen as a rather severe man preoccupied with politics and overburdened by religion.[28] This is due, importantly, to the fact that most scholarly approaches to Gladstone's life and character fail to engage seriously and methodologically with the ways in which a complex, and ever shifting, array of Gladstonian 'representations' were created, disseminated, and perpetuated during his lifetime and beyond. Even the growing number of discussions focusing on Gladstone's attitudes to women and sex are not as attuned to issues of masculinity and (self) representation as they might be.[29]

Figure 0.1 John Tenniel, 'Critics', *Punch, or the London Charivari*, 14 May 1870. St Deiniol's Library Collection.

Furthermore, until the publication of David Bebbington's *Mind*, Gladstone's classical scholarship had been largely dismissed as amateurish and misguided;[30] his literary output has only sporadically attracted interest;[31] and there has been only limited analysis of his use of historical methods and approaches.[32] Moreover, historians have not, as a rule, taken sufficient notice of the shifts in Gladstone's religious opinions in the very last years of his life.[33]

Gladstone's religion

Biographers have never seriously questioned that Christianity formed the touchstone of Gladstone's world view – his own writings and contemporary opinion leave no doubt – and there are a number of important published studies of Gladstone's religious life, including Peter Jagger's study of his early faith;[34] Perry Butler's stimulating dissection of Gladstone's high churchmanship;[35] Boyd Hilton's exposure of the persistent influence of Gladstone's evangelicalism;[36] and David Bebbington's compelling case demonstrating the liberal tendencies of Gladstone's religion. Many studies – particularly Jonathan Parry's delineation of the role of religion in the collapse of Gladstone's first government[37] – carefully calibrate the connections between the spheres of faith and politics. Nonetheless, there is yet to be a full and equal integration of the important work on Gladstone's complex religious preoccupations into broader conceptualizations of his political life in the 1880s and 90s when he was establishing St Deiniol's.

Gladstone's theological development did not reach a certain point and then stop, any more than did his political evolution. Just as it is simplistic to see the latter as a simple peregrination from conservatism to liberalism, so it is with his theology. The key point of which one must remain aware is that the various terms which we try and use to define Gladstone's religious position at different times – evangelical, high church, liberal, and so on – were not only frequently contested by contemporaries but also are rarely sufficiently flexible for our purposes, and a reluctance to recognize this further obscures our historical perspective.

The first real attempt to explain, rather than try to explain away, such inconsistencies was Perry Butler's study of Gladstone's religious ideas and attitudes up to 1859. Butler began the important work of correcting such simplifications and confusions by demonstrating the transformative effect on Gladstone's religious, intellectual, and political being of the twin – and far from complementary – forces of catholicism and liberalism which galvanized his mission to serve the church from within the political sphere.[38] This uneasy alliance, made as 'a result of a profound political and ecclesiastical readjustment accompanied by not inconsiderable emotional upheaval', Butler argues, served to transform Gladstone's public religious position to that of liberal catholicism. Descriptions of Gladstone as a liberal catholic have not been overused – commentators have preferred the tried and tested label of high churchman – but use of the former soubriquet has the advantage of recasting the tension and complexity, which clearly characterized Gladstone's private and public faith, as essential qualities to be analysed rather than irresolvable problems to be ignored. Butler presents a persuasive and sensitive portrait of Gladstone's religious persona during his first 50 years, but only speculates on how the remainder of Gladstone's career might look, if viewed through the critical lens of liberal catholicism, and his focus remains on Gladstone's politics. Butler's revisionism initially had a limited impact on subsequent studies, leaving scholars such as Richard Shannon, for example, to continue characterizing Gladstone's mature theological position as defensive, and St Deiniol's as his 'bastion of defence' against contemporary attacks on orthodox Christianity, expanding Philip Magnus's claim that the library's 'purpose was to promote "divine learning" and to combat unbelief'.[39]

However, a thorough investigation of the theological underpinnings of Gladstone's liberal catholicism, and a survey of its impact on the second half of his life, is provided by Bebbington's *Mind of Gladstone*. Bebbington corroborates and extends Perry Butler's thesis with evidence mined from Gladstone's spiritual life; in particular his work is based on exhaustive readings of Gladstone's sermons and other theological writings. Bebbington argues that, following the disappointment of his high hopes for Tractarianism and his intensifying dislike for what he saw as an increasing authoritarianism in Roman Catholicism, coupled with the effects of a sharp spiritual crisis in 1850–1, Gladstone's theology developed a more humane character in the years that followed. Without repudiating important aspects of his earlier religious positions, Bebbington contends, Gladstone began to be increasingly receptive to liberal theology and teaching, and to demonstrate liberal influences in his own apologetics. In particular Bebbington stresses the central influence of the eighteenth-century broad church bishop of Durham, Joseph Butler (1692–1752), on this evolution. Gladstone had himself described Butler as one of his four 'doctors' (significant role models or guides), but later commentators increasingly associated the philosopher-theologian with inspiring some of Gladstone's more conservative later apologetics.[40] In particular, Gladstone's two-volume edition of Butler's works, published in 1896, was judged outmoded and traditionalist even by late Victorian standards, and was taken by many as proof of Gladstone's unremitting theological conservatism late in life.[41] Following Jane Garnett's valuable reassessment of the role played by Butler's moral philosophy in late-nineteenth-century theological debate,[42] and building on her observation that Gladstone's edition of Butler, rather than being the result of researches undertaken in the 1880s and 90s, was based on work 'done half a century before',[43] Bebbington demonstrates how the broad thrust of both Gladstone's epistemology and later apologetics had a great deal in common with the contemporaries Garnett quotes. Gladstone's proposition in the 1880s of a liberal *via media* inspired by Butlerian principles, Bebbington further argues, links him with 'a trend of thought just beginning to gather force at that time among younger clergymen, the liberal catholicism of Charles Gore and his *Lux Mundi* circle that blended high ecclesiastical claims with wide intellectual and social sympathies'.[44]

For all Bebbington's painstaking research, some – even those deeply sympathetic to his project – nevertheless remain unconvinced. Frank Turner, for example, has recently judged that 'Bebbington makes a strong but not altogether convincing case for seeing Gladstone as a broad churchman.'[45] While the thrust of Turner's response is misdirected, Bebbington leaves himself open to the criticism that he overstates the liberal influence over Gladstone by drawing his evidence in the first instance from Gladstone's private manuscript writings, and by providing no indication that its effect was either particularly far reaching, practical in nature, or indeed more widely recognized. Moreover, although he refers to the social and family connections which linked Gladstone and the liberal catholic *Lux Mundi* group in Oxford, and points to the fact that they were both influenced by wider liberalizing trends, Bebbington neither makes explicit their direct intellectual engagement nor investigates the *Lux Mundi* group's substantial involvement in the St Deiniol's foundation. Chapter 6 of this book will show the reality and importance of both and demonstrate how St Deiniol's was perhaps the single most important practical outgrowth of Gladstone's liberal catholic sympathies.

Approaches to reading Gladstone

One way to attempt to challenge the assumptions and blind spots detailed above is to attempt to develop and use a genuinely interdisciplinary methodology. It is difficult to overestimate the complexity and constructed nature of human stories such as Gladstone's, particularly in light of now well-established post-modern and post-structuralist critical theories about the self-reflexivity, constructed nature, and contingent operation of historical identities and narratives. The influence of such critiques has already encouraged many historiographical shifts, away from the exclusive and 'objective' concentration on social forces and groups traditionally seen as the originators of identity – social class, writers and intellectuals, political élites, and so forth – towards myriad instances of the dissemination, reception, renegotiation, and subversion of meanings taking place among shifting and frequently elusive audiences.[46] The effect of the 'linguistic turn' has not made a huge impact on Gladstonian studies, although, as Mark Nixon's recent work on liberal historiography demonstrates, there is considerable scope and need for the deconstruction and reconfiguration of Gladstonian identity and historiography along such lines.[47]

One academic field, which is both centrally relevant to the study of Gladstone's library and reading and well grounded in such theoretical approaches, is that usually classified under the names of 'book history' or 'the history of reading'. Still regarded as a new discipline, its seminal texts date back to the mid-twentieth century. Richard D. Altick's *The English Common Reader* and Richard Hoggart's *The Uses of Literacy*, both published in 1957, have, for instance, been widely influential and remain revered.[48] Important refinements have nonetheless occurred during the last two decades, including a decided shift away from sole concentration on the production and circulation of texts towards the interrogation of textual reception and consumption, a move which, once again, reflects the underlying influence of literary and cultural theory.[49] Pioneers in this endeavour include Roger Chartier and Robert Darnton,[50] and their calls, not only for increased recognition of the historical and cultural complexity of activities such as writing, publishing, reading, book collecting, and library ownership, but also for the opening up of new areas of investigation, have fostered a huge expansion in this area of scholarship.[51] For instance, a considerable contribution has been, and is being, made to the history of reading by scholars of gender and women's history,[52] as well as by those interested in readers, class, and status.[53] Moreover, there is a small but ever burgeoning body of literature which seeks to explore the links between reading, books, and visual culture.[54] The value placed on evidences of reception and the shifting and unpredictable behaviours of audiences by scholars of reading has much to offer and teach the reader of Gladstone. A perennial question for the student of reading is whether or not it is possible, in the words of Roger Chartier, to 'organize this indistinguishable plurality of individual acts according to shared regularities'.[55] Some historians have made general claims on the basis of very specific reading responses left by Gladstone, and yet in many cases these have been made without a broader understanding of how and why Gladstone read in general. This book sets out to provide a survey of that broad and rich context, in order not only to undergird but also to challenge the significance of isolated individual pieces of reading evidence.

This study, by examining Gladstone in the context of his library, aims to cut through many long-established categorizations of Gladstone, and to offer a wide-ranging cultural reading extending beyond the boundaries of traditional political history or intellectual biography. In so doing, it draws on insights and methodologies drawn from literary studies, art history, the history and theory of reading and material culture, as well as theology and history. As no other in-depth study of Gladstone's library and reading exists, this project is both wide-ranging and detailed; simultaneously it aims to display to its readers both the breadth and potential offered by studying Gladstone from this perspective as well as providing a body of firm, new conclusions based on the library evidence. However, the creative tension it maintains between chronology and case study, introduction and detailed analysis, and historical and non-historical methodologies proves the most efficient and exciting way of encapsulating something of the sheer diversity and unfathomable complexity of this vital relationship.

Sources for reading Gladstone

The initial source for building up a basic chronology of Gladstone's pattern of book collecting and arrangement is the fourteen-volume edition of the *Gladstone Diaries*: 'the touchstone for all judgements of Gladstone'.[56] In the *Diaries* we have an extensive record of books, pamphlets, and articles which Gladstone listed as having read, which are collected together alphabetically in a separate section of volume 14 under the heading 'Gladstone's Reading'. In his introduction to this index volume, Colin Matthew explains the significance of such a record:

> I know of no other major figure who attempted to record, day by day, his or her reading over a lifetime ... Since a part of each day was systematically reserved for reading ... and since Gladstone read as eclectically as any Victorian, the record of his reading is a tour not only of Victorian high culture ... but also of the by-ways of nineteenth-century political, religious and literary life.[57]

The diary is essential to an understanding of the chronological development of the library. In its many entries are recorded not only detailed lists of Gladstone's reading but also evidence of book-buying in Britain and Europe, contact with booksellers, and the arrangement, housing, and cataloguing of his growing collection. It also provides information on visits to and comments on major libraries such as the Bodleian, the British Museum Library, and the *Bibliothèque Nationale*, as well as meetings with librarians and other bibliophiles. There are also many entries relating to Gladstone's reading methods. References were also made there to pornography and the use of reading with rescue cases.

However, the source is not without its limitations when used alone, as Colin Matthew stresses:

> There are gaps in this record of his reading. He recorded much – about 17,500 book and pamphlet titles, and in addition to that figure, many periodical titles – but not everything. Nor did he list newspaper reading.[58]

And, as John Powell reiterates, there is the need for 'the cautious use of self-referential evidence' such as the diary.[59] Moreover, as the indexed list of reading in the *Diaries* was not checked against the St Deiniol's collection when it was compiled – for reasons of time and money – its usefulness is somewhat circumscribed.[60] Many of its entries remain editorial conjectures, and the scope of most of the comments based on it are limited to the simple equation between Gladstone's having read a book and having expressed a broader interest in its subject in his diary or elsewhere.

The St Deiniol's collection thus offers the opportunity to expand on the diary evidence in several important ways. Firstly, it presents the prospect, within certain limits, of being able to confirm exactly which texts Gladstone read and owned. For example, not all of Gladstone's books have visible ownership signs such as bookplates and immediately recognizable annotations. There is also the question of the completeness of the collection. Some books, which were part of Gladstone's private library, remain at Hawarden Castle. Duplicates and different editions also pose problems, for St Deiniol's did not necessarily receive the copy listed in the diary, and Gladstone did not always own the books he read, or read the books he owned, as is the case with many book collectors. Secondly, and more importantly, the presence of Gladstone's marginalia within a significant number of these texts – a source which has hardly been used at all by scholars – offers a new and important perspective on Gladstone's reception of texts, and the relationship such reception had with his broader thinking. Furthermore, since the commencement, in February 2006, of a major Arts and Humanities Research Council-funded project to identify and catalogue electronically Gladstone's surviving books in the St Deiniol's collection and to map his annotations, this source's value and accessibility continues to be significantly enhanced.[61]

There has been significant dispute, among scholars of reading, concerning the usefulness of book annotation as a source, some arguing that it is unreliable and unfathomable, others suggesting that it offers privileged access to the reader's mind.[62] In a useful 1992 article on Gladstone's political marginalia, which includes an illuminating micro-study of Gladstone's reading of political biography based on several hundred books in the St Deiniol's collection, John Powell endorses the latter view.[63] Despite the limitations placed on Powell's study by the cryptic nature of Gladstone's annotation code, his work is rightly described by Heather Jackson as a 'fine' model for the study of annotation more generally.[64] Powell gives a thoughtful critique of the annotations as a source. He considers the problems of their often-cryptic nature, and the complex relationship between reader and text. It is dangerous, for example, to assume the direct influence of a text, 'for people sometimes retain the unexpected when reading, or come to a work for seemingly inexplicable reasons or for justifying a position already taken'.[65] Echoing Thomas Jones's earlier recognition that Gladstone's marginalia was 'evidence of an alert, critical, and encyclopædic intelligence', which 'might furnish fresh proof ... of the amazing contents of his voracious mind',[66] Powell nonetheless argues:

> They provide an unparalleled access to Gladstone's inner life, which better informs one's understanding of evidence drawn from traditional sources. They are tangible and verifiable, and therefore may properly be drawn within the scope of historical inquiry. Too, the marginalia further delineate the gap between Gladstone's public and private personalities, suggesting possible explanations for a number of questions which have resisted closure ... since his death. ... The marginalia help one to sense the instinctive personality, before the weight of observation, reflection, duty, and calculation began to impinge.[67]

Jackson usefully qualifies Powell's critique by questioning his assumption that all Gladstone's annotations 'express ... impulsive and unguarded reactions', and offer 'access to the inner life'.[68] As Jackson points out, not all annotations – Gladstone's included – are reflective of impulsive, unformed thoughts. They can sometimes be as cultivated and stylized as conversations.[69] Moreover, there are significant differences between annotation types; fly-leaf summaries and endpaper indexes cannot automatically be treated in the same way as marginal notes. However, Powell's interpretation rings true when one considers Gladstone's attitude to the documentary material that he was to leave behind him. Gladstone must have been aware that, after his death, his letters, diaries, and other writings would be used as references in written accounts of his life. He had, himself, aided researches into the lives of his deceased mentors and contemporaries by allowing access to his letter collections.[70] Yet he left no definite proscription on the use of his own papers, which, considering the content of his diaries, appears surprising. However, one source for which he did legislate was his marginalia. As Hulda Friederichs stressed in her account of St Deiniol's:

> None of Mr. Gladstone's annotations on the margins may be copied or quoted as illustrating his views on certain questions, since such quotations might convey an altogether wrong impression … Mr. Gladstone often jots down marginal remarks when an idea occurs to him while reading, though that idea may in no way represent his views.[71]

Gladstone's role as St Deiniol's first librarian undoubtedly behoved him to take a strong, public line on the practice of annotation, which, as Jackson observes, is 'taboo in the librarian's world'.[72] Nonetheless, this Gladstone-approved account supports the view that the annotations were examples of an unguarded Gladstone, a persona not so clearly to be discerned, for example, in his later, self-conscious autobiographical writings.

One of the most significant limitations placed upon Powell's annotation study is the absence of a definitive explanation of Gladstone's cryptic annotation code. The studies of Gladstone's annotations undertaken in this book, however, have had the advantage of being supported by Gladstone's own written explanation of his annotation code, which I discovered towards the beginning of my research.[73] Whereas previous scholars were forced, through sheer lack of evidence, to admit that 'the scholar will frequently be baffled by a variety of cryptic markings, and that these are better left alone as evidence',[74] this code has provided the means whereby we can be more certain in assigning meaning to Gladstone's succinct, and often apparently inscrutable, marginalia.

Reading Gladstone: A reader's guide

Reading Gladstone is made up of seven chapters divided into four parts. The aim throughout has been to combine chronology with theme, with

Chapters 1, 2, and 7, in particular, offering both narrative overview and thematic analysis. Chapter 1 provides the reader with an historical overview of Gladstone's collecting life from 1815 to 1896. It offers important insights into the ways in which Gladstone collected and organized books and examines his developing identity as a collector. Chapter 2 undertakes the important and necessary task of introducing Gladstone the reader in all his complexity by investigating in detail his reading methods and practice. It also introduces us to those important, distinctive, and influential rhythms which book collecting and reading introduced into Gladstone's life, all of which were affected by time, place, and relationships. Here we begin to understand why, and how, Gladstone formulated opinions, and accrued knowledge, about important topics of his day through reading, and we are thus prepared for seeing these rhythms at work in later chapters.

The heart of the book – Chapters 3–6 – seeks to analyse Gladstone's reading and book collecting as a son and sibling, as independent adult and head of his own household, and as elder statesman and founder of St Deiniol's Library. Chapter 3 investigates Gladstone's early book collecting and reading in more depth, placing it within the twin contexts of his family life and the bibliophilic and educational practices of the late-eighteenth and early-nineteenth centuries. Gladstone is seen growing up, searching for knowledge and identity through self-education, consuming and ordering texts in a pre-Victorian world dominated by romanticism, evangelicalism, and one family's vital and determined understanding of book culture. The chapter explores the family's explicit and, to an extent, problematic gendering of reading purpose and practice as a precursor to looking at Gladstone's search to establish an understanding of what role study, reading, and education should play in his life. Chapter 4 further advances the chronology of Gladstone's life and library through a study centring on the development and function of his private library. Whereas in Chapter 3, Gladstone's book collecting is discussed largely in the context of his family, Chapter 4 focuses on the development of his personal collection and its accommodation in the 'Temple of Peace' in Hawarden Castle – its most significant location – detailing its character, layout, use, function, and its overall importance to its owner. This chapter, and indeed the book as a whole, is concerned with important issues of privacy and intimacy, publicity and distance in relation to Gladstone's reading and book collecting. Hence it concludes with discussion of Gladstone's reading and collecting outside the domestic environment, represented by the Temple of Peace, and investigates the role of reading in his rescue work with prostitutes.

Part III, consisting of Chapters 5 and 6, provides a fully contextualized analysis of the last great transformation in the life of Gladstone's library: its re-birth as a 'public' cultural institution. Following Gladstone's own classificatory division of knowledge into the spheres of 'humanity' and 'divinity', Chapter 5 begins by examining his ideas for how reading and 'mental culture', as represented by libraries, reading rooms, and so forth, could function as promoters of, and sites for, educative and ameliorative liberalism in British society. The chapter further discusses his estimation of literature, and his understanding of 'history' as the key element that individuals, communities, and the Victorian state needed to cultivate, and its relation to his understanding of class, nationality, and community. Chapter 6 turns from 'humanity' and focuses on Gladstone's category of 'divinity', or 'divine learning'. It endorses the view that Gladstone should be described in his later years, not as an ultra-orthodox high church dogmatist, but as a liberal catholic churchman, on the basis of the evidence of an important aspect of the St Deiniol's foundation which has, up until now, been almost completely overlooked: the impact of Gladstone's relationship with the Oxford *Lux Mundi* group. These two chapters together lay bare the complex motivations behind Gladstone's decision to found a residential library in rural north Wales. Issues such as location, function, and the question of community are all addressed, as are questions of privacy and publicity in the case of Gladstone's 'public' library. The chapter concludes by reflecting on how the library represented the ultimate expression of Gladstone's lifelong commitment to contribute to the extension of human knowledge: to enlarge the text. The complexity of this public–private dichotomy attains even more prominence in the final section of the book: 'Transforming the Reader'. Chapter 7 focuses on changes in the public representation and reception of Gladstone as an intellectual during his life. It interrogates – via extensive analysis of visual imagery – the interplay of perception and representation between Gladstone and his publics, and it also integrates the public image of Gladstone's library into our broader understanding of the development of his popular appeal.

This book provides the first in-depth chronological and thematic study of Gladstone's lifetime of book collecting and library building. It revises, and fully contextualizes, the history and significance of St Deiniol's Library, integrating it within the broader context of Gladstone's intellectual and religious life, while simultaneously offering a significant extension to our understanding of Gladstone's later theology and ecclesiastical relationships. By studying Gladstone in the context of his library, this study presents a fresh perspective on his popularity through study of visual representation and analysis of his intellectual and scholarly persona. In addition, this project reinstates an important body of evidence to a prominent place in Gladstonian studies, from which it has too long been missing. It also fulfils a bridging function between the evidence of the books Gladstone owned – his organization, reading, annotation, and opinions upon them – and the wider circumstances and character of his life and career.

Part I Reading the Reader

1
Sacred Dramas: The History of a Collection, 1815–96

On 29 June 1892, Gladstone began what was to be a particularly uncomfortable stay at Dalmeny House, Lord Rosebery's residence to the west of Edinburgh. Awaiting the outcome of the July general election with some trepidation, Gladstone's usual reading programme was hampered, not only by worsening cataracts in his right eye, but also by an injury to his 'left & only serviceable eye' sustained in Chester four days previously. There to visit the city's Liberal club, Gladstone had been hit in the face by a piece of hardened gingerbread flung by a 'middle aged bony woman ... with great force and skill'. Bizarre and amusing as this incident sounds, its results were not: Gladstone was confined to bed for three and a half days and undertook the journey to Scotland 'in dark spectacles'. After suffering an unpleasant relapse during his visit to Glasgow on 2 July, when: 'I thought small thin flat scales were descending upon me: & afterwards observed with some discomfort that there was a fluffy object floating in the fluid of my serviceable eye', Gladstone 'determined to forswear for the time continuous reading, and limit my eyework on papers & material for speeches to *"le strict necessaire"*'.[1]

With Rosebery in a foul and obstructive mood, Catherine Gladstone unwell, ominous electoral prognostics, and reading almost entirely prohibited, Gladstone turned in semi-desperation to an endeavour he had long been deferring: 'that quasi Autobiography which Acton has so strongly urged upon me'.[2] This he began with 'some recollections of my infancy and earliest childhood' in which memories of Liverpool and Scotland featured prominently.[3] These were suitably patchy and disconnected, and Gladstone was about to move on to discuss his family's history, when he recalled an incident to which he clearly attached substantial importance:

> Before quitting the subject of early recollections I must name one which involves another person of some note. My mother took me in 181[5] to Barleywood Cottage, near Bristol. Here lived Mrs. Hannah More with some of her coeval sisters ...
>
> During the afternoon visit ... Hannah More took me aside, and presented to me a little book. It was a copy of her *Sacred Dramas* and it now remains in my possession with my name written in it by her. She very graciously accompanied it with a little speech, of which I cannot recollect the conclusion (or apodosis). But it began: 'As you have just come into the world, and I am just going out of it', etc.[4]

Reminiscing once again, this time in an 1896 letter to his successful bookseller-friend, Bernard Quaritch,[5] Gladstone reiterated the importance of the occasion, fixing it as the moment when, as a five-year-old boy, his book collection began: 'The ... book ... longest in my possession, was presented to me ... in 1815', he wrote, adding that: 'My purchases commenced a few years after that time'.[6]

The inexorable spirit of collection

Following such an initiation, Gladstone embraced the collecting habit enthusiastically. The presence in St Deiniol's Library of his copy of Thomas Frognall Dibdin's advice manual, *The Library Companion* (1824),[7] suggests that Gladstone deliberately planned an extensive collection from an early stage, and was eager to follow appropriate, gentlemanly advice when doing so. Everywhere he went, in his youth and early manhood, Gladstone bought books, and his diary entries abound with references to his purchases. Thus, the fifteen-year-old Eton boy recorded: 'Bought at a book sale Goldsmith's Works, and Breton's China. Much pleased with purchases.' A month later, he paid off his bill – undoubtedly considerable – at T. Ingalton's, the Eton bookseller.[8] Over the following year or two, he was endlessly 'out – looking over a stock of books', frequently making 'a considerable purchase', then: 'Out again – shopping'![9] These patterns continued in later life: 'No figure was more familiar than his to the dealers in old books in London', wrote Wemyss Reid: 'He would spend hours poring over their well-thumbed stores, not disdaining even the poorest collections.'[10] When he was abroad, Gladstone also prioritized the purchase of books. Over the years he was 'busy on the book stalls' of Paris, Milan, Florence, Rome,

Naples, Turin, Cologne, and Cannes, both buying for himself and for others: in July 1837, for example, he was out in Cologne 'bookbuying for Mr G[ladstone]., R[obertson].G[ladstone]., & [the] Carlton Club'.[11]

Such foraging was not always pleasurable – collecting having its share of disappointments, frustrations, and anxieties – as Gladstone was to experience:

> Hunting for books: in Rome: what a labour! For example: for the Statutes of the Sapienza, Petrucci (bookseller) referred me to the Propaganda: the Propaganda to the Stamperia Camerale: and the Stamperia to the printing office: the printing office back to an upper floor of the Stamperia: where I went at one, & it was closed for dinner: again at five, & it was shut for the night.[12]

While Gladstone was clearly a speculative, and sometimes a compulsive buyer, he was not wholly indiscriminate. Many references mention searches for specific works, for instance, when in Athens in 1879, he 'went to S.P.C.K.s Office and hunted up the Sikes Tracts'.[13] Moreover, he was both knowledgeable and astute. In June 1898, one George Angus repeated a Brighton bookseller's anecdote 'as to the keenness of Mr. Gladstone's collecting eye': 'He took up a French book, from, said the bookseller, the library of Catherine de Médicis. "But there's no fleur-de-lis in the top lozenge," objected Mr. Gladstone.'[14]

Gladstone patronized numerous booksellers during his lifetime, including Parker's in Oxford, William and Charles Tait, Manners and Miller – both of Prince's Street, Edinburgh; John Leslie, theological bookseller in Great Queen Street, and Westall's & Co., off the Tottenham Court Road, in London. As well as visiting booksellers in person, Gladstone made extensive use of their catalogues: perusing them at home, marking the volumes he wished to purchase before returning them by post.[15] Edward Hamilton drew attention to Gladstone's vanity as an author-collector when he noted: 'it was a special interest to him, when he went through the catalogues, to see if any of his own works were included among the lots, and at what price they were marked'.[16]

There was an undeniable tension between the 'ardour' and 'inexorable spirit of collection', and the 'considerations springing from the balance-sheet' which frequently troubled Gladstone.[17] He endeavoured to be a prudent collector and, for the most part, succeeded in being so,[18] scrupulously recording when he thought himself extravagant. On one occasion in Florence he was, 'Again at the Booksellers', flying (for me) rather high'.[19] His private papers are littered with annotated catalogues and accounts calculating the cost and value of books. Some of these clearly indicate that he sold off or exchanged books to make way for new ones: for example, in one rough note he added in '11 vols in exchange' to balance his proposed purchases.[20] In addition, Gladstone habitually insisted on a ten per cent discount for cash on second-hand books.[21] In his public comments on book collecting – while he recognized that: 'Book-buyers of the present day have immense advantages in the extended accessibility and cheapness of books'[22] – Gladstone remained utilitarian in his conceptualization of the collector's position and responsibilities. In 'On Books and the Housing of Them', *Nineteenth Century* (March 1890), Gladstone's fullest exposition on the subject, he criticized 'when bindings of a profuse costliness are imposed ... upon letterpress which is respectable journeyman's work and nothing more ... The paper, type, and ink ... and habiliment ... ought to be adjusted to one another by the laws of harmony and good sense'.[23] In addition, his attitude to the proliferation of printed matter at the *fin de siècle* was quasi-Malthusian:

> In every two years nearly a mile of new shelving will be required to meet the wants of a single library. But, whatever may be the present rate of growth, it is small in comparison with what it is likely to become. The key of the question lies in the hands of the United Kingdom and the United States jointly. In this matter there rests upon these two Powers no small responsibility.[24]

Such rhetoric was undoubtedly influenced by Gladstone's ongoing battle to maintain control over his own collecting, but it was also prompted by the recognition that the world of book collecting had changed radically in 80 years.

Early collecting

Things had been very different for the young Gladstone, whose early purchases were largely made with the financial support of his family,[25] who also gave them houseroom.[26] Perhaps because of this dependence, his own early personal collecting went along with tireless work on his father's libraries. All the while, Gladstone bought considerable amounts on his own account, expenditure in which he was encouraged by his parents.[27] During his careers at Eton and Christ Church between 1821 and 1831, the range of his acquisitions went far beyond the standard set texts that he was required to purchase. Moreover, his collection was further swelled by gifts.

Books were integral, not only to the work, but also to the ritual of Eton life. On leaving the college in 1827, therefore, Gladstone was given 'the traditional morocco-bound book',[28] plus various other 'leaving books' from school friends.[29] By far the most precious of these volumes was 'a copy of Mr. Hallam's Constitutional History in quarto, presented ... by his son, Arthur.'[30] Although intended, at the point of gift, to display the status of both giver and recipient, and to represent friendship, these volumes were far from being merely representational in Gladstone's eyes. When they entered his collection they became part of an organic system of organized knowledge, often to be read and annotated at a later date than that of receipt, for reasons far removed from the circumstances of their original acquisition.[31] The immediate effect of this bibliophilic ceremonial was, however, to inspire Gladstone to a flurry of personal book-buying and reading following his arrival in London on 4 December 1827, when he immediately 'bought books & read'. The size of his early collection was clearly unusual necessitating as it did both the construction of custom-made bookshelves for his rooms at both school and university,[32] and for Gladstone to make a very early attempt at cataloguing, in order to keep it under control.

Ownership and organization

There was a practical and rational side to Gladstone's book collecting, which ensured that he was concerned with what happened to a book once it had been purchased. Purchase, to Gladstone, was only the beginning of the true collection: arrangement, organization, maintenance, and use were of equal value and importance to the true bibliophile.[33] Gladstone was always keen to get his books bound as quickly as possible; for example, in Naples in 1850 he: 'Sent the little library I have gathered off for binding which is done here well and cheaply'.[34] Such precipitateness was not always possible, but Gladstone regularly combed his collection 'for the binder', shipping off the resulting volumes 'with all directions'.[35] Once a book was bound, it 'must ... be put into a bookcase', wrote Gladstone in 1890, reflecting his lifelong belief that the proper furnishing of his book rooms ought to be prioritized.

In common with many readers and annotators, one of the first things Gladstone did on buying, or being given, a book, was to paste his bookplate, or write his name, in the front of it, not only to establish and publicize his ownership, but also to personalize the book's character still further.[36] Gladstone's regular bookplate was of relatively small size, with a simple, armorial design,[37] with his signature, 'W. E. Gladstone', in italics underneath.[38] Gladstone's use of this bookplate appears to have been most concentrated in his boyhood and youth; it is much more likely to appear in books which Gladstone acquired during this period of life, when issues of ownership and its assertion are particularly strong.[39] Gladstone regularly wrote his name in his books, usually, but not always, as an alternative to inserting his bookplate. This would typically take the form 'W. E. Gladstone', unaccompanied by any reference to date, or location of purchase. Occasionally, Gladstone would elaborate, at this stage, on the provenance of the book, particularly if it was second hand. Thus, in a copy of the 1664 edition of Erasmus's *Colloquia*, Gladstone appended to the original purchaser's inscription: 'Samuel Powell Purser / bought this book on the 11th day of July being Saturday / in the year of grace 1840', the ironic, and somewhat competitive, comment: 'and sold it very soon after / WEG'.[40] Even such a brief annotation reveals something about Gladstone's personality, and his attitude to his books. Although we know that he sold, and even reportedly destroyed, books, he clearly considered himself a committed owner, willing to take both pride in, and responsibility for, husbanding his collection.

Once the marks of ownership had been made, books could be read. However, in order for them to be efficiently used, and perhaps lent out, they needed to be organized. As long as Gladstone collected books, he simultaneously organized them with, what Richard Shannon calls, a 'taxonomic passion for systematising, classifying, ordering, arranging and allocating that was one of the abiding characteristics of both the private and public spheres of his life'.[41] As Gladstone made clear in his 1890 article, the successful maintenance of a library and book collection depended on efficient and methodical organization. Essential to this project's success were the twin tasks of classification and cataloguing.

The process of classification is, for the librarian, one of the most imaginative of tasks. While cataloguing focuses on recording the tangible, classification offers opportunities to create maps of knowledge which are essentially intangible, personal, and poetic.[42] Gladstone recognized this personal aspect, believing that 'the arrangement of a library ought ... in some degree to correspond with and represent the mind of the man who forms it', admitting himself 'guilty ... of favouritism in classification', and 'sensible that sympathy and its reverse have something to do with determining in what company a book shall stand'. He also sensed the poetics of classification, especially when its harmonies were ignored, such 'as ... in at least one princely mansion of this country, where books, in thousands upon thousands, are jumbled together with no more arrangement than a sack of coals'. Instead:

> In a private library ... books ... ought to be assorted and distributed according to subject ... It is an immense advantage to bring the eye in aid of the mind; to see within a limited compass all the works that are accessible, in a given library, on a given subject; and to have the power of dealing with them collectively at a given spot, instead of hunting them up through an entire accumulation.

Nonetheless, classification – as Gladstone recognized – was a question 'more easy to open than to close', as categories of size, language, and so on, always transect simple subject divisions. Therefore, his method of classification was also practical: 'Economy, good arrangement, and accessibility with the smallest possible expenditure of time' were his watchwords.[43] Texts were to be classified both according to their format, and their subject matter, with books, pamphlets, letters, newspapers, accounts, original memoranda, abstracts, and manuscript books kept separate.[44] Books, as bound volumes, were the least troublesome of all the categories, for, 'being easily classified and found', they were able 'almost to find their own way from tables to shelves'.[45]

As early as 1825, Gladstone was recording lists of books read in his diary, but the first references to cataloguing date from 1826.[46] At home for the school holidays, he occupied himself with assiduous reading, punctuated, among other things, by errands for his parents, sketching, and archery. On 5 September 1826, perhaps diverting himself from worry about his sister Anne's latest illness, Gladstone 'wrote [a] catalogue of books'. This is unlikely to have been the first such project, as his elaborated comment, dated 9 September 1826, shows: 'Wrote Catalogue of books, alphabetical as I find no other way answers'. The following year, Gladstone, again at Seaforth: 'Made some additions to my book Catalogue'.[47]

Although Gladstone furnished his own room with books at home,[48] and played a principal role in the planning, stocking, and organization of his family's formal libraries, it was a number of years until Gladstone was either responsible for fully financing his purchases, or had a separate library room that he could call his own. Hence funds to purchase specifically named gentlemanly essentials, including books, for Gladstone's lodgings at the Albany, his first independent establishment as a young bachelor MP, were provided by his father.[49] While his marriage to Catherine Glynne in 1839 made Gladstone feel more independent – he expressed obvious pride in 1840, both in his collection, and in his new status as a family man, when '*our* first bookcase [was] put up' at the couple's first marital home, 13 Carlton House Terrace[50] – he remained heavily dependent on his father for both funding and accommodation. Although Catherine and William were encouraged to treat her ancestral Hawarden Castle as home, the presence of Gladstone's brother-in-law Stephen, and the venerable Glynne Library of *incunabula* and eighteenth-century treasures, meant that there was only limited space available for Gladstone or his books. Thus, while his father lived, Gladstone continued to regard Fasque as his principal residence. Taking full advantage, he stored much of his burgeoning book collection in Scotland and still combined work on his own books with those belonging to his father.[51]

Gladstone's most sustained attempt to catalogue his book collection took place in this phase of his collection's history. It began in 1845, when he and Catherine were in London awaiting the birth of their second daughter.[52] On Saturday, 26 July, Catherine went into labour, and Gladstone, unable to concentrate on his usual regime, occupied himself, firstly by 'sorting pamphlets', and then, 'recommenced a catalogue of my books'. This, he admitted, was 'a formidable undertaking, but one that I can carry on when not enough settled for steady work'. Gladstone's reaction to the birth, which occurred at 2.30 am the following morning, was joy mixed with concern: 'The gift is great so is the responsibility; is it now enough if ever there is to be a release from the toils that now enclose?'[53] Gladstone continued his cataloguing project during the succeeding days, amidst lingering concerns about Catherine's health.[54]

The catalogue is divided into three sections, headed: 'Theology, Ecclesiastical History and Biography'; 'Secular Literature; Division I; English Language'; and 'Secular Literature, Division II; Foreign Languages, including Classics'. Thus, it provides a snapshot of the core of Gladstone's early collection, as well as the basic, classificatory division between theological and secular material which would continue to characterize it.[55] On 1 August 1845, Gladstone recorded: 'Finished the Theological part of my Catalogue', transferring to the 'Sec[ular] Dept.' in subsequent days. After two week's consistent attention, he 'Entered Part III' on 9 August, and finally 'Finished my Catalogue' on 12 August 1845. It had taken him 18 days. A few days later, he recorded yet more 'bookbuying', and work 'on books'.[56] It is clear, both from the surviving catalogue and Gladstone's diary, that he continued to make additions to it. Further entries were made on the catalogue's left-hand pages, and, in his diary for 1849, he recorded a further spate of cataloguing, again, while in London.[57]

The death of Sir John Gladstone in 1851 resulted in something of a crisis for Gladstone and his books, a circumstance partly brought on by Gladstone's attempt to persuade first his eldest brother, Thomas, and then his father, to agree to a division of the Gladstone inheritance on Sir John's death. He proposed that the baronetcy should go to Tom but that he should have Fasque. This Machiavellian plot came to nothing, however, and Tom duly inherited both title and estate. Nonetheless, the survival of a number of sharp rejoinders in the family papers ordering Gladstone to abandon his 'claims', and the swift removal of Gladstone and his 5000 books from the Scottish house testify to the seriousness of the disagreement.[58] The dispute thus enforced what proved to be the most consequential upheaval in the young family's life – a permanent move to Hawarden Castle. Stephen Glynne, having no family of his own, agreed to accommodate his sister, brother-in-law, and their family at the Castle on a more permanent basis and set about expanding the house to accommodate them. This move also turned out to be one of the most significant moments in the history of Gladstone's books, the majority of which were, for the first time, brought together in his own principal private residence.

Consecrating the Temple of Peace

Gladstone was used to spending whole days busied with his book collection,[59] but the move to Hawarden presented a challenge of librarianship greater than any he had ever before experienced. Gladstone's study was initially located in 'a large room on the first floor, with a northern aspect',[60] and work began there in earnest in October 1854. Initially his priority was in erecting 'bookcases or rather bookholders' to receive 'the first fruits of the 5000 vols that are to come here'.[61] For this work Gladstone employed David Bailey, the member of a respected Hawarden family of carpenters and builders who were to do similar work for him for the rest of his life. Book-sorting and stowing then commenced seriously over Christmas. Gladstone, 'in a chaos of some 2000' volumes, enlisted the help of sons Willy and Stephen, until finally, 'a third bout carried me through most of the work of arranging books ... The number I have here must be over 5000'. He then arranged 'with Bailie [sic] for more book-room', and his 'evening closed with a short retrospect

Figure 1.1 'The Study, Hawarden Castle', G. B. Smith, *The Life of the Right Honourable William Ewart Gladstone* (London, Paris and New York, n.d.), vol. II, p. 257. St Deiniol's Library Collection.

& exam[inatio]n'.[62] The work proved both strenuous and exhausting; on the following day (his 45th birthday) Gladstone recorded: 'Resumed work on my books *more moderately*'.[63] On 3 January 1855, he eventually 'finished the whole affair', and 'found them ... 5185 Vols' in total.

The contents of Gladstone's library were moved again in the 1860s, to a purpose-built location on the ground floor of the Castle (Figure 1.1). Wemyss Reid described how, 'in the year 1864 an addition was made to the Castle, a spacious library with bedrooms above being built at the north-west angle of the house'. The name 'Temple of Peace' was inaugurated by the family to distinguish Gladstone's study from the Castle's original library, 'the large and cheerful room, looking south and west'.[64] The room was thus named after Vespasian's *Templum Pacis*, which was built in Rome between 71 and 75 AD, and incorporated a library, housed treasures acquired following the sack of Jerusalem and by Greek artists, and was described by the elder Pliny as one of the three most beautiful monuments in Rome.[65] In August 1864, Gladstone's newly constructed 'Temple' was far from beautiful, however. After examining 'the new rooms: especially with a view to the vast undertaking of moving', Gladstone spent two months preparing for the translation, 'for the lower room is *raw*'.[66] 'The beginning of moving effects & books from above occupied most of' 19 October; he had 2 000 volumes 'down, & placed in the new "Temple of Peace"' by the 22nd, but still faced the formidable task of 'importing all the bookcases from above'.[67] In August 1865, Gladstone took to the cataloguing task again, undoubtedly spurred on by the move. On 16 August, he began a 'catalogue of my Bibliotheca Homerica – after arranging it', an undertaking which he completed two days later.[68] He then worked '2 or 3 hours on Catalogues which I am attempting of some minor branches of my Library'.[69] Gladstone's 'minor branches' included privately printed books,[70] *incunabula*, aldine books, bibliographical works, dictionaries and books of reference,[71] grammars, ethnology and ethnological philology, works relating to universities and public schools, works connected with Shakespeare (a sizeable collection),[72] epitaphs, and county histories.

In its new location, Gladstone's library continued to expand. In 1866, while in London, Gladstone worked 'at packing books' in preparation for ferrying them to Hawarden, and in 1872 he was again unpacking books 'in the Temple of Peace'.[73] Expansion necessitated both more space and more bookcases with Gladstone even considering the construction of 'a *crypt* under my library' in 1869.[74] Bailey was summoned to the Castle in April 1874, at which time he and Gladstone engaged in 'much busy measurements & arrangements for more stowage of papers & for an addition of 1100 volumes'.[75]

Gladstone's defeat as prime minister in 1874, and subsequent resignation as Liberal leader, placed additional pressure on the Temple of Peace. Gladstone deemed necessary the sale of 11 Carlton House Terrace,[76] its furniture, and 'part of my collections' in view of the loss of his official income,[77] and early in March 1875, he began sorting out his London books, packing those he wished to keep, and sorting and arranging others prior to valuation.[78] The 'Library of the Right Honourable W. E. Gladstone', which auctioneers Sotheby, Wilkinson, and Hodge found 'standing on the shelves at No 11 Carlton House Terrace' and duly valued 'at Six Hundred and Seventy Pounds (£670) (exclusive of the Hansard's Parliamentary Debates)', was, as Gladstone later described it to Lord Acton, a 'useful library' of 'political and historical ... volumes'.[79] The library's eventual purchaser was George Grenfell Glyn, second Baron Wolverton (1824–87). Wolverton, described by Matthew as one of Gladstone's 'old cronies', was a banker, Liberal Chief Whip 1868–73, Paymaster General in Gladstone's second ministry, and a staunch supporter of Home Rule.[80] Their professional relationship had deepened following a visit by

Glyn to Hawarden in 1867, which left Gladstone with the impression that 'he has ... much improved on this closer acquaintance'.[81] Thereafter a close confidant, Wolverton's advice was sought during deliberations over resignation in both 1873 and 1874–5.[82] Despite his consistent discouragement of Gladstone's efforts to resign from politics, Wolverton nonetheless represented a calming and reassuring influence, 'hearty ... and refreshing in proportion'.[83] It was therefore a trusted aide and friend to whom Gladstone sold his books. They agreed the sale in principle at an early stage, and on 24 March (the day the valuation took place) Gladstone 'saw Ld Wolverton & arranged finally with him for the transfer of my library to the satisfaction of both'.[84] Their subsequent correspondence suggests that Wolverton did not purchase Gladstone's parliamentary debates.[85] As a politician, he would have owned a sizeable collection himself and perhaps found, as Gladstone did, that there was 'but little sociability in a huge wall of Hansards'.[86] However, a later rough note written by Gladstone lists £820 having been received from Wolverton. In addition Gladstone recorded sending several locked boxes containing court dresses, papers, and a collection of coins, medals, and miniatures to his friend.[87]

Whatever the full extent of Wolverton's purchase, Gladstone had still only divested himself of a portion of his library; there were still many books which he had not sold. This considerable influx of books (and bookcases) he spent much of the 1875 recess integrating into his Hawarden collection before any further sustained intellectual work was undertaken.[88] As a result, lack of space became so critical that Gladstone began to commandeer space beyond the confines of his library. Thus on 18 May 1875 he was looking over other rooms 'with a view to the planting out of my library', and three days later was working 'hard on setting up bookcases in the supplemental T[emple of] P[eace],[89] unpacking bookboxes, & placing books'.[90] Many commentators were both amused by the rapid growth of Gladstone's collection, and intrigued by his often ingenious attempts to house it efficiently.[91] Particular attention was directed towards his design and use of a three-faced, projecting bookshelf.[92] The design's uniqueness, as Gladstone himself explained, was due to the inclusion of 'an end-piece ... that is a shallow and extremely light adhering bookcase ... which both increases the accommodation, and makes one short side as well as the two long ones ... present simply a face of books'.[93]

Despite even such ingenuity, Gladstone struggled to keep his library in order. Problems of space were exacerbated by the fact that Gladstone's collecting was increasingly supplemented by gifts from publishers, admiring authors seeking reviews, and the general public. As a reporter for *The Sketch* posthumously explained:

> Publishers were astute enough to recognise the value of a post-card of commendation from 'your faithful servant, W. E. Gladstone,' and accordingly despatched numberless new books to the indefatigable statesman. Authors of high repute and otherwise – especially otherwise – would present Mr. Gladstone with autographed copies of their books, and usually he replied graciously.[94]

Such unsolicited gifts raise the question of whether or not, as Gladstone's collection matured, it fully reflected his personal tastes. However, Gladstone's attitude to review books or books from authors with whom he was not personally acquainted was selective, and was largely dictated by practical rather than intellectual considerations. As David Williamson observed: 'Many of these volumes he did not preserve in his own select library after reading, for they would have soon swamped even the capacious shelves arranged on Mr. Gladstone's own adroit plan of accommodation'.[95] However, as was perhaps only to be expected, there were always individuals or groups who sought to engage Gladstone in further dialogue via letter. *The Young Man* described the eclecticism of his post as follows:

> Autograph and birthday books, manuscripts, novels, poetry, essays on every conceivable subject, schemes for the government of the universe, inventions, medicines, testimonials, are all placed in a box for future return when demanded.[96]

Most commentators were dismissive of such so-called rubbish. The London correspondent of the *Birmingham Daily Post* was in particular appalled by 'the persistence of uninvited spiritual advisers in addressing Gladstone. I am told that not a day, and scarcely a post, passes without some of these personages intruding themselves.'[97] However, it does seem that Gladstone was quite prepared to communicate or at least take note of such correspondence. Edward Hamilton, for instance, noted that Gladstone did not view his more miscellaneous correspondence so negatively. Instead, 'he regarded it as an indication of the drift of public opinion, and of the questions on which the attention of the country was principally fixed'.[98]

A further problem was represented by the mass of papers which Gladstone accumulated as politician, author, and public figure. As with his book-sorting, Gladstone was constantly occupied with arranging and organizing these, and was forever formulating new ways of managing them.[99] One day in 1868 he wrote: 'Spent much of the forenoon in making a list I hope complete of my publications & corrected speeches, and in putting them all together'. In February that year he 'set seriously to work upon my books & papers wh[ich] will find me much to do before I establish Cosmos & get rid of superfluities', several days later setting 'aside ab[out]. 3000 vols of pamphlets of the shambles!'[100] On 17 March 1874, he again referred to work 'on *Chaos* for Kosmos', and in 1875: 'Resumed moving & arranging papers: I must give to this business, & my library, 2 to 3 hours per diem'.[101] Gladstone's determination to keep papers and memoranda both secure and separate motivated the planning and construction of the 'Octagon' in the 1880s. Built at the northwest corner of the Temple of Peace, and named after a room at Seaforth, this fire (but not damp) proof annexe housed all Gladstone's papers until their final dispersal.[102] The construction of his muniment room eased pressure on space in the Temple of Peace, but burdened Gladstone with yet more work. 'It will seem small in my journal', he wrote in 1888, 'but [it] must take much of my time for many weeks', and as late as 1893 he despaired: 'Worked in the Octagon. But my papers overwhelm me. I am like a little mole, who has cast up an enormous hill'.[103]

Mary Drew later reminisced about the extent to which her father's collecting habit literally invaded the life and space of the rest of the family:

> Quickly the room filled; one by one each piece of extraneous furniture disappeared to make way for low bookcases suited to serve as tables and to hold volumes of abnormal size ... They overflowed into the vestibule, they ran along the passage into the billiard-room; this involved the disappearance of the billiard table. Prizes were offered for the discovery of possible new spaces for bookcases.[104]

Hawarden Castle was literally being overrun with books. This situation was cheerfully tolerated by Gladstone's family, but as he aged, the question of what would happen to the collection after his death began to press. The practical necessity for Gladstone to dispose of his library before his death was obvious: his collection was a very personalized, working library and it was unlikely that his children would either be able to find space or use for its more abstruse elements. Moreover, Gladstone had a horror of libraries being broken up, as his campaign to save Lord Acton's library from dispersal in 1890 indicates.[105] It seems logical, therefore, that Mary should have continued her narrative by suggesting that Gladstone:

> Often pondering, as he did, how best to benefit his fellow creatures, how to bring together readers who had no books and books who had no readers, gradually the thought evolved itself in his mind into a plan for the permanent disposal of his library.[106]

'The Meditated Foundation'

Serious discussion of Gladstone's plan for a library foundation began in the summer of 1886. He first told his second son, Stephen, who, as the Rector of Hawarden, was an obvious confidant. Stephen in turn wrote to his brother Henry on 4 August 1886:

> He plans to leave his library to the Church of England as a legacy – together with a sufficient endowment to let it become a centre of study and learning ... He thinks of building a Library in Hawarden, future railways will make it soon very convenient for Liverpool etc. He doesn't want this talked of. Isn't it fine? He has been maturing it for many months. He thinks when the Ch[urch]. is disestablished (& in Wales it soon may be) that places of learning will be greatly wanted.[107]

Between 1886 and 1888, with the help of Stephen and eldest son, Willy, Gladstone searched exhaustively for a suitable site in Hawarden village.[108] During this period, his ideas about the form the projected institution was to take remained nebulous, but nonetheless, by April 1888, the idea was fully occupying his mind. His enthusiasm and increasing absorption in all things bibliographical is plain from his journal entries alone. For instance, on 5 April 1888, during one of his periodic later visits to Oxford, Gladstone visited the Bodleian Library and had a lengthy meeting with its librarian E. V. Nicholson. During the course of this interview Gladstone, on the spur of the moment, sketched out on the back of an envelope a plan for mobile shelving he thought might be of use to the library.[109] Seven months later, following further discussions in Oxford when, for the first time, Gladstone's plans were revealed to individuals outside the family, his vision for the library was committed to paper, also for the first time.[110]

During the summer of 1889, Gladstone recommenced his search for a library site in Hawarden, concluding it successfully that September.[111]

Simultaneously, he planned the layout of the new library. 'My ground floor is to be Theological & planned for 25000 volumes', he recorded on 21 August 1889. Having eventually decided to erect only a temporary structure, which could be moved or re-configured if future circumstances demanded,[112] Gladstone purchased a galvanized iron building from a Mr Humphreys of London and construction was soon underway, supervised by the faithful Bailey.[113] Gladstone threw himself into the task of planning the library and its future, designing bookcases based on the three-sided design he had developed for the Temple of Peace.[114]

The 'grand transfer' of books began on 21 December 1889 when Gladstone 'sent off my first instalment to Saint Deiniol's'.[115] He henceforth threw himself into the move with the same energy that had always characterized his library work, curtailing his customary afternoon walks in order to receive and organize the books on their arrival at St Deiniol's, work in which he was aided by his daughter Helen, who was home from Cambridge for Christmas.[116] At the end of January 1890, Gladstone estimated that he had 5700 volumes in place in the library. By September, the figure was nearer 10,000, and shortage of space necessitated a doubling up of books on the first room's swelling shelves.[117] Gladstone's attention then turned to the second room. Bookcases were fixed and, at the beginning of October 1890, Gladstone recorded: 'I have now *in situ* bookcases for 22 [to] ... 24000 volumes: & full 12000 carried up.'[118] The work proved heavier going in November as the library suffered storm damage, and Gladstone found himself preoccupied with 'the awful matter of Parnell'.[119]

In external appearance, the library, which lay on a north-south line to the north west of the existing building, was 'not a thing of beauty' (Figure 1.2).[120] With its small spire and gabled ends, it resembled the mission churches which constituted the usual function of Mr Humphreys' iron buildings and was affectionately known as the 'Tin Tabernacle'. Internally it was a condensed version of the Temple of Peace, dominated by the same buttressed shelving, desks and chairs, and decorated with a small selection of pictures and medallion portraits (Figure 1.3).

In a memorandum written in 1892, during his fraught visit to Lord Rosebery's house,[121] Gladstone set out 'to give an idea of the principle & method of arrangement ... upon which the books of this library have been placed', and to describe the classification scheme and its layout in the tin library. He referred to the two rooms as 'North' and 'Southern', but

Sacred Dramas: *The History of a Collection* 39

Figure 1.2 The Exterior of the 'Tin Tabernacle' (1890). Flintshire Record Office Photographic Collection.

Figure 1.3 The Interior of the 'Tin Tabernacle' (Divinity Room) (n.d.) Flintshire Record Office Photographic Collection.

it can be clearly seen that the fundamental division between divinity and humanity, which characterizes the memorial library, was in existence from the very beginning. Here, the arrangement of his books mirrored the progress and fluctuating preoccupations of his personal religious life; thus school, university, 'Church and State', Anglican devotion, foreign theology, church history, varieties of unorthodoxy, and other religions succeeded each other consecutively on the shelves. In the 'Southern' humanity room, the chronological constitution was also quite striking. English history and literature made up the largest sections, but divisions on romance and poetry, Scotland, the classics, history and, of course, Ireland remind one not only of Gladstone's abiding preoccupations but also of specific phases of his life and career. In order to indicate that this interpretation is not merely fanciful, in 'On Books and the Housing of Them' Gladstone pondered:

> whether the arrangement of a library ought not in some degree to correspond with and represent the mind of the man who forms it. For my own part, I plead guilty ... of favouritism in classification. I am sensible that sympathy and its reverse have something to do with determining in what company a book shall stand. And further, does there not enter into the matter a principle of humanity to the authors themselves. Ought we not to place them ... in the neighbourhood which they would like [?][122]

Despite setbacks and distractions, Gladstone remained totally committed to the task of setting up the library, and, over the next couple of years, time spent at Hawarden was dominated by the project. During August 1891, for example, he was working there almost every day. As more of his books were transported to the new buildings, Gladstone not only engaged in practical work at the library but also read there.[123] John Morley recalled: 'Mr. Gladstone sat reading in the corner' of St Deiniol's, where no one dared disturb him except Petz, the black Pomeranian, who 'when he considered that the horses must be kept waiting no longer, pushed his little cold nose against the master's hand, and suggested an immediate adjournment of the sitting".[124] Moreover, Gladstone's immense pride in his project ensured that, from October 1889, practically every visitor to the Castle was taken along to view and admire the new building. Lady Charlotte Ribblesdale's recollection of the 'Tin Tabernacle' leaves little to the imagination:

Whatever the fate in store for it, I could not help feeling a sense of waste at this large collection of books isolated on a bleak hill in a scattered district. It seemed to me too sanguine a hope that the few cabinlike living rooms would ever be occupied by resident pupils from distant parts. Mr. Gladstone was wise in making the building of a temporary description – corrugated iron has few obligations. He was very proud of the economy of the space inside, which, on the buttress plan, holds the maximum of books within the minimum of space; if anything, the passage room is run too fine for comfort. He told us that he had taken every measurement himself.

The heating apparatus is another subject for congratulation, also planned by himself. It consists of one small stove, which is on such approved principles that the heat is supposed to extend equally to all extremities. We found this to be a fond illusion; the cold was intense, and it was almost piteous to see M. Waddington [a guest] shivering and longing to be back in a comfortable house.[125]

In February 1894, Stephen Gladstone announced in the parish magazine that 'St. Deiniol's opens provisionally on February 2nd to receive any who come to Hawarden for the purpose of theological study and wish to avail themselves of Mr Gladstone's New Library and ... hostel'.[126] Everything promised well when the first resident arrived that Easter.[127]

Despite increasing infirmity, Gladstone presided over the formal establishment of the St Deiniol's Trust. Since 1889 Gladstone had envisaged a board of trustees for the library and he returned to the question again in 1891, once most of his books had been transferred and the hard work of arranging them eased.[128] The year following the library's official opening, Gladstone met the proposed trustees and 'discussed ... the particulars',[129] and a month later endowed the library with almost £40,000 in bonds and stock.[130] 'May God of His mercy prosper it', he wrote in December 1895, just before the library was formally constituted by deed of trust on 1 January 1896. The St Deiniol's project had thus moved, with only momentary hindrances, from inspiration to institution within ten years.

Gladstone actually handled the transmission of power over the library rather poorly, promising control of it first to his son Stephen (whom he made chair of trustees), then to his son-in-law Harry Drew (who was made acting warden), before choosing his permanent successor himself.[131] Such contrariness produced a deal of bad feeling and the uncomfortable circumstances surrounding the Trust's institution contributed to some underlying problems in the practical establishment of the library, which are discussed in Chapter 6.[132] In his last diary entry, written on his 87th birthday, Gladstone wrote: 'I have ... got St. Deiniol's very near its launch upon the really difficult and critical part of the undertaking'.[133] The library had, of course, been 'launched' for over two years, but what Gladstone really referred to here was the period in the library's existence when he would no longer be alive to oversee its management. Gladstone's concerns about its future were only to be expected. At 87, his faculties were failing and he was unsure how his brainchild would survive without his guiding hand.

Gladstone reserved a significant residuum of his private collection in the Temple of Peace, where he continued to work:

> I have sent to the new building by far the larger number of my books (a number estimated at about 25000): but I retain at the Castle mainly for my own use a smaller portion (perhaps 6000) including some important branches and many select works. The two should be regarded as eventually in substance one, subject perhaps to some special exceptions.[134]

From the very beginning of his collecting life, Gladstone had been taught both to associate book collecting and ownership in terms of human interaction and to understand their ultimate purpose as the generational transmission of knowledge. When Gladstone reached that stage when he recognized himself as one 'who must shortly quit the scene of life', he demonstrated this shared understanding of book culture by replicating Hannah More's action on a grandiose scale, by bequeathing the majority of his books to the nation. More's gift was not one of those many volumes which made the transition from Hawarden Castle to St Deiniol's – its sentimental value undoubtedly prevented its relinquishment – remaining instead in the Temple of Peace. Nonetheless, the memory of its gifting had clearly played a part in the final act of the history of Gladstone's collection: on the same day that he recalled and wrote about his meeting with More, on a sheet of 'Dalmeny Park' notepaper, Gladstone also 'wrote notes respecting St Deiniol's'.[135] Furthermore, it was in the Temple of Peace, surrounded by his remaining books, that Gladstone interviewed Gilbert Cunningham Joyce, who, in October 1896, he appointed as St Deiniol's first permanent warden.[136] Providing Joyce at this meeting with a written list of the library's aims for his future reference,

Gladstone in many ways echoed the circumstances of his collection's inception at the moment when, to all extents and purposes, he relinquished control of it. As he told Quaritch that year, 'speaking generally, I have retired from the list of purchasers'.[137] At Gladstone's death two years later, *Sacred Dramas*, together with his other remaining books, constituted the most appropriate of backdrops to his first lying in state.

2
Rhythms of Reading

On 3 July 1832, the brothers John and William Gladstone found themselves stranded without post horses in the village of Balzers, Liechtenstein, a staging post between Austria and Switzerland. Like many well-to-do young men of their age, they were engaged on a 'grand tour' of Europe, and having spent the previous five months making leisurely progress across the length of France and Italy, were finally about to embark on their journey homeward. After being made to wait for over an hour by an obstreperous postmaster who claimed not to understand English, John finally lost his temper and launched into a tirade of abuse. His volley of oaths succeeded, where entreaties had failed, in re-awakening the postmaster's dormant command of English, and before long, John was subjected to a violent physical assault. William was at first oblivious to the excitement. Unlike his brother, he had sought to make the most of the enforced delay by catching up on his books, and was occupying himself by reading in the stationary carriage. On hearing 'a stamping of feet', he emerged and joined his brother in the fray, which was soon dangerously out of hand: no sooner had William hauled off the postmaster, but the 'execrable Postillion' set upon John once more. Only after John introduced a second line of argument – in the shape of a brace of pistols – was the conflict moderated into a 'Tongue war'. The brothers reached Milan four days later relatively unscathed. John, 'jealous of the honour of our concern', took up the matter with Director of the Post (who predictably did nothing) whereas William – who in the intervening time had 'finished Fox's speeches' and begun 'Volney's ruins' – seems to have been more interested in: 'Inquiring in divers shops about books and other things'.[1]

This story demonstrates how Gladstone strove to maintain his habits of reading even in the most trying of circumstances. It signals, moreover, quite how well-established, integral, and essential these routines were to Gladstone – even as a very young man. This chapter explores how Gladstone fitted reading and study into an increasingly busy timetable, by tracing the development and function of, firstly, his reading style, and, secondly, some important, distinctive, and influential rhythms, which not only anchored his domestic and spiritual lives, but also underpinned and structured his 'public' existence. It shows how critical is a recognition of these styles, rhythms, and relationships in understanding Gladstone's continual negotiation between different spheres of his life, and how they facilitated and aided him in the formation of opinion and in the creation of knowledge. It also introduces us to instances where these rhythms were challenged, as on this first trip abroad.

Reading style

Gladstone, as many of those who knew and observed him could testify, 'was hardly ever, except in company and on dress parade, without a book. To his reading there was never an end.'[2] As Lord Rosebery once reportedly observed, Gladstone was, '"as a learner and as a reader, ever with his books, ever among his books; ever trying to learn something, as if he had ... eternity before him in which to work."'[3] Such descriptions presented what was, in many ways, a paradoxical situation: a man with immense public and professional responsibilities who yet managed to find the time, not only to read constantly, but apparently to absorb a great deal from the books he read.

Despite extensive coverage and discussion of Gladstone's reading, some confusion has persisted regarding the place of reading in his busy life. Some commentators described him as a slow, deliberate reader: *The Young Man* magazine, for example, described his method of reading as 'more that of the tortoise than the hare', elaborating: 'He cannot read rapidly, nor has he ever acquired the fine art of skipping; he cannot boast, like Carlyle, of reading a page of Gibbon "with one flash of his eye."'[4] Gladstone's private secretary, Edward Hamilton, took the same line, observing that he 'read slowly and most conscientiously. He never skipped a page or a line.'[5] However, others such as Thomas Wemyss Reid, stressed the speed with which Gladstone read: 'His friends declared that he devoured books rather than read them, so rapid was the process of perusal.'[6] Whatever their view, all such commentators were left having to explain how Gladstone could be both 'an exceptionally thorough reader', and nonetheless get 'through a great deal of reading in a short time'.[7] For, as Hamilton noted, 'the number of books through which he plodded every year was astounding',[8] and, as Wemyss Reid was forced to admit, 'no one who has had occasion to discuss with him any particular volume could find reason to doubt that he had made himself thoroughly master of its contents'.[9] *The Young Man* suggested the paradox could be explained by Gladstone's habit of deciding, on the basis of a few pages, 'whether the book is worth reading, and if not, after a few pages it is cast aside'.[10] Thomas Archer and Alfred Story explicated the phenomenon by 'the quickness with which he seized points of importance', and 'the retentiveness of his memory'. Furthermore, they noticed his practice of annotation, and also his habit of composing flyleaf summaries in some books.[11] They were not the only ones to detect, and assign importance to, Gladstone's method. The *Literary World* observed in 1891: 'There have been comments made lately by various writers depreciating Mr. Gladstone's literary judgements. Whatever else may be said for them it is certain, we think, that they are not hastily formed, for in his reading, as in all else, he is strictly methodical.'[12]

Gladstone's reading was generally accepted to be omnivorous, but those who periodically accused him of reading indiscriminately were wrong to do so. Gladstone could be incredibly focused in his reading, with particular matters of current interest or research leading him into bouts of concentrated work. W. Roberts of the *Bookworm* described Gladstone's preparations for an address on poultry farming: 'He was found by a friend with twenty or thirty books on the subject, which he had specially ordered, and in a week or two had made himself almost complete master of all the manners and ways of these animals.'[13] While Arthur Woodward, describing the contents of the Temple of Peace in 1898, noted that, judging by levels of annotation, 'books bearing on marriage and divorce have received his closest attention'.[14]

Gladstone developed an elaborate, intricate, and precisely ordered methical system of reading to ensure the most profits were gained from study. Gladstone's diary with its lists of reading, surviving books and marginalia, epitomes, as well as contemporary descriptions of him, total a well-preserved record of the text-processing system by which he sought to map the raw, epistemological data which could fulfil his, and others', immediate and future intellectual needs.

These methods were clearly established at Eton and Oxford. When reading books, especially those on academic subjects, Gladstone would read regularly (rarely missing a day), take notes, or make an epitome, and re-read to secure his knowledge and his opinion of the text. Thus in 1833 he mused, when analyzing Arthur Hallam's gift of his father

Henry's *History of England*: 'My method has usually been 1. to read over regularly – 2. to glance again over all I have read, and analyse'.[15] James Brinsley-Richards' description of Gladstone's reading practice at Oxford depicts a disciplined but not unrealistic regime. Gladstone's many irate annotations to his copy reveal this to be a largely inaccurate piece of writing;[16] however, the following anecdote escaped unmarked.

> After his guests had dispersed, Gladstone was always ready to apply himself to a few hours of vigorous reading ... Gladstone never dawdled over his books. He set himself a task and toiled until he had finished it – though one of his rules was never to infringe on the seven hours which he allotted for sleep. The men who wreck their healths by hard reading are those who sit up half through the night with pots of strong tea at their elbows and wet towels round their heads. Gladstone worked regularly and never had to put himself on the *aeger* list, or to lie late a-bed in the morning snatching fitful eyefuls of sleep.[17]

Gladstone was keen, when he read things, to remember them accurately. As we shall see, it was essential to him to cultivate a working knowledge of and an accurate memory for texts in order to employ and transmit his knowledge to others. Thus he expressed some frustration, for example, when he had to read Quintilian 'now afresh, as I have lost almost all recollection of my recent perusal. Book memory & life memory *non bene conveniunt*'.[18] He would learn some things he read by heart, particularly poetry. Thus he recorded 'getting by heart' Tennyson's *Guinevere* in 1859.[19] As well as learning from the books he read, Gladstone liked to contextualize his reading; to know where, when and why he had read a book. This was one of the important functions of the book lists recorded throughout his diary. He was clearly lost when he could no longer see to compile these. Thus he lamented in 1894:

> While I enjoy the relief from the small grind of the Daily Journal, I think it may be well still to note ... books read. For a main difficulty with me now is to know *where* I have read this and that: and a list will be a help.[20]

Re-reading texts was to Gladstone 'an event in life', which 'suggest very much',[21] not only indicating Gladstone's acknowledgement of the tendency for readers to respond differently to texts at every re-reading, but also testifying to his affection for a reading world in which favourite texts satisfyingly interrelated like old friends.

Annotation

Essential to Gladstone's reading method was the distinctive system of annotation that he used. This was made up of marginal annotation, characterized by a code of brief, symbolic marks occasionally elaborated by textual commentary; fly-leaf summaries; and hand-written indexes of varying lengths. W. T. Stead described Gladstone's use of it in practice:

> When he reads a book he does so pencil in hand, marking off on the margin those passages which he wishes to remember, querying those about which he is in doubt, and putting a cross opposite those which he disputes. At the end of the volume he constructs a kind of index of his own which enables him to refer to those things he wishes to remember in the book.[22]

Taken together, such elements provided a consistent framework by which Gladstone could efficiently organize and record his lifelong reading. They also supplied convenient maps by which he could navigate when returning for those re-readings he made to secure his understanding and opinion of texts.

By using a code, Gladstone was not an unusual annotator. Between c. 1750 and 1820, responding to the development of the critical edition, as well as increasing trends towards the circulation and publication of marginalia as 'literature', many readers had increased both the amount and critical tone of their written comments in books.[23] However, this partial transformation of the annotation – from private, scholarly aid, to public, argumentative commentary – made other readers increasingly zealous in guarding their privacy. As a result, encoded annotation became more prevalent in the period during which Gladstone was formulating his reading method.[24] Gladstone's code is not an elaborate example of this type of cipher, based as it is on marginal lines – the most basic signs of attention – and other conventional symbols like the question and exclamation marks, and the cross. However, whereas most annotators who experimented with codes quickly abandoned them, Gladstone consistently used his basic code, with only slight elaboration, until the end of his life. In this respect, *pace* Jackson, he was unquestionably unique.[25]

We know that Gladstone developed his individual annotation code at a very early stage, thanks to the survival of his handwritten 'key' to it, complete with definitions, at the back of the second volume of his ten-volume set of John Locke's *Works*.[26]

notice.....|

/

special notice....*NB*

/

n. [note] with approbation...+.

/

disapprobation..X,=.

/

special do. [ditto]..... XX, XXX.

/

a doubt....?

/

a reservation or qualification ....ma [the Italian word for 'but'].

/

disbelief or surprise ...!

(at statement, or, <u>manner</u> of statement)

Gladstone's definitions are not surprising. For example, Colin Matthew lists, among abbreviations used by Gladstone as a diarist 'X' and '+'. [27] These he translated as 'rescue work done this day', and 'prayer, usually when on a charitable visit or plus', respectively. The marks are the same as those used for book annotation, and the general positive and negative connotations accord with Gladstone's definitions, immediately suggesting the existence of a very intimate relationship between Gladstone's reading and his other pursuits.

The key itself is not complete; Gladstone did not define here all the marks which he frequently used. One very commonly used symbolic annotation not featured is a 'v' sign, which is almost certainly a tick of approval. Other known annotation marks that are not defined include obvious elaborations, such as a double line beside text denoting emphasis; various combinations of the listed marks; as well as more obscure symbols such as '^', which possibly represents disapproval, or missed words;[28] a back-to-front question mark, and a sloping hyphen. It is likely that these represent later additions to the basic code. Nonetheless, Gladstone's extant classifications provide solid points of reference and, in addition, his memorandum, 'On Keeping Books and Papers' (25 November 1837), offers further gleanings as to the style and purpose of his annotations. He occasionally, for example, used slight underlining. This he noted, in the context of abstracts, 'very much assists the eye if bold, and further, if proportioned to the prominence of the fact or expression underlined ... assists the eye'.[29] Moreover, the way in which the key is laid out is similar to that in which Gladstone habitually constructed book abstracts:

> Do not write them in lines continuously – but begin a fresh line and mark the place with at the left hand thus.
>
> /,
>
> if you please, either at each new fact or wherever the subject takes a turn, or any very observable circumstance is recorded.[30]

Gladstone's key can be dated to February 1836 by means of his first annotation in the same volume, which is a quotation from Dante:

> Lì si vedrà ciò che tenem per fede,
> non dimostrato, ma fia per sè noto
> a guisa del ver primo che l'uom crede.
>
> Paradiso II.43.[31]

Gladstone had read some Locke at school,[32] but his first reading of Dante's *Commedia* did not occur until 1834, confirming that the book's annotations were not made at Eton. The volume enclosing the key contains part of Locke's *An Essay Concerning Human Understanding*, commencing at Book II, Chapter 23 to Book IV, Chapter 4. According to his diary, Gladstone began reading this work on 11 December 1834, while in Edinburgh, only days before he received his first 'serious call' from Sir Robert Peel to be Junior Lord of the Treasury.[33] Responsibility of office presumably curtailed the reading, for he only resumed study of the *Essay* in December 1835, during another stay in Scotland.[34] His reading continued in London, whence he returned in January 1836 as a backbench MP who took little part in parliamentary proceedings, being distracted by his lingering, and ultimately hopeless, infatuation with society beauty, Caroline Farquhar.[35] Crucially, Gladstone's reading list for 25 February 1836 records: 'Locke [on] U[nderstanding] (began B.IV) – Dante Paradiso I, II (+)';[36] the quoted lines from 'Paradiso' II are written on the third page of the second chapter of Book IV of Locke's *Essay*. Moreover, Gladstone made use of the code system in the diary entry itself, and the first use of the code in the text of Locke – a '|' and 'NB' combined – occurs in the very next chapter of Book IV, with the symbols being consistently employed throughout the rest of the volume.[37]

Gladstone's code provided him with a form of shorthand by which he could quickly express his opinion about what he was reading without taking too much time from the reading act itself. As can be seen from the key, where negative marks outweigh positive ones, Gladstone read, or rather annotated, with the expectation that he would be critical of what he read. This analysis operated on a number of levels, with Gladstone not only being critical of arguments put forward by the author but also alert to typographical and factual errors, which he would also correct as he went along. This tendency was noted by Edward Hamilton, who observed that, in general, Gladstone 'was decidedly critical about the style of others, and most exacting about grammatical correctness', adding that he 'was always on the look-out for it when he was reading'.[38] The essentially critical character of Gladstone's annotation is borne out by the fact that, in general, the less Gladstone agreed with a text, the more likely he was to annotate it profusely.

There were occasions when Gladstone's code proved, on its own, inadequate for the expression of his feelings about a text. In these cases, either short comments would be added in the margin, or more extensive musings would feature in the day's diary entry or in separate notes, if the book was being epitomized. In addition, if Gladstone had more to say about a particular work once he had finished reading, he would regularly inscribe a fly-leaf summary. These summaries form the second important feature of Gladstone's annotation system. The inscription of such mini-reviews was, as Jackson notes, typical practice among 'conscientious readers'; recommended by no less a personage than Michel de Montaigne.[39] Gladstone's summaries, which were usually specifically dated and signed with his initials, fall into similar categories to those cited by Jackson. Firstly, there are the spontaneous, and frequently humorous, responses to the material read, serving as both as an immediate outlet for derision or admiration. These are usually presented as imagined dialogues with future readers, but sometimes they appear to address the author directly. Such an example can be seen in Gladstone's copy of William Carlisle's *An Essay on Evil Spirits* (1827), which Gladstone read in 1885:

> The author has a title to the credit of sincerity[,] labour and self denial (p. 175): but is too much given to anathema and to rambling, and might have given the entire gist of his argument on evil spirits in the compass of a few pages. WEG S. 27. 85.[40]

Fly-leaf reviews also served as *aide mémoire*, both in Gladstone's private reading, and as tools for his writing and reviewing. One particularly extensive and eclectic annotation – which begins as a summary judgement and turns into a research note for himself – is preserved in the first volume of Gladstone's copy of William Cobbett's *History of the Protestant Reformation* (1829).[41] It reflects Gladstone's growing interest in the history of the English reformation, a fascination which resulted in several periodical articles during 1888–9;[42] his predilection for personal reminiscence; as well as his taste for high-flown, critical rhetoric:

> A 'rollicking'[,] impudent, mendacious book; most readable; with great art and felicity of narrative, the author spontaneously exalting, as he wrote, in his command. Here truly is a man master of his work, not servant of it. Take the description of Bishops North and Tomline in Parr. [paragraph] 124, b: a masterpiece.[43]
>
> After all, considering the sugared optimising tone, and the enormity of abuses, which had prevailed, a book of this kind had its uses.
>
> Query compare Cobbett with Defoe: and in some respects with Bunyan. Carlyle calls him healthy: the least appropriate surely of epithets.

> I have personal recollections of him in his very last days: the most grandfatherly of men, with singularly gentle and pleasing manners. The Tussaud figure (say 20 years back) was excellent. WEG N. 29. 87

The other main component of Gladstone's system was his regular provision of a handwritten index at the back of his books. Until the late-nineteenth century, most books were published without an index, obliging the assiduous reader to compile their own.[44] Such personalized indexes can reveal much about reading practice, for example, the level of readers' interest; the order, number, and purpose of readings; and the selection of and interest in particular topics.[45] Gladstone's indexes, when they appear, vary greatly in length and complexity. Some readings generated only a couple of page numbers accompanied by brief captions,[46] others several pages of detailed notes, others none at all. Sometimes Gladstone would compile a new index on re-reading a text; at other times he would simply make additions to an existing one. It is clear that Gladstone paid significant attention to printed indexes when they were provided, and would correct errors or omissions, just as he would in a book's margins. One entry he was particularly assiduous in inserting or elaborating was 'Gladstone, W. E.'. On Christmas Eve, 1884, he even went so far as to complain to John Murray, on finishing reading the *Croker Papers*, that 'the Index is rather *thin*'.

> I find in it two references following my own name. I have noted in the text at least twelve. What is more important, such a point as the authorship of the Waverley Novels p. 351 is not noticed except under Croker, where it might not be looked for.[47]

Once again Gladstone here indicated his self-consciousness as a reader, as well as his high estimation for a good, well-compiled index. While Gladstone was far from unusual in compiling his own indexes, according to Jackson's analysis, his ability to go beyond single lists of chronological references, grouping topics instead into separate areas, demonstrated particularly strong habits of mind.[48] And, by his frequent use of his own subject headings rather than the words of the original author, Gladstone showed himself to be an 'unusual and noteworthy' indexer.[49] It is not uncommon to come across other jottings on Gladstone's endpapers, the significance of which is not always easy to ascertain. These include mathematical sums and diagrams, short poems or hymns, and – apparently random – lists of names. While in some cases these annotations can be related to the subject matter of the book, in others, it seems that the text concerned – being close at hand – was simply being used as a convenient notebook.[50]

Taken together, Gladstone's annotation system of encoded marginalia, fly-leaf summaries, and personalized indexes (supplemented by other endnotes) signified that he had, in his own library, an individual filing system for the information his books contained and his opinions on them. The techniques of annotation he developed went some way towards ensuring that he could read efficiently and profitably during those times he could allot for study, but, in addition, he developed a number of important temporal and subjective rhythms in his reading life, an examination of which will form the rest of this chapter.

Rhythms

Reading rotation

Fundamental to the organization of Gladstone's life – including his reading – was his belief that rotation and alternation were key to both productivity and refreshment. From his practice of book rotation, with which we will deal in a moment, to his attitude to recreational and religious holiday, one can see Gladstone aiming to maintain the pace and productivity of his working life by ensuring that the regular daily and yearly structures of which it formed the principal part also contained activities which promoted invigorating change. Moreover, the attempt to keep up such rhythmical routines was one way in which Gladstone tried to make sense – both to himself and others – of the notion that his public life had equally important private, spiritual, and scholarly dimensions.

A number of Gladstone's contemporaries drew attention to his practice of book rotation, a habit for which they provided a range of explanations. W. T. Stead recognized that Gladstone's frequent exchange of reading matter was a technique by which he kept his mind fresh and his attention engaged: 'Mr. Gladstone usually has three books in reading at the same time, and changes them from one to the other, when his mind has reached the limit of absorption.' He also suggested that such reading practice formed 'a necessary corrective to the tendency to think only of one thing at one time, which sometimes in politics leads him to neglect that all-round survey of the situation which is indispensable to the Prime Minister'.[51] David Williamson argued that by using this rotational method, Gladstone 'managed to accomplish much more than the man who confined himself solely to solid volumes'. The role of 'light fiction' was seen as crucial by Williamson – who recorded 'seeing Robert

Louis Stevenson's "Treasure Island" in Mr. Gladstone's hand, when he was on his way to Osborne to kiss hands as Prime Minister' – as providing a refreshing contrast to the more academic texts Gladstone was wont to read.[52]

Reading fictions

Literature, and more particularly the novel, was certainly treated by Gladstone as a distinct category of book to be read at different times, places, and in different ways from others. Novel-reading was both an individual and a social activity. Gladstone read novels to himself to aid relaxation. For example, George Smalley noted with some approval Gladstone's novel-reading just a few hours before delivering an important speech at Midlothian in August 1884: 'Like the trained athlete, ready for a great physical contest, the great political gladiator knew that the last hours before the contest ought to be spent in relaxation.'[53] Novels as well as poetry were also regularly read aloud to family and friends – indicating once again how far social and communal reading continued to hold an important role in nineteenth-century reading practice.[54] Members of Gladstone's household would freely exchange novels between themselves, especially those just published, with a less restrictive concept of ownership than that applied to other types of book. Thus Mary Drew records several members of the family, including her father, passing round and commenting on *The Vulture Maiden*, the English translation of a German novel by Wilhelmine von Hillern.[55] Moreover, just as fiction was read differently by Gladstone and his family, so it was regarded as more disposable. This, and the family's greater interest in Gladstone's literature collection as opposed to his historical or theological ones, offer some explanation for literature's comparative under representation in the surviving St Deiniol's collection.[56] Having said this, there were key exceptions to this rule. Gladstone's lifelong love of the works of Scott and Shakespeare, for example, meant that they were classed very differently, being carefully catalogued and preserved. Scott was also one of the few authors (others included the revered Aristotle and St Augustine) for whom Gladstone would change his rotational practices, exclusively reading his works in concentrated succession.[57]

A further way by which Gladstone sought to maximize the amount of daily reading was by filling up any spare moments he had with one of his current books.[58] It was Gladstone's long-established practice to carry round at least one such book in his pocket; a habit that was affected neither by increasing familial and state responsibilities nor by widening acquaintance. Following their double wedding to Gladstone and Lord

Lyttelton in 1839, Catherine and Mary Glynne discovered that such reading habits were irremovably entrenched. As Catherine's daughter Mary later recorded:

> She [Catherine Gladstone] used to tell us, long afterwards, that it was something of a shock to both sisters when, after marriage, any little waiting time, as at the railway station, which during their engagement would have been spent in love-making, was now spent in reading – both husbands carrying the inevitable little classics in their pockets. Out it would come and quickly engross the owner.[59]

A similar, although perhaps less galling, experience befell Gladstone's friend Ignaz von Döllinger:

> 'We began talking on political and theological subjects,' writes Dr. Döllinger, 'and became both of us so engrossed with the conversation that it was two o'clock at night when I left the room to fetch a book from my library, bearing on the matter in hand. I returned with it in a few minutes and found him deep in a volume he had drawn out of his pocket – true to his principle of never wasting time – during my momentary absence.'[60]

Such spontaneous readings ensured that the activity punctuated Gladstone's whole day. However, there developed particular rhythms and timetables, which, rather more systematically, structured his reading habits, and gave a particular constitution and character to his daily life.

Reading days

The Young Man, when describing the book rotation system by which Gladstone ensured 'variation of his reading', also made sure to comment on the 'order' of reading which Gladstone imposed on himself, and the way in which different readings were undertaken at different times of day.

> Last summer, for instance, the three books he had on hand, at one time, were Dr. Langen's Roman History (in German) for morning reading; Virgil afternoon, and in the evening a novel.[61]

The substantial and ever-increasing public interest in Gladstone's routine, apparently generated by people's amazement at his legendary energy and productivity, meant that many descriptions of Gladstone's daily routine, and the part that reading played in it, have survived. Wemyss Reid observed: 'Each minute had its employment, each book (of the many he read in the day) its appointed hour'.

By the orderly management of his time he effected an all-round economy of days, hours, and minutes that is probably unparalleled. This it is that explains the immense amount of reading that he got through, and also his astonishing recollection of what he had read.[62]

Harper's New Monthly Magazine noted that, 'In the library the Premier spends nearly the whole of such portion of the day as is occupied within-doors.'[63] Via such descriptions, it is possible to reconstruct the typical reading day of the mature Gladstone. Differences, of course, pertained depending on where Gladstone was. His schedule in London, at the height of the parliamentary session, was different to that in Wales or Scotland during parliamentary recesses. It differed again when he was occupying high office, serving as a back-bencher, or in retirement. It is also important to recognize that the bulk of these descriptions come from the very end of Gladstone's reading life when he was arguably least active. Nonetheless, it is fairly easy to apprehend Gladstone's preferred routine.

Most contemporary accounts began their description of Gladstone's daily schedule in Hawarden with his attendance at morning prayer at the parish church of St Deiniol. This ritual remained a fixed point in Gladstone's day until his very last year, when, according to W. T. Stead, he began to spend an extra two hours in bed reading and preparing work before rising at ten and moving to his library for 'correspondence or literary work'.[64] In the prime of life, however, Gladstone's working day frequently got underway before his church service. In January 1888, the family's German maid, Auguste Schlüter, recorded that Gladstone was regularly in his study 'by 7.30 a.m.' when she worked in Hawarden.[65] Church was usually followed by breakfast,[66] and then work (including reading), from ten o'clock until two o'clock. This, as George Potter noted, 'seems to have been Mr. Gladstone's long-settled habit', since his Oxford days.

> At Oxford he was an exception to undergraduate life, and did not break off his morning studies at the regulation luncheon hour of one o'clock. It mattered not where he was, in college rooms or in country mansion; from 10 a.m. to 2 p.m. no one ever saw William Ewart Gladstone. He was locked up with his books. From the age of eighteen

to the age of twenty-one he never missed these precious four hours except when he was travelling.[67]

Gladstone was famously impatient of meals curtailing all aspects of his routine, not just his reading. There are written accounts of him leaving puddings to cool on the lunch table in order to economize on time,[68] and punctuating picnics with 'some pamphlet upon a question of the day'.[69] Lunch, taken at two o'clock in Hawarden, would be followed by more reading unless the presence of visitors led to the substitution of such solitary study with conversation or a walk.[70] It was noted by some that Gladstone's afternoons in the late 1880s and 1890s, following the foundation of St Deiniol's, were spent arranging books in the tin library.[71] Lewis Apjohn suggested that even the rituals of the family dinner were sometimes bypassed by Gladstone in favour of more reading: 'At times he came down to dinner and dressed for the meal. Often it was served to him in the library.'[72]

It was Gladstone's long-established habit to read in the evenings, by natural light if possible, and if not by the aid of candlelight – as early as 1823 we find him writing to his father to tell him, 'I am now reading pretty hard. The long evenings encourage reading.'[73] However, the levels of intensity of work after dinner clearly varied. Some claimed that, 'Eight o'clock saw him once more engaged in a stiff bout with Aristotle, or plunged deep in the text of Thucydides.'[74] Others described this period of reading in somewhat more restful terms: 'After dinner he returns to his sanctum – a very temple of peace in the evening, with its bright fire, armchair, warm curtains, and shaded reflecting candle. Here, with an occasional doze, he reads until bedtime, and thus ends a busy, fruitful day.'[75] During a visit to Hawarden in January 1891, Algernon West recorded Gladstone behaving in a way that falls somewhere between the two previous descriptions. While 'we went into the drawing-room', West recorded in his diary, Gladstone retired 'to his "Temple of Peace" (which he begged me to consider as my own) to read Dunckley's *Melbourne*, also Justin McCarthy's *Peel*, which he did not like so much as his *History*'.[76] Other commentators claimed that Gladstone stuck to reading literature in the evenings, and could be persuaded to remain in company if 'guests are present with whom he wishes to talk',[77] or if a game of backgammon was suggested.[78]

It also appears that at least half an hour of Gladstone's evenings was allotted to reading newspapers. Gladstone was accustomed to keeping abreast of current affairs via the daily and weekly papers, but, although essential, reading of this sort was neither intellectually challenging enough to merit regular inclusion in the diary's list of daily readings, nor sufficiently concise to satisfy Gladstone's desire to absorb essential information as quickly as possible. In some circumstances, he seems to have preferred to receive news via letter, being a more personalized and precise form of communication.[79] Nonetheless, both newspapers and the bulk of correspondence signified work for Gladstone and were avoided if at all possible when he was trying to devote himself to either holiday or concentrated study. For example, when he visited Oxford, he would leave both correspondence and newspapers untouched until his return home.[80] The only time when he can have said to have 'devoured' the papers was when he was travelling through continental Europe on his grand tour. For the most part, he was able to access English-language newspapers in public reading rooms or in the homes of friends, but when such sites were unavailable, he did feel it keenly. Thus, on reaching Genoa in March 1832, Gladstone 'Walked out – discovered a reading room with English news. We have none since leaving Paris – and I need not say that the remainder of the afternoon was devoted to devouring it. It only served to excite a craving for more.'[81] Again, when in southern Italy, access to newspapers all but dried up, a state of affairs which maddened the young Gladstone both eager for and fearful of receiving news of the Reform Bill's second reading in the Lords. On his return to Rome, Gladstone hurried immediately to Monaldini's, a print and bookseller in the Piazza di Spagna specializing in English books and papers, 'and devoured his whole stock of Galignani's'.[82]

Matthew notes Gladstone's close relationships with the personnel of the *Daily Telegraph*, and later the *Times*, and sponsorship of the regional press,[83] but makes no reference to Gladstone's personal reading preferences or techniques *vis à vis* the news. According – rather predictably – to W.T. Stead:

> Mr. Gladstone in the matter of newspaper reading stood midway between Mr. Balfour and Mr. Bright. Mr. Balfour read nothing; Mr. Bright read every word in a morning newspaper, devoting regularly two hours a day to its perusal. Mr. Gladstone usually reads one newspaper regularly. It used to be the *Pall Mall Gazette* before it changed hands, and latterly it has been the *Westminster Gazette*. The *Times* Mr. Gladstone has never read regularly.[84]

Harper's New Monthly Magazine claimed, in 1882, that Gladstone had all the London papers forwarded to him in Hawarden but spent no longer than half an hour surveying them. The *Pall Mall Gazette*, it asserted, was a favourite.[85] The *Pall Mall Budget* – as expected[86] – later agreed that the *Gazette* was Gladstone's favoured evening paper, suggesting the reason why he could afford to spend so little time on newspaper reading was because his secretaries 'when he is in office, go through every paper, and extract things as it is necessary he should see'. This suggests that Gladstone engaged in highly mediated forms of reading as well as those intense personal engagements with which he is more often associated. In addition to the *Gazette*, the *Budget* claimed, Gladstone 'takes the *Standard*, and, of late years, since it began to oppose his policy on the Irish Question, the *Daily Chronicle*'. In addition, 'he dips into the *Spectator* and the *Guardian* among the weeklies'.[87] Henry Lucy noted, in the *Strand Magazine*, that the *Spectator* also fell out of favour following its defection over Home Rule.[88] However, the careful preservation at St Deiniol's of a run of the Church of England's *Guardian* attests to Gladstone's sustained favouritism for at least one newspaper.

Known for needing a good night's sleep, Gladstone continued his reading at bedtime, 'keeping some book at his bedside, neither too light nor too heavy, and treating of something as far removed as possible from the subjects occupying his mind'.

> On returning from the House in the small hours, tired and excited, he would have a cup of tea, and then resort to this reading remedy, which was hardly ever known to fail if he was in his usual health.[89]

If he was confined to bed through illness, however, Gladstone also sought respite in reading – usually something familiar and well loved, which would bring him comfort and amusement. Thus, in 1873, when 'my upper jaw ... sent me to bed early', he wrote with grim humour: 'I took to reading [Scott's] "Old Mortality"'.[90] Gladstone also resorted to reading in the middle of the night when suffering from insomnia. In January 1883, when he was only getting between three-and-a-half to four-and-a-half hours sleep per night, Gladstone again turned to Walter Scott and 'Read The Antiquary (in the night)' to try and remedy his sleeplessness.[91] Gladstone did experience illnesses and conditions which prevented him from reading. Gladstone regularly suffered from severe eyestrain, which worried his doctors and infuriated him as he hated not being able to read. In 1849 he recorded: 'My eyes suffered from the light today – reading is at an end except the paper – which is a kind of necessary'.[92] His struggles with failing eyesight towards the end of his life, which affected both his public and private lives, make painful reading.[93] In 1893 he wrote to B. W. Currie, the banker, that 'my sight is now impaired so that when speaking I obtain hardly any assistance from ordinary written notes, and have to depend almost entirely upon memory alone',[94] and privately he noted: 'Much change in my reading power since I read [Henry] Esmond'.[95] He was unable even to read by candlelight,[96] and his incapacity also made it difficult for him to maintain his habitual book lists. In December 1894 he recorded: 'I had a fall over one of the drawers of my writing table, on my forehead, with the whole weight of my body'. He tried to continue his book listing but, due to 'Il Male Occhio', he conceded 'No: I *cannot* do it'.[97]

Gladstone's routine when in Downing Street was somewhat different. It revolved around a weekly mid-morning 'breakfast' to which people in whom Gladstone was interested, or from whom he felt he could learn, were invited. As such, these breakfasts constituted part of one of Gladstone's most important strategies for accruing knowledge.

Reading people

Notwithstanding the many descriptions of Gladstone reading alone, his reading was not wholly private and individualistic. Communal and public reading, especially in domestic environments – whether for spiritual or leisure purposes – formed a key part of Gladstone's experience as a reader, and he clearly enjoyed discussing what he had been reading, even with the least receptive of companions. Furthermore, different genres, texts, and individual reading performances were often associated with different people or groups, for example, as we shall see in Chapter 4, his association of Tennyson's poetry with fallen women. The association of reading and relationships, therefore, is a crucial one in understanding Gladstone's mind and motivation over his long career. Some of the most significant relationships he had, ones which influenced him politically and intellectually as well as privately and emotionally, began with or were cemented by reading.

Perhaps the earliest such reading relationship, which Gladstone made outside his own family, was with Arthur Henry Hallam, who not only charmed him personally but also, according to Gladstone, had a considerable formative intellectual impact upon him. In a reminiscitory article on Hallam, written not long before his own death, Gladstone publicized the personal debt he felt he owed his friend. As well as being regular participants in the school's debating society, Hallam and Gladstone regularly breakfasted and took walks together, 'often to the monument of Gray, so appropriately placed near the "Churchyard"'. At these meetings, the two would engage in discussions 'largely of an argumentative character', during which, Gladstone recalled, many of his youthful intolerances were broken down under Hallam's broadening influence. Furthermore, Gladstone recalled how he had been 'plodding on the beaten and dusty path' before his revelatory relationship with Hallam opened his eyes to a true appreciation of literature. Hallam, who read – as Gladstone later aimed to do – 'largely, and though not superficially, yet with an extraordinary speed',[98] crucially introduced his friend to his lifelong love of Dante.[99] He was also the means by which Gladstone was introduced to the person and poetry of Tennyson, a reading relationship which, as we will see later, generated both explosive political, and disquieting personal, consequences. For his part, Gladstone later thought, Hallam was making use of his mind (and those of similar friends) 'as anvils on which to beat out the thoughts engendered in his own'.[100] In the aftermath of Hallam's death, Gladstone had spoken both of the 'elevating effects derived from intercourse with a spirit such as his' which would, he felt, have worked 'powerfully and for good' in the wider world had Hallam lived.[101] As it was, Hallam's influence lived on, not only through Tennyson's *In Memoriam*, but also in Gladstone's reading habits and practice. Gladstone's intellectual breakfasts at Downing Street, his long, disputatious walks with house guests, and wide range of correspondences were, in many ways, carried on in homage to Hallam's practice of using others' minds as intellectual anvils.

It thus became Gladstone's practice, when opening up a new subject, to contact those of his friends with knowledge or potential advice about what to read or how to interpret what he read. Sir Walter Phillimore, in his eulogy on Gladstone as scholar in the *Fortnightly Review*, gave a good example:

> I have a letter in his own hand dated May 14th, 1886, asking me what the civil law view was to the necessity of an official resignation being made always to a superior. I thought some rather recondite analogy was wanted for the action of his proposed subordinate Irish Parliament ... but a P.S. told me that the interpretation of a curious passage in Dante turned on my answer.[102]

Gladstone's relationships with Antonio Panizzi (1797–1879), principal librarian of the British Museum;[103] Lord Acton;[104] and Ignaz von Döllinger[105] all fell into this category. Neither did Gladstone solely ask advice of trusted friends. Although he was often overwhelmed by the numbers of gift books he received from strangers, if a book or subject interested him, Gladstone did not hesitate in entering into dialogue with the sender. As Ewing Ritchie recorded:

> The Rev. Dr. Robertson, of Venice, having sent Mr. Gladstone a copy of his second edition of 'Fra Paolo Sarpi,' in returning thanks from Hawarden, Mr. Gladstone writes: 'I have a strong sympathy with men of his way of thinking. It pleases me particularly to be reminded of Gibbon's weighty eulogy upon his history. Ever since I read it – I think over forty years ago – I have borne to it my feeble testimony by declaring that it comes nearer to Thucydides than any historical work I have ever read. It pleases me much to learn that a Sarpi literature has appeared lately at Venice. If you were so good as to send the titles of any of the works or all works on the subject, I would order them; and I should be further glad if you would at any time thereafter come and see them in a library with hostel attached, which I am engaged in founding here.[106]

Gladstone's practice of asking friends, acquaintances, and even strangers for such advice, was, once again, partly a time-saving device. Gladstone, as prime minister, had so little time to accrue knowledge via conventional means that any opportunity which presented itself – to elicit useful summaries of work in progress, or advice on further reading – was enthusiastically taken up. Moreover, his position as premier ensured he could attract almost anyone he wished to meet and interrogate. There are several accounts of his Downing Street breakfasts, which became an institution. W. T. Stead, in his 'Character Sketch' of Gladstone, published first in his *Review of Reviews* and republished in booklet form following Gladstone's death, described M. Chevalier, the French economist, and his Belgian counterpart, M. de Laveleye, being invited to breakfast to meet Gladstone and Bright. Gladstone clearly used such meetings as an opportunity to speak about books, although not always to the delight of his guests:

> On another occasion, on the eve of Lord Wolseley's departure for Egypt, Mr. Gladstone mortified his guests, who included Lord Wolseley, by talking obstinately about nothing but the best binding for books.[107]

This anecdote accords with Wemyss Reid's description of Gladstone's habit of fixing, in conversation, on a particular issue in which he often remained interested to the exclusion of everything else:

> A characteristic of his was that he was deeply interested in one thing at a particular moment ... Many can doubtless remember how, on

the appearance a few years ago of the 'Life of Cardinal Manning,' Mr. Gladstone, having read it with his usual avidity, made it for several weeks the chief topic of his conversation. No public events sufficed to drive it from his mind ... I remember that chancing at the time to meet Mr. Gladstone at a London railway station, as he was on the point of leaving town for Hawarden, I found myself instantly involved amid the noise and bustle of the place in a discussion upon the book and its merits.[108]

Here again, as well as observing Gladstone's characteristic obstinacy, it is possible to see the way in which he sought, partly by means of his position, but also by force of will, to stick rigidly to the terms of his routines and interests, rather than complying with those of his acquaintances, a species of politeness in which he had literally no time to indulge.

Let it not be thought that, amongst Gladstone's reading relationships, those he had with men either predominated, or were automatically more important. As Gladstone himself observed, 'friendships with women have constituted no small portion of my existence',[109] which truth has been well corroborated by his biographers, most recently Anne Isba and Jenny West.[110] For all his well-entrenched reading habits as a bachelor, it is vital to recognize how profoundly Gladstone's reading life was influenced and shaped by women, both within, and far beyond his family circle. As Chapter 3 shows, Gladstone's earliest reading experiences were powerfully shaped by his mother's feminine, spiritualized influence; while reading and books provided an enduring bond in his relationship with his two sisters, despite the interventions of separation, illness, addiction, and death. Although it has been suggested that Gladstone's marriage to Catherine Glynne did not immediately affect his reading practices, as Susan Pearce asserts, marital relationships have an important influence on collectors and their collecting.[111] Indeed, we have already seen how Gladstone responded to the birth of his daughter by working on his books. Moreover, the effect of Gladstone's marriage on his book collecting, and *vice versa*, offer further evidences of the importance of women in Gladstone's reading life.

Catherine Glynne's reading was certainly affected by her relationship with Gladstone. Before her marriage she had steeled herself to read and memorize parts of *The State in its Relations with the Church* (1838), a daunting task which Roy Jenkins rather patronizingly suggests was due to her 'growing absorption' in Gladstone rather than youthful intellectualism.[112] Despite her recognition and appreciation of Gladstone's scholarliness, as we have seen, his extreme and casual bookishness proved something of a rude awakening to Catherine immediately after their marriage. Biographies of Catherine Gladstone frequently stress her complementary role as helpmeet to her husband; the enabler of an independent intellectual no less than a political life. For example, Edwin Pratt elaborates:

> His health and his happiness were for Mrs. Gladstone a sacred trust, and whether he was the Prime Minister of England or only a scholar in his library was a matter of detail which made no difference either in her profound devotion to him or in her watchful care.[113]

Such representations suggest that it was Catherine's work and wifely devotion that facilitated Gladstone's time-consuming reading by effectively denying herself an intellectual life. 'Her function', as described here, 'was to manage the details', and relieve 'him of any of those troubles or worries' and leave 'him perfectly free to make his speeches, *to read his books*, or to take his rest as he felt inclined'.[114]

While it is important to recognize the role played by servants, as well as partners and children, in facilitating intellectual work,[115] it is unlikely that Catherine consciously denied herself intellectual stimulation for the sake of her husband. Although her reading habits differed in both volume and style to his, Catherine Gladstone was intimately involved in the book-life of the household. She occupied a desk in the Temple of Peace in Hawarden Castle, borrowed books from its shelves both for herself and others. She was, as her daughter Mary made clear, 'in the habit of reading aloud to her children in later years', noting in particular that 'Scott's novels were read in that way'.[116] By so doing, Catherine was communicating a love of literature, which she fully shared with her husband, to their children. Readings of Scott had featured centrally in the married couple's early relationship. In the weeks prior to their wedding in 1839, Gladstone recorded, 'read ... Kenilworth, aloud with dearest'; on both their wedding night and on the succeeding day he read the sentimental and chivalric 'Marmion to her'; and during their honeymoon, he 'read Lady of the Lake (aloud)'.[117] The following year, Gladstone recorded reading both *Rokeby* and *Lord of the Isles* to Catherine.[118] Bible reading was also an important feature of their first years of marriage. Again on their honeymoon, Gladstone recorded that he had read the 'Bible *with* my Catherine: this daily practice will I trust last as long as our joint lives'.[119] Indeed, there are numerous references to joint Bible-reading between 1839 and 1874. Other reading, by Gladstone to his wife,[120] occurred more intermittently. Gladstone had, soon after his marriage 'ruminated on plans of reading for C. & myself which now at least ought to take form. It is high time to recommence application', but such joint readings never matched the intensity of Gladstone's own programmatic reading schedule.[121] Not at least until it became necessary, because of Gladstone's blindness, for Catherine to read to him.[122] 'Many kind friends have read books to me', Gladstone wrote, but 'Dearest C has been my chaplain'.[123]

Gladstone's Sunday reading

Contemporary commentators drew regular attention to Gladstone's punctilious Sabbath observance and the special reading habits which were associated with it. 'From Saturday night to Monday morning', recorded *The Young Man*, 'Mr. Gladstone puts away all business of a secular nature, keeps to his special Sunday books and occupations, and never dines out that day unless to cheer a sick or sorrowful friend.'[124]

Gladstone's determination to maintain a different routine on 'the Lord's day' in order to '*quell* the remaining excitement of the week, and effectually reduce it to peaceful exercises on matter [sic] of religion' was established at early stage.[125] The day's regime was structured around his attendance at two (or sometimes three) church services and hearing one or two sermons.[126] When at home, Gladstone would endeavour to abstain from academic or political work, travelling, or frivolous entertainment, limiting his activities to those he deemed appropriate to the day, such as conversing with friends and family, or engaging in some light physical exercise. The bulk of his time away from church was spent either in reflecting on what he had heard there, conducting household worship, or in further reading.

Gladstone took his position as family pastor extremely seriously. He led prayers, usually in the evening, in both his father's and his own establishments over the years,[127] even publishing a prayer manual for family use in 1845.[128] Even more remarkably, he wrote a large number of his own sermons which he regularly delivered to his entire household at Sunday evening prayers held at a quarter to ten. More than 200 complete and fragmentary manuscripts survive, written substantially between the 1840s and 1860s, mainly for his London household at 13 Carlton House Terrace.[129] These documents, as David Bebbington has demonstrated, 'lay bare the speaker's religious assumptions and sometimes his social and psychological premises too' as well as revealing 'the most deep seated shift in his convictions during the 1850s and 1860s'.[130]

Gladstone sometimes found it impossible to follow his ideal Sunday rituals rigidly. If away from home, he was sometimes forced to travel on Sundays or live with habits and customs which were incompatible with his brand of Sabbath observance, particularly when travelling in Europe or attending country-house parties. However, Gladstone demonstrated more flexibility when it came to prosecuting political work. If matters were pressing, he would not hesitate to work on the Sabbath, defending such decisions by remembering that St Augustine had considered that 'useful labour on the Day of Rest' is 'preferable to the frivolities of recreation'.[131] Moreover, the difference between types of work appropriate and inappropriate to a Sunday was not always easy to discern. 'The service of God', Gladstone observed in an article on 'The Lord's Day' written in 1895, 'is necessarily performed within the area which is occupied by this world and its concerns'. As such, any attempt to maintain the distinctiveness of Sundays necessarily involved a degree of compromise. Gladstone's explained his formula for deciding whether or not a certain activity was appropriate as follows:

> All that ... most vividly brings home to us the presence of God, all that savours most of the emancipation from this earth ... is matter truly proper to the Lord's Day. What it is in each case, the rectified mind and spirit of the Christian must determine.[132]

This was a remarkably broad prescription, setting no hard and fast rules – each case should be considered on its merits – and potentially allowed the Christian to do or consider things that were not intrinsically religious on a Sunday. The only requirement was that the activities undertaken should prompt the individual to a consideration of spiritual things.

We can see this prescription being followed remarkably clearly in Gladstone's lifelong practice of dedicated Sunday reading. This displayed an overtly religious character, clearly distinguishing it from his more eclectic weekly diet.[133] It was, as one might expect, dominated by the Bible – described by him on one occasion as '*the* Book' – the reading of which was, to Gladstone, a religious duty.[134] A large version was kept open for this purpose in his dressing room at Hawarden.[135] To this he habitually added further sermons, devotional works, as well as books on theology and church history – all of which reading influenced his own homilies.[136] While Wemyss Reid (and others) claimed 'no secular books were read',[137] it is clear from Gladstone's diaries that no such complete exclusion existed. In line with his formula, Gladstone would certainly not have read anything either intentionally hostile to Christianity or which diverted his mind from godly things on Sundays, but the breadth of what he did allow himself to read – for example, works on spiritualism – was quite remarkable.[138] Moreover, not all Gladstone's Sunday reading was monastically solitary: Auguste Schlüter recorded in her diary the household practice of reading in the garden on summer Sundays.[139]

Reading aloud has been described as 'the most pervasive form of mutual education',[140] and was an activity in which Gladstone delighted to participate.[141] It was not only a common after-dinner entertainment, but also, as we have seen, for Gladstone, a religious and patriarchal duty. This, together with an understanding of its philanthropic qualities, encouraged Gladstone to take such readings outside the family context, and to read aloud to strangers. Ewing Ritchie, for instance, recorded one perfectly respectable occasion when Gladstone 'came ... and talked and read' to a London crossing-sweeper who had fallen ill.[142] However, texts are rarely to be restricted to such respectable contexts, and there were significant reading experiences for Gladstone that were neither polite, religious, nor domestic; ones which he regularly shared with women other than his wife. A combination of his belief in the philanthropic power of books, with his own tendency to resort to different kinds of reading in response to emotional crisis, led Gladstone to engage in readings to and with fallen women over an extensive period. While most of these encounters were brief and unremarkable, others – such as that with Laura Thistlethwayte – were of tremendous significance for Gladstone's reading experience and will be explored in more depth in Chapter 4.

As the discussion has so far made clear, reading and reception can be significantly altered by the company the reader may keep.[143] It also begins to highlight the extent to which these activities may be influenced by location. Hence, it is important to review the ways in which 'place' made a difference to the way Gladstone read.

Reading places

We have already seen indications that Gladstone's reading was profoundly influenced by place. His Sunday rituals were, for instance, prone to alteration because of travel or residence in unfamiliar or uncongenial surroundings; it has also been observed that his Hawarden routines differed from those followed in London. It is clear that, while some of these changes were enforced, others – such as the neglect of post and newspaper reading in Oxford – were deliberately established by Gladstone in order to create or emphasize divisions between different areas of his life, particularly to differentiate work, leisure, or study time. Moreover, it is possible to identify a number of key reading places that were of particular importance to Gladstone over the course of his life. Some, such as Fasque and Penmaenmawr, were associated with particular periods. Others, such as Oxford, influenced much longer spans of years.

It will be argued below that Oxford was, spatially, intellectually, and theologically, the site of St Deiniol's genesis. As such, it is important to survey Gladstone's on-going relationship with his *alma mater*. Oxford's influence on Gladstone's sense of self and on his intellectual development was tremendous. The *idea* of Oxford was important throughout his life, as can be seen in Gladstone's dedication to the University in *State in its Relations*, as well as in his dying message to its vice chancellor,[144] but the place itself: its buildings, atmosphere, scholars, and publishers, were equally significant. The scholarship which emanated from the city was crucial in influencing Gladstone's broadening from the evangelicalism of his youth to a species of high churchmanship soon after graduation.[145] Although in later years Gladstone played down the impact of Tractarianism upon him, its influence is clear in his diary, and he noted the significance of this period and its Oxford contacts in his *autobiographica*.[146]

Following his election as MP for Oxford University in August 1847, Gladstone's visits to Oxford took on a more public and political flavour, frequently consisting of endless rounds of visiting, canvassing, and testy discussions about university reform.[147] He did occasionally manage to escape 'the usual *giro*'[148] – on more than one occasion retreating to Cuddesdon, where he could reacquaint himself with 'old & loved scenes'.[149] He also found time to keep up with the latest theological developments – hearing Benjamin Jowett's 'very remarkable, but unsettling' university sermon on 25 January 1852 – and used his position of privileged access to interrogate Oxford's heads of houses concerning his all-consuming Homeric researches in 1857.[150] In 1859 he was made an honorary fellow of All Souls, an auspicious occasion marked by a series of lavish dinners and – less conventionally – a reading of various pornographic works in the college's Codrington library.[151] Although Gladstone would make use of All Souls as an Oxford base in later years, he did not visit the city at all for a decent interval after his acrimonious rejection as member for the University in July 1865. However, when in 1870 his niece by marriage, Lavinia Lyttelton, married Edward Stuart Talbot (1844–1934), the recently appointed first warden of Oxford's newest college, Keble, Gladstone was provided with reason to resume his visits,[152] one result of which would be the determination of the future of his Hawarden library.

Hawarden was, of course, of central importance to Gladstone's reading life and dictated many of its rhythms. Gladstone made a conscious distinction between the readings he undertook in the family home and those made in his London houses. For example, he began reading Scott's *Peveril of the Peak* (1822) on 1 October, 1860, while at Hawarden, left it behind during a short visit to London (where he read Wilkie Collins' *The Woman in White*), resuming *Peveril* on his return.[153] Similarly, he left Scott's *St Ronan's Well* behind in Hawarden when returning to London on election business in 1857.[154] Several months later, he repeated the same procedure with *The Heart of Midlothian*, reading almost every day, only breaking off when away from Hawarden.[155]

Although from 1851 onwards, Hawarden Castle represented home for Gladstone and his growing family, it remained owned by and shared with Catherine Gladstone's brother Stephen. Furthermore, as Gladstone's country residence, it was both increasingly a site for political entertaining and for significant amounts of necessary public business, contesting its status either as a place for private scholarship or for family relaxation. When one adds to this the family's regular and extended stays with Catherine's sister Mary and her family, at Lyttelton's Hagley Hall, it is not surprising to find the Gladstones' seeking to institute a separate holiday routine from *c.* 1855, which involved decamping to the North-Wales coast for extensive periods. This pattern was undoubtedly also introduced for health reasons. As well as Gladstone's enthusiasm for sea-bathing (recorded faithfully in his diary) and walking, both he and Catherine were sensitive about the health of their children; Agnes had only narrowly escaped death from erysipelas in 1847 and was still delicate, and the couple had lost Catherine Jessy to meningitis in 1850. It was not without some relief, therefore, that Gladstone observed the instalment of a 'healthy happy party' at Penmaenmawr, their chosen seaside retreat, on 3 September 1855.[156] The resort was both far enough and different enough to give the family privacy – Gladstone noted significantly in August 1867 that 'we are nine, all together, *and alone*'[157] – and a change of air. It was also easily accessible (by carriage and train) to Hawarden in case of emergency. This familiar routine, followed almost every summer between 1855 and 1874, and intermittently in succeeding years, also gave Gladstone the opportunity to institute distinct patterns of holiday reading. He could establish a settled base with a good collection of books, read and write in a sustained manner, and still remain within easy reach of his main library. Gladstone, as he did at home, set apart an area for work – in the early trips this was more often than not one corner of a room, or a portion of the dining table, but in later years he frequently commandeered a room for himself.[158]

As well as Gladstone's concern to improve his children's health – evidenced by his encouragement of vigorous exercise, sea-bathing and boisterous play – he was also keen to use holiday time helping his children with their education. He would typically assist the boys with their classical studies, and give scripture lessons to the girls.[159] Teaching (as is often the case) stimulated his own appetite for study and research: thus working through Aristotle's *Politics* with Willy (begun on 3 September 1860) he began 'a paraphrasic translation of the Politics'.[160] This endeavour had to be suspended until the following year, no time being available in Gladstone's increasingly busy work schedule.[161] For reasons such as this, Gladstone's desire to escape from the cares of state while in Penmaenmawr was very strong – he described the receipt of a 'Terrible parcel of letters & papers from London' on 11 August 1868 – but he could not disguise his underlying guilt at leaving such responsibilities aside. Thus, in 1855, after departing from 'this pleasant sojourn: where I have lived too happily for one who thinks as I do about the course of events & the responsibilities of needless war', on his return to Hawarden, Gladstone 'Sat up late reading the detailed accounts from Sebastopol: wh[ich] were for England grievous.'[162] While on 25 September 1859, he surreptitiously luxuriated in working 'on Translations in German & English: an agreeable way for a C[hancellor]. of [the] E[xchequer]. to pass his time.' On other occasions, he was forced to interrupt his holiday by pressing political business. Thus in September 1859 he was obliged to return to Hawarden for an impromptu conference with Cobden on French foreign policy.[163] It is no wonder, therefore, that he was jealous of what time he could spare for study – even momentary illness was resented: 'An evil night from an attack of diarrhoea & sickness made this a *dies non* as to all outward work: I could not even read.'[164] Acutely aware of the precious nature of such vacations, Gladstone would often set about such holiday tasks with almost more intensity than those which occupied his working life. For example, in a letter written in 1886 to the sometime editor of the *Daily News*, Henry Lucy, Gladstone related that his 'ambition during my "holiday" has been to give eighteen hours a week out of seventy, or one-fourth, to the prosecution of a study of which the Olympian Religion is *a* central part'.[165]

Gladstone could and did, however, distinguish between study and 'pure holiday'. It is not true to say that he had no other method of relaxation than replacing one type of work with another (a regular description of him in contemporary biographies). Thus, we find him in September 1860 admitting that a diet of Aristotle, Tacitus, Luigi Tosti and Madame de Sevigne – in addition to 'my business' – was 'a little hard ... so I may let in some lighter material'. He duly replaced the French work with a pirate story in *Tales from Blackwood*, before launching onto a fresh burst of Walter Scott.[166] Moreover, he sometimes admitted to feeling tired of politics *and* study: 'I still feel much mental lassitude', he observed after having left Penmaenmawr for Balmoral, '& not only shrink from public business but from hard books. It is uphill work.'[167]

When Hawarden and North Wales became as much if not more publicly associated with Gladstone's professional image than London – an integral part of that reconfiguration of Gladstone's image discussed in this book's final chapter – further careful delineations were needed in order to maintain and refresh the differentiation between 'public' work and 'private' leisure. In contrast to Gladstone's 1867 exultation over being 'alone' with his family, 1868 saw a change of atmosphere at Penmaenmawr. On 10 August, the Gladstones arrived at the station at half past five to be met by a party of working men who 'amid much enthusiasm', drew their carriage all the way to their holiday home. Gladstone 'thanked them briefly' before retiring, but it was the sign of things to come. Later that holiday, the family 'entertained some 90 to 100 men & boys of the Craig Llwyd Quarry', who presented Gladstone with an address and sang. Again, 'I spoke in answer'.[168] By 1874, 'All seem to know and greet us',[169] a familiarity undoubtedly aided by Gladstone's sessions with photographers both on this trip and on the one before.[170] They left as they had arrived, 'with very many kind tokens of good will',[171] but were not to visit Penmaenmawr again until 1882 when invited by Lucy Cavendish. Once more, there was a 'speech to a large gathering at the Station' before departure.[172] In addition to increased publicity, Gladstone found it ever more difficult to put off work. Thus in 1868 he 'Worked on Homer. But *public* business takes half my working day or near it.'[173] By the time of their final visit – a brief stay in the midst of February 1887 – the resort was a resort no longer.[174]

In part to counter such pressures, from 1877, an increased variety was exhibited by the Gladstones on holiday. As the couple aged, stays in

Penmaenmawr were supplemented by at least five cruises, several residences in Brighton, more regular trips to Europe including extensive, and increasingly frequent, sojourns first with the Stuart Rendels in Cannes, and later with George Armitstead in Biarritz.[175] As suggested at the outset, extensive periods of foreign travel potentially created the most significant challenges to Gladstone's rhythms of reading, and it is with an examination of Gladstone's reading during such journeys that we conclude.

Foreign travel

In common with an increasing number of his contemporaries, Gladstone travelled extensively as a tourist in both Britain and Europe.[176] Undertaking such lengthy and elaborate journeys presented many challenges, especially to a young man who thrived on order and daily routine. Problems of accommodation, transport, illness and so forth, could, at best, disrupt long formulated plans and, at worst, place travellers in considerable physical danger, as demonstrated by the Balzers *contratent* described at the outset. Like many other similar journeyers, Gladstone made a detailed record of his movements, instituting a separate journal in which he could record places visited, people met, and things read at much greater length than was his custom.[177] While this was physically distinct from his daily diary, the latter digest was not wholly laid aside: matters of a very personal nature – usually relating to his spiritual life and self-opinion – were still recorded 'secretly' here. This was a necessary continuance; both the tone and content of Gladstone's travel journals indicate that they were written, at least in part, with an eye to being read by others. For instance, it is evident from the journals detailing Gladstone's grand European tour of 1832 that he and John had received advice about places to stay and visit from their eldest brother Tom. In his turn, Gladstone systematically rated the hostelries in which the brothers stayed (in some cases noting how badly bitten he had been by fleas), gave tips as to where tasty and (more importantly) economical meals were to be had, provided lists of local attractions not to be missed by the novice traveller, and made crucial, corrective updates to 'several of the books much used by Tourists'.[178] Gladstone continued this approach during his second European tour in 1838–9, largely spent in southern Italy and Sicily, and was rewarded by sections of his travel journal being included by John Murray in his hugely successful series of travel guides.[179]

Among the changes travelling entailed to Gladstone's routine, curtailment of and alterations to his reading habits were amongst the most serious, as can be seen from his diary's list of daily readings. These lists, usually so remarkable for their length, variety, and consistency, altered significantly when Gladstone was travelling. Accustomed to having a sizeable library at his disposal, Gladstone could only carry a relatively small number of books with him on such peripatetic trips, necessarily curtailing the breadth of his reading. As he discovered in both 1832 and 1838, libraries and reading rooms were often readily available for consultation,[180] but the demands of 'lionising' (and, in Gladstone's opinion, his propensity for indolence) meant that only short periods of time could realistically be 'rescued' for reading.[181] As a result, we find Gladstone regularly complaining about the lack of progress he has made with his reading while abroad. 'As to reading', he wrote on reaching Lyons in February 1832, 'such as I have been able to accomplish in the evenings & in the carriage (but *here*[182] my performances are very trifling from inability in my eyes)[183] has been Moliere, Bourrienne [*Mémoire ... sur Napoléon* (1829)] at intervals, Manuel du Voyageur [Milan, 1818], French Grammar, Shelley and Coleridge – but very little of any.'[184]

Moreover, luggage space and reading time had to be made for books of practical use for the tourist: language texts and travel guides. Gladstone was a natural linguist and took pains to improve his knowledge of the languages he would need during his travels.[185] In consequence, grammars and dictionaries formed part of his travelling library from the outset. Thus he was: 'Employed in "cramming" French phrases' on the outward channel crossing in February 1832, an unwise choice of occupation which brought on 'dismal presages of sea sickness'.[186] Similarly in Italy, he was regularly to be found rehearsing Italian grammar,[187] and was well enough organized in Venice to equip himself with the German equivalent in preparation for the return journey through Austria and Switzerland.[188] This purchase did not profit him greatly however; he soon found himself, talented as he was, stuck fast in a grammatical bog, *'roking'* (steaming or smoking like an overworked horse) and as 'blind as a mole'![189] On the whole Gladstone did not feel the limitations of his travelling library too keenly, although in Florence in 1838 he wished he had taken 'Rio's book' – as indeed the author had advised him, rather than relying on his 'memory & notes'.[190]

Gladstone had more ambitious reasons for wishing to improve and perfect his linguistic knowledge beyond that of furnishing himself with necessary everyday vocabularies and phrases. He maintained a high level of sermon attendance on the Continent in both 1832 and 1838–9; if anything he increased it both to compensate for his limited access to reformed religious books and his eye strain. In order to understand and comment on the theological intricacies of such expositions, Gladstone needed to equip himself with highly specialized vocabularies. Furthermore, he frequently wished to interrogate preachers, librarians, museum and gallery attendants, and other locals, sounding their views on complex matters such as the state of education and religion in their respective countries, conversations which required considerable linguistic flexibility. Gladstone did not spend as much time as he would have liked improving his language skills: 'I make but little time for Italian', he lamented in March 1832.[191] One reason for this was because, in order to orientate himself successfully, a considerable amount of time had to be devoted to studying travel guides.

Gladstone was an inquisitive, independent-minded, and interactive traveller. His reading and use of tourist guides and maps, those other essential reference works included in his luggage, reveals both his desire to be informed about the foreign environments in which he found himself, and also his determination not to be passively reliant on such information. He and John bought and annotated maps, inscribing on them their actual or projected peregrinations. William described the process at the start of their stay in Genoa: 'Bought a map: investigated by our books the principal objects, at least a selection of them: traced them on the map, and numbered them to be visited in order, according as they lie. This plan we have found the best, both on this and other occasions.'[192] He noted inconsistencies and possible errors, for instance, suggesting that Heinrich Keller (1778–1862), the cartographer of their map of Switzerland, had inaccurately demarcated the borders between the Rheinwald and Schams areas![193]

If Gladstone sometimes took issue with map makers, he did so far more readily with travel writers (although it is important to note that he was also often unconsciously influenced by their writing).[194] Some of their productions Gladstone appears to have carried with him from England, such as Marianna Starke's *Information and Directions for Travellers on the Continent*, the eighth edition of which was published in 1832. Others, such as Johann Gottfried Ebel's traveller's guides to Germany and Switzerland, he bought *en route*. Gladstone included comments on these texts both for the practical benefit of his own future readers, but also because he wanted to establish and authenticate himself as a knowledgeable traveller, able to expose the shortcomings of recognized authorities. The final words of his travel journal Gladstone devoted to inscribing his opinion of his seven most frequently used travel books. Ebel's volumes received commendation, as did Joseph Forsyth's, *Remarks on Antiquities, Arts, and Letters during an excursion in Italy*, 3rd edn (Geneva, 1824) despite the fact he found it lacking in moral tone. Others were judged less satisfactory. Daniel Wilson's *Letters from an Absent Brother* (London, 1825) 'ought never to have been published', pronounced Gladstone, as 'the work is extremely hasty: style diffuse: descriptions overdrawn: statements frequently erroneous.' Edward Burton's *A Description of the Antiquities and other Curiosities of Rome,* 2nd edn, 2 vols (London, 1828) was deemed 'faithful and full of information ... but dry & hard' because it 'seems only [to] view that [most] wonderful of city [sic] as a collection of sights', while Henry Matthews' *The Diary of an Invalid* (Paris, 1825) was dismissed as tasteless.

Gladstone expected his guides to be accurate, comprehensive, with a sufficiently detailed coverage; a writing style characterized by liveliness and imagination, and the whole tempered by both taste and moral principle. Mrs Starke (1761/2–1838),[195] whose works were to provide the model for John Murray's guides, fell short on many of these points and duly received the most consistent criticism throughout the 1832 journal (and came in for more in 1838–9). Gladstone, while acknowledging that the book was 'generally useful', somewhat smugly pointed out hotels Starke had missed,[196] her inaccurate recording of mileage and prices,[197] and her failure to convey local colour.[198] He lost patience with her entirely in July, when, at the top of the Splügen Pass he raged:

> Mrs. Starke's description of this passage is nothing less than a disgrace to her book. Amongst other varieties, she seems to confound the two roads: & I suppose has never travelled either. Nothing in her book ... has met my eye, which can be compared to this misdescription: – except her Sonnets.[199]

Mrs Starke's sonnets probably compared unfavourably with the other poetry Gladstone was reading during the course of his trip: works by Shelley, Coleridge, and Wordsworth. Gladstone travelled with poetry for a number of reasons. A few were practical – a book of poems is 'the most profitable of all others in a carriage to one who cannot read there much or long'[200] – but most were aesthetic.

It is clear from his journals that Gladstone conceived of his grand tour, not only as an opportunity to view and collect fine art and to observe continental religious practices; it also served as a kind of literary excursion. He made a point of visiting places associated with particular writers – Voltaire's villa near Geneva,[201] Dante's grave in Ravenna, and the graves of Shelley and Keats in Rome. To this should be added two failed attempts to find Edward Gibbon's house in Lausanne,[202] an abortive effort to track down Sir Walter Scott in Rome,[203] as well as a successful meeting with Alessandro Manzoni during his 1838 visit.[204] Gladstone read poetry in order to heighten his travelling experience, to excite his imagination, and to facilitate comparisons between the character of the written works and the scenes that had inspired them. Thus, when surveying the Wurmer Loch (a gorge near Santa Maria, Switzerland) in 1838, Gladstone observed that the sight 'would have aided Dante with materials for the construction of his Inferno', before going on to 'read Dante, on the mountain, while waiting for the carriage 8000 feet high. (In Par. III. IV)'.[205] And, at 'the beautiful lake of Thrasymene', he 'longed for [Richard] Trench's poem' to heighten his experience.[206]

In some places, Gladstone thought himself able to detect (or so he thought) tangible echoes of even earlier writers' inspiration. Southern Italy and Sicily, in particular, represented an opportunity to encounter classical civilization almost unchanged.[207] Indeed, he seemed genuinely surprised when, in 1838, 'some peasants grinned with contempt at me, or with surprise at least, when I was plucking from a blackberry bush', noting, with some disappointment, that 'Virgil's declaration is no longer true, vaccinia nigra leguntur. Ecl[ogues]. 2.18'.[208] Undeterred, and armed with Virgil's works, Gladstone used the Roman poet as a guide – frequently finding more to please him than in the pages of Mrs Starke.[209] When at Pozzuoli, near Naples, in 1832, Gladstone had struck a conspicuous pose reading Virgil from the back of a donkey, all the while comparing the poet's vision with the scene before him. His local guides tried their best to capitalize on his enthusiasm, taking Gladstone to see a variety of 'original' sites including 'the Sibyl's baths' and 'the Elysian fields'. However, their hopes of extra payment for these additional excursions were to be disappointed, as the well-read Gladstone considered their stories 'ridiculous'! Nonetheless, he did judge that 'the face of the country [is] still corresponding in many particulars, notwithstanding the violence of volcanic action'.[210] He came to a similar conclusion in Sicily in 1838. Gazing into the Castelventrano valley near Segesta, Gladstone 'Read 3[r]d Aen[eid]. with pleasure.'[211] And again, when gazing into Etna's crater, Gladstone's experience of the natural wonder was once again shaped by his Virgilian frame of reference, his journal containing various quotations from the poet, and extensive affirmative commentary on the accuracy of his descriptions.[212] As well as Virgil, Gladstone found allusions with a host of other ancient texts including Juvenal, Homer, Sophocles, and Thucydides. Looking out from his window in the Albergo del Sole in Syracuse in 1838, Gladstone seemed

> to see the proud and gilded galleys of Athens struggling to enslave the hardy ancients of this city, the long banks of oars, the decks crowded with armed men, the deadly grapple and the chequered incidents of those great and gallant seafights which the pen of Thucydides much to our labour but more to our delight has immortalised.[213]

Elsewhere much was changed of course, not least in Rome. Here the decayed remains of the once-great empire were the object of much contemplation by Gladstone. He was much struck by Shelley's description of Rome as both 'beauty and decay',[214] and on one occasion sat amidst the ruins of the Forum to read *Aeneid* VI, the book in which Virgil describes Aeneas' descent into the underworld. Rome's 'humiliating ... mass of ruins' had powerful lessons for the observer, Gladstone reflected, especially for a citizen of the nineteenth century's largest and most successful empire.

> For amidst this utter ruin and desolation, we should remember, that it is on the ruins of no common tyranny that we stand, but of the most vast and most abiding empire that the world ever saw. Now, all its pride is level with the dust, and the remaining chambers of its palaces are buried under the fragments of their own ruins.[215]

Here Gladstone's attention shifted from those rhythms of reading which shaped his days, his years, his relationships, and his travels, to a contemplation of the equally complex and fluctuated rhythms of history, full of import for the conduct of the present – a process which represented, in Gladstone's case, an equally familiar and lifelong pattern.

Part II Making the Reader

3
The Gentleman's Inheritance, 1809–36

Visitors to an impressive exhibition of portrait miniatures at the South Kensington Museum in 1865 might have noticed Liverpool artist Thomas Hargreaves' representation of a young girl and boy, loosely embracing in a leafy glade. The image, part of an eight-piece loan, is not exceptional in its composition or technique: the bodily proportions of the girl in particular are crudely represented. Yet, the compelling pensiveness of the faces might have attracted even those tiring of such minute imagery by number 1028 in the catalogue.[1]

The large dark eyes the children share and their attitude of simple affection suggest a sibling relationship. The boy appears the elder; he stares directly at the viewer while his sister's unfocused gaze drifts to her left. Most arrestingly, the boy points didactically to the text of a small book lying open on his sister's lap. With her attention diverted from the book (presumably chosen for her edification) her teacher-brother has assumed the task of educating the observer, drawing our attention both to his own proficiency in reading and his precocious desire to share that knowledge with others.

The miniature (Figure 3.1) represents one of the earliest known authenticated likenesses of William Gladstone,[2] pictured with his younger sister, Helen Jane (1814–80). The image represents a stage of his reading and book-ownership that is both largely uncharted but also potentially important. It references those formative years which he spent living, learning, and reading with his family in Liverpool and Scotland; constructing his selfhood in the context of an affluent merchant household, largely in a pre-Victorian world; a world which in part pre-dates his own diary record.

When Gladstone was born on 29 December 1809, he entered a family for which books, in their reading, ownership, and display, were important

Figure 3.1 Thomas Hargreaves, *William and Helen Gladstone* (*c*. 1816). C. A. Gladstone.

commodities. What is more, a taste for bibliophily and serious reading was actively encouraged by both Gladstone's parents, albeit with somewhat mixed results and within ambiguously gendered frames of reference. We know that William was, in terms of time and scale, to outstrip both his parents and siblings in his love, collection, and reading of books, but many of his lifelong bibliographical practices and intellectual priorities were shared with and learned from his family.

Bibliomania in the family

Gladstone was the fifth child and fourth son of two émigré Scots, John Gladstone (1764–1851), a lowlander from Leith, and his second wife, Anne Mackenzie Robertson (1773–1835), a highland woman from Dingwall.[3] We know that John Gladstone amassed a sizeable book collection with which he furnished the libraries of successive family homes. The late-eighteenth and early-nineteenth-century context in which this collecting took place was the site of widespread and impassioned debate about both education and reading. It saw the beginnings of mass education with legislation for the education of lower-class children,[4] the Sunday school movement,[5] an increase in the amount and availability of instructive children's literature and didactic popular fiction,[6] mounting popularity for the educational theories and methods of Locke and Rousseau (and for critiques of them by radicals and feminists)[7], as well as witnessing a library revolution in both the public and private spheres.[8] 'Public' libraries for the wealthy grew out of debating clubs and gentlemen's societies. For instance, John Gladstone's adoptive home of Liverpool opened a library for 'Gentlemen and Ladies who wish to promote the Advantage of knowledge' in 1758, which claimed to be the first of its kind in Great Britain.[9] Concomitantly, there was an unprecedented growth in the popularity of private, domestic libraries, reflecting the emergence of this apartment as a key space for both everyday living and formalized entertainment, and as a vehicle for the display of wealth, status, cultivation, and gentility. Distinctively furnished with books, busts, especially designed furniture, and other elegant accoutrements of learning, the library represented 'a perfect blend of comfort, civilization and choice taste' for Britain's propertied classes, and, during the last two-thirds of the eighteenth century, libraries of this sort were being built on an unprecedented scale.[10] Guides to good (and acceptable) reading were freely available to novice library builders – who were encouraged to learn from sale catalogues of great libraries, largely acquired by centuries' worth of aristocratic collecting – in order to ensure the social currency of their acquisitions.[11] However, such collectors were not without their critics, and were regularly diagnosed with 'bibliomania' – an extreme species of book-collecting typified by indiscriminate and excessive expenditure.[12] Benjamin Disraeli's father, Isaac D'Israeli (1766–1848), sharply satirized 'bibliomaniacs' in his *Curiosities of Literature* (1791–1823).

> The BIBLIOMANIA, or the collecting an enormous heap of books without intelligent curiosity, has, since libraries have existed, infected weak minds, who imagine that they themselves acquire knowledge when they keep it on their shelves. Their motley libraries have been called the *madhouses of the human mind*; and again, *the tomb of books* when the possessor will not communicate them, and coffins them up in the cases of his library ... where volumes arrayed in all the pomp of lettering, silk linings, triple gold bands and tinted leather ... and secured from the vulgar hands of the *mere reader*, dazzling our eyes like eastern beauties peering through their jalousies![13]

John Gladstone's enthusiasm for books was, undeniably, in keeping with his ever more genteel existence, as were his art purchases, his essays in church patronage, and his progressively grand houses. He bore a striking resemblance to Mark Girouard's Victorian merchant, for whom 'there was increasingly present the vision of ... an estate in the country, a glistening new country house with thick carpets and plate-glass windows, the grateful villagers at the doors of their picturesque cottages, touching their caps to their new landlord'. Nevertheless, John Gladstone's gentleman's library was not to be like that described by D'Israeli – purely for show and impractical. While his library had not only to look impressive, it had also to exist as an important educational resource for his children (principally his four sons) and contain the books which would prove most useful to them. For, just as Girouard's merchant, John Gladstone looked forward to 'his sons at Eton and Christ Church and his ... daughters teaching in the Sunday school'.[14]

The first library Gladstone would have known was that of his birthplace, 62 Rodney Street, Liverpool (then No. 1). It was built by John Gladstone during 1792–3 for his first wife, but was really shaped by his family with Anne. During the period when their children were being born, John purchased books, drawings, and pictures to ornament the house, estimating in 1814 that his books alone were worth £400.[15] Gladstone retained few memories of Rodney Street, but he found Seaforth, the draughty house on the Mersey estuary to which the family moved in 1815, a very stimulating environment.[16] It featured regularly in his early diary record as the family home to which he returned, usually twice or three times a year, in school and university vacations.[17] Seaforth was, moreover, the house in which Gladstone's love for reading, his passion for organizing books, and his enthusiasm for discussing their contents first took shape. Whenever he returned home, Gladstone's invariable priority was to get into the library. This was not always to engage in concentrated reading – on 2 August 1827, he only managed to 'read various books idly in the Library' – but it was a place to which he was irresistibly drawn and in which he could unwind. Thus, on 7 December 1826, despite being tired, 'having slept very little on the road', William set about 'getting the Library to rights' as well as reading 'part of the Confessions of Ireland & ... Tomline's Life of Pitt'.[18]

The other residents of Seaforth quickly recognized, and sought to harness, William's bookish enthusiasms, and he was appointed by his siblings to the post of Seaforth's nursery librarian in 1818.[19] The position was one that he keenly prosecuted and in which he was ably supported, when absent at school, by his deputy, Helen Jane.[20] William's determination to exercise total bibliographic control did not stop with his siblings' books. His ambition was to monitor the reading of the entire household, including the servants. His project, to build up a small servants' library in 1829, was one that he planned and executed with the support of his mother, and which was clearly didactic in emphasis. On 29 September 1829, he recorded having been 'in Town, riding', and selecting 'books from the Christian Knowledge List for a servants' Library, & arranged with my dear Mother about them'. The following month he 'made a list of the books for the servants'.[21]

Gladstone was not only buying books for the house's main library, but also for the personal use of his parents.[22] As a self-made man and autodidact, John came to rely heavily on his Eton-educated son for bibliographical advice, in order that his collection should be both worthy and function as an up-to-date educational resource.[23] Nevertheless, negotiations between the testy patriarch and his precocious son over book purchases were not easy, with them not always seeing eye to eye on matters of quality or finance. In February 1824, Gladstone wrote to his mother: 'I hope my Father has not forgotten a gentle hint I gave him that while the hundreds are rolling in, a few ... might without inconvenience by vested in Books.'[24] By November that year, John appeared more acquiescent, asking for his son's comments on a list of sale books: 'Many of them seem to be valuable and useful Books, & proper to constitute a Library', Gladstone diplomatically replied.[25] Five years later negotiations were still proving difficult: in October 1829, Gladstone attended a Liverpool book sale with his father and complained 'there long – a very bad day'.[26]

Other members of the family also found William's zeal somewhat exasperating. Thomas (1804–89), John and Anne's eldest son and heir,[27] did not share the heightened intellectual curiosity common to William and his two sisters. The following letter illustrates Tom's lack of interest:

Dear William,

I beg a thousand pardons for my neglecting to send you the list of my Library before now, but I really have had a good deal to do since the holydays. Robertson is writing to my Mother, who is I hope by this time better than she was when Ann [sic] wrote. Excuse brevity and with best love to Helen and Johnny. Believe me to be y^r very affec^t Brother

I shall write to Johnson   Thos Gladstone.[28]

This letter underlines how far William's desire for knowledge and order extended beyond the sphere of his own book collection. He had obviously been pestering Thomas – preoccupied with his own affairs at Eton – for some time. In return, Tom mocked his nine-year-old brother's bibliographic (and political) precocity by addressing his belated note to: 'The Rt. Hon. W. Gladstone, Librarian &c, &c, &c'! The list Thomas sent was neither extensive nor detailed; unlike William, he did not see fit to arrange his inventories alphabetically or to group subjects together, indicating both his lack of time and interest. It reflected the required classical reading of the student (Virgil, Homer, Ovid, and Horace), the influence of his evangelical Christian home (the Bible, *Moral Tales*, and Edward Young's poetical *Night Thoughts* [1777]), and the familiar English language 'classics' of the early-nineteenth century (poetry by Scott, Southey, and Cowper).

It was at Seaforth where Gladstone forged the earliest and most influential of his reading relationships with women: those with his mother, and his two sisters, Anne Mackenzie (1802–28) and Helen Jane, with whom he had the closest and most intense of relationships. Gladstone's mother's role in the literary interests and education of her family were, as might be expected, more privately than publicly orientated.[29] The activities of Anne Robertson Gladstone were both important and influential, but they were – as we shall see – also less straightforwardly recognized or represented than those of her husband. Numerous scholars have convincingly demonstrated that Anne was the driving force behind the family's evangelical Christian character, with its strong emphasis on the textualities of the Bible, religious literature, and personal journalizing. It has also been made clear elsewhere how influential she was over William's religiosity and practice.[30] Her own private reading habits were, as were her son's, dominated by her religious interests: family letters reveal that her favourite texts were such as *Daily Bread*. Spiritual material was supplemented by works like *The Scotch Gael*, indicating that her nationality, as well as her religion, featured strongly in her own sense of identity (a combination which also displayed itself in her youngest son).[31] But Anne's influence was not completely restricted to the private sphere. She knew members of the Clapham Sect, including William Wilberforce, whose opinion of her Gladstone later recorded:

> I am sure they loved my mother who was love-worthy indeed ... [In] 1833 I had the honour of breakfasting with Mr. Wilberforce a few days before his death, and when I entered the house, immediately after the salutation, he said to me in his silvery tones: 'How is your sweet mother?' He had been a guest in my father's house some twelve years before.[32]

Anne was instrumental in acquainting her son with a group influential, evangelical, and educationally minded, being the means by which her son William was personally introduced to Hannah More in 1815. More, who noted that children 'bring into the world a corrupt nature and evil dispositions which it should be the great end of education to rectify', was in the vanguard, with Maria Edgeworth and others, in producing popular didactic literature which aimed to compete with the unregulated moralities of chapbooks and broadsheet tales.[33] William was an obvious target for such didacticism, and duly received his copy of her *Sacred Dramas*. There is no doubt that More also made an immediate, as well as a more lasting, impression on him: he recorded reading nine works by her between 1825 and 1840.[34] What is equally clear is that his mother was instrumental in perpetuating the influence of More's circle in her particular domestic environment, for example, by casting William in the role of the child evangelist so commonly represented in evangelical texts,[35] and by encouraging the introspective, autodidactic, and self-examinatory aspects of his learning techniques. The most important of these was his journalizing – a very common feature of evangelical and Nonconformist upbringings – to aid spiritual self-examination, encourage careful reading, interpretation and analysis, as well as intellectual self-improvement.[36]

Of his brothers and sisters, William was closest to the eldest and youngest: Anne Mackenzie and Helen Jane. Anne Mackenzie was the eldest of John and Anne's children and is most frequently remembered for her religious influence on the young William.[37] It is clear that she was an intelligent young woman, reading French and studying Italian, as well as being keen to debate theology with her youngest brother. She too was an enthusiastic reader, almost certainly increasingly so as her health deteriorated throughout the later 1820s, and other activities became proscribed; her room at Seaforth, to which she was increasingly confined, was furnished by 'heaps of books on the tables'. She shared William's love for Scott and admired Byron.[38] She too was plainly aware of the educative power of the domestic environment over the public sphere: 'The power to do well cometh from the home', she told William (at Eton) in 1824.[39] William was devastated by her death at the age of 26. On Sunday, 22 February 1829, he recorded his sorrowful return to Seaforth, where he 'found all in great grief' and 'saw the pale remains of dearest Anne'. Characteristically, Gladstone responded to his emotional turmoil by resorting to his books and struggled to maintain continuity through his reading schedules. Thus, later the same day he 'Began Sumner's Apostolical teaching' and, several days later, in a poignant bibliographic tribute to his dead sister, he and Helen 'made ... an inventory of dear Anne's books'.[40]

This youngest sibling, Helen Jane, was not only equally intelligent but also an independently minded girl. She asked William to teach her Latin when only a little child (suggesting Hargreaves had indeed caught the true state of their relationship in his miniature). Helen and William grew increasingly close, especially after Anne's illness began, and remained so into the early 1830s. William's relationship with Helen followed the one he had had with Anne very closely. They read about and discussed together many of the same topics, including baptismal regeneration,[41] and, after Anne's death, they entered a pact to monitor the conduct of the other.[42] In adulthood their relationship was stormy, and one in which books and reading were both uniting and dividing factors. Helen's intense spirituality and lack of fulfilment in the family home drew her to Roman Catholicism, to which she converted in 1842.[43] Gladstone's reaction to her decision was periodically marked by intransigence and vindictiveness. On one occasion he lost his temper completely when he discovered that she had been using religious books from their father's library as toilet paper![44] However, when they did get on, Helen and William's relationship continued to be dominated by books and reading.[45] Following her death in 1880, part of Gladstone's process of grieving for her (as it had been for Anne) was to sort through and reflect upon the library she had collected. On 17 January 1880 he recorded: 'walked awhile after dusk. Until then, and again after dinner to near midnight worked on the large mass of effects, especially the books, of which I arranged I think about 1200'. The following day he 'made an examination of all the books of devotion: it was very interesting & important & set forth the whole history of her mental transition since 1870. I packed all these Volumes apart. They show she died at one with us as before'.[46] However spurious was Gladstone's judgement that Helen had died in communion with Canterbury, his deduction based on her library shows how very seriously he regarded a book collection as reflective of its owner's mind and development, as well as a useful source for trying to understand it. Thus, on the 19 January, Gladstone 'Read through the uncut Vol. on Morphia-Craving … & resumed work on Books & effects (which are a huge chaos) as also upon papers', prior to their sale on the 20th and 21st.

Educating the public man

The domestic atmosphere in which Gladstone was brought up, and which influenced his understandings and practice of book culture, was thus feminized in important ways. Many of the texts produced by the circle with which Anne Gladstone had contact, and which she introduced to her children, were addressed specifically to women and girls. Of the nine texts by Hannah More that Gladstone recorded reading in his diary, two focused specifically on female education and behaviour: *Strictures on the Modern System of Female Education* (1799; read 7 December 1834) and *Hints Towards Forming the Character of a Young Princess* (1840; read 30 October 1840). Exemplary child characters who described keeping diaries (in works such as M. M. Sherwood's *The Fairchild Family* [1818]) and teaching in Sunday Schools (which Gladstone did)[47] were commonly women. The encouragement of even such regulated autonomy among children was deeply ambiguous, considering the dependency such minors shared with women and servants in the context of the patriarchal family. This ambiguity, coupled with the need for male children (unlike their mothers or sisters) to change their status and become more independent over time, made the position of boys within the domestic sphere particularly problematic. Women writers were as aware as their male contemporaries of the social advantages of an Eton education for boys.[48] Edgeworth, in *Practical Education*, advised parents in the 'middle ranks of life' to consider the 'large public schools' as a way of expunging their (male) children's 'rusticity' and 'provincial dialects', also insisting that school holidays were to be monitored and not be allowed to degenerate into 'dissipation and idleness'.[49] Such advice can also be read as recognition that boys' removal from the feminized home space was a necessary stage in their development as men.[50] However, the difficulties involved in achieving a smooth transition were – as we shall see in Gladstone's case – not inconsiderable.

In old age, Gladstone did not recall much in the way of formal teaching having emanated from either of his parents: 'My father was too much occupied. My mother's health was broken.'[51] Nonetheless, the letters that passed between the three of them during these early years clearly show the careful consideration Gladstone always exhibited towards their opinions on educational matters, as well as revealing the whole family's disputatious interest in matters educational. Before we compare the feminized influences on the young Gladstone's reading outlined above, with those masculinized ideas which emanated from his father, it is important to note that these gendered influences, while distinct in many ways, were neither mutually exclusive nor always oppositional. John and Anne shared many ideals and there is considerable evidence that John regularly consulted his wife and other children over William's dilemmas. For instance, on 17 November 1827, he wrote to William 'after consulting with your mother and sister', sent a joint letter with his wife the following day regarding William's tutoring, and, on 29 October 1830, promised to discuss the thorny question – of whether or not his son should continue his mathematical studies – with Anne and their eldest son.[52] Nonetheless, the final say usually remained his. In March 1828, for example, he decided that William should go to Seaforth to spend his vacation in mathematical study, rather than gratify his wife's wish that he should join them in Edinburgh, a plan John thought (perhaps following Maria Edgeworth's advice) 'would never do'.[53]

John's position as principal arbiter was reflected in the extreme levels of deference William habitually reserved for John's opinions. When thanking his father for sending him an edition of the *Liverpool Courier* in February 1823, Gladstone added the assurance that 'indeed I always read everything you send me'.[54] Later the same year he wrote with news of his success at Eton:

> My beloved Father,
>
> As I promised my Brothers to write to someone at home to-day, to inform you of the result of our Trials for getting into the fifth-form, I cannot choose a fitter person than the Patriarch (or Governor) of No. 5 Grafton Street: and I hope you & all will be happy to hear that I have got into the fifth-form, and that I have taken sixteen places.[55]

None fitter indeed: John Gladstone remained fiercely loyal to the patriarchal traditions of his Scottish heritage, seeing himself – as Checkland notes – as 'a Highland chief' who 'regarded himself as the head of his clan (including his wife's kinsfolk)'.[56] Naturally, he had a very well-developed idea of the characteristics that should mark out his sons' education and reading, being firmly convinced that their future careers and social position were dependent on both. Between 1820 and 1822, he had unfolded his views to Tom, who clearly bore the brunt of his father's substantial ambitions for his family, in a series of letters. John expressed himself with all the zealous passion of one to whom formal education has been denied and the anxiety that was habitual, as John Tosh has argued, to the nineteenth-century father seeking to plan his son's future life.[57] Note in particular how the pronoun changes from 'we' to 'I' in the following excerpts, indicating the direct and personal nature of this advice from father to son.

> A greater proportion of eminent and distinguished men have been sent forth into the World from Eton than any other Seminary in the Kingdom, we therefore did not hesitate in selecting for you this School, tho' the most expensive ...

It is our anxious wish to give you a right direction to your mind ... I wish I were more competent to the Task, but *none* such fell to my Lot when at your time of Life, I can therefore only speak from information and observation, not actual experience ...

Education is now so general that everything is expected from a Gentleman. He is expected to possess every acquirement, to speak Modern Languages, to have a knowledge of Science generally, to know something of the Fine Arts, with a well cultivated mind and a deep sense of the Duties he owes to his Creator and his fellow Creatures ...

In Classical acquirements you should become acquainted with the nature and composition of those languages ... and ... the style and manner of the most intelligent and accomplished Scholars and Orators of the Ancient Schools of Greece and Rome. On these your taste ought to be formed and from them your mind should be stored with useful and important knowledge, ... you ought to acquire the habits of application, of close thinking and investigation of subject, and that of tracing every effect to its cause ... Your Studies (Classical) ought also to give you a taste for reading, and a desire for general knowledge, which you will be at no loss for time to gratify.

When you have leisure for general reading, I would recommend History in preference ... If either at the Bar or Public Life, it is absolutely necessary to possess and intimate acquaintance with not only the history and constitution of your own Country, but every other ...

At Eton you have abundant proof in the conduct of others what may be done there. Look to Mr Canning who, whilst storing his mind with Classical and General Knowledge, was distinguishing himself by literary composition.[58]

Part of the essential preparation for life in the public sphere, in John Gladstone's view, was wide and 'general reading'.[59] Although Tom was being given every advantage by being sent to Eton, he would need to self-direct his learning and reading in order to achieve that highly tuned working knowledge that his father saw as necessary for a professional career. Such attitudes permeated the educational theories of the day and showered their diffused influence over popular literature for both children and adults. In order to emulate characters like Mary Wollstonecraft's heroine in *Mary, A Fiction* (1788), who was 'left to the operations of her own mind' considering 'everything that came under her inspection, and [thus] learned to think',[60] and to avoid the fate of those like Edward Waverley, who, in undisciplined fashion, 'drove through the sea of books, like a vessel without pilot or rudder',[61] it was taken for granted that Tom needed self-discipline and natural curiosity in order to learn.

John's first three sons found it hard to live up to such high expectations. Tom endured a difficult, and at times miserable, five years at Eton before advancing first to Christ Church, and then to a political life, being elected Tory MP for Portarlington in 1833.[62] The second son, Robertson (1805–75), who was to become mayor of Liverpool in 1842, began studying at Eton, but was relocated by John to the family business, and replaced at the college by William.[63] Nevertheless, he did not go without further education. John Gladstone deemed that appropriate mental training was as necessary for a merchant as for a lawyer or politician. Thus Robertson was sent back to his parents' ancestral country, to study at the College of Glasgow for two years.[64] In his second term of study there, he received his parents' permission to learn to play the flageolet, on the proviso that he devoted no more than half an hour a day to the hobby. Furthermore, he was advised to stop reading novels: 'After you have finished *Peveril*', wrote his father, 'I would wish you to give up the subscription to the circulating library. It is only calculated to tempt you into light reading.' Robertson was also instructed to keep careful account of his spending and keep his handwriting plain.[65] However, parental advice did not deter Robertson from reading: in 1831 William referred to a 'book-commission' undertaken for his elder brother.[66]

John and Anne's third son, John Neilson Gladstone (1807–63), was a somewhat remote figure who refused to follow his father's predetermined plan, forging a successful naval career before settling into the life of a country gentleman and backbench MP (for Devizes from 1852–63).[67] John always got on well with William, accompanying him amicably on his 1832 grand tour, but they drifted apart in later years.[68] Nonetheless, he clearly shared in his family's liking for and common exchange of books; in an early diary entry, William recorded receiving '10 little books from Dear John'.[69]

Unlike his elder brothers, it is evident that the Gladstones' youngest son enthusiastically embraced the challenge he had been set. Gladstone developed into a voracious reader at Eton. Although he was generally happy there, he remained singularly unimpressed by both the low standard of religious practice,[70] and the inadequate levels of intellectual rigour at the College – often using echoes of his father's rhetoric to either praise, or criticize.[71] On leaving, he informed his father that his Eton education had left him 'wretchedly deficient in the knowledge of modern languages, literature and history', the very subjects which John Gladstone felt should supplement the classical education of a proto-public man.[72]

In the face of such deficiencies, it is not surprising that John Gladstone impressed on his boys the importance of self-discipline and self-motivation in learning, and that William habitually read more widely and for much longer than either syllabus or school debates required.[73] Gladstone read much modern British history (including Clarendon, Hume, Burnet, Coxe's *Walpole*, and Tomline's *Pitt*), which was useful not only for filling in historical gaps in his schoolwork but also for the school debates to which he was an enthusiastic contributor. In addition, he kept up a formidable programme of private religious reading built around daily study of the Bible – read extensively on Sundays and sometimes in Greek – thus maintaining the influence of his evangelical home.[74] This said, we should not overemphasize the uniqueness, or precocity of Gladstone when at Eton. The annotations in his surviving school books demonstrate characteristics common to children's marginalia. His books were bound with interleaved pages – a common practice at the time – to allow him to insert parallels, which he frequently made in ink, betokening their status as officially sponsored insertions designed to last. The school books also contain many drawings – once again, a common characteristic of children's books – including doodles, caricatures of masters, diagrams, and field placings for cricket![75]

Gladstone was not exclusively receiving advice and instruction from his father. Talk of books, reading, and religion recurrently occupied the correspondence of Gladstone with his mother. Despite the distance, Anne was keen to monitor William's reading following his departure for school: 'My opportunities of study are indeed desirable,' he reassured her in 1822, '& you may be sure that I will use them all to the best advantage I am able. I sensibly feel the truth of what you send in your last kind letter, & I will, please God, endeavour to take the good advice which it contains.'[76] He was evidently happy to submit to his mother's vigilance, later agreeing to put off reading Scott's *Peveril of the Peak* until Easter 1823, a significant sacrifice for him considering his love for the author's work.[77] It is interesting that Gladstone's mother (unlike his father) seemed to regard *Peveril of the Peak* as inappropriate reading for her sons, suggesting an awareness of, and uneasiness with, the competing and ambiguous models of masculinity on display in Scott's Waverley novels.[78]

Just as her husband, Anne Gladstone entrusted William with book-buying commissions – he was searching for a suitable new Bible for her personal use in 1825 – while he enthusiastically regaled her with stories of his own purchasing.[79] The letters between them appear, as they are catalogued, to be much fewer in number than those between father and son.[80] There are, in fact, are a good many 'hidden' letters from Anne, incorporated into her husband's epistles. As she herself explained, it was John's practice to write and then, if space remained, allow his wife (or his daughters) to fill up the blank paper. There are also examples of John overwriting his wife's letters. Such private epistolary traditions are very revealing of the patriarchal nature of the Gladstone household. Their content is even more demonstrative of it.

Gladstone undertook a period of intense cramming before progressing to Oxford, under the tutelage of the Revd Dr J. M. Turner of Wilmslow. Considering the shortcomings of his Eton education, this appears to have been an understandable move, but it was clearly also common practice.[81] During these preparations William demonstrated how much his father's educational discourse had influenced him, commenting in a letter to Tom that, 'though Mathematics are undoubtedly of great importance ... their relative importance in the scale, compared with that of Classics, is most decidedly, and considerably, inferior'.[82] Gladstone spent the years 1828–31 at Christ Church, Oxford, reading *Literae Humaniores* and Mathematics. The family letters of this period in particular enlighten the systematically gendered tensions in Gladstone's attitudes towards study, and their origin in his relationship with his parents. The letters between Gladstone and his father are characterized by the importuning, the giving, and the receiving of advice on reading, political questions, school work and life choices. At each stage of Gladstone's Eton and Christ Church careers, discussions took place between them as to William's future course. Most of this correspondence was driven, on William's part, by his feeling the 'great responsibility' of acting 'merely on the strength of my own view of the question, without consulting others'.[83] He was unable (or unwilling) at this stage to act independently, and still deferred to John Gladstone as the *pater familias*.

In a lengthy letter of August 1830, in which Gladstone revealed to his father his wish to become an Anglican clergyman, he described his mounting sense of vocation thus: 'Day after day it has grown upon & into my habit of feeling & desire'. This emotional description, accompanied by an unfavourable comparison of the secular world with the kingdom of God, is followed by a crucial passage that reveals Gladstone's sense of his mother's influence on his nascent vocation:

> I have scarcely mentioned my beloved Mother in the whole of this letter: for though little has ever passed between us on this subject

through the medium of language, & nothing whatever, I believe since I last spoke with you upon it, yet I have long been well aware of the tendency of her desires, long indeed before my own in any degree coincided with them.

Then, anticipating his father's reaction to such an expression of sensibility, Gladstone toyed with the idea that his 'statements' might 'be false, or exaggerated, or romantic, or impracticable', and prayed that he might 'through you [his father] instrumentally ... be brought back to my right mind, & taught to hold the truth of God in all its sobriety as well as in all its force'.[84] John's reply to his son was far more sympathetic and restrained than William could have expected.[85] In it he reiterated his opinion that the role and sphere of a clergyman was overly 'circumscribed & limited', when compared to 'those Professions, or pursuits, which lead to a more general knowledge, as well as a more general intercourse with mankind', and accordingly provide the entrée into 'Public life'. However, John promised William that, if his feelings had neither changed after leaving Oxford nor on return from his grand tour, 'I shall not oppose your <u>then</u> preparing yourself for the Church', afterwards reiterating that the decision 'will then rest wholly with yourself'.[86] Gladstone's mother wrote several days after her husband, having, significantly, rejected 'an offered corner of yr dear Father's last letter'. Her epistle expressed obvious delight in William's choice. She described the projected event as 'so essential' to her 'comfort', and concluded, 'I look to you – as to a stronghold'.[87]

Despite her faith that her son would hold firm to his intentions and so realize her long-cherished hopes, her desires were to be overwritten, just as her carefully penned letter was by her husband.[88] William, filled with an enthusiasm for politics ignited during the rumbustious reform debates of 1831, abandoned his clerical ambitions in favour of a career in public life. At this point, and far more decisively than he ever had before, Gladstone echoed his father's language, and relegated his mother's, in his letters. 'What was then written', he told his father in January 1832, 'I wrote under impressions of my judgment, associated perhaps with a larger share of emotion than is ordinarily incidental to my mind'. Now, he continued,

> I am free and happy to own, that my own desires as to my future destination are exactly coincident with yours in so far as I am acquainted with them – believing them to be a profession of the law with a view substantially to studying the constitutional tranch [*sic*] of it, and an

experiment as time & circumstances might offer on what is called public life.[89]

In the midst of the familial clamour inaugurated by the duke of Newcastle's approach to William in 1832, Anne admitted defeat. 'Yes dearest William', she wrote in postscript to yet another of her husband's letters, 'you have been indeed called from quiet into direct action – What an armour it requires.'[90] In contrast, John praised William's attainment of his masculine maturity; exuberantly following his successful election two month's later with the words: 'You are now a Public Man'.[91] Anne's influence over her youngest son's choice of career was thus ultimately subordinated to that of her husband's.

For all the father's triumphalism at his son's attainment of manly independence, Gladstone was, as we will see, never entirely free of the tensions that had so plagued him. This was partly, of course, because the idea of a transition between a private, feminized world of the home, and a public, masculine space beyond was straightforward neither in theory nor in practice. Gladstone's Oxford years, as academically successful and lastingly influential as they were,[92] left the young man with considerable gaps in that knowledge-accruing project in which he constantly engaged; lacunæ he felt acutely once he was thrown into the disorientating worlds of Westminster and London Society. Gladstone thus found it necessary to educate himself, principally through private reading, in ways which he hoped would both equalize the tensions existent between the two ideals of education he had inherited, and vindicate his decision to follow his father's advice.[93]

The principal venue for Gladstone's period of remedial study was once more his father's library, which had by this time been removed to Scotland. John Gladstone had begun searching for a suitable Scottish estate as early as 1820, a quest that intensified following his rejection as parliamentary candidate for Liverpool in 1823. He eventually settled on Fasque, near the village of Fettercairn in Kincardineshire, purchasing the house and estate for just under £80 000 in 1829–30.[94] Gladstone had begun his first visit there on 20 August 1833,[95] being 'much pleased with ... the interior of the house', 'lionising' both 'within and without' enthusiastically the following day. He was clearly struck by the house's romantic setting, and made the most of his opportunities to walk over the estate.[96] However, Fasque was not only important because it proffered opportunities for numerous squire-like pursuits, but also because it proved conducive to reading, study and, in particular, to that self-education and self-organization Gladstone craved.[97]

Between 1833 and 1851, William habitually spent the August to October parliamentary recess at Fasque, during which he often read aloud or acted as secretary to his father.[98] In the autumn and winter of 1835 Gladstone went to Fasque and, in Colin Matthew's words, 'undertook what represented, in scope and intensity, almost a second education'. Matthew interprets this move as a response to the Tory defeat and Gladstone's own disagreement with Aberdeen over West Indian education,[99] but this was a project that William had been planning for some time. He had already embarked on a punishing regime the previous year. Thus, on 14 August 1834 he was 'arranging ... books & meditating great doings, to work 2 h. (at least) before breakf[ast] – & go to bed at 11'. However in October 1835, conscious that the previous month had been 'one of much disorganisation', Gladstone sought to impose 'exercise and discipline' and extended his habitual reading period to cover the whole day, aiming to read and write for at least nine hours, sometimes working for eleven or more, efforts which, not surprisingly, resulted in eyestrain.[100] He focused on a wide range of serious theoretical texts, reading history (Hume's *History* again); biography (reading and re-reading Boswell's *Life of Johnson*); politics (Tocqueville's *Democracy in America*, and Aristotle's *Politics*, which he found of 'immense value for all governors and public men');[101] law (Blackstone); ancient literature (Plato); modern philosophy (Francis Bacon and Locke's *Essay Concerning Human Understanding*); theology (St Augustine's works and Thomas Chalmer's *Bridgewater Treatise*); and there was, of course, Dante. He finished the *Paradiso* for the first time in March 1836, when back in London.[102] The previous month he had inscribed the key to his system of annotation. By so doing, Gladstone was taking stock of how far his mind had developed, not in a self-congratulatory manner, but in order to judge how much work still remained to be done. It was an intimation both of methodical intention – this was how he planned to systematize his future reading – and also an admission of perceived ignorance: how much there was still to learn and discover from the many texts with which he had yet to engage, and how much more 'moral' he could become in the process.

One further spur for the period of intense work which had preceded this moment was undoubtedly the grief Gladstone felt over the loss of his mother, who had died at Fasque, her family around her, on 22

Figure 3.2 Alexander Munro, 'Sketch for John and Anne Gladstone's Memorial, Fasque', May 1854, GG MS 450. C. A. Gladstone.

September 1835. A fascinating postscript on the nature of the Gladstone family's gendered consciousness, and the place of Anne within it, is offered by a series of drawings produced in 1854 by Alexander Munro (1825–71) for John and Anne's memorial in St Andrew's Episcopal Church at Fasque.[103]

Commissioned and adapted by Tom (by then Sir Thomas) Gladstone, the original sketches (Figures 3.2–3.3) represent the couple praying in the family library.[104] John, with head resting on his right hand, occupies the dominant, central space throughout the series, while Anne's role, as both reader and supplicant, was increasingly subordinated during the memorial's design process. It was not John's position as religious patriarch that ensured this; in fact Anne was more easily integrated into the newly emphasized religiosity of the final composition (Figure 3.4).

Figure 3.3 Alexander Munro, 'Sketch for John and Anne Gladstone's Memorial, Fasque', June 1854, GG MS 450. C. A. Gladstone.

It was the need to represent, in a public context, John Gladstone as the dominating presence and sole actor in the family's library – conventionally recognized as a masculinized space – even though his wife's influence over her children's reading and education certainly had the potential to equal if not to exceed his. It was this role of library-reader and educator, rather than of intercessor, which required a more overtly autonomous male representation. It is important to note the gendered iconography deemed to be required, by both son and artist, in the public representation of the domestic library space, which highlights the existence of inconsistency and tension between the public representation (male dominance and autonomy) and the private reality (feminized influences) of the library sphere. It also echoes the conflict, which will be further explored in later chapters, that Gladstone felt when trying to

Figure 3.4 Alexander Munro, *The Gladstone Memorial, Fasque* (1854). C. A. Gladstone.

reconcile the ideal circumstances of study in a private, isolated, and spiritualized setting, with the moral imperatives of study which were public, relevant, and engaged. A union of the two was not, as we shall see later, an easy one to achieve or maintain, but it was nonetheless one to which Gladstone adhered, and with which he worked, throughout his life.

4
A Place of Deceptive Tranquillity: Gladstone's Temple of Peace

In 1998, Archbishop Robert Runcie described a 'deceptively tranquil' library 'set in a small village amidst quiet countryside'. He called its tranquillity 'deceptive, because to stand amidst its books is an ... encounter with the restless, brooding intelligence that was William Ewart Gladstone'.[1] Although he described the 'decorous Gothic architecture' of St Deiniol's, his words more accurately invoke the experience of visiting Gladstone's study in Hawarden Castle. This spacious room, located on the ground floor of the west-wing of the house, is preserved very much as Gladstone left it. Letters, pens, ink-stained wipes, desk toys, and untidily stacked books litter the desks: the visitor, trespassing in an eerie silence, endlessly expects the return of the library's owner, who appears only temporarily absent. Only the pungency of decaying calf-skin, dust, and old polish betrays the age of the room's contents. The site of over 40 years of reading, work, and relaxation, it remains the clearest physical trace of Gladstone's private gentleman's library.

Nevertheless, the tranquillity, privacy, and gentlemanliness of the Temple of Peace are proved deceptive by the evidence the study-library provides of those contests between privacy and publicity, temperance and temptation, openness and obsession, which characterized Gladstone's life. Chapter 3 examined Gladstone's immersion in his family's book culture, his youthful keenness to organize and run the family's libraries, and the ways in which these experiences influenced his maturing identity. Attention now turns to the collection over which he had personal control. Part one of this chapter focuses on the layout and use of the Temple of Peace itself. Here we examine not only Gladstone's arrangement and use of his library, but also his textual relationships with immediate family, friends, and neighbours, investigating the significant use made of the Temple of Peace by readers other than

Gladstone, the scale and character of which has not previously been documented.

Discussion of the impact of Gladstone's private library's impact upon others leads to a consideration of Gladstone's reading and textual relationships beyond the Temple of Peace. As has been made clear by other biographers, the years during which he was establishing the Temple included ones of severe crisis for Gladstone – both politically and personally.[2] They saw the escalation of his rescue work among prostitutes, and his consistent, albeit tortured, reading of pornography. Attention is given here to Gladstone's relationships with prostitutes because of the significant part reading played in them: an aspect not usually given any prominence. Such reading is both intrinsically significant, but also throws into relief, along with his reading of pornography, what kinds of reading were possible and held desirable for the private library space, and which were not. If Gladstone's library in Hawarden was a haven of peace, how far were other reading contexts regarded as unpeaceful or even transgressive, needing to be kept strictly separate? How far were both the public and private aspects of Gladstone's library governed by notions of what behaviour would be publicly acceptable? It is these questions which occupy the second part of this chapter.

Inside the Temple

Due to the widespread publication of detailed descriptions, often accompanied by photographs and engravings, as well as the survival of many of the room's features, we can be fairly confident in describing the physical appearance of the Temple of Peace during Gladstone's lifetime.[3]

The apartment, lit by three large windows and possessing two fireplaces, was completely lined with bookcases (Figure 4.1). Those on the north, east, and west sides, were of Gladstone's individual design and jutted out into the central space. Those on the south wall were slightly more ornate, having been introduced from London in the 1870s. A number of free-standing cupboards, small bookcases, easels, easy chairs and a chaise-longue, occupied the room's central space. Towards the west end, benefiting from the light admitted by two large windows, lay Gladstone's two desks; a third, used by Catherine Gladstone, was positioned at the east end of the study, in line with the room's north window. The Temple of Peace was not only a repository for Gladstone's books, but also home to a complementary collection of art objects. Principal amongst these were the portrait busts and medallions placed

Figure 4.1 Temple of Peace, Hawarden Castle (c. 1880). Flintshire Record Office Photographic Collection.

on top of the room's bookcases,[4] supplemented by numerous small pictures, ornaments, as well as Gladstone's growing collections of walking sticks and axes.

It is more difficult to be sure how Gladstone arranged his books in the Temple as no specific classification and layout schemes survive for it.[5] Moreover, while Gladstone's study still contains many of his own books, the bulk removal to St Deiniol's in the 1880s, and the posthumous introduction of other volumes by Gladstone's surviving family, makes it almost impossible to deduce with any accuracy the room's original classificatory layout. However, Gladstone's cataloguing divisions give us some indication of how the Temple's books were originally organized. As discussed in Chapter 1, Gladstone established three main sections comprising: Theology, Ecclesiastical History and Biography; Secular Literature in English; and Foreign Language Secular Literature, including Classics, as well as a number of minor subdivisions.[6] A contemporary description of the room's arrangement by subject noted that Gladstone's 'theological works', which 'form an appreciable proportion … are collected in one particular corner of the room', with separate 'departments' being 'assigned to the works of Homer, Shakespeare, and Dante'.[7] This again accords with Gladstone's expressed preference, not only for thematic divisions, but also 'for individual men as centres of subdivison'.[8]

Superficially therefore, Gladstone's Temple of Peace – stocked with its chairs, busts, and books – was a typical private gentleman's library,[9] but there are important ways in which it challenged this stereotype. As Gladstone knew and articulated, the collection and arrangement of a library was an opportunity to acknowledge a particular heritage and follow a distinct plan. The Temple of Peace's visual vocabulary paid homage to established conventions in library decoration, including multiple references to classical civilization, and to the early Italian renaissance centred on Dante. However, it was principally equipped as a practical, working room, not to exhibit status or superficial knowledge. Gladstone's furnishing of his study in Hawarden was far more economical than that he had undertaken for his various London residences, implying a less pressing need to conform to fashion or to impress visitors by show.[10] The room contained few chairs, and the desks were sturdy, square, and sacrificed grace for storage space. For his plain, buttress-style bookcases constructed by Bailey, Gladstone drew, not on the domestic library tradition, but on the academic, citing a 'great example of it ... in the noble library of Trinity College, Cambridge'.[11] Their simple design reflected a deliberate decision by Gladstone:

> It has been a fashion to make bookcases highly ornamental. Now books want for and in themselves no ornament at all. They are themselves the ornament ... The man, who looks for society in his books, will readily perceive that, in proportion as the face of his bookcase is occupied by ornament, he loses that society; and conversely, the more that face approximates to a sheet of book-backs, the more of that society he will enjoy.

Furthermore, Gladstone's insistence on fixed shelving, which flew in the face of the bulk of contemporary bibliographical advice, was very much a statement of personal opposition to the gentlemanly tradition. In 1890 he reiterated that, for this arrangement to be successful, it 'requires that each person owning and arranging a library should have a pretty accurate general knowledge of the sizes of his books'.[12] This statement clearly disassociated Gladstone and his library from those moneyed bibliomaniacs who did not know, or use, the books they collected. This was not only a direct repudiation of current fashionable trends, but also differentiated the Temple of Peace from the arrangements at Fasque House and Hawarden Castle, whose main libraries

Figure 4.2 The Library at Fasque (2002). C. A. Gladstone. Photograph: the author.

contained highly ornate shelving, were designed to impress, and had important social and semi-public functions.

Fasque library served as one of the principal living rooms for the Gladstone family, located as it was on the first floor of the west-wing of the house, adjacent both to the house's main staircase and extensive drawing room (Figure 4.2).

Ostensibly unchanged until recently, it consisted of a large and elegant main library, and a turret room where, in later years, Gladstone would apparently retire to read when he and his brother Thomas were at odds over politics.[13] In the principal space, comfortable chairs flanked the fireplace, over which hung a portrait of John Gladstone's political hero, George Canning. Chaises longues provided seating in the first and third windows, and the central light overlooked one of two elegantly shaped and decorative desks. The bookcases, in line with the normal arrangement recommended by manuals,[14] lay against the wall and consisted of shelves lit by scalloped lamps and base cupboards. Their tops were peopled by busts of politicians, philosophers, literary and historical figures.[15]

The busts that adorn the Temple of Peace's bookcases likewise form a pantheon of ancient and modern scholars and politicians, including Canning, Wellington, Dante, Homer, and Socrates.[16] However a striking divergence – both from the norm and certainly from the Fasque scheme - is the prominence of close friends, contemporaries, and family members in the group. The politicians – including the fifth duke of Newcastle and Charles Canning – are all ones Gladstone knew. They are interspersed with family members: Gladstone's father is placed between Wellington and Canning senior, and his eldest son Willy stands close by. A florid earl of Beaconsfield (moulded in terracotta by Moyniham), keeping an ever-vigilant watch over Gladstone's political desk, is by far the most surprising personage in this category.[17] Even the prominence of Homer and Dante represents Gladstone's 'favouritism' at work rather than a more generalized representation of inherited knowledge. Women are also well represented. As well as mythological figures like Athene, Gladstone's wife, eldest daughter Agnes, Queen Victoria, Charlotte Stuart (wife of Charles Canning), and Gladstone's confidante, Harriet, duchess of Sutherland, are included.[18] Unlike Fasque's matching set of busts, this is a very personal collection.

In Hawarden Castle's main library, books harmonized with, rather than dictated, the overall decorative scheme, and signs of the room's multiple functionality abounded in the form of writing and tea tables, and musical instruments (Figure 4.3). As such the room was almost indistinguishable from the Castle's drawing room. Wemyss Reid's

Figure 4.3 The Hawarden Castle Library (n.d.). Flintshire Record Office Photographic Collection.

description of the library terrace as a favourite spot for photographs further signalled its semi-public function. Moreover, Reid's report positively stressed Gladstone's physical distancing of himself and his books from the Castle's library and the largely pre-1800 collection it contained.

> This room, which is lined with bookshelves on two of its walls, has always been the principal 'living-room' of the castle. Mr. Gladstone's own books have never intruded themselves into the Glynne library, but filled his own room.[19]

This all suggests that Gladstone's Temple of Peace was designed to function in quite a different way from the gentleman's library that privileged appearance over content; the public image over private use.[20] However, even though Gladstone sought to keep private and public work physically distinct by the maintenance of separate 'literary' and 'political' desks in his library, the difficulties of separating such spheres, however desirable in theory, were all too real.

Using the Temple: private or public acts?

It goes without saying that the principal user of the Temple of Peace was Gladstone himself. The bulk of the texts he recorded reading were undoubtedly in his collection, and the work he did there was clearly undertaken for his own personal satisfaction. Such activity afforded him relaxation,[21] stimulation,[22] achievement,[23] and, ultimately, peace: 'Worked on arranging books: after (I guess) 30 hours my library is now in a passable state and I enjoy, in Ruskin's words "the complacency of possession, & the pleasantness of order"'.[24] The majority of diary entries suggest that he was working alone and privately, and this image of separateness was one perpetuated, not only by the room's lack of an obvious social function, but also by contemporary descriptions of it. As Mary Drew observed:

> As a kind of pledge of sanctity, the 'Temple of Peace' was the name chosen for the room set apart for his books. Conversation in the ordinary sense of the word – though many an important consultation and interview took place there – was strictly prohibited, but members of the family, or friends staying in the house, were at liberty to make use of the room for purposes of study or reading, and so absorbed was its owner that he was usually quite unaware of their presence.[25]

Mary suggested her father allowed others to enter his private space, but denied their existence, or certainly resisted their influence, an impression supported by Wemyss Reid: 'Here would Mr. Gladstone be seen, entirely oblivious of anyone's presence, either seated in his arm-chair by the fire, or of later years extended on a narrow sofa'.[26] The only vigilance was provided, it was sometimes suggested, by Gladstone's black Pomeranian, Petz.[27] However, Gladstone's relationship with visitors was not so straightforward. Although he clearly lacked a conventional desire to exhibit a grand or ornate library, and could adopt the rhetoric and behaviour of the reclusive scholar,[28] the desire to show off his treasured book collection and impress those of like mind was strong. Thus he recorded in 1860: 'The Company visited the "temple of peace" ... & inspected my library',[29] and the following year his friend 'Sir J[ames] L[acaita] paid a Bibliographical visit to me in the Temple of Peace: & some good things were discovered'.[30] Gladstone was also willing to give over his library, when necessary, for practical domestic use. Thus in 1874 he recorded: 'Tidying room: which tonight officiates as drawing-room'.[31] Moreover, Reid's observation, quoted above, had followed a description of how the Temple of Peace fulfilled a very public function – as a lending library:

> Here everyone was welcome, provided he observed the rule of silence; and no more peaceful shrine for reading or writing could be imagined. The shelves were open to all on condition of an entry being made, in a book kept for the purpose, of each volume taken out, with name of borrower and date of borrowing and return.[32]

The two-volume borrowing register to which Reid refers survives in Hawarden Castle, offering compelling evidence of the public character of Gladstone's private library. Together its two volumes cover the years 1860–96, from the institution of the Temple of Peace to the years when Gladstone was no longer able to read. This chronological span, and the fact that very few entries were made in the second register after 1894, immediately indicate that Gladstone required and maintained a powerful level of control over the borrowing in his library – or at least the proper recording of it – while ever physically capable of doing so. The fact that Gladstone instituted borrowing registers at all is in all ways remarkable, and poses questions about whom he encouraged and permitted to use his library. Domestic librarians were advised to provide means by which to monitor borrowing, for example, the anonymous *Practical Economy*, 2nd edn (1822) suggested tickets be left on shelves in place of consulted or borrowed volumes,[33] but the Temple of Peace scheme bespoke a far higher level of surveillance.

The first register, with its light-coloured hardback cover, spans the years 1860–9. It is inscribed on the front, in Gladstone's hand: 'Register of Books taken out from W. E. G.'s library'. On the first page, Gladstone established the following categories for borrowers: 'Name of Person', 'Date of taking out', 'Name of Work', and 'Date of return'. The second volume (1870–96) is also hard-backed. Apparently untitled for many years, Gladstone wrote on the front in 1894, clearly in some frustration, 'NB All entries to be made in Ink'. This may have been provoked by borrowers ignoring long-standing instructions, but it is also likely that Gladstone, who was losing his sight, was unable to read entries made in pencil by this date. If this is the correct interpretation, it indicates Gladstone was used to making regular checks on borrowing right up until his last years.

Analysis shows that, between 1860 and 1896, 201 individuals borrowed books from the Temple of Peace. They made 1992 separate entries and borrowed 2306 volumes with an average rate of between 60 and 70 volumes per year.[34] Out of the 201 individual borrowers, 52 remain so far unidentified by sex and 43 by category (either family/household, friends/colleagues, or neighbours). The largest group of users was, as might be expected, drawn from Gladstone's family and household (59/201). In that grouping, Gladstone's children were the heaviest borrowers, with Mary Drew alone recording 252 separate entries, 13 per cent of total borrowings.[35] This is unsurprising as she was known to contemporaries as 'an alert reader' and assistant to her father in his 'literary labours', and she herself clearly displayed her passion both for books and for her father's library, both privately and in public.[36] She shared Gladstone's opinion that books were important household possessions being, for instance, critical of Ferdinand de Rothschild's Waddesdon Manor, in which she found herself 'much oppressed with the extreme gorgeousness and luxury', principally because 'there is not a book in the house save 20 improper French novels'.[37] Other significant family borrowers were Catherine Gladstone's nephews and nieces from both the Lyttelton and Glynne families. As Gladstone's children, nephews, and nieces married, they in turn introduced their husbands and children to the borrowing habit, especially in the cases of Agnes Gladstone and Lavinia Lyttelton. Catherine Gladstone made the fewest entries (25) of the nuclear family and began with her husband's translation of Farini's *Roman State*,[38] although, having a desk in the Temple of Peace, Catherine arguably had less need to borrow than the others. The family/household category is closely followed by those deemed to be neighbours of the Gladstones (57/201), many of whom borrowed as families. Thus we have William Jacobson (1803–84), Bishop of Chester and his family, the Burlinghams (family of a Hawarden physician), and the Wades. Visiting friends and colleagues were not far behind (42/201), but they generally borrowed fewer books as usually only visiting for short periods.

Gentlemanly space? Issues of gender and class

It is thus already clear that the Temple of Peace played a significant role as a lending library in a sphere that extended well beyond the private and familial. However, some of the most interesting and startling insights offered by this evidence are on the subject of the gender and class character of Gladstone's library. Kate Flint has described the library and the bedroom as the most contested areas in the Victorian and Edwardian house. She cites Robert Kerr's description of the library, written in 1871, as:

> Primarily a sort of morning-room for gentlemen rather than anything else. Their correspondence is done there, their reading, and, in some measure, their lounging ... the Billiard-room ... is not unfrequently attached to it. At the same time the ladies are not exactly excluded.

As Flint rightly observes, 'Kerr's grudging vocabulary suggests that they are not exactly welcome, either'.[39] Representation of the library as an overwhelmingly male preserve was commonplace within advice literature published during the period when Gladstone was establishing and using his library. Books like Kerr's *Gentleman's House*, Charles Eastlake's *Hints on Household Taste* (1869), and Mary Haweis' *The Art of Decoration* (1889) all engaged with and reinforced long-established ideas about the gendering of household space. Kerr made the ideal gender character of the library even more explicit. He described how '"for a man of learning", one must either constitute the library itself as a study, or add one, with a secluded position, no door of intercommunication with any other room "(except possibly the Gentleman's-room)", so that it becomes "now essentially a private retreat"'.[40] In his analysis of the Victorian country house, Mark Girouard follows such contemporary distinctions: 'The mistress of the house had her boudoir to work in' and 'the master, his study or business room. The drawing room (or rooms) was considered the ladies' territory, but the gentlemen were allowed in; the opposite was the case with the library'.[41] This goes beyond even Kerr's description and clearly over generalizes. Not only were women allowed into Gladstone's study-library – as Ishbel Gordon, marchioness of Aberdeen and Temair recalled in 1935, 'my thoughts turn to some of those talks in his own library, so rightly called "the Temple of Peace"'[42] – at least one – Catherine Gladstone – possessed a desk there. Girouard goes on to illustrate the prevalence of a clear 'male preserve' in the Victorian country house, consisting of consecutive ground floor rooms: library, billiard room, gentleman's business room, lavatories, smoking and gun rooms. However, while his assertion that the billiard room was 'the nucleus' of the male domain might be true of houses such as Waddesdon, it has already been shown that, at Hawarden Castle, the development of the study was significantly privileged over that of the billiard room, which lost both its table and its function under the relentless advance of Gladstone's books.[43] More recent, theorized analyses of the study space, while problematizing the notion of a rigid division and policing of spheres, have still tended to favour arguments for the marginalization of women and children. The central thrust of Martin Danahay's thesis in *A Community of One* is that the life of the writer – self-represented as autonomous – is in fact dependent on and safeguarded by the cocooning protection of women and the labour of domestic servants.[44] While Trev Lynn Broughton, following Philippa Tristram (who in turn draws on Robert Kerr) continues to stress the importance of sex segregation in the Victorian household and women's liminal presence. By deploying the evidence of carefully worked (auto)biographical texts, almost to the exclusion of other sources, such work necessarily replicates a very stylized picture of the study's nature.[45] This is – as we shall see with Gladstone's study – a crucial aspect of its historical existence, but an aspect nonetheless.

Evidence from the Temple of Peace borrowing registers shows clearly how integral women were to the life of the library and how important such a resource was to them. Of the borrowers whose sex we can identify, 82 were women compared to 65 men. Six out of the top ten borrowers were women and there were more female borrowers than male in the family/household and neighbour categories.[46] Where members of the same family borrowed, the women frequently borrowed more. Two good examples are, firstly, the Jacobsons. Both wife Eleanor (18 entries) and daughter Katherine (a massive 59 entries) outborrowed the Bishop (14 entries). Secondly, Miss Caroline Smith of Hawarden Rectory outborrowed the Revd E. Smith almost ten to one. Although the largest female borrowers were of an equivalent class to Gladstone, there were a significant number of lower class women who regularly borrowed from the library. From among the household, Miss W. R. Syfret, the governess, (29 entries),[47] Miss Auguste Schlüter, Catherine Gladstone's lady's maid and part-time housekeeper, (16 entries), and Lucy Phillimore, Gladstone's nurse, (5 entries) regularly borrowed books. From the village Mary Burnett (wife of the Hawarden Land Agent) appears 20 times, and Elizabeth Potter, wife of a local farmer, twice. Members of the family also frequently took out books on the behalf of others. Many of these 'others' were women (like Mrs Bagshawe, Mrs Chamberlain, and Mrs Isaac) and, one may surmise, were locals who were ill, elderly or otherwise incapacitated. They may even have been rescue cases.

The reasons behind women's use of the Temple of Peace are likely to have varied significantly between individuals and classes. One obvious suggestion, particularly for Gladstone's daughters, was the lack of public educational facilities. Beyond the often-limited instruction offered by governesses or private tutors, educational opportunities for upper-class girls were uncertain.[48] The wealth of potential knowledge offered by a well-stocked library must have been irresistible to intelligent and diligent women like Mary and Helen Gladstone. However, even with such a resource, women could not always make the best use of it. Not only had families and individuals to resist contemporary gendered assumptions about the library space, but about reading itself. Gendered debates about reading simmered on throughout the nineteenth century and characterizations of women's reading were often derogatory. In 1880, W. H. Davenport Adams pronounced, 'it is said that a ... woman may be known by the company ... she keeps; a truer index to character is the books' she reads, and, as Kate Flint explains, 'to read actively, rather than to absorb sentiment passively like a sponge, was popularly considered, in the 1840s, to be adopting a masculine rather than a feminine style of reading'.[49] However, Mary and her sisters were lucky. Not only did they have unlimited access to their father's library, they also received his guidance. Lucy Masterman suggests that Gladstone – worried that Mary's reading was too diffuse, and more emotional than intellectual – 'tried to press for a male University standard of study',[50] and, as Anne Isba has recently re-emphasized, Gladstone was consistently supportive of his daughter Helen's studies and subsequent academic career.[51]

Having shown conclusively that women were not only allowed but positively encouraged to use Gladstone's library, and that they enthusiastically made use of its resources, it is necessary to discuss an important aspect of the library's use which was almost exclusively male. At least 23 of the total number of individual borrowers (over 10 per cent) were clergy, drawn from the entire Anglican hierarchy from bishops to curates.[52] There were a substantial number of clergy among Gladstone's close family and household who borrowed from his library: his son Stephen; brother-in-law Henry; sons-in-law Edward Wickham and Harry Drew; three Lytteltons; his chaplain H. G. Henderson and, perhaps most significant of all, Lavinia Lyttelton's husband Edward Stuart Talbot,[53] who became the most prolific male borrower from the Temple of Peace (102 entries). Local clergy are also well represented in the registers. For example, the Revd Edward Austin (1824–70), priest at nearby Broughton, made 18 entries; Edward Bickersteth Ottley (1853–1910), curate of Hawarden, 39 entries; the Revds G. Hockley and William West – also Hawarden curates – are also listed. Clergy wives and families borrowed too, but it is clear from other supporting evidence that clergymen, especially local incumbents and curates, enjoyed privileged access both to the Temple of Peace and to its owner. During the 1920s, the Revd J. Drew Roberts recalled this for *T. P.'s & Cassell's Weekly*.

> At Hawarden, when I was a young curate, in 1896, both Gladstone and Mrs. Gladstone were extraordinarily kind to me and my colleagues ... We curates at Hawarden were not expected to speak of politics at the Castle; but we could not be wrong in talking theology. I well remember how one of us presumed to know the facts about some question concerned with the Trent Council, and an argument began with Gladstone, who disagreed. Gladstone rushed the young man out of the room and into his 'Temple of Peace,' where he kept his 30,000 books. They returned together, roaring with laughter, after looking up the authorities. It appeared that the curate was right and Gladstone wrong; by no means a usual conclusion to a disagreement.[54]

Although this story relates to the year in which recorded borrowing ceased from the Temple of Peace, it usefully illustrates Gladstone sharing his resources with others, and depicts the sort of male bonding in which he clearly engaged with clergy-friends and neighbours. The fact that the Temple of Peace consistently operated as an important educational resource for clergy during these years is important new information in itself. However, as Chapter 6 will demonstrate, awareness of such a function is fundamental to a proper and revised understanding of the motivation for Gladstone's foundation of St Deiniol's Library.

All the clergy who borrowed books from Gladstone's library would have been drawn from a class roughly equivalent to Gladstone's own. Passing reference has been made to individuals from lower classes borrowing books from the Temple of Peace, both within Gladstone's household and outside, and before proceeding further, it is important to say more about them.

As Chapter 3 showed, Gladstone and his mother set up a separate, servants' library at Seaforth, bought exclusively from S.P.C.K., and clearly intended to be didactic. Gladstone established a similar collection in his own first household. On 24 April 1840, he once again went to 'S.P.C.K. to choose [a] servants' library'. He clearly took his time over it; the next entry on the subject dates from over a year later when he 'made inventory of & arranged the little library for the servants: about 60 vols'.[55] The establishment of a separate household library accorded with other efforts Gladstone made to monitor and control the morality of his servants. He regularly read religious texts (often of his own composition) with and to the servants.[56] He 'wrote servants' rules', and frequently noted with sadness when premarital sex or unbelief were practised in his household.[57] With regard to an instance of the latter, he wrote, when at Hawarden in 1857: 'We conversed on the case of T. Turner [a servant]: it appearing that one of the servants in the house is an unbeliever: Eli, the reading youth'.[58] Gladstone's description of Eli as 'the reading youth' may be read in several different ways, not all negative. Although he clearly sought to control the morality and religious conduct of his household through reading, there is no evidence that Gladstone objected to his servants improving themselves, for example, he himself taught one French in 1834.[59]

There is no evidence that Gladstone's servants' library was expanded in later years but, as we have already seen, servants were allowed to borrow freely from among Gladstone's own books from 1860 onwards. Thus F. Hampton (a relative of William Hampton the butler) borrowed *Pickwick Papers* on 26 October 1861; a governess, Miss Scott, borrowed *The Female Jesuit*, *Life among the Madocs*, and *Kidnapped*, and Nurse Lucy Phillimore took out *Ernestine*, *History of St James' Square*, *Robert Frampton*, as well as *Footprints of the Apostles*. This suggests, either that Gladstone's attitude to his servants' reading relaxed considerably over the years, or that the monitoring of morality we see displayed in the diary was only one aspect of a multifarious approach to household management.

Thanks to the preservation and publication of her diary,[60] we can consider in a somewhat broader context the use one of Gladstone's servants made of his library. Auguste Schlüter (1849–1917), a Hanoverian woman, joined the Gladstone household as maid to Gladstone's daughters Mary and Helen in 1867 aged 17. She served the family for 23 years, occasionally as housekeeper, and as Catherine Gladstone's maid, in between Mary's marriage and her own return to Germany in 1890. As K. D. Reynolds observes, Schlüter's frequent role as chaperone provided ample opportunities for her 'to witness, and mimic' her employers' lives.[61] Reynold's judgement is not exactly borne out by the surviving diaries: Schlüter was both a sensitive and an intelligent woman in her own right, harbouring a strong desire to improve herself. She learned French in 1878, ostensibly to help Helen practise conversation but clearly mainly for her own satisfaction, as Helen had departed for Cambridge the previous year. By 1879, Auguste was 'attending my night school with great pleasure twice a week'.[62] Her employers not only encouraged Auguste's self-cultivation but also turned her skills to their advantage, for instance enlisting her help for 'the gentlemen secretaries when they have to deal with German letters', a task which she found very interesting.[63] An ardent reader, she enthusiastically shared many of Gladstone's religious interests, although she once admitted that 'I fear I always find other books more interesting' than the Bible![64] She certainly joined him in his penchant for sermon attendance.[65] The influence of 'our dear gentleman', as she called him, seemed marked in other areas too: in August 1878, she read Harriett Jay's *The Queen of Connaught: a story* (London, 1875), describing it as a 'very interesting' Irish tale,[66] and in 1888 she recorded 'kind Mr. Gladstone' lending her 'a most delightful book' while in Italy (where she also emulated his practice of buying books).[67] She recorded reading a wide range of other novels in her diary – from Louisa May Alcott's *Little Women* to George Eliot's *Felix Holt* – a taste which she also shared with her employers.[68] One of her official duties was to read to Mrs Gladstone,[69] and she was obviously included in the family's novel-reading circle on fairly equal terms. In November 1879, she 'read out in the evening a delightful book called *The Vulture Maiden*', which, as we have seen, Gladstone and his daughter Mary had also read and discussed,[70] and in June 1880 she read Rhoda Broughton's *Red as a Rose Is She*, describing it as 'very light written'. Mary Gladstone, who read the novel after Auguste, described it less politely: 'well written but flippant to excess'.[71] Auguste was not undiscerning, however. Cruising aboard Donald Currie's *Pembroke Castle* in 1883, she recorded that Miss Fisher was reading aloud Bertha M. Clay's *Which Loved Him Best?* (c. 1880): 'one of those sensational novels, but very fair for a voyage'.[72] As shown here and elsewhere in her diary, it is clear that, in addition to reading with her employers, Auguste and her fellow servants read together regularly: when staying with Mrs Hampton, Gladstone's housekeeper at Hawarden, in 1886 she noted there was 'nothing I liked more than arriving home after a good walk and taking our tea, and then for a jolly read – this was after both our hearts'.[73]

Faced with her mother's failing health, Auguste resigned from her post in the autumn of 1890 and returned to Germany. Once there, she described what 'a wrench' it had been to leave her beloved Gladstones, with whom she remained in contact – exchanging letters, books and photographs as they had been accustomed to do – until the Great War and her death in 1917 intervened.[74] A good part of the poignancy of Auguste's record – particularly her last letter written just before her death and not received by Mary Drew until after the cessation of hostilities – comes from the inevitable contrast it reveals between the servant's adoration for the woman who had 'cheered and brightened' her life, and her employers' friendly encouragement, always tempered by a natural sense of superior class distinction. Auguste, despite being included in both the confidences and the educated pursuits of her well-to-do charges, remained a paid employee (as she was sometimes painfully reminded).[75] The family were clearly sorry to part with her – Gladstone wrote that her resignation was a matter of 'very serious concern' to him – but her position of inequality continued unaltered; Mary, on later reading Auguste's diary, allegedly observed condescendingly on 'the way she gives us all back seats while she occupies the front seat'.[76]

By allowing women like Auguste Schlüter access to his books, and by encouraging their mental cultivation, Gladstone ran the risk of awakening feelings and aspirations that were potentially incompatible with their station in life. Yet he advocated reading and study, not only to members of his own household, but to a much wider constituency of working people. Ample evidence survives as to Gladstone's encouragement of learning and 'mental culture' among Hawarden residents, but most of it is related to his support of separate institutions such as the Hawarden Institute, which will be investigated in the next chapter. Evidence from the Temple of Peace registers adds substantially to this picture (despite obvious difficulties of identification) by showing that some ordinary local residents were borrowers in their own right. Some clearly became so after the family had borrowed for them. For example, after Catherine Gladstone borrowed 'Hirell' in '3 vols' for a Mrs Chamberlain in December 1872, she signed out a further six books herself. Others were apparently fully independent borrowers like Elizabeth Potter and Samuel Mason of Hawarden.

The implications of Gladstone's decision to open his library in this way are profound. On the one hand, it offered the possibility for a personalized contribution to that 'manifold humanity' which meant so much to him. On the other, by inviting outsiders into his library Gladstone was taking a significant risk. Moreover, he also took substantial gambles in his reading practices when venturing outside the Temple of Peace. So far this investigation has traced the organization and use of the Temple of Peace. We now turn to consider those categories of Gladstone's private reading which contrasted, sometimes most uncomfortably, with those he practised within its walls.

Outside the Temple

Gladstone's libraries were, as we have seen, not only home to his books but also to works in his art collection.[77] However, the relationship between library space, reading, and art seems to have been inspirational as well as locational.

During Alexander Munro's execution in marble of his *Paolo and Francesca da Rimini* (1852; Birmingham Museums & Art Gallery), Figure 4.4, commissioned following the Great Exhibition of 1851, Gladstone lent Munro his 'Dante criticism' to refer to while working.[78] The finished piece was, as the artist knew, destined for the library at 6 Carlton Gardens.[79] However, Munro wished Gladstone to view the sculpture at his studio 'before it gets to your library', in case he wished to make any last minute adjustments before its highly significant placing. The sculpture depicts the moment when Paolo and Francesca, who have been reading the tale of Lancelot and Guinevere, are finally overcome by their mutual passion; the line 'Quel giorno piu non vi leggemo avanti' is carved round the base of the sculpture.[80] There was a striking correspondence between what John Gere calls the 'restrained but intense eroticism' of the work and Gladstone's own textual relationship with fallen women.[81] For, as Matthew points out, the years surrounding the Munro commission (1850–3) were characterized by 'highly charged encounters' with prostitutes.[82]

Gladstone and 'fallen women'

Gladstone first recorded contact with prostitutes at Oxford, and engaged in rescue work, with varying levels of intensity, between 1828 and 1894.[83] One memorandum preserved with the diary manuscripts shows how Gladstone, in discoursing with such women, found himself

Figure 4.4 Alexander Munro, *Paolo and Francesca* (1853). Birmingham Museums and Art Gallery.

in repeated danger of deviating from the immediate subject of rescue and, more ominously, becoming sexually excited. He also found it hard to break off such encounters immediately when he perceived such dangers. Gladstone indicated that much of his excitement came from the consideration of, rather than an engagement in, the forbidden. However, Gladstone believed 'that either of these is adultery in the heart', and berated his inability to repel 'with firmness, singleness', and 'entireness of purpose', the solicitations with which some of his 'cases' clearly bombarded him.[84] Gladstone was deeply worried by the contradiction between his sexual fulfilment in marriage, which he described as 'an ideal above the ordinary married state', and his sexual fantasies about other, forbidden women, which 'still beset me as snares and pitfalls among which I walk'.[85]

Discussion of Gladstone's mission to 'fallen women' has been ongoing since his death. With the exception of the circumstances surrounding the Wright Case of 1927, early commentary made by both supporters and opponents was muted.[86] Scholarly coverage began in the late 1960s with the work of Steven Marcus and Ronald Pearsall, and increased significantly following the publication of the *Gladstone Diaries*.[87] Gladstone's tortured diary entries and associated memoranda, as well as his limited 'declaration' of marital faithfulness given to Stephen Gladstone just before his death,[88] have inspired repeated questioning of both the motives behind and the conduct of Gladstone's rescue work. There is no doubt that in seeking out prostitutes Gladstone was inspired by a Christian desire to save both souls and bodies from the degradation and sin which prostitution signified to him and to most contemporaries.[89] However, there remains one aspect of Gladstone's relationship with his rescue cases, which, in the context of this study, merits further investigation: the incidence and significance of Gladstone's reading with them.

Reading and book giving had always constituted a regular part of Gladstone's philanthropic activities. The evidence of the Temple of Peace and its borrowing registers in particular serves to lend credibility to some later and popular anecdotes about Gladstone's philanthropic work, which are frequently now dismissed as hyperbolic fruits of the Gladstone 'myth'. The following is a particularly good bibliographic example:

> Hence he prayed, with the prodigal son brought to him by his sorrowing mother, and in his own "Temple of Peace", saw him restored, and witnessed him afterwards reformed. He visited the cross street sweeper, who told to the vicar concerned and interested, that Mr Gladstone had been to see him, and had read a bit of Bible to him, and afterwards had knelt down and prayed with him.[90]

It is not therefore surprising that the reading and gifting, particularly of religious books should have occurred in the context of Gladstone's rescue work. Indeed, in 1852, he 'took £2 with a copy of Jer[emy]. Taylor['s] Holy Living to E. Watson's – my promised aid', noting several months later of another rescue case, 'A. L.', that 'The Jer. Taylor had proved most acceptable' to her.[91] In 1856, he 'Saw Milligan & gave [her a]

Bible & Pr[ayer Book]'.[92] However, Gladstone's gifts were not restricted to religious works. He gave women works of literature, both classics and popular novels. For example, in 1852, he: 'In ev[enin]g saw E.C. & C. Morgan: with *better* conduct than heretofore. Gave each an Uncle Tom'.[93] Whether this was a reward for their good conduct, or had further moral purpose, is unclear. The motivation for the gift of an edition of Shakespeare in 1858 was made more explicit: 'Saw Rigby – gave Shakespeare for a practical purpose: & advised [her] to think of emigration'.[94] What is apparent is that Gladstone appeared to give books that he himself had read and liked. Jeremy Taylor's *Holy Living* and *Holy Dying* had been known and profitably read by Gladstone from childhood, while *Uncle Tom's Cabin* was a novel he admired. It is clear that Gladstone considered that gift books could transmit practical advice to their recipients. Shakespeare may not superficially have anything to do with emigration, but the idea that reading Shakespeare might broaden a woman's mind and thus lead her to reassess her life is not too spurious a connection to assume that Gladstone made. The gifting of books to prostitutes continued over many years. Thus, in 1873, Gladstone went 'Shopping: & sent books to Mrs Heaphy', and as late as 1887, 'Carried another book to … Clifton' who was, unfortunately, 'absent'.[95]

There was limited opportunity for extensive personal engagement between Gladstone and his rescue cases while he merely gave them books. However, when readings (in addition to conversations) occurred between Gladstone and these women, opportunities for mutual education arose. The texts read varied; some mirrored those chosen by Gladstone as gifts. Thus, in February 1876, Gladstone recorded 'readings' of 'Longfellow and Shakespeare' with 'Dalton'; three months later he 'Saw Phillips & read Hamlet'.[96] It appears that, in the same way as with his gifts, Gladstone read aloud texts that he himself liked and enjoyed.

By far the most significant and potentially dangerous texts for Gladstone in his encounters with fallen women were by Tennyson. Gladstone first read poetry by Tennyson in October 1829, after having been introduced to him by Arthur Hallam, and 'liked it exceedingly'.[97] However, the effect of such juvenilia was as nothing compared to the impact of *Idylls of the King*, which Gladstone devoured in 1859.[98] That year he read 'Tennyson, Tennyson, Tennyson', going on to acclaim the author and his work publicly in the *Quarterly Review* in the October, having requested to be allowed to review 'his late work [which] has laid hold of me with a power that I have not felt … for many years'.[99] As Bebbington makes clear, and as will be explored further in the next chapter,

Gladstone was attracted to these poems because of the way Tennyson 'brilliantly blended the national with the universal, the human with the Christian'.[100] However, it is equally obvious that Gladstone's personal emotional response to the poems, especially to *Guinevere*, was just as important and certainly had implications for his use of these texts during his rescue work. In July 1859, Gladstone: 'Read Guinevere – twice or thrice over & with much emotion', admitting the following day that 'Tennyson ... has grasped me with a strong hand'. Throughout the time when Gladstone was avidly reading Tennyson and composing his review article on the poems, he was engaging in rescue work; experiences which became intermeshed. The day before he read *Guinevere* with 'much emotion', he had seen a prostitute called Stewart and had indicated that the encounter had been problematic for him by inserting his 'X' of disapprobation in his diary entry. The succeeding days were again taken up with intense study of *Guinevere*, which, of course, relates the story of an archetypal and idealized 'fallen woman'.[101]

The eroticization of Gladstone's reading, and with it, his attempts to rescue certain fallen women, intensified when he met a woman called Marion Summerhayes. It is clear from Gladstone's diary that he was attracted to her as an individual, not merely as a 'case'. For example, on 30 July 1859, he 'Saw Somerhayes [*sic*]', whom he described as 'full in the highest degree both of interest and of beauty'. He continued to read Tennyson over the next week, before seeing Marion again to make quite a remarkable request: that she should sit for a portrait. On 6 August, Gladstone recorded that he 'saw Summerhayes resp[ecting the] picture &c', and noted that hers 'is a very peculiar case: & merits what I wrote of it to Mr Dyce'.[102]

The resulting picture, Figure 4.5, now entitled *Beatrice*, formally *Lady with the Coronet of Jasmine* (1859; Aberdeen Art Gallery) represented the model as Dante's Beatrice and expressed the fantasy-fusion of Gladstone's reading and his rescue work. Gladstone read to Marion as he had done to her predecessors, and, during September 1859, when he was writing his Tennyson paper, their relationship became very emotionally charged. Just before the family's annual trip to Penmaenmawr in September 1859, Gladstone, aware of the relationship's increasing inappropriateness, decided that 'My thoughts of S[ummerhayes] require to be limited & purged.' However, his work on Tennyson made such a resolution difficult to keep. When called back to Hawarden to see Cobden, Gladstone also wrote to Marion.[103] By the 15th he had returned to the coast and his Tennyson studies,[104] but the following day he repaired to London where, as well as writing, Gladstone spent four

Figure 4.5 William Dyce, *Beatrice,* or, *Lady with Coronet of Jasmine* (1859). Aberdeen Art Gallery.

and a half hours (from 11 a.m. to 3.30 p.m.) reading Tennyson's *The Princess* to 'M S[ummerhayes]', during which interview he noted that he was 'much & variously moved'. On the 17th Gladstone recorded: 'Saw M.S. a scene of rebuke not to be easily forgotten.'[105] Despite this, he saw Marion again two days later, between '6 ½ and 7 ½' and again 'at 11' when he 'brought d[itt]o to D[owning]. St for 1 hour, esp[eciall]y. to see the pictures.' All the while he continued with his work on Tennyson, reading parts of the *Idylls* on the 18th and *The Princess* on the 20th on which day he returned to Wales once more. On the 21st and

22nd he 'Wrote on Tennyson', and read 'Tennyson's In Memoriam', finally finishing the 'revision of my Tennyson MS' on 23 September. He was back in London on 24th and spent between '8 ½–10 ¼ with M S winding up.' On the 26th there was further meeting which elicited the opaque diary observation: 'the case is no common one ... To me no trivial matter, for evil or for good.'

Despite the obvious perils inherent in his textual relationship with Marion Summerhayes, Gladstone continued his practice of reading Tennyson dangerously with fallen women. Thus, in 1865, he 'Saw H. Hastings: & read the whole of Guinevere aloud. X', and, in 1876, he 'Read Guinevere – aloud' in front of Mrs Thistlethwayte 'with undiminished admiration'. Whether this was of the poem or his hostess is unclear but he repeated the reading in 1877. After dining with Laura, they 'went for an hour to the Alhambra where there was the prettiest & best ballet I ever saw. Then read Guinevere aloud'.[106]

Gladstone's relationship with Laura Thistlethwayte – the recently retired courtesan who first captivated him in the 1860s – was another of Gladstone's key reading relationships with women, and was in quite another league to his relationship with Marion Summerhayes. As Jenny West has recently highlighted, their early relationship both began with, and was further developed by, the exchange of texts. In 1866–7, Laura sent Gladstone examples of her poetry and hymn writing, while he bestowed upon her printed copies of his speeches.[107] Much of the relationship's early intensity was fuelled by Laura's promise, in July 1869, to send Gladstone the specially written 'personal history' which became her autobiography. This she temptingly serialized in at least 28 parts, between September 1869 and January 1870. Gladstone, who, as West demonstrates, clearly instigated the work's writing, read it in a state of heightened anticipation and consequent emotion, devouring most of the first 23 parts on receipt, during a lengthy stay at Balmoral in September 1869. It is hard not to agree with West that Gladstone, undoubtedly conversant with similarly pitiable and titillating life stories through his rescue work, found the opportunity to read such material in the privacy and comfort of his study rather than 'on dark street corners' or in prostitutes' shabby dwellings, overpoweringly exciting. Regularly losing sleep over its pages, and begging its author to send him new instalments without delay, reading Laura Thistlethwayte's autobiography teetered tantalizingly on the uncertain border between risk and respectability.[108]

Beyond this central act of knowledge-sharing, Gladstone and Laura's relationship continued to be marked by reading experiences. His visit to the Thistlethwaytes' house at Boveridge, Dorset, in December 1869, which scholars concur in describing as the emotional highpoint of their relationship, and during which Gladstone and Laura spent significant periods alone together, was punctuated by respectable acts of reading – Gladstone declaiming Longfellow's poems aloud and Captain Thistlethwayte delivering a sermon.[109] West also usefully draws our attention to an incident which both illuminates our understanding of Gladstone and Laura's relationship, and his response to fictional literature. She describes, for example, his 'unease' on reading Elleray Lake's *Longleat* (1870) – a tragic tale of adultery and its consequences – which he passed immediately to Laura on finishing it. As with his reading of Tennyson to rescue cases, Gladstone was here seeking a way of vicariously and indirectly communicating his feelings about both the dangers and the pleasures of his relationship with Laura without having to articulate them in his own words. Contact between the two continued until Laura's death in 1894. While it undeniably lessened in intensity, the relationship, as West has shown, remained an important one to them both for much longer than previous biographers have recognized.[110] Moreover, its bibliographical element somewhat surprisingly proved to be one of its most durable aspects: in her will, Laura left her last home, Woodbine Cottage in Hampstead, to be a miniature St Deiniol's, 'a Retreat for Clergymen of all denominations true believers in my God and Saviour and literary men'.[111]

Reading with fallen women was clearly another aspect of Gladstone's reading life that exhibited significant tension, similar to his desire to possess books and yet exercise economic restraint. In this case, Gladstone's understanding of reading as a purifying, educative, and moral activity (witnessed in his encouragement of it among his servants) was tested when morality and immorality became confused. In addition to Gladstone's long-standing habit of reading with fallen women, there was a further category of forbidden, and this time solitary, reading in which Gladstone engaged, the pornographic, which it is necessary to consider.

Pornography

There is no evidence to show that Gladstone collected pornography.[112] His diary indicates that he read it outside the confines of his own library; indeed he was anxious to note down that such books were 'library books', in other words, borrowed.[113] Moreover, as Gladstone saw reading and book collection explicitly as moral endeavours, this alone would make the collection of pornography extremely problematic and undesirable.

As Colin Matthew points out, many of the texts Gladstone regarded as pornographic would not appear so now. However, this does not diminish the anguish Gladstone clearly felt, or lessen the impact of his self-loathing after engaging with such texts. The earliest reference to such reading and its impact was made in 1830 after Gladstone had read some pornography at a book sale. 'Self disgusted & with reason', he wrote. He then went on to record reading to his mother, clearly showing the firm demarcation which existed in his mind between different categories of reading.[114] In common with his approach to other reading matter, Gladstone drew up rules by which he hoped to guard against reading unsuitable material.[115] However, he clearly found it hard to abide by them. Thus, in 1847, he recorded: 'Reading Petronius. A clear offence ag[ains]t my rules of Oct. 26. 1845'. He read Petronius' poetry again in 1850, but made no such observation.[116]

When buying second-hand books, Gladstone clearly took it as a recommendation of the text if it had been previously owned by someone he knew. However, this practice did not serve him very well in 1848 when he bought a copy of French stories and poetic fables. Writing in Italian in his diary, Gladstone revealed:

> I bought this book because it had within it the name of Mr. Greville, to whom it had belonged: and I began to read it, and found in some parts of it impure passages, concealed beneath the veil of a quite foreign idiom: so I drank the poison, sinfully, because understanding was thus hidden by a cloud – I have stained my memory and my soul – which may it please God to cleanse for me, as I have need. Have set down a black mark against this day.[117]

Despite his resolve, Gladstone undertook more reading on 15 May: 'I should have sheered off at the first hints of evil – may these be the last of such base explorations'. And on the 18th: 'I read sinfully, although with disgust, under the pretext of hunting solely for what was innocent; but – criminal that I am – with a prurient curiosity against all the rules of pious prudence, and inflaming the war between the better qualities of man and the worse'.[118] In his own mind then, Gladstone's reading of pornography was rationalized in a similar way to his conceptualization of his mission to fallen women. Gladstone told himself that he read with the intention to uncover and draw out whatever truth or goodness existed in a text (whether woman or book) but then was disappointed with himself when finding so simple a rationalization was often impossible to live up to in practice. In 1848 he 'Wrote ... at night a separate Mem[orandum]. on a sad subject', in which he expressed his frustration with his inability to cope with these aspects of the pursuit of knowledge, which was, in general, so fundamental to his existence.

> The pursuit of knowledge, the desire of estimating different periods & states of the moral and religious life of man, the hope of doing good to persons living in sin: of all these I had utterly failed to discern the proper bounds, and had sometimes perhaps often lost even these from view when once upon the train of thought on imagery of which they might have first effected the introduction.

As well as his own moral weakness, Gladstone blamed overwork as a factor in his inability to resist such books. He then revealed the immediate motivation behind this particular episode of tortuous memorandum-writing:

> This very night ... I saw a book ... marked 'Rochester's poems' and looked at the contents then at some of the verses which were his, and in this I acted against my Resolution though I believe I did not actually read what was evil: but looking on through the rest of the book – which at first appeared more innocent – I found two vile poems, and of these with disgust I hope but certainly with a corrupt sympathy I read parts under that very pretext ... of acquiring a knowledge of the facts of nature & manners of men.[119]

There are references both to reading and trying to avoid 'dangerous pages' well into the 1880s,[120] but always on the proviso of seeking for an elusive moral purpose. Thus, in 1852, Gladstone 'saw the infamous work of (Pseudo) Meursius', and looked at it again the following day because 'the Preface professes a moral aim'.[121] Whether we believe Gladstone's reasoning or not, either in this case or with regards to his relationship to fallen women, is in a sense immaterial. This was how he rationalized his behaviour to himself and, as such, it is important evidence of the way he engaged with and responded to texts.

*

This discussion of Gladstone's private library and reading has underlined once again that its 'private' character is not to be taken at face value. There were distinctly public aspects to the institution and to the reading that went on there, but there were different levels of privacy – some relating to the private but respectable domestic sphere; others to more secret and transgressive domains. On a superficial level, Gladstone's collection and the place in which he housed the bulk of it were symbols of a gentlemanly tradition extending back centuries. However, Gladstone's Temple of Peace reflected history on a far more personal and self-consciously engaged level. This neither involved a simplistic dismissal of tradition nor the denigration of outward appearance; there were many occasions on which Gladstone's library was made available to others to be the object of suitably well-informed admiration. Moreover, even though Gladstone clearly enjoyed the adoption and projection of a reclusive, unworldly scholarly persona – a characteristic to be explored further in Chapter 7 – one has the impression he was never as unaware as he appeared of what was going on around him. This is made more than evident by the borrowing registers that survive. These documents not only testify to Gladstone's organizing personality, but also to the high level of surveillance he instituted and maintained over his books. This was not a totalitarian or narrow control however. The Temple of Peace as lending library boasted a very broad range of borrowers who read books from all categories in Gladstone's collection. The library was not a space exclusively designed for and used by upper-class men. There were clearly identifiable male and female users, as well as representatives from a variety of social classes among the list of borrowers. Bearing in mind what has been observed about Gladstone's collecting habits, it is not at all surprising that he should wish to maintain personal control over who used his library and how they used it.

Control and the transgression of boundaries are also central concepts for understanding the readings that took place outside the Temple of Peace. As well as looking at who, and what, was allowed into Gladstone's library, we have explored what was kept outside it. Despite the new information presented here of the high level of openness and inclusivity of Gladstone's library, there were clearly limitations to the kinds of reading that were possible, and that were held desirable, within the Temple of Peace. Even when reading alone in the Temple, one gets the sense that Gladstone was working within a tightly monitored and controlled domestic frame of reference, openly accountable to his wife, family, and peers, joining in their dislike of 'improper French novels' and in their efforts to monitor the morality of servants' reading. However, as we have seen, Gladstone found it more difficult to control and monitor his own reading beyond the confines of his private library.

Beyond the Temple of Peace, the boundaries of what was and was not acceptable became increasingly blurred. On one level it was usually straightforward to distinguish between forbidden texts and those with moral purpose. However, Gladstone's problems were most severe when it was discovered that the same texts could be read both in respectable and dangerous contexts. Thus reading Tennyson could both be a decent after-dinner familial entertainment but also, in other contexts, and with other readers, an activity which threatened such domestic respectability; disrupting all notions of control and moral certainty.

The image of Gladstone guiltily perusing illicit material in the bookshops of Europe, or reading Tennyson dangerously in prostitutes' garrets, superficially seems as far from the snug domesticity he enjoyed in the Temple of Peace as it is possible to get. However, even though his reading experiences inside and outside the Temple appear so divergent in content, motivation, and impact, it is striking that, in many ways, they were the expression of the same overpowering impulse of collection which Gladstone, even in Hawarden, found stimulating, frustrating, and occasionally uncontrollable. His 'collection' of women was undertaken in similar ways to his collection of books – he sought them out and established distinct and regular patterns for the activity. In his own mind, the pursuits shared moral and epistemological functions: the revelation, discovery, and the learning of truths, the provision of opportunities to act upon them, and the medium by which to transmit them to others. It is this underlying connection that firmly establishes the status of the Temple of Peace, and the mutating collection housed within it, as a place of very deceptive tranquillity.

Part III St Deiniol's Library

5
Humanity: Libraries, Literature, and Liberalism

As summer progressed towards autumn in 1889, the relative peace of Hawarden village was more than usually disturbed. Local residents had, by this date, become largely immune to the periodic busyness and clamour emanating from train loads of inquisitive tourists, making for either church or park in search of Mr Gladstone. The substantial festivities surrounding the Gladstones' Golden Wedding that July had been greeted with appropriate, but not unwarranted, levels of celebration, and even the sight of Mr Gladstone himself paying repeated visits to an expanse of open ground near the parish church had done little to excite their interest. Over the last few years they had, after all, become accustomed to seeing various members of the family purposefully touring the village on estate business. The first indication that something very different was afoot was given by the arrival of a large consignment of building materials all the way from London, followed by the pegging out and gradual construction of what looked like a galvanized iron chapel. That this new building was not to serve as a place of worship was apparent by the time winter came. Not long after building had finished, a seemingly endless procession of vehicles began to shuttle between the Castle and the tin edifice, depositing load after load of books which, upon their arrival, were taken inside to be placed on new bookshelves by Mr Gladstone personally. The sheer scale of this removal, which was to last for almost two years, left no one in any doubt that an institution of some note was being established, and speculation was rife as to its purpose. Rumours abounded, and the idea quickly formed that the foundation would soon function as a reading room for the village, before the appearance of a short letter in the December issue of the parish magazine put paid to any such notions.

'With reference to the small structure of corrugated iron which I am now erecting near the church', Gladstone wrote:

> I address to you these few lines with the view of obviating any misapprehensions among my fellow parishioners ... The building is simply a repository for books, with the additions necessary for due care-taking, and will be in no wise suited for the purposes of a reading room.[1]

However much this epistle initially deflated the spirits of Hawardeners, they were somewhat heartened when they discovered that the repository's contents were hardly suitable reading material for their hard-won leisure hours, being largely theological in character.[2] With some measure of relief, they soon returned to observing, with characteristic detachment, ensuing developments at the curious institution they would soon know as 'St Deiniol's Library'.

Uncertainty as to both the origination and ultimate purpose of Gladstone's foundation was not limited to his fellow parishioners. Many of the visitors to the Castle who were taken to view St Deiniol's professed themselves confused, with Lady Charlotte Ribblesdale confessing herself irritated that Gladstone 'had not ventured to tell himself, far less anybody else, what was to be the ultimate end of this library' at the time of her visit in 1892.[3] Gladstone was undoubtedly vague, if not secretive, about what had inspired his foundation and his plans for its development. He told a group of Yorkshire Liberals, visiting Hawarden in 1895 in order to present 'an oak bookcase containing nearly three hundred volumes of valuable books intended for the use of the Hawarden St. Deiniol's Library', that his vision was 'still in embryo'.[4] He was equally reticent with close friends and colleagues: Lord Stanmore, then Sir Arthur Gordon, recalled that Gladstone 'always spoke rather mystically' about his new library, 'saying it "would shape itself", "time would reveal", etc.', and, when pushed, all Gladstone would offer by way of either confirmation or denial was: "'You're not far out, not far out," ... and on a subsequent occasion ... "Not far from the mark, not far from the mark."'[5] Such reticence bordered on the unhelpful. Surely, if the library was to have even a semi-public function, it required that the world at large should have a clear idea about its purpose? Gladstone did draw up a leaflet to advertise the library at an early stage. It was broad in its characterization of suitable readers: 'students (lay and clerical, of any age), inquirers, authors, and clergy, or others desiring times of rest', but this information was evidently still only 'sent to such of Mr. Gladstone's friends as are interested in the scheme'.[6]

In due course, however, the institution began to acquire a higher profile in the press, ever eager for news of how Gladstone was spending his retirement, and, following the statesman's death and the designation of St Deiniol's as his key national memorial, publicity material also began to be issued directly by Gladstone's family and the new library's administrators. All these accounts agreed that much of its importance derived from the fact of it being Gladstone's library. Such commentators were, by the 1880s, well accustomed to making connections between Gladstone's political liberalism, his library, and reading, and many readily represented St Deiniol's as a further outgrowth of Gladstone's inclusive politics and the fruit of his popular Liberal agenda, characterizing it as a public library in essence. Friederichs described the library as 'a scheme of public utility which has been in Mr. Gladstone's mind for many years', closely linking the library's foundation with his political and intellectual liberalism: 'Thus it will be seen that in this his munificent gift Mr. Gladstone has acted on the same large-minded and large-hearted principles to which he has adhered all the days of his life'. The library, Friederichs stated, had been founded 'on the broadest and most liberal lines' providing an explicit political impetus to a largely private action, and stressed the fact that even the books remaining at the Castle stayed publicly available. She further highlighted the '"liberal" tendency' of Gladstone's trust arrangements, especially his provision that 'Trustees and officials may be men or women, married or single' together with 'the ample power given to the Trustees to make the Foundation "move with the times"'.[7]

Mary Drew suggested that her father's primary intention had been 'to bring together readers who had no books and books who had no readers', and J. C. Story echoed this populist rhetoric by telling his readers that: 'Mr. Gladstone's books became one of his treasured possessions; yet for years he cherished the intention of presenting them to others'. Story further described the library as an act of 'great benevolence' and 'joyful sacrifice' on Gladstone's part, given 'for the use of the public' in the broadest sense of the word. 'It should hardly be necessary to say', he confided, 'that studious persons, of whatever class, residing in the neighbourhood, as well as strangers from afar, are equally eligible'.[8]

This vision – especially Story's insistence that those 'residing in the neighbourhood' would be welcome to use the library – jars awkwardly with the tone of Gladstone's letter to this very constituency, in which he not only denied that the library was for their use but also that it was a reading room at all. It neither supports the idea that Gladstone created St Deiniol's as a kind of advance memorial to himself, nor does it appear to accord with certain other alternative visions that were simultaneously circulating, which presented the library within a religious, rather than a political, frame of reference.

In this chapter we will examine the background to this anomaly, and investigate the case for understanding St Deiniol's as an outgrowth of Gladstone's interest in, and work for, the public proliferation of libraries, reading, and mental culture – a sphere which we can broadly correlate with his elevation of the concept of 'humanity' to a position of key importance in his liberal outlook.

The humanistic reader

> So human and personal did a book seem to Mr. Gladstone that it gave him real pain to see it carelessly used, or illtreated – laid open on its face, untidily marked, dog's-eared, thumbed. And in arranging his friends on the shelf, no squeezing or even coaxing was allowed; they must fit with nicety, not wasting space, but in no way uncomfortably housed.[9]

So Mary Drew summarized her father's attitude to books. To him they were almost living and breathing things, requiring great and constant care, facts reflected, as we have seen, in the solicitous way in which Gladstone organized and tended his book rooms and their contents. The treatment of books as companions to be loved, cared for, and talked to, has been marked as a fairly common trait amongst readers, and Gladstone clearly exhibited many of these shared characteristics.[10] However, he constructed his anthropomorphic characterization of books on a far grander and more publicly conscious scale. Books were to be cherished because of the moral work that they were designed to undertake: 'They are first and foremost among the *compages*, the bonds and rivets of the race ... the history of books cannot ... be separated from the history of souls', he wrote in 1890,[11] adding, six years later, 'book collecting ... is a vitalizing element in a society honeycombed by several sources of corruption'.[12] The genesis of these ideas can be traced back to Gladstone's own experience of book collecting and understanding of the function of the library, but even more fundamentally, to his philosophical understanding of the functions of study and the ways in which knowledge is propagated.[13]

It is well known how much value Gladstone placed on the institutional role of the Christian church as the preserver, improver, and transmitter of the aggregated spiritual inheritance of humankind. What is less often recognized, but equally important to our understanding of his epistemology, is the value Gladstone accorded to other institutions, such as libraries, which in their own way fulfilled similar preservative and educative functions. Gladstone even saw bookshops as far more than simple locations for purchase. For instance, when in Turin in 1850, Gladstone's bookshop visits were valuable, not so much for the books which he purchased 'in moderation' there, but for the conversations he was also able to conduct. Book shopping 'has the advantage', he wrote, 'of giving one the means of intercourse with an intelligent class', adding that, of five intelligent conversations he had had on Piedmontese affairs, 'two were [with] booksellers'.[14] A similar level of cultural exchange could be experienced in libraries; for example, in June 1832 he visited the University library in Bologna where he 'conversed much with a very intelligent Italian, who seemed connected with the management'.[15] As well as valuing such commerce, Gladstone believed that one could also glean much from studying the collections, catalogues, and classification systems of libraries themselves.

Gladstone visited and used libraries other than his own throughout his life. He regularly viewed libraries as a tourist both at home and abroad,[16] took a dedicated interest in the libraries of his friends and social peers,[17] especially those which he considered somehow innovative or out of the common,[18] made use of a wide variety of collections, and was active in administering and running a number of such institutions.[19] Moreover, as well as publicly promoting the political cause of libraries,[20] Gladstone privately donated books to those that he thought in need.[21] One of the first that Gladstone used or visited outside the family home was Liverpool's Athenaeum library, an institution of which his father was a prominent member.[22] While at Oxford, he used both university and college libraries,[23] and was given some degree of responsibility over Christ Church library.[24] When he was an MP, Gladstone regularly used the House of Commons library,[25] and additionally supplemented the resources of his own private collection by making use of those available to him at the British Museum,[26] and the London Library, of which Gladstone was a founder member, with responsibility for recommending the institution's initial purchases of ecclesiastical history.[27] He was also very well acquainted with continental libraries, making it a priority to visit and assess as many of them as possible from the very outset of his 1832 grand tour. Thus, on 2 February, he toured Ghent's public library, followed his arrival in Paris nine days later with a trip to see the *Hôpital des Invalides* library, which housed 18, 000 volumes given by Napoleon. On 27 February, he compared the library in Lyons to that of Christ Church: 'perhaps twenty feet longer ... but not near so fine', on 3 March he was touring the University library at Turin, on the 9th he visited that of Genoa, and by the 22nd he had surveyed the Laurentian library in Florence. In April he inspected the libraries of the Vatican and the English College in Rome, and in June he toured libraries and archives in Bologna, Ferrara, and Venice.[28]

These tours had a specific, educative purpose in Gladstone's mind – equivalent in many ways to his fact-finding attendance at overseas church services. Gladstone wanted to know how accessible accumulated knowledge preserved in libraries was to the communities surrounding them. He therefore frequently made attempts to discover both how inclusive the libraries he visited were, and also how all-embracing were the collections to which the reader had gained access. On the first point, Gladstone was favourably impressed by the European libraries which he visited as a young man. He was permitted to use the University library in Bologna, noted that admission to the Doge's Palace library and its 83, 000 volumes in Venice was 'liberal, here & elsewhere', found that the 'Biblioteca Ambrogiana' in Milan, which had been founded in the seventeenth century as the first European library offering universal access, still possessed its 'liberal constitution' being 'open to all, something it furthermore shared in common with the city's 'Brera Palace, or Royal Academy ... where everyone is admitted to read'.[29] Once inside these libraries, however, Gladstone discovered – by interrogating their catalogues and custodians – that the laudable theory of open access was not necessarily followed in practice. Thus in Turin, at the beginning of March 1832, Gladstone visited the University court and library. After examining its treasures – 'an old Bible of 1573, ... a Testament of 1569 ... [and] a beautifully illuminated "life of Christ"' – Gladstone turned to the catalogue:

> On examining the Catalogue, I found that there were some works of Protestant Divines there ... I remarked this to a keeper of the Library who went with us, and he said 'Yes, they had them, but generally kept them locked up.' I asked him whether they would not show them to a priest who desired it. They said, that they would to an old priest, but certainly not to a young one![30]

Similarly, when Gladstone visited the Vatican library that April, he recorded another such conversation, observing humorously that the Custodian 'declared there were no Protestant books there! And when I found in the room with open shelves the name of Calvin, [he] said it must be another'![31]

Visits to bookshops also revealed significant information about these matters. Thus he was assiduous in conversing with as well as purchasing from a Milanese bookseller in 1832:

> Went out and completed a purchase of Italian books ... I asked a bookseller with whom I was dealing the price of Martini's Bible (with notes) when complete.[32] He named a sum between one & two hundred francs. 'Nothing cheaper?' 'The cheapest Bible with notes costs 45 to 50 francs'. 'And is there no cheaper Bible to be had?' 'Yes, Diodati's: for 18 or 20.' 'Can this be easily procured?' 'No: for it has no notes and is prohibited'.

The Protestant Gladstone smugly concluded: 'I think when no Bible is purchasable under 45 or 50 francs, we may without breach of charity say, that the Bible is, virtually, kept from the poor'.[33]

Gladstone was, however, just as interested in the humanity divisions of the libraries which he visited. When surveying Napoleon's library at *Les Invalides*, Gladstone paid particular attention to its history section because he was concerned to gauge how far the French had sought, and were continuing to seek, to extirpate the memory of the 'old Bourbons', researches which caused him to reflect that:

> It is a melancholy event in the history of nations when they think themselves compelled to blot out a period from their history ... The life of nations is given to be used like that of individuals ... but here we see a severing of those links which united us to other times, whereby we hold communion with the dead, and may hope to imbibe the rudiments of a kindred spirit.[34]

Libraries were, for Gladstone, not simply places where history was to be preserved for its own sake; they were also sites where the minds of the living ought to commune with the dead, draw on their accumulated learning, and hence receive enlightenment. Moreover, they were, as he so frequently found during his investigations, also extremely vulnerable sites, offering only the most fragile and tenuous of connections to the past and its knowledges, ties which could easily be broken not only by the self-serving actions of governments and religious authorities, but also by a lack of altruism on the part of the individual thinker.

Gladstone did not, however, exempt himself from the latter failing, he had experienced first-hand the contradictions existing between the ideals of scholarship and the realities of public life on both individual and communal levels. As early as 1846, he had reprimanded himself for losing sight of the altruistic purpose of scholarship:

> It has now become a very important part of my duty to take care that the absorption of my time in study, which is a great delight to me, do not also become a snare & an occasion for the unsuspected, & even therefore vigorous, action of selfishness. The remote idea of the fruits of study, as intended in some way to reach others, is not a sufficient remedy: and by flattery it has in itself the seeds of another disease. Let me by God's help therefore have this matter always before mine eyes! Today perhaps was my best with reference to this subject: I had but about 4 hours of reading against near 8 of what had direct reference to God or to my fellow creatures.[35]

This conceptualization of how knowledge and culture are ideally transmitted made Gladstone hypersensitive to his own failures to live up to it. For instance, on his 65th birthday, he reiterated his concerns when considering whether or not his engagement in the papal infallibility controversy was really fulfilling the ends for which study had been designed.[36] Moreover, it also made him very aware of others' failures encountered during his reading. Thus, when, on 30 December 1874, Gladstone finished reading George Eliot's *Middlemarch* and commented: 'It is an extraordinary, to me a very jarring, book',[37] he was not only, as Richard Shannon points out, referring to Eliot's 'depiction of the wastes and futilities of lives and ambitions skewed and spoiled by muddled religion and misdirected science',[38] he was also commenting on the incorrect relationship between knowledge and action represented in the book. In the character of Edward Casaubon, we see someone whose preoccupation with intellectual endeavour is completely divorced from an understanding of any obligation to act upon knowledge obtained. Casaubon is eminently qualified to express other writers' opinions, based on his exhaustive summaries and epitomes, but he neither responds to them creatively nor allows them to inform his own views. As a result, his endless research, conducted amongst the 'dark bookshelves' of his library, is rendered pointless, and he makes no meaningful response to the social and moral world around him. In this he is unfavourably contrasted with his wife Dorothea, who regards scholarship as offering endless opportunities for informing life.[39] Gladstone's unsettled response to the book was rooted in the way he related the negative portrayal of Casaubon and his barren scholarship to his own altruistic understanding of humanistic study, as well as his residual uncertainty about the uncomfortable dualism in his own situation as a scholar-politician.

In Gladstone's lengthy response to Mary Augusta Ward's best-selling novel of religious doubt, *Robert Elsmere* (1888), published in the *Nineteenth Century*, we are provided with further evidence for Gladstone's continuing preoccupation with such tensions.[40] The novel's central theme, the process and consequences of a young liberal Anglican clergyman's loss of faith in the historical truth of Christianity, realistically personified the intellectual struggles of a whole generation of late Victorians and created terrific impact with thousands finding its three volumes a painful, and yet compelling, reading experience. Reporting to Mary Drew in March that 'Mama and I are each of us still separately engaged in a death-grapple with *Robert Elsmere*', Gladstone had initially regarded 'with doubt and dread the idea of doing anything on it',[41] but when published, Gladstone's review generated almost as much debate as the novel itself, both in Britain and the United States, and significantly boosted its sales. Although he commented on the novel as a work of literature, Gladstone devoted the bulk of his review to a critique of Ward's handling of Robert Elsmere's abandonment of orthodox Christianity in favour of theism, which was, of course, what made the book such a debating point. However, the philosophy as well as the theology of *Robert Elsmere* explicitly challenged the touchstone of Gladstone's personal intellectual life: the conjunction and cross-fertilization of strong faith with scholarship.

As Stefan Collini has noted, a significant part of *Elsmere*'s exploration of faith and doubt was shaped by that atmosphere, which pervaded intellectualized public expressions of Victorian morality, in which the abhorrence of selfishness and the desire to cultivate altruism were powerfully mixed.[42] Moreover, the novel is also deeply concerned with matters of epistemology: ways of knowing, varieties of knowledge, the diachronic processes of acquiring knowledge and the consequences of possessing it. What must Gladstone have thought as he read the following description, one of the most impressive in Mary Ward's long novel, which depicts the visit of the eponymous hero and his former

Oxford tutor to the library of Murewell Hall, treasured possession of his parish patron, Roger Wendover, a well-known but hermit-like and sceptical intellectual?

> Robert held back the hangings over the doorway leading into the rest of the wing, and, passing through, they found themselves in a continuation of the library totally different in character from the magnificent room they had just left. The walls were no longer latticed and carved; they were closely packed, in the business-like way, with books which represented the Squire's own collection, and were in fact a chart of his own intellectual history ... The room seemed instinct with a harsh, commanding presence. The history of a mind and soul was written upon the face of it; every shelf, as it were, was an autobiographical fragment, an 'Apologia pro Vita Mea'.[43]

This quotation is representative of an important and conspicuous literary device, frequently used throughout the novel, by which Ward charts characters' intellectual development through a description of their books and the spaces in which they study them, placing the individual's attitude to knowledge at the centre of the novel's preoccupations.[44] It was not only the level of knowledge attained that interested Ward, but also the ways in which knowledge was procured over time, and the ways in which it was used. Like Eliot, Ward was emphatic that the acquisition of knowledge should not be an end in itself and, in the characters of Oxford don Edward Langham and Squire Wendover, the author presented the perils of pursuing great knowledge for no purpose other than for its own sake. Langham, of whom Robert says: 'It is no use ... expecting you to preserve a moral sense when you get among books,' is without a sense of emotional responsibility to others, and Wendover, although he possesses a fine library, is incapable of social or moral action, scoffs at Robert's belief in a divine Christ and – just as Casaubon takes no interest in Dorothea's schemes for cottage building – knows nothing and cares less for the sufferings of his tenants. Moreover, it is in Wendover's library that the eponymous hero finally rejects the comfortable but redundant security represented by its collection of inherited knowledge in favour of social action after recognizing that the library, as well as being a place of enlightenment, can also be a 'symbol of that absorbing and overgrown life of the intellect which blights the heart and chills the senses'.[45]

Gladstone had no sympathy for Wendover's lack of landlordly duty – noting that, although Robert has persuaded him to clean up Mile End, this action 'does not indicate any permanent change in the social ideas of Mr. Wendover' – nor would he have considered either his or Casaubon's use of knowledge appropriate or desirable. However, unlike the majority of *Robert Elsmere*'s reviewers, Gladstone considered that Wendover, who he described as 'the supreme arbiter of destinies in the book', was 'somewhat unkindly treated' by his creator. Gladstone felt it unfair that the possessor of such a 'rich library' should end by losing his mind, echoing the book's hero's regret: 'What learning has perished with him! How vain seems all toil to acquire!' – and the words, as they passed through his mind, seemed to him to ring another death-knell'.[46] For Gladstone, the deaths of Wendover and Casaubon did indeed ring another death-knell, that of inherited knowledge itself, for both represented wasted opportunities to continue the cumulative knowledge project that libraries and collections ideally signify. It is not surprising that Gladstone, out of office and engaged in making his own contribution to the expanding scope of human knowledge when he read both novels, should have been disturbed by the personal implications of the fates dealt out to these fictional intellectuals, simultaneously concerned, as he was, with whether or not his scholarly life would prove 'as worthy as my public life' in either his own estimation or that of the wider world.[47]

However, Gladstone was also concerned with the wider implications of such fictional representations, because of his conception of the function of literature, his worries about the impact on readers of novels such as this, and his continued belief that – as he expressed it in 1890 – books, by their very nature, are 'in a certain sense at enmity with the world'.[48]

Endangered truth: the social responsibilities of literature

Gladstone was not an uncritical reader of fiction, having a firm idea of both writing quality and adherence to literary form. He had a strong sense, for example, of what constituted a novel. Thus, after he had received and read a copy of the first collected edition of Thomas Love Peacock's works, sent by an admiring clergyman, Gladstone wrote on the fly leaf of volume 1: 'That Mr Peacock's novels have been much in vogue, is testified by this reprint in 1875. I find them unreadable, and hardly entitled to be called novels at all.' Once Gladstone had decided that Peacock's fictions did not qualify as novels, they were nonetheless plundered for information of 'historical value'.[49] Gladstone believed that, in order for literature to be judged as truly great, it should offer exemplary forms of character and ideal patterns of behaviour which the reader could admire and seek to emulate. As such, literature should offer a harmonizing counterpoint to the Christian gospels and their work. Two of the most significant producers of this type of writing, in Gladstone's estimation, were Sir Walter Scott and Alfred Tennyson.

Walter Scott was the dominating English language literary influence on Gladstone. He read his works with phenomenal regularity throughout his life – being particularly fond of the Scottish novels – and defended Scott's qualities as a writer even when he was distinctly out of fashion with the reading public at large.[50] In 1906, Mary Drew claimed her father's enduring love for Scott was determined by the writer's commitment to achieving a 'sense of harmony' and 'fitness in literature', and his 'presentation to mankind of, not the ugly, the unnatural, the cruel, the base, but the lofty, the beautiful, [and] the ideal.'[51] In 1868, Gladstone had conveyed the essence of these beliefs to an audience of Welsh schoolchildren at Hawarden. The reason, he told them, why he believed Scott had 'exceeded most of the literary men that the world has produced' was his ability, not only to communicate historical facts, but to call 'forth from the sepulchre the dry bones of former ages … causing them to live and move before us, and us to live and move among them, as if we belonged to them and they belonged to us', so inspiring readers to identify personally and engage deeply with the past.[52] Also an advantage and an attraction in Gladstone's eyes was the universal accessibility of Scott's works. For those few that might not be able to afford a set of Scott for themselves, Gladstone believed that they should be able to find them in their local library. As he wrote in the set he presented to the Hawarden Institute: 'No library should be complete without a set of Sir Walter Scott's novels in full. Accordingly, I present this set to the Hawarden Institute.'[53] And this was not just a directive that he gave with reference to working-class readers. When addressing the well-to-do library owner, Gladstone pleaded: 'not only for Homer, Dante, Shakespeare, but for Johnson, Scott and Burns, and whatever represents a large and manifold humanity' as classificatory subdivisions.[54] Gladstone saw such authors' works as – potentially – easily accessible, civilizing, and spiritualizing influences over the next generation, but only if it would heed them. In his 1868 Hawarden speech, Gladstone had noted, with some concern, Scott's apparent waning popularity among the young, calling it a 'public misfortune',[55] underlining his understanding of Scott's literary inventions as knowledge that had direct relevance to public as well as private domains. As he was to reiterate in 1885: 'It is a degradation to man to be reduced to the life of the present', adding, 'never will he cast forth his hope, and his views, and his efforts towards the future with due effect and energy, unless at the same time he prizes and holds fondly clasped to his heart the recollections of the past'.[56]

Gladstone's belief – that the imaginative revival of mediaeval chivalric and Christianized ideals could have widespread and beneficial effects on contemporary society – also lay at the base of his immediate and lasting admiration for the poetry of his near contemporary, Alfred Tennyson. In his enthusiastic 1859 *Quarterly* article, Gladstone contended that the *Idylls*, and most particularly *Guinevere*, represented 'the highest point which the poetry of our age has reached'.[57] His review was, however, not completely adulatory, incorporating as it did a strong attack on the climax of *Maud* (1855), which Tennyson had written in direct response to the Crimean war, and which Gladstone interpreted as endorsing war as a social panacea.[58] Reliance on such 'partial and narrow aspects of ... truth' were, in Gladstone's view, unlikely to provide a sound basis for the exercise of the individual's moral duty in the world, especially if that individual were a public figure. Tennyson's duty to his 'public' was therefore something Gladstone felt he had to remind the poet laureate, in the conclusion to his original onslaught:

> Mr Tennyson is too intimately and essentially the poet of the nineteenth century to separate himself from its leading characteristics, the progress of physical science, and a vast commercial, mechanical, and industrial development ... We fondly believe it is his business to do much towards the solution of ... how to harmonise this new draught of external power and activity with the old and more mellow wine of faith, self-devotion, loyalty, reverence and discipline.[59]

This passage clearly illustrates Gladstone's understanding of Tennyson as a social poet of great potential, poised to reach the heights of Scott *et al.*, and it was clear that Gladstone's annoyance with *Maud* had not for a moment outweighed his enthusiasm for Arthur: 'it is ... human in the largest and deepest sense; and therefore ... universal'. He firmly believed that Tennyson, 'by his own single strength, has made a sensible addition to the permanent wealth of mankind'.[60] It also illustrates his increasing tendency to analogize Tennyson's poetic vocation with his own political one.[61] However, Gladstone's vision of the poet and politician working in harmony to raise the moral character of Victorian Britain was not to materialize. Although Gladstone had persuaded Tennyson to accept a barony and enter the House of Lords in 1883, fully expecting him to support the Liberal cause, Tennyson refused to take a party seat, energetically opposed many of Gladstone's initiatives, and regularly criticized him in verse, particularly over questions to do with defence and the governance of Ireland. The most damaging of these poems was the long and vitriolic *Locksley Hall Sixty Years After*, which was published in the *Times* on 31 July 1886. A loose sequel to *Locksley Hall* (1842), it revoked the latter poem's optimistic endorsement of progress and constituted a savage indictment of Gladstonian liberalism. Specifically, Tennyson denounced Gladstone's duplicitous political philosophy, symbolized by his Home Rule campaign, which had not only dispatched 'old political common-sense' but heralded the demise of civilization, in the form of heraldry, poetry, and history (lines 249–50).

In his full-scale review of the poem, published in the *Nineteenth Century* as '"Locksley Hall" and the Jubilee' in January 1887, Gladstone sought to refute Tennyson's criticisms by offering a panoramic review of the improving measures enacted during the preceding half century. The resulting litany, of course, undertook to validate Gladstone's political career in the aftermath of the June defeats and his resignation as prime minister, but it also gave him a chance to restate his commitment to learning from the knowledge of past generations.[62] Calling upon the memory of the mutually admired Prince Albert to support him, Gladstone defended his endorsement of popular government as the only way by which 'the Future might effect some moderate improvement upon the Past, and mitigate in some perceptible degree the social sorrows and burdens of mankind'.[63] Politically expedient as this undoubtedly was, it was also reflective of a wider intellectual vision. Gladstone wrote to his son, Willy, on 8 July 1886: 'The whole business is historical, and will come up again in the future, probably at no distant day ... I grieve that England will seemingly not learn the lesson written in the book of fate until she has to learn it with more or less of pain and shame'.[64]

In 1887, Gladstone reiterated his conviction that 'No greater calamity can happen to a people than to break utterly with its Past ... for ... we dislocate the axis of the very ground which forms our own point of departure'.[65] His twin beliefs that the past is the defining other of society – knowable and educative – and that 'every generation of man makes its own addition' to that cumulative, human experience, were at the root of his admiration for literary figures such as Scott and Tennyson who held such potential influence over 'the nature and destinies of man'. Thus, in his review of *Sixty Years After*, Gladstone was able to write: 'The multiplication and better formation of the institutions of benevolence among us are but symptomatic indications of a wider and deeper change: ... acknowledgement of the great second commandment, of the duties of wealth to poverty, of strength to weakness, of knowledge to ignorance ... of man to man'.[66]

The duty of 'knowledge to ignorance' was, from the middle of 1886, something Gladstone was evermore determined to champion. The problem was, of course, that, by rejecting Gladstone's Home Rule bill, parliamentarians had suggested that they did not share his understanding of how progress was to be achieved, or indeed understood – an irritating fact which convinced Gladstone that lack of support for Home Rule amongst MPs and the general public was a result of widespread historical ignorance. From the bill's defeat, Gladstone seemed obsessed by this idea, and of the need to convince colleagues, opponents, and the general public of its relevance to current issues. He thus supported schemes to make revisionist Irish history more widely available, steeped himself in Irish texts, and produced a substantial body of articles and reviews on historical themes. During 1887, for example, he published six other historical articles, including one of the first for the fledgling *English Historical Review*. Repeatedly, Gladstone reiterated the need to supply 'the people of Great Britain with the historical information, in which their "titled" and "educated" leaders are so woefully deficient'.[67] His first task, therefore, was to try and re-educate these public men.

Reading and the public man

Such a programme was, in fact, one Gladstone had long sought to implement, not only amongst professional public men, but also among those occupying that position through birth and duty. Thus in 1872 he had written privately to Queen Victoria, continuing their long and tortuous discussions over a suitable public role for the Prince of Wales, and had urged her to encourage her son 'to adopt the habit of reading':

> The regular application of but a small portion of time would enable him to master many of the able and valuable works which bear upon Royal and Public duty. Though the Prince's turn appears to move towards that kind of training which is acquired by oral intercourse and by active life, the serious difficulties which are encountered in this direction might weigh in favour of a partial application to the study of books.

Gladstone's suggestion fell on deaf ears. The Queen replied: 'she has only to say that the P. of W. has *never* been fond of reading & that from his earliest years it was *impossible* to get him to do so. Newspapers & *very rarely*, a novel, are all he ever reads.'[68]

Sixteen years later, and two years after the defeat of his first Home Rule bill, Gladstone spoke at the opening of the Gladstone library in the National Liberal Club in May 1888, to what he hoped would be a more receptive audience. Despite being perilously elevated on a chair to ensure his audience a good view, Gladstone eloquently summarized what he felt a library ought to embody for the public man. Not 'a mere place to lounge in', not 'simply a repository of novels and romances', a library should be:

> a rich treasure-house of all that can fertilize the human mind and enable men to devote themselves either wholly or partially to the high pursuit of politics to make themselves worthy of discharging the true duties in connexion with that pursuit in a befitting manner.[69]

Quoting Macaulay, he further reminded his listeners of the beneficial effects of turning from 'the changeful and worrying circumstances of the world' and the inconstancies of human relationships, to a 'tranquil and fruitful' communion 'with the great spirits of the dead through the ... works they have bequeathed to us'. Due to their constant and unchanging nature, Gladstone represented books as a social panacea, 'a living protest in an age ... too much addicted to practical materialism ... on behalf of ... mental life'.[70] Gladstone reflected on the sources of knowledge routinely available to the politician, recognizing that, beyond 'a mere handful' of professionals or leisured individuals who had the time and money to devote to the study of politics, most non-stipendiary politicians habitually relied on daily and monthly journals for their information and sometimes, he added, their principles. Even though the Houses of Parliament had greater access to reference material and information digests than ever before, Gladstone alleged MPs' knowledge of politics and, in particular, of history, had not markedly 'improved upon the practices of our ancestors'. Envisioning the politician's ideal relationships – with both knowledge and with the public – as analogous with a market in which imports and exports are balanced, Gladstone pressed his political colleagues to 'import' as much through reading as they habitually 'exported' through speaking.

> If you wish to treat political subjects in the manner in which they ought to be treated, if you wish to bring to them the knowledge by

which they ought to be illustrated, if you wish to provide yourselves with all the instruments which will aid you in forming sound judgements and in expressing them after they have been formed, depend upon it that can only be effectually done by combining study and reflection with the rapid and constant expression of ideas, which is our duty in the circumstances of the time.[71]

This 'duty' of the public man – to be constantly publicizing his opinions – was also, as Gladstone understood it, a dangerous 'snare' if, by so doing, he 'goes very suddenly out of his own line and delivers very positive judgements on a subject to which he has not applied his mind'. Thus Gladstone's recommendation – to lawyers and clergymen as well as politicians – was:

> that every man in his own measure and degree ... should endeavour to equip himself for the consideration of ... politics ... by reaping and garnering the knowledge which a study of other times and the study of other countries will afford him, and by making use of it in order to enlarge the scope of his judgements, to increase, not to diminish, the allowances that he is disposed to make for what he may think the aberrations of opinion in others, and to give greater solidity and greater durability to his own conclusions.[72]

Despite the perils of selfishness and greed, the creation of such truly liberal public figures, Gladstone held, was facilitated by the use of history. Beyond holding a central place in national culture, history now occupied an augmented place in the universities, and was, as a result, the subject of an increasing number of books being published in English. It is no surprise to find that Gladstone dwelt on this in the numerous university and school addresses which he gave. For example, in his 1879 Rectorial Address at Glasgow University, Gladstone had urged his listeners to study history, 'the most potent and effective of all the instruments of human education', because it 'gives us far larger materials of judgment upon human conduct, and upon the very springs of action, than any present experience can confer'.[73]

The acquisition and reading of texts – contemporary as well as those penned by former generations – would ensure that the politician's library was both a 'liberal and bold' resource; 'a great and powerful instrument of mental education'. In a manner entirely characteristic of Gladstone's mature liberalism, this enhanced mental education was seen by him as essential, not merely for the individual politician, but for the amelioration of the wider community which he served:

> It is an ennobling incident ... when you are enabled to labour at once for the concurrent interest of millions ... It is a blessed lot if we are permitted through that channel ... to do a little ... towards diminishing the sum of misery in the world, and towards making our fellow-creatures happier and better.[74]

As can be seen from his own sale of his library of useful books to Wolverton, rescue of Acton's great library, and disquiet when reading of figures such as Casaubon and Wendover, Gladstone had a horror of library books lying unused on their shelves, or even worse, being misused. He warned members of the National Liberal Club in 1888 not to let their new library exist merely as 'a library of demonstration'. 'Unfortunately', he opined:

> there are a multitude of houses in this great country, especially rural residences, where the library appears as a matter of course, and as a matter of form, but where the venerable books which occupy its shelves are rarely disturbed from the repose of ages ... and rarely shower down upon the incautious man who should imprudently move them from their places the clouds of dust which is their common, almost universal, inheritance.[75]

Gladstone would also later call upon such 'wealthy men' to facilitate the extension of the 1850 public libraries legislation to rural districts by their own benevolence.[76] On neither count, of course, could he himself could be accused of neglect. His enthusiastic use of his library, and his making the Temple of Peace accessible as a neighbourhood lending library were both well known. Moreover, Gladstone's own later rhetoric sought to position the book as an item which should not only be affordable and accessible to all; it also stressed the fact that it was, by its circumstances of manufacture, a product of the skilled working classes. With this in mind, we turn to examine Gladstone's ideas about the mental culture of working people.

Gladstone and working-class reading

At the conclusion of the 1886 election campaign, Gladstone had made his most famous and forthright statement on class in Britain in a speech at Liverpool. In this address, Gladstone contrasted what he saw as the increasingly illiberal and self-interested 'classes' and the hardworking 'masses', the backbone of the nation's progress and prosperity. The Liberal party was opposed, he announced 'by a compact army ... of the classes against the masses'. 'It cannot be pretended', he continued,

> that we are supported by the dukes, or by the squires, or by the Established clergy, or by the officers of the army, or by a number of other ... respectable people ... I am not about to assert that the masses of the people ... are necessarily, on all subjects, better judges than the leisured men and the instructed men who have great advantages for forming political judgements ... but ... upon one great class of subjects ... where the leading and determining considerations that ought to lead to a conclusion are truth, justice, and humanity, there ... all the world over I will back the masses against the classes.[77]

This address constituted a startlingly straightforward statement, rarely to be found without substantial qualification, in any of Gladstone's speeches. These words well-reflect Gladstone's fundamental and spiritual repugnance for conflict between social groups and nations, as well as his ceaseless concern with the idea of humanity. Of course, the speech also reflected his fresh disappointment in the refusal of Britain's political establishment to grant life to the one particular 'great' subject he had in view: Irish Home Rule, and it was clearly an attempt to inculcate support at a more popular level. However, Gladstone's praise of and appeal to those he described as the 'masses' was, as we shall see, driven by educative preoccupations similar to those with which he had harangued the 'classes'. There were certainly similarities between the rhetoric and themes which Gladstone employed when talking about books and reading to working-class audiences, and those he used to 'public men'. Thus he pointed out to working men their ameliorated access to books, telling an audience of working men at Buckley in 1878:

> When I was a boy I used to be fond of looking into a bookseller's shop, but there was nothing to be seen there that was accessible to the working-man of that day ... Those books are accessible now which formerly were quite inaccessible. We may be told that you want amusement; but in reading the works of such authors as Shakespeare and Scott there is the greatest possible amusement in its best form ... I want you to understand that multitudes of books now are constantly being prepared and placed within reach of the population at

large ... having subjects of the greatest interest, and which enable you at a moderate price ... to go straight into ... the sanctuary of the temple of literature – and become acquainted with the greatest and best works that the men of our country have produced.[78]

It is unsurprising that Gladstone should have here stressed the beneficial effects of his removal of the so called 'taxes on knowledge', facilitated as Chancellor of the Exchequer in 1853–5 and 1860–1,[79] a campaign which had become correlated in the public mind with franchise extension and issues of representation.[80] However, he also adapted his well-worn analogy of knowledge as a balanced transaction:

The mind of man, some people seem to think, is a storehouse which should be filled with a quantity of useful commodities which may be taken out like packets from a shop, and delivered and distributed according to the occasions of life ... No doubt you are to cull knowledge that is useful for the temporal purpose of life; but never forget that the purpose for which a man lives is the improvement of the man himself, so that he may go out of this world having, in his great sphere or his small one, done some little good to his fellow-creatures, and laboured a little to diminish the sin and the sorrow that are in the world.[81]

Gladstone had long expressed interest in the development of public libraries and encouraged working people to improve their 'mental culture'. For instance, he supported and donated a small collection of books – now lost – to the Hawarden Institute in 1875,[82] and after Gladstone had visited 'the great [Forth] bridge' in 1884, he reciprocated the workers' gift of an axe with a number of entertaining and improving volumes.[83] Believing as he did in the need for remedial and class-transcending conciliation and mutual sympathy to redress wider social and political imbalances, Gladstone specifically supported further education and self-improvement amongst the masses. This was to begin by achieving unity in the individual – between mental cultivation and physical well-being, the latter being a central goal of many working-class institutes – and then to foster unity in wider spheres.[84] It was, firstly, to better equip working people to decide important political and moral questions amongst themselves – note his observation to the Buckley Institute members that 'whatever your political opinions are they will be all the better, all the more intelligent, and all the more moderate for being brought by contact into competition with those of your friends'.[85] Secondly, it was also designed to enhance community relations between classes. Thus, in a speech to the Hawarden Institute in 1893, he expressed the hope that its chief role would be 'to produce a sense of unity ... among all the various classes that make a local community'.[86] Such sentiments were reiterated on numerous other occasions when Gladstone spoke at local institutes and libraries, which he also supported with generous gifts of money and books.[87]

For all his positive views about public access to libraries, however, Gladstone firmly conceptualized book collection as an elitist and leisured activity, open only to those who had the money, time, and domestic workforce to sustain a working library. For instance, in his 'On Books' article, he set out to disillusion any would-be collector:

> The purchase of a book is commonly supposed to end, even for the most scrupulous customer, with the payment of the bookseller's bill. But this is a mere popular superstition. Such payment is not the last, but the first term in a series of goodly length. If we wish to give to the book a lease of life equal to that of the pages, the first condition is that it should be bound ... then ... the book must of necessity be put into a bookcase. And the bookcase must be housed. And the house must be kept. And the Library must be dusted, must be arranged, should be catalogued. What a vista of toil, yet not unhappy toil![88]

In 1896 he wrote, concerning his own collecting:

> The regiment of Book Collectors stands in no need of recruits, and even if its ranks were thin, I doubt if I am qualified to enlist. I have in my time been a purchaser to the extent of about thirty-five thousand volumes, and I might therefore abide a quantitative test: but, as I fear, no other. A book collector ought, as I conceive, to possess the following six qualifications: appetite, leisure, wealth, knowledge, discrimination, and perseverance. Of these I have only had two, the first and the last, and these are not the most important.[89]

Moreover, although characteristically self-deprecating about the quality of his collection, and anxious to point out that he was himself 'a beggarly collector', Gladstone was clearly proud of his 'few specialities'. His correspondent, Bernard Quaritch, argued that his friend was at least more concerned with typographical elegance and fine bindings than he himself cared to admit!

Furthermore, Gladstone remained as uncertain as many of his educated contemporaries about the implications of allowing the masses freedom of access to unrestricted knowledge.[90] Consider, for instance, his lukewarm response to Matthew Arnold's 1869 characterization of culture as a potential social leveller. Arnold had written that culture's aim was 'to do away with classes; to make the best that has been thought and known in the world current everywhere; to make all men live in an atmosphere ... where they may use ideas, as it uses them itself, *freely, – nourished, and not bound*'.[91] Gladstone read the 'Preface' to *Culture and Anarchy* and approved Arnold's recommendation of 'culture as the great help out of our present difficulties ... turning a stream of fresh and free thought upon our ... notions and habits', marking the passage twice with his '+' sign of approbation.[92] Arnold's definition clearly accorded with Gladstone's understanding of civilization as articulated in 1862 to the working men of Chester. 'Civilisation', he here propounded:

> Resides in man himself ... It lies in the strengthening of his faculties ... in clearing and raising his convictions ... in the refinement of his tastes, it lies most of all in the improvement of the practical habits of his life ... ever studying to be ... orderly, diligent, modest, and affectionate, with a good conscience before God and man.[93]

On one level, Gladstone and his promoters encouraged independence amongst the electorate. During the first Midlothian campaign, for instance, he called on the people to engage intellectually with the theories which legitimized politics.[94] Nonetheless, Gladstone the omnivorous, moralistic reader, and obsessive librarian, was also preoccupied with controlling and organizing knowledge – an impetus which was intriguingly displayed during the Home Rule crusade by the production of Gladstone bookmarks to cultivate a direct and intimate association between the matter read and Gladstone's person and politics![95] Moreover, this tendency was particularly active when considering questions of working-class access to knowledge. In Chapter 4 we speculated that the free access Gladstone allowed to the Temple of Peace might create tensions for those working-class individuals who used it. When he invited outsiders into his library – whether in person or through the medium of print – Gladstone possessed only limited control over what such persons would do with the information and knowledge they found there, and over the invasive public gaze which such openness might attract. What is clear is that, as its librarian, Gladstone was caused a fair amount of anxiety by the way in which such borrowers sometimes played free and easy with his prized collection. As a result he tightened up the library's rules: insisting that his borrowing registers were kept up-to-date, had their entries made in ink, and restricted the length of the borrowing period. In 1888 the *Pall Mall Budget* made reference to this curtailment:

> At one time this liberty was unlimited; anyone could take a book out and keep it an indefinite period, provided that he simply left an acknowledgment of having borrowed the book. This privilege, however, was so much abused by some persons that a few years ago a rule was laid down limiting the time for which a book might be kept to one month. With that exception, however, the Hawarden Library is still the free loan library of the countryside.[96]

Further evidence of Gladstone's general concerns about what working-class access to reading should entail is to be found in his speeches on the subject. At the opening of the Saltney reading and recreation rooms in 1889, Gladstone indicated his belief and expectation that the Saltney men would principally only 'learn all ... about ... different industries ... because it is through these industries you may ... aim for honourable advancement, and ... improve the advantages of your position in life'. He went on to outline his conception of a workman's correct field of aspiration and opportunity, which was quite clearly vocational and limited to that 'employment of position to which *others* may call you':

> Every workman has a fair chance to make himself useful and do himself good by keeping his eyes open, observing his work and the conditions under which he performs his work, and to study how these conditions can be met, how labour can be economised, how useful products can be brought to the services of the earth and fitted for the service of men, and thus provide better means of executing the works that they have in hand ... That is a fruitful field, and a field open for workmen – a field in which many ... a working man has gained advantages to himself and done great service to his fellow creatures.[97]

Gladstone did recommend the study of history to these listeners, just as he had to his fellow politicians – 'To every Englishmen the history of his own country should be followed with the greatest interest' – but the scope of his suggestions was far more limited and clearly dictated by considerations of public order. Thus he recommended study of the lessons of both the French Revolution, which he described as 'the most vast and the most terrible series of dangers known to ... history', and the American Revolution, which had inaugurated a governmental system characterized by 'the love of freedom *together with respect for law and the desire of order*'.[98] Over a decade earlier he had impressed upon Buckley Institute members the fact that their institution should cultivate moderation, 'self-restraint and self-government'.[99] Here also he advised restrictions in the reading of the labouring class: 'It is not to be supposed that working men, on coming home from labour, are to study Euclid and works of that character; and it is not to be desired unless in the case of very special gifts'.[100] And his call to enlarge the text in 1887 was carefully qualified to include only 'those of us, I mean, whose branch of labour belongs to or includes that world'.[101]

There remained for Gladstone something inscrutable, unpredictable, and potentially dangerous about the working classes, which could only be controlled by good (self) government. Gladstone was clearly uncertain about what working people would contribute to local and national life if given unrestricted opportunities during their ever-increasing hours of leisure. At St Martin's Free Library in 1891, he characterized the library as part of a 'war against ignorance, ... brutality ... [and] idleness', but made clear that, because of the 'severe and continuous' nature of manual labour, these pitfalls remained a particular danger to the worker in search of 'relief'.[102] Essentially, it was Gladstone's view that the working classes were to be respected and rewarded with political and financial responsibility only where they had demonstrated a suitable level of fitness for the receipt of such benefits.[103] They were to be well organized in the service of the nation and its prosperity, cultivated and educated as befitted their station in life, and willing to bear misfortune in a noble and orderly manner. Note his commendation to the Chester men of the distressed Lancashire cotton workers' attitude of 'universal and unbroken reverence for public order'.[104] Such selfless behaviour, reflecting the workers' trust in the institutions of their country to govern well on their behalf, was the route to both social peace and communal growth.

Neither were such advantages and trusts to be regarded as unalienable rights. Despite the adulation which he had received as a result of his abolition of the knowledge taxes, and which he traded on regularly, Gladstone had no compunction about reinstating such restrictions if he felt public order to be at risk. As Marie-Louise Legg has shown, 'freedom of expression as a safety valve might be acceptable in Britain ... [but]

this policy could not be so easily translated to Ireland, where the behaviour of both landlords and tenants was uncertain'. Despite having abolished taxes on knowledge in Britain ten years previously, a major plank of Gladstone's 1870 Peace Preservation Bill was a raft of measures to control the Irish press. Attacked as a direct assault on legitimate nationalism, and as further evidence of Gladstone's tendency towards inexplicable and hypocritical changes of mind, he nonetheless refused to back down.[105] Defending himself in print, Gladstone spoke of the dangers of giving unregulated power to an unstable constituency, whose recent admission to the franchise had exchanged 'a certain and well-disciplined support for a doubtful and many-sided chance'. In the same piece he also considered the potentially dangerous effects of uncontrolled popular passion on the masses: 'when it does operate upon a mass of men, a very formidable case may conceivably arise. It is difficult to reason with the passion of an individual or a few, with those of a multitude once aroused, it is impossible.' This was, as he then crucially made clear, rooted in the masses' 'inferior information and capacity' which the better informed had to try and influence and control, but certainly not leave to its own devices.[106]

With this in mind, it is no surprise to find Gladstone making clear at both Hawarden and Saltney his belief that peace and progress depended on mutual recognition of and respect for separate social and intellectual spheres as much as on the cultivation of mutual sympathy between classes.

> I do entreat you to lay to heart the great importance of this subject ... every one of you in your separate spheres ... and that every one of you will consider it part of his personal duty to exert himself in his own sphere for the purpose of bringing members of all classes ... within the precincts of the institution.[107]

Although communication and free association were to be encouraged, 'unity' was to be achieved by the individual exerting himself within 'his great sphere *or* his small one'.[108] Moreover, Gladstone was keen to emphasize in these speeches his own distance from the sphere occupied by institute members. At Saltney, Gladstone noted the infrequency with which he undertook such 'neighbourly' duties, and, at Hawarden, Gladstone expressed the hope that the Institute's library would 'be found most valuable to *your* community', indicating his understanding that Hawarden was the site of multiple, and possibly mutually exclusive, communities. Colin Matthew observes that Gladstone 'did not "play the squire"' in Hawarden; 'I love them not' was his comment as he tried to stop the annual Hawarden bazaar.[109] These attitudes undoubtedly contributed to Gladstone's reluctance to make known the purposes of his St Deiniol's foundation to his local community.

'The library was not for them'[110]

In 1898, J. Ewing Ritchie noted that St Deiniol's 'is in no sense a public institution', rather it 'is intended to afford to clergymen and others an opportunity of quiet study'.[111] Despite the popular liberal glossing given by commentators such as J. C. Story and Hulda Friederichs to their accounts, St Deiniol's Library was neither designed for the village in which it was built, nor for the use of those ordinary people who had borrowed from the Temple of Peace. If we look more closely at the printed descriptions of the library and its surroundings, we see that, in fact, few commentators had actually seriously disputed this and presented to the reading public a very exclusive, private, and élite institution. Mary Drew, for all her rhetoric about bringing 'together readers who had no books and books who had no readers', also described St Deiniol's as: 'A country home for the purposes of study and research' and 'for the pursuit of divine learning'.[112] Hulda Friederichs described the residents' hostel similarly: 'Standing outside St. Deiniol's Library door, and looking straight ahead, you have before you an old world entrance to a country house'. Furthermore, Friederichs, by implication, suggested the type of reader that would be made welcome at the library. Flowers gave a 'welcome', she wrote, 'to all who may walk along the gravel walk that leads from St. Deiniol's Church to the Hostel, and then onward to the library', but the reception was very different for those who might approach from the street:

> There was at the beginning only a somewhat undefined country path across the green field separating the library from the high road. Now a wide, neat, gravelled walk, at the end of which a new iron gate prevents the 'man in the street' from too easy admittance into the precincts of the library, leads up to the very door.

Friederichs went as far as to describe an actual example of this exclusion, relating how, during the *Westminster Gazette*'s photo shoot at the library, Gladstone's retinue tried to 'keep ... off' an Irishman, who had 'come all the way from Ireland on the chance of seeing Mr. Gladstone', suggesting once again a limited correlation between Gladstone's popular liberalism and his library foundation.[113]

However, even if the locals were not to be allowed open access to the books of St Deiniol's, it might still be expected that the institution should to some extent memorialize the grand old bookman who had founded it. The translation of collections from private to public hands is sometimes motivated by concerns with self-memorialization and immortality,[114] and, as stated at the outset, some commentators have argued that Gladstone was consciously seeking to create his own memorial by founding St Deiniol's.[115] Despite the fact that Gladstone founded the library only a decade before he died, and the testimony of some contemporaries stating that they believed he would have been pleased by the choice of the library for his national memorial,[116] there is no evidence to suggest he was so preoccupied with his own legacy that he created St Deiniol's as an advance memorial. In her 1906 promotional article for the memorial library, Mary Drew made clear 'how little', in her opinion, 'Mr. Gladstone ever realised his position in the hearts and minds of mankind, and the interest that might belong to relics connected with his youth'. While, as Chapter 7 will make clear, Gladstone was not this disingenuous, the anecdote with which she illustrated that claim does little to support the claim that Gladstone was keen to memorialize himself through his books. She described Gladstone taking:

> A quarto MS. book bound in red leather, in an excellent state of preservation ... with beautifully written mathematical notes and diagrams. These he neatly cut out, and, presenting the book to a member of his family, expressed a hope that now he had removed the already used pages, it might be of some service. One page of diagrams in the middle of the volume had luckily escaped his notice, and for this and the early autograph signatures the book is treasured in a manner very contrary to his expectations.[117]

In Gladstone's opinion, the St Deiniol's collection was important because of the accumulated knowledge it contained and represented, not because he had owned the books or that they displayed signs of his ownership.

It is therefore clear that Gladstone's foundation was not the outgrowth of Gladstone's political liberalism, at least as it was popularly understood, despite superficial attempts to make it appear so. As we have seen, Gladstone was preoccupied by an intensifying belief in the need to rediscover for society the importance of universal humanistic truth during the 1880s, and supported the aim of the public library movement to facilitate universal access for readers to books, but St Deiniol's was not designed to meet this latter need, and neither should we be surprised when we review Gladstone's continued reservations about the reliability of the informed masses. Gladstone had from the very beginning intended the iron building to be a reading room adjoined by a hostel for the accommodation of visiting, not local, readers; the tin library was not to serve as a reading room as they would have understood the term: for relaxation after work and newspaper reading. For whom then, was this 'country home' designed, and what, if any, Gladstonian liberalism did it embody? In order to answer these questions, we need to turn from an examination of humanity to divinity: the subject of the next chapter.

6
Divinity: Gladstone, Oxford, and *Lux Mundi*

As the previous chapter made clear, Gladstone's St Deiniol's foundation was neither a straightforward outgrowth of his political liberalism, an attempt at self-memorialization, nor an altruistic contribution to the public library movement. Instead, despite his reticence on the subject of its purpose, all the indications which Gladstone gave to close friends and family suggested a central religious motivation. For instance, Algernon West recorded in his diaries during a visit to Hawarden in 1891 that 'Mr. Gladstone was rather in a pessimistic frame of mind on the state of society and was not, he said, over-sanguine as to the continuance of belief, and feared that the "seen," such as riches and luxuries, was eclipsing the "unseen."

> The best way he knew to combat such dangers was to encourage reading, and with this sense of duty before him he was trying to found a library in Hawarden, where he hoped there would some day be 40,000 volumes.[1]

Despite such evidence, uncertainty has persisted concerning the exact nature of both the library's religious impetus and mission. The unsettled debate about Gladstone's theological views and ecclesiastical alliances in the 1880s and 90s has been a contributory factor, as has the ambiguity which surrounded Gladstone's foundation and its early history. In order to begin to explain some of these uncertainties, we need to return to Oxford in the year 1868.

'A real home'

On St Mark's day, 1868, the foundation stone of Keble College, Oxford was laid. As early as 1845 a scheme had been discussed for a new Oxford foundation on religious lines, but it remained unimplemented until the death of John Keble in 1867. Plans were henceforth put into motion, formulated and spearheaded by Edward Pusey, who used the occasion of the foundation to voice his fears for the future of religion in Oxford, and his somewhat lofty and austere hopes for the College.[2] June 1870 saw the official opening of Keble, the marriage of Edward Talbot and Lavinia Lyttelton, and Talbot's installation as warden. It was, in the words of Pusey, 'an act of faith'.[3]

On 13 November 1872, Gladstone began his first visit to the new college, renewing his acquaintance with both Pusey and Liddon, recording that the former 'behaved with all his old kindness and seemed to have forgotten the Temple business, or rather as if it had never been'.[4] More importantly, Gladstone was soon struck both by Keble's character as 'a real home', and as a venue for spirited academic debate,[5] and, by the time of his next visit in November 1874, he was fully engaged with the vibrant circle that surrounded the Talbots. As Lavinia wrote enthusiastically on 9 November:

> You ought to hear of the success of Uncle William's visit – he is just gone off with every sort of hearty good wishes to us & the College. He arrived on Saturday afternoon not very well, but quite up to any amount of talk, & we had a capital Munich, Dollinger & Bonn talk, Edward & all, & then at 9 came Dr Mozley for the first of many consultations over a scheme of Uncle W's own promoting the editorship of a series of books on eirenic writers from before the Reformation.[6]

William Whyte has recently described Keble as 'the culmination of the Oxford Movement', asserting that, through Butterfield's 'variegated brick', the College 'aggressively asserted its independence from a supposedly corrupt university'.[7] In many respects, this characterization is accurate: Pusey's vision for Keble College had been that 'besides a simplicity of life here, there will be a religious tone', both appropriate to its namesake, and intimating its separateness.[8] However, the public statement of Keble's place and mission in Oxford was only fully realized with the official opening of the new hall and library on 25 April 1878.[9] At this important event, alternative visions for the College's future were articulated publicly, which draw our attention both to the uncertainty which pervaded high-church circles about the future of Anglo-Catholicism, and to Gladstone's forward-looking religious position.[10]

The day began with Holy Communion, an occasion which Gladstone found 'very striking'. This was followed by the library opening, lunch in hall and associated speeches, 'mine a long one', recorded Gladstone, 'proposing Prosperity to Keble College'.[11] In his address, Gladstone discussed the principles that Keble represented and, in doing so, explicitly revealed the extent to which his high churchmanship had broadened out between the 1840s and the late 1870s. He fully endorsed Pusey's ideal of simplicity but, despite his obvious respect for John Keble's Anglo-Catholic credentials, Gladstone's vision of the college's future was markedly different:

> It has been truly said that this is a college for special purposes, and as a college for special purposes it is open to special criticism ... and ought not to shrink from that criticism. There would, in my opinion, be no greater calamity than that we should see formed in Oxford any new college characterised by fanciful peculiarities, or any new college open ... to the charge of being sectarian.[12]

Gladstone had been concerned about the rise of partisanship in Oxford since the 1840s, vigorously attacking its pernicious influence in *Church Principles* (1840).[13] In his 1878 Keble speech, Gladstone chose to revisit the painful Tractarian split and discuss its still-contested legacy. He proposed – somewhat controversially considering the occasion – that Newman had been 'greater than either' Keble or Pusey in terms of his religious and intellectual influence over Oxford. However, as he went on to clarify, this influence was largely negative. Newman's secession had not only destroyed the Oxford Movement, it had also destabilized the whole intellectual basis of Anglicanism. Newman had thought his way to Rome and then abandoned thought, and the repercussions of his mental journey had been 'to throw all the brightest and noblest intellects of the University as wrecks upon every shore'.[14]

By the 1870s, Gladstone was increasingly articulating concerns about the need to rebuild Anglicans' confidence in an intellectually grounded and liberated Christianity.[15] While he regretted that the ways of seeking knowledge familiar to Newman, Keble, Pusey, and himself, as well as the institutional frameworks in which they had been fostered, had all been undermined, he nonetheless believed that the only way forward for Anglicanism was for it to become intellectually broader and academically reinvigorated. Else it risked being destroyed by what Gladstone, and many of his contemporaries, saw as a further assault on its intellectual foundations by an aggressively marketed scientific-agnostic worldview. 'This disposition', he had told an audience at Liverpool College in 1872, 'is boldly proclaimed to deal alike with root and branch, and to snap utterly the ties which, under the still venerable name of Religion, unite man with the unseen world, and lighten the struggles and the woes of life by the hope of a better land'.[16] In his Keble speech he reiterated his concerns about the distrustful atmosphere in existence between academic disciplines:

> The knowledge of the age, and the active and successful pursuit of some particular branches of knowledge, has led to an overestimate of their comparative importance and to a desire to invest them with a domination to which they have no title, and to a character to which they cannot pretend.[17]

Drawing on his understanding of the epistemological debates surrounding Hume's appraisal of the role theory, belief, and conjecture play in the creation of systematic knowledge,[18] and his faith in the efficacy of Butler's arguments for probabiliorism,[19] Gladstone defended the validity of reasoning and thinking theologically and, crucially, argued for a reconciliation between Christianity and modernity to be achieved through ecumenical co-operation. Hence the staff of Keble should not give 'too exclusive an ecclesiastical character to the college', and needed to realize that their institution had been set up to 'meet ... special and pressing dangers' emanating, not from the outside, but from the inside: the insularity, backwardness, and fear which cause disorientation, confusion, and the desire to create immutable truths.[20] In contrast, Gladstone argued, college members should maintain religion as their 'groundwork and centre', but 'around that centre ought to be grouped ... every accomplishment ... that can tend to the development of human nature'. He continued:

> There has been noticed appropriately the notable conjunction of Keble College with the [University] museum over the way. It has been well said that they are a representation of the sacred and secular at Oxford; and if the sacred and the secular do come to be compared ... Keble College would have no reason to look upon the issue with dread. But it is an illustration of the harmony which ought to prevail ... between the branches of education within this great university.[21]

By adopting this conciliatory approach to truth and knowledge, Gladstone was publicly allying himself with liberal, not conservative religious, opinion, and, by speaking so at Keble, he was addressing an audience amongst whom were those who would seek to inaugurate the revival within Anglicanism for which Gladstone called.

Lux Mundi

The *Lux Mundi* group was a party of Oxford clerical friends and colleagues who met regularly to discuss theology. Originally dubbed 'the holy party', they became known by the title of the famous collection of theological essays which they published in 1889: *Lux Mundi*, meaning 'the light of the world'.[22] Charles Gore (1853–1932),[23] first principal of Pusey House, was the driving force behind both the group and the book, writing the preface and the eighth essay, but the majority of his associates – more than half the *Lux Mundi* contributors – were, or had been, associated with Keble: Warden Talbot, Sub-Warden Walter Lock (1846–1933), William James Heathcote Campion (1851–92), John Richardson Illingworth (1848–1915),[24] Arthur Lyttelton (1852–1903), and Aubrey Lackington Moore (1848–90). Other group members and contributors were associated with Christ Church: Henry Scott Holland (1847–1918),[25] Robert Campbell Moberley (1845–1903), Francis Paget (1851–1911),[26] and Robert Lawrence Ottley (1856–1933).[27]

Of the eleven *Lux Mundi* contributors, Gladstone recorded contact with all but three and, with the exception of W. J. H. Campion, all those who had been at Keble. This interaction ranged from occasional meetings, such as that with Walter Lock whom he met at Keble in 1883, to his familiar and regular dealings with his nephew, Arthur Lyttelton.[28] Gladstone's comments on the group were universally positive. His diary remarks are characteristically brief, but they indicate not only personal admiration but evidence of intellectual engagement. Gladstone's recorded opinion of Charles Gore was particularly auspicious. In January 1885, he described him as 'a person of very great promise',[29] and called Lord Acton's attention to the 'society of twenty Tutors formed for Theological study under or with him' at 'the Pusey Institute' in Oxford.[30] Gladstone also greatly admired Talbot, who formed the vital link between Gladstone and the *Lux Mundi* group as a whole, describing him in 1881 as 'a fine fellow', and in 1884 as 'a model of dispassionate uprightness'.[31] Gladstone held a particularly high opinion of Talbot as a priest (in his view 'the first of callings'), and as a preacher,[32] having no doubt that Talbot should and would go far in the church: 'He is excellent: & will make a mark.'[33] They agreed on matters of faith,[34] and Gladstone increasingly relied on Edward's judgement on administrative matters, especially regarding the question of disestablishment. In 1877, after discussing the 'pending crisis in the Church', Gladstone recorded: 'He can hardly be too much prized', and, in 1881, Gladstone declared himself 'strongly confirmed' in his opinions 'by E. Talbot'.[35] In turn, Talbot regarded Gladstone as the greatest layman in the Church. He wrote to Herbert Gladstone in 1924: 'I preserve quite unchanged the reverence for the great Christian statesman, and the gratitude for having been in a measure brought up at his feet.'[36] He took pains to introduce Gladstone to the work of other members of the group, giving him, for example, a copy of Aubrey Moore's 1883 paper entitled 'Evolution in its relation to the Christian Faith', following a visit to Keble.[37]

Even before he was ordained, Talbot had seen himself as a liberal, writing to sister-in-law Meriel Lyttelton: 'Be free, be liberal, be courageous!'[38] He argued for the efficacy of 'the "broad" views of our own day', clearly articulating the difference he perceived between the Anglo-Catholicism of the first generation Tractarians, and that of his own generation. In 1917 he wrote:

> There is a ... difference between Keble's time and thought and our own. His seems so much the more solemn and searching. Yet we have gained so much by what we have learned since the Tractarians; and they seemed to gain their solemnity by the exclusion of much which is so genuinely a part of Christian truth and life in fruit and application that ... we should try to retain some of the Tractarian severity (I am afraid I don't) while opening one's heart to the value of freer, larger, more instinctive things from which they shrank.[39]

The *Lux Mundi* group have been categorized as pioneers of liberal Anglicanism, firstly because the circumstances surrounding the publication of *Lux Mundi* created a well-documented rift between the contributors and the older Tractarian generation,[40] and secondly, because of the substantial impact made on later theological thought by the incarnational theology[41] to which they subscribed.[42] The *Lux Mundi* group's interpretation of the Tractarian tradition was unmistakably liberal in its impetus and emphasis. The aim of publishing their essays, in the words of Charles Gore, was 'to attempt to put the Catholic faith into its right relation to modern intellectual and moral problems',[43] a phrase which expressed nineteenth-century religious liberalism's central tenet, and excited opposition from many who thought that spiritual truths could be precisely stated and ought to be accorded universal assent.[44] Nevertheless, the *Lux Mundi* essayists, like Gladstone, remained fundamentally 'catholic' in a very real sense – Michael Ramsey, for example, is careful to categorize their era as one in which 'conscious doctrinal reconstruction began' – upholding a traditional high-church theology and ecclesiology, and regarding themselves as orthodox.[45] However, Gladstone was also on the side of *Lux Mundi* when it came to Christianity's need to forge a new relationship with modernity. As early as 1869, Gladstone had told Henry Manning: 'I profoundly believe in a reconciliation between Christianity and the conditions of modern thought, modern life, and modern society';[46] his Liverpool speech three years later had resonated with parallel ideas,[47] and his Keble address, as we have seen, strongly reinforced them. Moreover, testimony to his affiliation with *Lux Mundi* also came from members of the group itself. Henry Scott Holland, for example, later indicated how closely Gladstone's religious agenda had accorded with his own and that of his associates:

> If Mr. Gladstone had retained his rigid Evangelicalism, he might have contented himself with denouncing the facts as the work of the Devil. But he had read Bishop Butler. He had found the Fathers. He had absorbed the rich Creed of the Incarnation, in all its fullness, in its largeness of historical preparation, in its superb honour for flesh and blood. He was bound to respect man in his self-manifestation. Therefore, his new effort lay in reconciling his own intense belief in the Catholic Church according to the form in which it had come down to him in England, with his ever-growing sense of the sanctity of life, as it revealed itself in freedom.[48]

Holland explicitly linked Gladstone with the *Lux Mundi* project by highlighting his incarnational theology, his flexible endorsement of catholicity in Christian doctrine, and his recognition of the importance of history.[49] Furthermore, such reminiscitory characterizations are supported by earlier annotation evidence, demonstrating Gladstone's favourable reception and response to the theology of his most influential *Lux Mundi* contacts: Charles Gore and Edward Talbot.

Charles Gore: inspiration, doctrine, and ecumenical education

On 31 January 1890, Gladstone, once again in Oxford, first recorded reading *Lux Mundi*, noting his approval of 'Gore's Masterly paper' therein.[50] In his *Lux Mundi* essay entitled: 'The Holy Spirit and Inspiration', Gore had addressed the question of scriptural inspiration and, controversially for one brought up a high churchman, acknowledged the claims of radical biblical criticism. Although he maintained that scripture was inspired, he asserted inspiration was not the miraculous communication of unknown facts, and did not guarantee historical truth. Furthermore, he stated that the Old Testament was a product of its time and that the Bible should be read in the spirit in which it was written.[51] If there was one area in which Gladstone remained influenced by his early evangelicalism, it was his attitude to the Bible, which he defended, at length, in *The Impregnable Rock of Holy Scripture* (1890). Why and how, then, did he approve of Gore's position in *Lux Mundi*? The broader context of Gladstone's 1890 Oxford visit is important for understanding his position. While there, he sought to prepare *The Impregnable Rock* by engaging directly with the biblical criticism that Gore welcomed. On arrival he read Gore's essay, followed by Liddon's condemnation of what the latter saw as Gore's capitulation to criticism,[52] as well as holding discussions with specialist biblical critics such as Samuel Rolles Driver (1846–1914) and Thomas Kelly Cheyne (1841–1915).[53] When Gladstone reiterated Gore's position on scriptural inspiration in his book, therefore, his high opinion was based, not merely on the circumstances of their social interaction, but rather on a balanced engagement with and evaluation of material from both sides of the debate.[54]

Gladstone maintained this intellectual respect for Gore. In March 1893 he read his *The Mission of the Church* (1892), placing an '+' in his diary.[55] This work further confirmed for Gladstone how different Gore was from the original Tractarians, and his strenuous endorsement strongly indicates how far his own views were also distinguished from theirs. He wrote enthusiastically to his son Stephen on 20 March 1893:

> I have been reading with great delight Mr. Gore's 'Mission of the Church'. I do not know when I have seen so much matter in so small a book and in general so admirably stated ... he ought to be advanced and I should be glad if he resigns his present employment [at Pusey House]. He is a much broader man than Dr. Pusey, with rather a different work to do – and the association with the name does him some injustice.[56]

Gore's book consisted of four lectures given at St Asaph, Flintshire, in June 1892. Over the course of his talks, Gore had expounded his vision of the church's mission in theology and to society, and explored questions of Christian unity and Anglican responses to 'independent and hostile opinion'. He presented a traditional, high-church interpretation of the Anglican church as fully apostolic. As claims to apostolic status depend on a conception of unbroken tradition and reliance on scriptural authority, Gore unsurprisingly stressed the importance of upholding Anglican traditions and gave the Bible a prominent role throughout.[57] Central to this understanding of church tradition was the system of doctrine, which summarized and defined belief. Gore identified the creeds, with their stress on the incarnation, the ministry of the Holy Spirit, the resurrection, and judgement, as the primary source of belief instruction for Anglicans. However Gore also underlined the value of the catechism, Ten Commandments, the Lord's Prayer, the sacraments (principally baptism and the Eucharist), and, in qualified terms, the 39 articles.

Gladstone's estimation of the importance and character of Anglican doctrinal structure was very similar. He had defended the importance of doctrine in 1888, typifying it as an important 'provision made through the Church of Christ for the perpetual conservation and application of its living powers'.[58] However, although he described himself as:

> One altogether attached to dogma, which I believe to be the skeleton that carries the flesh, the blood, the life of the blessed thing we call the Christian religion ... I do not believe God's tender mercies are restricted to a small portion of the human family ... I was myself brought up to believe that salvation depended absolutely on the reception of a particular and very narrow creed. But long, long have I cast those weeds behind me.[59]

That Gladstone accepted an overzealous adherence to, or teaching of, doctrine could be, and had already proved itself, harmful was confirmed in the closing comments of his 1894 review of the autobiography of the theosophist Annie Besant:

> It cannot be denied that upon ... doctrines rash things have been said, with the intention of defending them, but with a great lack of wisdom in the choice of means for making that defence effectual ... The ... causes [of] which may require the exercise of careful and constant criticism over the forms of language in which Christian doctrine has to be inculcated, and the application of a corrective and pruning process to retrench excesses unwittingly committed by believers.[60]

Gladstone therefore believed that the solution lay in a future concentration on Christianity's 'cardinal and central truths'.[61] Gore too, although he held a traditional and conservative conception of Anglican structure and doctrine, did not see the church's role as unchanging.

He thought it should be capable of 'varied adaptation to the different needs of different ages', maintained a strong insistence on doctrinal conformity, but, like Gladstone, disagreed with the proliferation of doctrine for its own sake. The more the church limited its doctrinal structure to the essentials, the better equipped it would be to meet cultural change. He consequently argued for greater inclusivity amongst all traditional parties of the church. Exclusive 'views of truth' and concentration on favourite doctrines – sacramental grace for high churchmen, atonement and justification by faith for evangelicals, and good moral living for broad churchmen – indicated 'foolish one-sidedness' and sustained divisions. Such conflicts limited the church's ability to present a united message in times of crisis.

He argued that education was the key to lessening Anglican divisiveness and aiding ecumenical understanding. Following Gladstone's friend Döllinger, Gore argued that 'common education, promoting friendliness among those who are to be clergy of the Church or ministers of different religious bodies, may do much good'. He asserted that education, in the broadest sense of communication and association, was already softening party divisions, leading 'men of different schools ... to know, understand and tolerate one another better'. Gore furthermore advocated an interdisciplinary approach to study, which would counter the 'one-sided teaching, or the neglect of parts of the truth' that so often aggravated party divisions. This then was what the 'temper of theology ought to be', he said, 'the temper of appreciation'.[62]

Gladstone shared Gore's belief that the Anglicans' approach to other opinions should be to 'endeavour to see as much good in them as possible'.[63] As we have already seen, Gladstone had long endorsed open-mindedness and toleration in the pursuit of knowledge, as well as according it spiritual and moral relevance. Furthermore, his public statements at Liverpool and Keble, which Gore's writings echoed strongly, make it increasingly difficult to characterize Gladstone as a curmudgeonly reactionary, or to miss the affiliation he so obviously had with the broad sweep of liberal Anglicanism. Further corroboration of Gladstone's intellectual leanings towards liberal catholicism is offered by his engagement with Edward Talbot's work.

Edward Stuart Talbot: history, kenoticism, and the evolving Christ

All the essayists who contributed to *Lux Mundi* were, and still are in critical terms, overshadowed by Charles Gore. However, Edward Talbot was of equal importance to Gladstone's intellectual involvement with late nineteenth-century liberal catholicism. Talbot's contribution to *Lux Mundi* was 'Preparation in History for Christ', and, although Gladstone did not record it in his diary, he read and annotated Edward's essay in his own copy of the book.[64] Talbot's essay aimed to show how the incarnation exemplified the universal nature of religion.[65] He suggested that the universal tendency to ascribe godlike attributes to humanity reflected a unique appreciation of the true terms of engagement between humankind and the divine. He pointed to the value placed on higher human qualities in classical philosophy and the Hebrew prophecies in which 'the strange vision of a human king with Divine attributes ... strain[s] towards some manifestation of God in present nearness'.[66] Gladstone marked this passage with two heavy vertical lines in the margin, meaning a special degree of notice. Well he might notice it, for Talbot's thesis echoed the great theme of Gladstone's unfinished work on Olympian religion, and mirrored almost exactly arguments he had made in his article on 'the Unity of History' in 1887:

> There was one country in the world [Greece] where, for centuries before the Advent, it had been the prime pursuit of Art to associate deity with the human form; and ... where this practice spontaneously grew out of the prevailing and fundamental idea of the established religion. This aim led the artist ever upward to surmount imperfection and to reach upward after perfection. And though the finite could not incorporate the infinite, yet ... actual performance was advanced to a point in the presentation of form, such as to supply a model for every country or age.[67]

Talbot related his thesis, as Gladstone had done, to the evolutionary historicism inherent in Victorian intellectual culture. Modern students and enquirers were interested in change and movement, he argued, but simultaneously retained a need to see 'the beauty of process', and to discern pattern and meaning in change. The mind, 'in the fullest sense of the word', is 'not the mere critical understanding, but the whole spiritual and rational energy'.[68] This desire to construct an evolutionary aesthetic, informed by romantic philosophy, to match an evolutionary science is where the religion of the incarnation, to Talbot and Gladstone, became ever more central.

In terms of *Lux Mundi*'s Christology, Gore's embryonic kenotic theory has been the primary focus for the book's readers. In his essay, Gore had argued that the eternal word of God, *logos* or Christ, had deliberately limited the knowledge of his human incarnation, Jesus of Nazareth, to that of a human being of his time.[69] Gore would develop this idea in his later work, but even hints at such a conclusion were controversial. However, Talbot suggested something equally, if not more, radical in the following depiction of an evolving Christ.

> The beginnings of life, as we know them, are laid in darkness: they emerge crude and childish: the physical and outward almost conceals the germ of spiritual and rational being which nevertheless is the self, and which will increasingly assert itself and rule. It may be so with that organism which God was to make the shrine of His Incarnation.[70]

Gladstone passed over this astonishing passage without comment, just as he had Gore's observations on kenosis. Incarnational theology of this type had featured in his lists of reading during previous visits to Keble,[71] and, moreover, he had long accepted that the human aspect of Christ was fully subject to time, temptation, and change. As David Bebbington has conclusively shown, the increasing prominence of 'humanity' in Gladstone's thought was deeply rooted in his Christology. Deeply affected by his spiritual crisis of 1850–1, Gladstone's faith became far more focused on the person and life of Christ, rather than on the institutional life of the church. In seeking to conquer his own trials and temptations, Gladstone meditated on those of Christ, drawing inspiration from what he saw as Christ's perfection of his human nature through suffering. This in itself was a radical idea – orthodox Christian teaching insisted on the absolute sinlessness of Christ – which had a lasting effect on Gladstone's attitude to humanity as a concept. By hinting that 'the incarnate Christ, in his weakness under testing, had greater moral stature than God in the abstract', Bebbington argues, Gladstone demonstrated the high and fixed place to which the category of humanity had been elevated in his thought.[72] Gladstone's estimation of the dignity of human nature itself increased as a result of this heightened appreciation of its potential for progressive improvement. As such, Gladstone was not only exhibiting clear sympathies with liberal Christianity, but he was also identifying himself with broader contemporary currents of thought – expressed by writers such as Arnold, Tennyson, and others – which explored the history and progress of human civilization. As Bebbington has shown, particularly compelling evidence is offered by Gladstone's positive review, published in *Good Words* from January to March 1868, of J. R. Seeley's *Ecce Homo* (first published anonymously in 1866), in which he defended the author's exploration of the humanity of Christ in the face of much dogmatic opposition.[73]

Gladstone, 'profoundly moved' by the book, criticized negative reviewers of *Ecce Homo* for their 'determined adhesion to fixed and unelastic modes of thought' which have 'unhappily, put a dead stop to any real investigation of the work in its general bearings',[74] and differed sharply in his interpretation of the work from other, even appreciative, readers.[75] Engagement with the work further affirmed Gladstone's renewed and strengthened affinity with a human Christ. His annotated copy of this work includes '+'s by the following quotations, anticipating both the kenoticism and humanism of *Lux Mundi*.

> [+ and double line:] This temperance in the use of supernatural power is the masterpiece of Christ ... This repose in greatness makes him surely those most sublime image ever offered to the human imagination ...
> [+:] Christ raised the feeling of humanity from being a feeble restraining power to be an inspiring passion ... humanity changed from a restraint to a motive.[76]

The following passage, which actually describes John the Baptist, also illustrates those characteristics of struggling humanity that appealed to Gladstone:

> He was a wrestler with life, one to whom peace of mind does not come easily, but only after a long struggle. His restlessness had driven him into the desert, where he had contended for years with thoughts he could not master, and from whence he had uttered his startling alarum to the nation. He was among the dogs rather than among the lambs of the Shepherd. He recognised the superiority of him whose confidence had never been disturbed, whose steadfast peace no agitations of life had ever ruffled. He did obeisance to the royalty of inward happiness.[77]

It is not difficult to see why Gladstone identified his position with that of John when he read this passage, reminiscent as it was of his own vocational struggles, sense of isolation, and unpopularity. However, the fact that he wrote the name 'Lancelot' in the margin – the knight who 'would indeed have been more than human' had he 'been unstained', gives a fascinating indication of the extent of the intertextuality which profoundly shaped Gladstone's intellectual world.[78] Reading of *Ecce Homo* not only combined with thoughts of the Arthurian legends, but also with extensive work on Homer, all of which served to focus Gladstone's mind on the value of the human condition, and illustrates to us something of the way his mind interrelated those liberal catholic concepts of 'divinity' and 'humanity' which underpinned his St Deiniol's foundation.

St Deiniol's Library

Rejection or regeneration?

Links have previously been proposed between the foundation of St Deiniol's library and Gladstone's Oxford connections. Pritchard concludes that the germination of the St Deiniol's project took place shortly after Edward Pusey's funeral in 1882, where plans had been discussed for the establishment of an institute in memory of the Tractarian.[79] This, as Henry Parry Liddon later wrote, was envisaged as 'a College of Clergy in Oxford, … a centre of religious faith, theological learning, and personal sympathy' based around Pusey's surviving library and constituting 'the most fitting Memorial of one whose whole heart was devoted to the preservation of the Faith, and whose days had been spent in fighting its battles in Oxford'. In the final words of his biography, Liddon articulated the hope that the work of the memorial would continue 'to impart new spiritual energy to the English Church', and it is clear from the surviving evidence that Gladstone always intended that St Deiniol's should have at least this function.[80] Moreover, he also considered a future for it as a 'College of Clergy', and the Pusey House model was directly referred to during the formulation of the library's Trust.[81] However, there are limits to the equivalence. Gladstone was advised by close associates not to base St Deiniol's on the Tractarian memorial. G. W. E. Russell, for one, felt 'the distinctiveness, individuality, and characteristic features of the Foundation would be lost' if St Deiniol's was too closely associated or even eventually merged with Pusey House.[82] Furthermore, Gladstone himself had serious enough reservations about the institution to suggest he would not have adopted it as too slavish a model. His disappointment with both Pusey House and its library,[83] and subsequent wish that Gore would devote himself to 'different work',[84] all indicate that he was planning something very different. Furthermore, both Pusey House and Liddon House (which was later established in London) were instituted first and foremost as memorials, whereas there is no evidence to suggest that this was the case with St Deiniol's. Besides, the nature of Gladstone's relationship with the Oxford liberal catholics makes the memorialization thesis unlikely considering the movement's emphasis on shaping the future of the church rather than enshrining unchanged aspects of its past.

Nonetheless, such evidence has not prevented associations being made between Gladstone's library and the latter impetus. Richard Shannon draws a direct link between St Deiniol's and Gladstone's desire to fight those aspects of Oxford thought which were apparently too radical for him. Thus in his biography Shannon states:

> It [St Deiniol's] was a concept quite characteristic of and conformable to Gladstone's long held prepossessions, but the immediate stimulus was the implications for Christian belief he saw dangerously present in such things as *Robert Elsmere*, the 'new lines of criticism' pressing hard, and needing to be resisted. Gladstone invited the Humphry Wards to Hawarden in September to witness, so to speak, Gladstone's preparations for his bastion of defence against them.[85]

Gladstone's engagement with Mary Augusta Ward and *Robert Elsmere* significantly took place at Keble just as his ideas for St Deiniol's were crystallizing.[86] The defensive tone of Ward's record of their meeting on 8 April 1888, and her side of their subsequent correspondence,[87] has distorted the way in which Gladstone's attitude to *Elsmere* has been assessed.[88] Firstly, Ward's testimony is not entirely reliable; she was clearly mistaken, for instance, in her belief that 'the new lines of criticism are not familiar' to Gladstone.[89] Secondly, commentators have neglected the substantial evidence, presented in Gladstone's review of the novel, of his preoccupation with Ward's diametric opposition of Christian belief as emotional and unintellectual, and theism as the rational outcome of rigorous, intellectual enquiry.[90] Gladstone, for example, took issue with Ward's presentation of Elsmere's intellectual development, arguing that, in fact, she showed no evidence of an intellectual process in Elsmere in either his renunciation of orthodox Christianity or his maintenance of a belief in God. Gladstone demonstrated this disparity by comparing the characters and fates of Wendover – who followed his scholarship to its logical conclusions in unbelief, and yet died insane – and Elsmere, who despite his researches in the squire's library, continued to defer to emotion in his decision making, providing arguments neither for rejecting Christianity, nor for remaining a theist, 'nobly kills himself with overwork' before passing 'away in a final flood of light'.[91] But the force of Gladstone's criticism was reserved for Ward's lack of engagement with scholarship:

> There is nowhere a sign that the authoress has made herself acquainted with the Christian apologists, old or recent ... If such be

the case, she has skipped lightly (to put it no higher) over vast mental spaces of literature and learning relevant to the case, and has given sentence in the cause without hearing the evidence.[92]

This criticism was meant to cut deep, for, as the niece of Matthew Arnold and a close associate of the liberal Anglicans in Oxford engaged in just this apologetic endeavour, Gladstone thought Ward had no excuse for being so ill-informed. Ward thanked Gladstone for 'the courteous & kindly way in which you have criticised the book & what it puts forward',[93] and sent him, by way of thanks, a handsomely bound copy of *Robert Elsmere*, containing pictures of the Lakeland locations which had inspired the earlier part of the novel.[94] The two had, during their earlier exchanges, also traded texts: Gladstone had sent Ward a marked copy of *Gleanings* with the hope that she would read his 'Life of the Prince Consort' and 'Courses of Religious Thought', while she had sent him her copy of T. H. Green's *Lay Sermons*.[95] Both of Ward's gifts were placed by Gladstone in St Deiniol's Library, further undermining the force of Shannon's characterization of the institution.

Gladstone next visited Keble in November 1888, his exchanges with Mary Ward fresh in his mind.[96] Before this visit, Gladstone's plans for the disposal of his library had been hazy, and discussion of them had been restricted to his immediate family. Now, he was anxious to move forward with his scheme. Significantly, Gore and Talbot were the first people outside this intimate circle to be informed. On the very evening of his arrival, Gladstone sounded Gore on the project.[97] He reacted with initial incredulity, complaining: 'Really it is a joke. Mr. Gladstone wanted to see me last night … about a scheme he has got for the furtherance of theological study amongst the clergy, as if he had no other thought in the world'.[98] By doubting his seriousness, Gore misjudged Gladstone, who spent the following day busily devouring Gore's *The Ministry of the Christian Church* (1888) to facilitate further debate.[99] On the 12 November, Gladstone held a: 'Full conversation with Warden [Talbot] & Mr Gore on [the] Meditated foundation',[100] and it was following this meeting that Gladstone wrote a memorandum laying down, for the first time on paper, his vision for St Deiniol's.[101]

Gladstone left Keble on 13 November 1888, but both Gore and Talbot followed him with letters in which they expressed growing enthusiasm for the library scheme. Gore told Gladstone that his experience at Pusey House 'encourages me in the belief that a library is an admirable basis of operations for an Ecclesiastical institution such as you propose', and: 'I cannot but feel ... that a great deal of good to religious learning may come of the enterprise'. Nonetheless, both men continued strongly to question Gladstone's choice of location. Gore accepted Gladstone's need to supervise the foundation personally, which would 'leave no doubt as to the place where the start of the undertaking should be', but maintained that:

> The ultimate situation of the library should be left an open question. Its first organization should be arranged so as to admit of its being ultimately moved, if it was found advisable, wherever its chances of usefulness would be greatest. I ... still incline to the opinion that on the whole it is more likely ultimately to be found workable in a town.[102]

Talbot's reaction was similar, if more conciliatory: 'I quite feel now that it would be best for you to proceed with the organisation of the library at Hawarden, though in a way which would make after transplantation possible & even probable'.[103] According to Gore, Gladstone – who had spent a considerable amount of time combing the village for a suitable site – was incensed by the suggestion of Liverpool. 'He never spoke another word for the next six miles of our walk, and I think I have never in my life felt so much like a whipped schoolboy. But I still believe I was right.'[104] Despite this reported disagreement, Liverpool was cited in the Keble Memorandum as 'the only possible town' site, although apparently only as part of a compromise.

One of Gladstone's primary motivations for instituting the library, and for locating it in Hawarden, was his belief that the church in Wales would soon be disestablished and would urgently require independent educational support.[105] Gladstone also wanted personal control of the foundation in his lifetime, which was a significant objection to situating St Deiniol's in Liverpool, but the fact that he began to entertain the possibility of a 'later transmigration' clearly reflected the level of influence Talbot and Gore had on him, as did Gladstone's eventual decision to build the library in galvanized iron, which was only ever going to be a temporary solution.[106] Furthermore, Gladstone remained aware of the challenge of the urban environment for the church, especially in Liverpool. Lady Charlotte Ribblesdale recalled in 1904 that 'Gladstone said that as a town it was very irreligious, and he had to bring home to it in consequence its duty as well as its capacity to build a cathedral.'[107] In a later memorandum Gladstone stated that he wished the library to provide assistance, from a distance if necessary, to that 'great city',[108] but he noted that 'an inhospitable atmosphere cuts off all idea of my personal agency'.[109] This undoubtedly reflected Gladstone's ambivalent, and frequently uncomfortable, relationship with the city of his birth, whose radical Toryism and religious sectarianism, intensified by the Home Rule question, would indeed have provided an inhospitable atmosphere for the kind of institution which Gladstone envisaged.[110]

Nonetheless, Gladstone's foundation of a rural library appeared to go against the prevailing trend of Victorian ecclesiastical interest – the cities, their heaving populations, and overworked clergy – which undeniably formed the basis of Gore and Talbot's objections, especially considering Gore and his associates' contribution to the resurgence of Christian Socialism in the 1880s.[111] However, there was a coincident strand of Anglican thought that identified the countryside – always its stronghold – as 'the pastoral ideal'.[112] Gladstone pledged that his library would provide 'aid to the local church', foresaw it might have a 'connection with ... local study', and form a 'centre of occasional instruction by Lectures'.[113] Moreover, he held a positive opinion of the advantages of an isolated rural location for similar institutions. In 1891, he defended the isolated situation of Glenalmond College, which he had helped to found in the mid-1840s, in similar terms:

> It may seem that it was a daring and a rash proceeding to attempt to found a college of this description at so great a distance from centres of population ... I dare say it may be said that ... a town offers a more popular and attractive site ... Undoubtedly ... proximity to masses of the population offers considerable advantage ... But ... there are some advantages ... that should not be overlooked with respect to ... [a] foundation ... in the country[:] ... the opportunity of free communication with nature ... larger liberty, and ... a practical acquaintance with the beautiful and romantic.[114]

This speech was aimed at schoolboys, but the emphasis given in Gladstone's first memorandum to St Deiniol's as a place of rest, holidays, refreshment, and retirement in many ways connotes popular idealizations of rural life and beliefs in the spirit-enhancing benefits of leisure. Hulda Friederichs propounded a similar understanding of St Deiniol's, suggesting that:

> The restlessness and roar of millionfold human life would be a disturbing element in any library intended for a Temple of Peace ... The perfect seclusion of the village; the ease with which it may be reached; ... the beauty and healthiness of the district; and also the

associations of the whole place with Mr. Gladstone; all seemed to point to Hawarden as the ideal situation for the Theological library.[115]

Moreover, Gladstone wished to establish an independent institution in St Deiniol's, in the same way as he had sought to establish a liberal and, in Scottish terms, an independent episcopal school at Glenalmond. In Gladstone's original memorandum, he tied in the library very closely to the idea of locality, but its central purpose was to be far more wide-reaching and universal in scope.[116]

The expectation of Welsh disestablishment largely legitimized the library's foundation in Wales but Gladstone consistently privileged intellectual over practical motivations. Lord Stanmore (formerly Sir Arthur Gordon) had questioned Gladstone on this point in 1892, and received an evasive answer.[117] Writing in a private memorandum the following year, Gladstone confirmed that there was more to his plan:

> I have not here principally in view the likelihood that ... the Church in Wales may be deprived or discharged of her temporal endowments, this constitutes a call for pecuniary aid with a view to the due and dignified maintenance of her ministrations ... I refer to a deeper & more searching need.[118]

He continued: 'a special necessity appears to have arisen at the present epoch requiring to be met by special means'. The 'necessity' was 'a severance between the Christian system and the general thought of the time'; one of the 'means' was to be St Deiniol's: an intellectual resource for a beleaguered and isolated church,[119] and Gladstone's personal contribution to the project that aimed to return 'the Catholic faith into its right relation to modern intellectual and moral problems'.[120] For there was clearly a coterminous vision being articulated by Gladstone and the *Lux Mundi* Group, of an ecumenical,[121] interdisciplinary, associationalist, clergy-led Christian culture; the growth of which would redress existing imbalances in Victorian intellectual life. Gore had written, in his *Mission* text, of what he understood to be the central paradox inflicting the relationship between theology and other intellectual disciplines, which Gladstone also recognized and acted upon in Hawarden. While the 'principle of faith is brought into exercise to some extent in all human life and knowledge', including the sciences, there remained a lack of dialogue between the disciplines to the detriment of all.[122] This mirrored one of Gladstone's enduring convictions about the need to restore a right relationship between theology and other disciplines, which he expressed and embodied most explicitly in St Deiniol's:

> Christianity is a religion adapted to the elevation and development of the entire nature of man, and, so far from seeing any antagonism between the prosecution of Divine knowledge and the prosecution of knowledge which is human and secular, in my opinion they never can be separated without disadvantage.[123]

In the combative intellectual climate of the late nineteenth century, Gore and Gladstone saw a clear choice for theology. Either it could continue a threatened withdrawal from current intellectual debate, prompted largely by ignorance and fear of new developments apparently antagonistic to faith, or it could stand its ground and keep the channels of communication open. To Gore it was a matter of 'duty' that Anglicans should learn from other branches of knowledge in order to assess more clearly their relative contribution to the sum of human knowledge.[124] This, along with Gore's call for Christians from different traditions to communicate and associate, was also central to Gladstone. Both preoccupations can be seen directly informing the structure of his library: the proximity of theological and secular texts on its shelves and the engagement in debate between both believers and non-believers in its hostel.

The most striking characteristic of the first library's classification scheme was the sheer broadness of its divinity section. The category 'Magic and Spiritism' was included in the very centre of the room, as well as 'Non Christian Religions', 'Pre-History', and the 'Philosophy of Man' and 'Of Nature'. Radically, Gladstone regarded these as major parts of his collection; minor sections, including such mainstream and 'orthodox' subjects as 'Epitaphs &c. Books on marriage &c. Hymns. Liturgies', were relegated down the hierarchy.[125] Several contemporary commentators stressed the breadth and inclusiveness of the St Deiniol's theological collection. David Williamson wrote: 'The choice of volumes was made on no exclusive basis, and I noticed the works of Churchmen, Catholics, and Nonconformists side by side',[126] and J. C. Story observed:

> The theological student who examines the books in the Divinity Room will be struck with the breadth of the donor's conception. Here is no sign of narrowness; nothing of the sectarian spirit; all is otherwise ... From Fetishism and Animism up to Judaism; from Judaism up to Christianity, in every phase and expression of the same, all may be traced, and the shelves, as they succeed one another, point the way.[127]

Figure 6.1 'St Deiniol's Library: the Warden's room', H. Friederichs, *In the Evening of his Days* (London, 1896), p. 122. St Deiniol's Library Collection.

Moreover, to look at surviving photographs of the original library and hostel, it can be seen how closely liberal catholic theories had been put into practice. The hostel was parsonage-like and yet, adjacent to an eclectic library, it challenged the priest to be both pastor and academic theologian. The warden was represented in quiet studious contemplation in his study reading (Figure 6.1). Smaller studies or carrels were provided for visiting readers but domestic space was shared: a communal dining room encouraged debate with the hope of increased mutual understanding, and the prayer room, although decorated, was not ostentatiously sectarian (Figure 6.2).

Circumstances thus enabled Gladstone's personal organization of the library within a well-known context, both harmonizing it to the needs of the locality, as well as offering the benefits of rest and retirement he himself had enjoyed in Hawarden to those further afield. There remained, nevertheless, questions over the future direction of an institution which the founder himself described as still in embryo. Gladstone expended time and energy considering the possibility that

Figure 6.2 'St Deiniol's Hostel: the prayer room', H. Friederichs, *In the Evening of his Days* (London, 1896), p. 141. St Deiniol's Library Collection.

St Deiniol's might house a religious community, a process which revealed not only the influence of but also the profound uncertainties which underlay the liberal catholic movement, and which had an important influence over later interpretation of the library's purpose.

The question of community

A significant revival of Anglican religious community life took place from the mid-Victorian period.[128] The impetus for this clearly came from the Anglo-Catholic wing of the church but there were specifically liberal catholic communities instituted, most significantly, Gore's Community of the Resurrection, founded in Oxford in 1887.[129] In his Keble memorandum, Gladstone had included among his 'higher' purposes the 'gradual formation of a body', and in 1893 he proposed that:

> The Trustees may place the Institution under the control of or in association with any Community or Institution having similar aims and may devolve on such community all or any of their powers; provided they shall be satisfied that the purposes of the Institution will thus be more effectively answered.[130]

It is important to note Gladstone's obvious caution here. As we have established, he was unhappy with the notion of study divorced from wider interaction. Whilst he was broadly supportive of lay, or 'third' orders, he was also somewhat unconvinced of the efficacy of religious life and worship conducted in seclusion.[131] In 1895, in a typical compromise, Gladstone approached an Oxford religious community – the Society of St John the Evangelist (SSJE), the oldest of the nineteenth-century Anglican foundations – for help and advice.[132] In return he received a detailed memorandum from R. L. Page, which addressed the practicalities of the library's association with a religious community.[133] Page stated that SSJE was unable to get practically involved itself,[134] but provided Gladstone with his opinions on the potential function of the library. Page also questioned Hawarden's suitability as a location. 'London, Oxford, Cambridge or (Durham) seem more suitable,' he wrote, 'as having the largest libraries, being seats of learning & more easy of access for persons generally'.[135] Page proceeded to set out a vision of St Deiniol's as a theological 'think-tank': a body of theologians giving advice and publishing on a range of theological issues to meet the needs of the church. He suggested that St Deiniol's might become a theological college, a retreat centre with clergy versed in 'ascetic theology', and a place of rest and help to the local clergy. This in part mirrored Gladstone's vision of how 'divine learning' might be successfully promoted but, in Page's opinion, because the library's endowment was insufficient to support a paid staff, an existing theological college or religious community should take over the running of the institution. Significantly, he proposed Gore's Community of the Resurrection.

Gladstone also received some strong advice against the idea of associating St Deiniol's with a religious community, reflecting tensions between understandings of St Deiniol's as either an independent, or a community-led, institution. G. W. E. Russell responded to Page's ideas with misgiving, pointing out that the presence of such a community would not guarantee learning. He estimated that monastic guidance would be 'undesirable' for both local clergy and for any future theological college students, concluding with the following indictment:

> St Deiniol's would necessarily become a mere creature of the Community, influenced and ruled according to the prevailing idea at the moment in the mind of the Superior or Community. The Founder's Hand would cease to operate; and the distinctness and individuality of the Institution would disappear as completely as if the library were bodily removed to Oxford.[136]

In a subsequent letter, Russell cast doubt on Page's assertion that a community would ensure permanence: 'I do not think that we can yet be assured of the permanence of the Cowley Brotherhood', he wrote.[137] Edward Talbot was also doubtful about Gladstone's idea of 'some form of community-life akin to that of Pusey House' growing up round the library.[138]

There was thus consistent and close involvement by liberal catholics in Gladstone's deliberations over the question of the library 'community' and staffing, but their contributions displayed inconsistency and disagreement. This was because of the fundamental paradox in founding what were essentially counter-cultural communities to further the liberal catholic aim of participating fully in and shaping modern life. The documentary evidence surrounding Gladstone's search for a warden for his library both shows how influential the liberal catholic nexus continued to be following its institution, but also demonstrates the problems that dogged efforts to realize the liberal catholic vision.

Henry Scott Holland wrote to Gladstone suggesting a member of the Community of the Resurrection, Mr Rackham, as a possible first warden. He added: 'it seems to me a real gain to associate this high venture for Theology, with the Company gathered under Gore's leadership, who have the cause so deeply at heart, and who are working toward the same ends in so congenial in spirit'.[139] However, despite his enthusiastic attitude to the library, Gore, as Community Superior, forbade Rackham's candidature, voicing a widespread anxiety among fledgling Anglican orders not to disperse before an enduring sense of community had been established.[140] Instead, he joined Talbot and Walter Lock in proposing a Keble man, E. W. Delahay, for warden.[141] Delahay did not, however, stand much chance of appointment: as well as Stephen Gladstone's judgement that 'Mr. Gore's man' was too young, he was engaged to be married.[142] As was made clear in the original advert for the wardenship, Gladstone was keen to appoint an unmarried man, ostensibly for reasons of space, but also because he was considering the possibility of a celibate community.[143] However, this criterion proved more difficult to satisfy than Gladstone anticipated, as a significant number of those who either applied or were suggested were married or engaged.[144] This was true of Arthur Cayley Headlam (1862–1947), then a young fellow of All Souls, who was Gladstone's first serious choice.[145] As a liberal catholic, Headlam was an ideal candidate for warden in view of the purpose of the institution. W. Saceday wrote to Gladstone confirming Headlam's – and by implication Gladstone's – liberal catholic credentials:

> He would approach matters very much from the point of view from which I believe that you would wish them approached – that of a High Churchman, progressive, independent and anxious to bring theories of doctrine into accord with the realities of things, but never rash in grasping at novelties.

He added more generally on the role of the library itself: 'I entertain great hopes as to the possibilities of the new foundation in helping to correct one of the weakest points in the English Church – a want of thoroughness in thought & study'.[146] However, Headlam ultimately decided that Gladstone's offer was one he 'could not accept ... on the terms you offered it'.[147] He had initially made clear he was unlikely to be suitable, both having resigned his fellowship in order to marry, and also having already accepted a parish elsewhere, but Gladstone had pressed ahead regardless because, he argued, 'the idea I wish to suggest is one generically so different'.[148] Headlam was unconvinced and told Gladstone, in his characteristically bald manner, that he desired practical, parochial work, not 'theology divorced from life', which was a brutal check for Gladstone who envisaged, of course, that St Deiniol's would directly counter this tendency.[149] He had from the beginning recognized the difficulties inherent in trying to achieve the 'gradual formation of a body' in Hawarden,[150] but Headlam's refusal so seriously questioned the direction in which Gladstone's plans were taking him that he was persuaded to abandon the idea of forming a community proper. Indicative of this change of heart is the fact that, in his negotiations with the eventual first warden, G. C. Joyce – another scholarly priest from the catholic wing of the church – Gladstone placed far less emphasis on devotional life than he had during his discussions with Headlam.[151]

St Deiniol's after Gladstone

Historically speaking, Gladstone's ultimate rejection of the idea of St Deiniol's as a counter-cultural religious community has not been made much of by commentators. Principally this has been because of his own family's disagreements over the institution's purpose following his death, and their key role in publicizing it. Mary Drew was the crucial figure here. After her father's death, Mary became chiefly responsible for publicizing St Deiniol's, and her version of its foundation and purpose was styled as the 'authoritative account', something which proved to be not only influential on but also misleading to both her contemporaries and later scholars. In her article promoting the library, Mary stated unequivocally that it was designed 'for the purposes of study and research, "for the pursuit of divine learning," a centre of religious life, a resident body of students, men of studious mind and habit, unfitted by various causes for active life or the turmoil of great cities'. She regarded the work of the temporary library as only in line with Gladstone's 'secondary purposes' for the institution; it was only with the completion of 'a permanent Residence for Warden and Students' or community that 'will arrive the real opportunity of fulfilling the main design of the founder'. Although she described the library as being 'open to thinkers of every class, even to those to whom the gift of faith has been denied, earnest enquirers, seekers, searchers after the truth that is divine', she maintained that:

> For 'the advancement of divine learning' he looked specially to the resident community. And the type of men that undoubtedly he had in view ... were men residing in religious bodies already existing and in working order, men who ... would do for their own generation what Pusey and Stubbs, Lightfoot and Westcott had done for theirs. Mr. Gladstone saw that ... it would be good to revive something of the methods of the wise of old. By their ... austere experience they had shown it could best be sustained by the spiritual discipline of the consecrated life, inspired and strengthened by corporate devotion and aspiration.[152]

This vision was far in advance of anything that Gladstone had himself articulated and, by privileging the qualifications of a withdrawn 'consecrated' community to form the heart of the library, Drew obscured much of the liberal catholic communitarian spirit that had informed Gladstone's project. Although Gladstone did not think 'luxurious living ... conducive to the well-being of the increased intellectual activity of those whom the institution is intended to benefit', this was a far cry from wanting it to be a place of ascetic denial.[153]

There were other versions of the story available. Prominent among these was that articulated by Stephen Liberty, sub-warden of the library between 1906 and 1910. His short introduction to the library, written soon after Drew's article, by implication took issue with her interpretation. He acknowledged her 'authority of intimate knowledge', but asserted: 'Foundations, however, like individuals, require a little time to "find their level"; indeed the Founder in this case himself wisely left it to future generations to decide ... the exact shape which his Institution should assume'.[154] His account concentrated on the role the library fulfilled for working clergy, which tallied more accurately with the original ethos envisaged by Gladstone and put into practice by Joyce:

> Here is a house which all the year round opens its doors to any man who wants to return for a long or short time from the burden and heat of action to the upper air of learning and resolve, which first sent him out into the world. In some cases a long stay and an extensive course of study would be found practicable ... but in cases (probably the majority) where this is not expected, it is, surely, something for the hard-worked or isolated parson to be able to come even for a week or two and turn over the new books, to discuss them in friendly intercourse with others either of his own or of a different standpoint, and generally to renew contact with the main stream of Christian thought ... The supplying in this way of an admitted need of the clergy is probably the most considerable, at any rate the most tangible, work that St. Deiniol's has yet been able to do.[155]

Gladstone's difficulty in combining the library and community ideas lay in a significant disjunction between their intellectual and theological rationale. Gladstone's central aim was for St Deiniol's to foster theology's engagement with the world by functioning principally as a periodical resource rather than as a place of permanent withdrawal for clergy.[156] Unlike SSJE, which 'was not called by human wisdom',[157] St Deiniol's was conceived as a response to contemporary moral and intellectual problems, and its primary aim was to effect a much needed rehabilitation of theology. Although Benson's vision of how SSJE should serve the Church – through mission preaching, retreats and teaching – to an extent accorded with Gladstone's, Benson's view that all intellectual study must be 'subservient to holiness and the love of God', was diametrically opposed to Gladstone's belief that the understanding and practice of religion was rooted in intellectual study.[158] Unsurprisingly, the religious community did not materialize. Gladstone did not set out to found such a community and, following his preferred candidate's rejection of the wardenship, essentially turned against the idea. Ultimately, however, although Drew did not see her ideal community installed at St Deiniol's, the authority of her 'intimate knowledge' significantly contributed to a consequent neglect of the library's liberal catholic context.

*

Gladstone's relationship with Keble and Oxford's liberal catholic revival, with its emphasis on an academically alive, doctrinally streamlined, confident, and broad Anglicanism, provides a context in which the foundation of St Deiniol's no longer appears so anomalous. It represented a natural and well-conceived response to the crisis of confidence afflicting Anglicanism rather than a defensive bastion against the circumstances of modern life. In fact, the evidence of Gladstone's liberal catholic connections and theological position make it unfeasible to describe Gladstone, as Colin Matthew did, simply as 'an orthodox sacramentalist with what was by the 1880s an old-fashioned view of heaven', 'an anglo-catholic' with residual evangelical tendencies,[159] or as Shannon's intransigent and defensive church conservative. Throughout his life Gladstone moved through several religious phases. He was brought up a strict evangelical, flirted with Tractarianism in his middle years, but all along he also developed deepening broad church sympathies and ended up a liberal catholic. His increasing broadness of religious outlook did not involve repudiating his previous positions, which in many important ways continued to influence him but, when one examines the textual evidence, one can see just how far he had moved. As this chapter has shown, he valued intellectual rigour and prized an open mind too highly to remain theologically unmoved in the face of multiplying 'modern intellectual and moral problems'.

One fascinating image of Gladstone, entitled appropriately enough *The Aged Reader*, (Figure 6.3), is firmly evangelical in its references: sombre Sunday best and right hand resting on the Bible,[160] but Gladstone's figure is integrated into the context of a late nineteenth-century gothic-revival church. Of the two images of Christ that fill the windows either side of Gladstone's head, the one on the right is immediately recognizable as William Holman Hunt's *The Light of the World* (1853). The first version of this painting has been in Keble College chapel ever since the day Gladstone made his long speech in 1878. The vaulting of this imaginary space is decorated with a criss-cross design also reminiscent of Keble. The tension between and within different Anglican traditions is marked in this composition just as it was in Gladstone's religious *mentalité*, but when confronted with either we are

Figure 6.3 'The Aged Reader', *William Ewart Gladstone* (Bristol, 1898). St Deiniol's Library Collection.

continually pressed to recognize the eclecticism, innovation, space, and depth which such a mixture afforded.

It has also been shown that that, while Gladstone was adamant about the intellectual rationale behind his decision to leave his books for the spiritual benefit of future generations, he was simultaneously unsure about how such an institution would be constituted and work in practice. When he confessed, in 1895, that 'It is an institution not yet fully developed', he was giving a fair assessment of the state of his thinking on its future, and was articulating a broader uncertainty felt by many liberal catholics about how an intellectual vision could be implemented in a relevant and practical way.[161] Nonetheless, despite the considerable problems which his vision faced, set within the class-related inconsistencies which afflicted liberal catholic ideology, we can clearly identify the central purpose for which St Deiniol's was founded and those for which it was not. It was not to be a 'public' library in the real sense, as can be seen from the careful hedging round of both its physical buildings and its intellectual rationale, rather it was there to nurture 'a learned clergy'.[162] However, neither was it designed, as Mary Drew would later argue, to be a permanent retreat from the world and its problems. Note Hulda Friederichs's 1896 description of the hostel as 'a congenial *temporary* home' for 'a student coming in from the busy world',[163] and the words of the Right Revd Dr Edwards, Bishop of St Asaph, spoken at the opening of the memorial library, which summed up the central aim of St Deiniol's:

> If the hearts and minds of men are to be won to the faith of Christ, there must be that scientific exposition of what we know of God and of his relations to the world, which can only be effectively given by those adequately equipped in Divine learning. And while the principles are clear and definite, they are pre-eminently broad and inclusive.[164]

St Deiniol's was then, the expression of Gladstone's theological and not his political liberalism. As has been consistently argued, although working compromises could be effected, tensions and inconsistencies remained in the engagement between these two species as well as in the constitution of liberal catholicism itself. Visions of how to effect change according to liberal catholic ideas were not always politically or morally liberal. For example, Charles Gore thought that the changing work of Christianity should be pioneered by 'a spiritual aristocracy', a vision which, in many ways, mirrored Gladstone's vision for St Deiniol's.[165]

As shown above, the earliest reference to Gladstone's plan made clear that the library was intended principally as a resource for the Anglican church, and the Keble memorandum indicated that this was heavily weighted towards the needs of both local and national clergy. It was the clergy who had borrowed books from the Temple of Peace and debated with Gladstone about theology who were to be the principal inheritors of his book collection and intellectual legacy. Men like these were, in his view, the future of the church; those who would change it by engaging in academic pursuits and practical pastoral theology. Whilst they were not to be kept isolated in community, they were still to be a powerful and influential clerisy. This vital distinction was illustrated by Stephen Liberty, who prefaced his short introduction to the library with the following quotation from Richard de Bury's *Philobiblion*:

> Having taken a survey of human necessities in every direction, with a view to bestow our charity upon them, our compassionate inclinations have chosen to bear pious aid to ... [a] class of men, in whom there is ... such hope of advantage to the Church, and to provide for them, not only in respect of things necessary to their support, but much more in respect of the books so useful to their studies.[166]

The late Victorian successors of such men were to be the inheritors of Gladstone's beloved theological book collection. In the same way in which he had sold his historical and political library in 1875 to one who would continue in his political stead, so Gladstone now bestowed his theological books on those who would continue the work he had begun in that sphere. In the light of our revised understanding of Gladstone's theological priorities, and their influence over the character of St Deiniol's, such a vision makes perfect sense.

The creative tensions observable in Gladstone's late Victorian liberal catholicism were thus also visible in his library. They also influenced its reception within the public domain. Both press and public had been coaxed and wooed into accepting Gladstone's intellectual life and library as outward signs of his public duty, and duly interpreted them as part of a popular Gladstonian liberal agenda. It is unsurprising, therefore, that St Deiniol's was incorporated into this familiar context rather than being interpreted through the more private, clerical, and somewhat anomalous liberal catholic frame of reference, which was never overtly publicized and would not necessarily have found favour had it been so. Even Mary Drew felt the need to publicize the library in popular political terms and one could argue that, in the end, Gladstone was the victim of his own success. So well had he integrated his scholarly image in this context that he had once again lost a substantial measure of control over it. Nonetheless, St Deiniol's remains by far the most potent statement of the broadness of Gladstone's spiritual and cultural vision. By the dynamic and selective creation of an appropriate material layout to epitomize and make sense of the knowledge that he had collected, imbibed, and used, he was making his own ultimate contribution to a lifelong ideal, that of 'enlarging the text' and 'extending the bounds of the common inheritance'.[167]

Part IV Transforming the Reader

7
Political Lotus-Eater to Grand Old Bookman: Re-presenting Gladstone the Reader

> It is easy in the world to live after the world's opinion; it is easy in solitude to live after our own; but the great man is he who in the midst of the crowd keeps with perfect sweetness the independence of solitude.
>
> Emerson[1]

By including this quotation in his biography of Gladstone, John Morley was not merely embellishing his subject with a generic valorization of political independence. He was also celebrating the ultimate, and in many ways surprising, success of a particularly idiosyncratic aspect of Gladstone's political praxis: his tendency to represent himself as, by turns, a scholarly recluse and a fully engaged public campaigner. As we have seen, Gladstone's library and reading were shaped by and conducted within shifting frames of reference in which notions of 'private' and 'public' jostled, often uncomfortably. It has been suggested that, following his entry into public life in 1832, Gladstone's continued attempts to negotiate satisfactorily between the two spheres generated considerable tension. In this chapter we will examine in more detail the multifarious and changing ways in which Gladstone's reading was both represented and received in public domains over his long lifetime. In many ways offering a counterweight to Gladstone's substantial musings on 'interior matters' that have been used elsewhere in this study,[2] the following analysis examines the fraught interplay between his understanding of what it meant to be an intellectual both in and out of politics – and others' attitudes to his intense intellectual life. Gladstone the reader was – increasingly so as he got older – incorporated into his popular political persona, with both his reading and library being described and celebrated in contemporary commentaries. However, it remains unclear how such usages functioned as part of those constant and changeable negotiations taking place between politician and audience, and what part they played in the constructions of Gladstone's image in the public mind.

The political lotus-eater

An anonymous author, writing for *London Society* in 1869, claimed the following had been general opinion of Gladstone as a young Peelite in the late 1830s and early 1840s:

> There was a kind of gentle languor and melancholy about him. He seemed a recluse, of scholarly poetic temperament. He was a political lotus-eater. His voice was called 'the echo of a voice;' the voice of one in whose breast all human passions were lulled. It was thought that he lacked the 'combativity' necessary for parliamentary conflict. It was thought that both his physique and his morale were against him.[3]

If one examines images of Gladstone made during the period here discussed, one finds visual support for such dismal prognostics. William Bradley (1801–57), a successful Manchester portrait painter patronized by the Gladstones, painted Gladstone twice between 1838 and 1844. The first portrait (1839; Hawarden Castle), (see Figure 7.1), bespeaks paternal pride, gentlemanly status, and intellectual romanticism.

There is little to indicate Gladstone's parliamentary calling, except perhaps the papers lying on the table. These are held down by an open book, which is an unidentifiable but convenient symbol of Gladstone's active scholarship and establishes the painting's intellectual priorities. The eyes of the viewer are drawn from book to the face of the pensive subject, whose unawareness of the viewer lends him an air of gentility, and reinforces the portrait's studied refinement. The pose is heavily charged with romanticism, reflecting as it does the complete introspection of the sitter.

Bradley had caught what Colin Matthew describes as Gladstone's 'highly romantic, even Utopian' conservatism of the 1830s, expressed in his church and state treatises and built upon a Coleridgeian 'cultivation of the inward man'.[4] However, Bradley's portrait sent mixed messages about the aspiring political thinker it represented. By 1839 romanticism of this sort was outmoded, and Gladstone's pose was particularly problematic. In its self-contained timidity – reminiscent of Antonio Canova's *Venus Italica* – it differed from the classical poses generally

Figure 7.1 William Bradley, *William Ewart Gladstone* (1839). C. A. Gladstone.

used for early Victorian male portraits, cutting a figure contemporaries would increasingly associate with female representation in both painting and photography.[5] Such associations problematized representing Gladstone as romantic reader and serious intellectual, especially for and in a non-domestic setting. Other early pictorial representations of Gladstone exhibited the same tensions, and such feminization of Gladstone's image was even more blatant in caricature. Throughout his life he was caricatured as a woman, but in later cartoons his masculine features were maintained. However in John Doyle's 'The New Christmas Pantomime' (1845; University of Manchester), Figure 7.2, Gladstone was represented as a fully feminine Columbine, dancing with his political mentor, Sir Robert Peel.

Figure 7.2 'H.B'. [John Doyle], *The New Christmas Pantomime* (1845). University of Manchester.

Attempts were made to address these representational problems by those who sought to celebrate Gladstone's early parliamentary success, including Peel and the commissioners of Bradley's second portrait, Eton College. For the latter commission, (1841; Eton College), Figure 7.3, Bradley maintained the same pose as the family portrait but added a heavy cloak to swell the slight frame and square the curving pose. Gladstone's face was made squarer and less delicate. While the classical column was retained, all references to books and reading were removed, toning down the scholarly emphasis; and re-centring the body as the pre-eminent marker of public masculinity.

Although the intellectual tone of Bradley's first portrait was deemed suitable for a private, domesticated setting, it was not viewed as entirely appropriate for a commemorative portrait of a politician, signalling the problems inherent in trying to integrate multiple, and not necessarily compatible, identities in representational form. Gladstone was a politician, but he was also a reader, scholar, and author. His published work and his position in the public eye, which excited comment and ensured portraits were of interest, brought his scholarly activities into domains where they could be discussed, criticized, and held up against the reputations

Figure 7.3 William Bradley, *William Ewart Gladstone* (1841). Provost and Fellows of Eton College. Photograph: the Courtauld Institute.

and productions of those individuals – men of letters and academic scholars – who relied on such intellectual capital for their primary living. His profile also invited comparison with those of his political contemporaries who combined their public duties with scholarly pursuits. However, it is evident that Gladstone's contemporaries experienced particular discomfort encountering the combination as it manifested itself in him.

Intellectuals in Victorian society

Conceptualizations of the 'man of letters' and the 'scholar' generated significant debate during the Victorian period. Many, including Thomas Carlyle and Matthew Arnold, attempted to estimate the place of intellectual activity in society. While simultaneously being preoccupied with properly defining 'manliness' in theory and as a code of conduct, laying emphasis on such things as moral courage, sexual purity, athleticism, and stoicism.[6]

The man of letters[7]

Carlyle articulated the most enduring concept of the nineteenth-century man of letters in 'The Hero as Man of Letters', one of the lectures published as *On Heroes, Hero-Worship, and the Heroic in History* in 1841, the year in which Bradley painted Gladstone for Eton.[8] In this address, Carlyle charted the influence of intellectual activity on human history, and analysed the power invested in those who communicate through the written word. Unlike the king, god, or poet, who had existed throughout history, Carlyle opined:

> The Hero as Man of Letters ... is altogether a product of these new ages; and so long as the wondrous art of Writing, or of Ready-writing which we call Printing, subsists, he may be expected to continue, as one of the main forms of Heroism for all future ages.[9]

Carlyle's presented his man of letters, not only as a creation of that state of modernity inaugurated by the genesis of print culture, but also as a key figure in both representing and actively communicating those heroic ideals he thought necessary to improve and civilize society. As both symbolic representative and active panacea, Carlyle's man of letters was the modern equivalent of the mediaeval priest:

> He that can write a true Book, to persuade England, is not he the Bishop and Archbishop ... of all England? I many a time say, the writers of Newspapers, Pamphlets, Poems, Books, these are the real working effective Church of a modern country.[10]

In his copy of Carlyle's lectures, Gladstone placed his '*NB*' of special notice by this section. His early years in parliament, resting as they did upon that agonizingly negotiated compromise between his spiritual vocation and aspiration to live a public life, were dominated by a particularly rigid conception of himself as a Christian in politics. It is therefore unsurprising that he should have read Carlyle with approval here. However, in Carlyle's view, the importance of the modern community of letters was epitomized by its functioning as a secular replacement for a church that was neither real, working, nor effective,[11] which is not an opinion Gladstone would have shared. His early intellectual priorities were heavily shaped by the trenchantly ecclesiastical and academic values he had encountered at Oxford, and shared little or no common ground with Carlyle's interpretation of the needs and values of modern society. As Colin Matthew notes, Gladstone's 'almost wholly theoretical' preoccupation in the 1830s was with 'obligation in State and Church ... with little or no reference to the circumstances of the day'.[12] By representing himself as an abstract scholar rather than as a man of letters, Gladstone assumed a mantle that was already deeply unfashionable.

The scholar

In the early to mid-Victorian periods, scholars were habitually regarded eccentric as at best and useless at worst. As Frederic Harrison wrote in his *Memoirs*, scholars were widely seen to 'suppress spontaneous expression' and were often 'ignorant and mindless men'.[13] In particular they were thought to show little evidence of those increasingly heroicized traits such as self help, hard work, and productivity, personifying instead such demonized characteristics as idleness, banality, and artificiality. Such negatively charged diametric opposition was also Carlylean. In *Past and Present* (1843), Carlyle contrasted the 'adroit' but ultimately ineffectual 'Man of Theory', and the apparently stupid but socially successful 'Man of Practice'.[14] Such celebrations of practical work implicitly questioned the image of the scholar and the writer as valid categories of true masculinity. In the event, Carlyle adeptly integrated his man of letters into this model by re-defining the literary in material terms as 'brainwork', but this still left the 'light adroit Man of Theory' open to question as a worker and as a man, intensifying the already clear distinctions that were understood to exist between men of letters and scholars.

J. R. Robertson, in an undated but much later study of Gladstone published in the *Free Review*, deliberately associated such prejudices with the name of Gladstone by expressing the – substantially exaggerated – opinion that the Oxford of Gladstone's undergraduate days had been 'furthest from valid knowledge and sane science' than at any time 'since the Middle Ages'.[15] Gladstone's most enthusiastic and public expression of intellectual association and debt had been made when he dedicated his first book to Oxford in fulsome terms, citing himself 'student of Christchurch' as well as MP for Newark. He had described Oxford as 'providentially designed to be a fountain of blessings, spiritual, social, and intellectual, to this and to other countries to the present and future times'.[16] This concept, of the university as an agent of the Christian gospel, differed radically from Carlyle's model for social and educational improvement by secular and non-institutional means. This dedication, and more importantly the text itself, provoked a host of negative reactions to Gladstone's literary endeavours; the effects of which were long lasting.

The State in its Relations was the culmination of Gladstone's theorizing about the nature of establishment during the 1830s. Heavily indebted to Coleridge, Plato, and Aristotle, the book proposed a confessional state, administered by an educated élite, or clerisy, and defined by its exclusive relationship with the national church.[17] The book was a public relations' disaster for Gladstone. It received scathing reviews from the literati, the most famous being Macaulay's virtuosic savaging in the *Edinburgh Review*.[18] The damage done to Gladstone's reputation was serious. As late as 1860, Walter Bagehot was still condemning the arguments which Gladstone had put forward in his first book in poisonous terms, criticizing him for deliberately placing himself outside the ecclesiastical and political mainstream and characterizing him, in Carlylean terms, as a scholar at odds with 'common Englishmen'.[19]

Gladstone's book also attracted the disapproval of parliamentary colleagues, which was potentially more serious in view of his junior political position. *State in its Relations* and its sequel *Church Principles* were idealistic and theoretical but, as Colin Matthew underlines, they were 'deliberately intended as a guide to Conservatives as they prepared for office'. However, Gladstone's vision was more far reaching than anything his fellow Conservatives, including Sir Robert Peel, envisaged. Peel was as pragmatic as Gladstone was idealistic, with a moderate, but not high, view of establishment.[20] Moreover, Peel had committed himself and Conservatism to appeal to the middle classes,[21] a decision Gladstone's endorsement of the higher abilities of an Anglican parliamentary clerisy to decide national religious matters seemed to oppose. Peel was so incensed by Gladstone's published position that he is said to have thrown the book on the floor in exasperation. Not only was Gladstone's approach perceived as naïve and foolish; such behaviour threatened to undermine party cohesion at a critical time.

Gladstone's reaction to the negative reception of his first book was to withdraw:

> How often, how daily, & this for how many years – ever since my feet were dipped in the turbid stream – do I ask inwardly of Him in whose lap is cast the lot of my destiny, 'shall I ever be a man of study and

of prayer, a man of the cell and of the lamp, of the chair, of the altar, shall I ever cast the burden from my shoulder and flee away and be at rest?'[22]

Gladstone's lifelong preoccupation with retirement was rooted in his understanding of a disjunction between the political opportunities that came before him and his own 'desires & designs in public life [that] lie along another line'.[23] Thus, when Peel offered him the vice-presidency of the Board of Trade in 1841, Gladstone accepted only 'to give himself to pursuits alien to his wishes & habits'.[24] In pragmatic response, Peel 'thought I had better leave the question suspended, & said that in the event of my finding the Govt. policy incompatible with my convictions of duty, my retirement upon such a ground ... would not be attended with the mischief of a retirement on account of general want of confidence'.[25] Peel was well aware of Gladstone's potential, but was concerned that it should be both directed and represented in appropriate and politically helpful ways. He was also keenly aware of the importance of image and concerned about political representation, visual as well as rhetorical. Before the establishment of the National Portrait Gallery and at a time when portraiture itself was suffering unpopularity, Peel was notable for building up a collection of portraits of distinguished contemporaries.[26] He commissioned a portrait of Gladstone in 1843 from John Lucas (1807–74), insisting on plain modern dress, at a time when classicism remained in vogue.[27]

The resulting three-quarter length portrait, Figure 7.4, which offers further evidence of what was seen as desirable in picturing the public man, represents Gladstone dressed in black with a white necktie against a dark background. It was exhibited at the Royal Academy in 1844 but received little attention. *The Athenaeum* judged the artist 'capable of producing a strong and characteristic likeness, and sometimes of rendering the mind, without which the most symmetrical arrangement of features is but a mark.'[28] Crucially the portrait makes no reference to Gladstone's scholarly activities. His left hand holds a parliamentary paper, establishing his identity to observers as yet unfamiliar with his features and also stamping upon him the priorities of his political chief, making him the epitome of the Peelite prescription: a committed servant of the electorate, open, unostentatious, and unromantic. His gaze is direct and earnest, the pose more open than that used by Bradley. The image exemplifies what James Eli Adams suggests was becoming 'a norm of "manliness"' at mid-century: 'honest, straightforward speech and action, shorn of any hint of subtlety of equivocation'.[29]

Figure 7.4 John Lucas, *William Ewart Gladstone* (1843). Glenalmond College.

Gladstone's romantic interiority and long-windedness were clearly at odds with this model. This is not to say Gladstone's public role as politician was incompatible with withdrawal to the privacy of his library, but public display of that withdrawal in representational imagery (or indeed any public or official context) challenged both the primacy of his role as a public man, and its effectiveness. The anonymity of Lucas' painting and its reception serves to underline the precariousness of Gladstone's junior status and the uncertainties surrounding his political reputation, which had not been helped by his (self) representations as a remote scholar and romantic reader, nor by his attempts to resign. Moreover, there is little indication that, at this stage, he himself saw any need to change his image. Indeed, when William Walker of London sought to make an engraving of him in the early 1840s, Gladstone directed him to use Bradley's 1839 painting as a source.[30] The mezzotint, published in

1845, actually exaggerated Bradley's pose and surrounded the sitter with additional accoutrements of scholarship. Moreover, Gladstone remained committed to expounding a particularly unpopular image of the scholar-politician in print.

The scholar-politician

At first glance, Gladstone appears neither unusual as a scholarly and bibliophilic politician, nor as a literary prime minister. Sir Gilbert Scott introduced Gladstone as a speaker at the Royal Academy dinner in 1877 as merely the third (after Derby and Disraeli) in a line of 'successive prime ministers who have made literature the solace of their scanty leisure, and delighted the world by their writings on subjects extraneous to State politics'.[31] A. J. Butler, citing Lord Derby's *Iliad* and fellow Conservative Lord Carnarvon's translations of Homer and Æschylus as illustrations, observed the fact it was 'quite usual' for leading statesmen of Gladstone's generation to pen classical translations.[32] Disraeli had, of course, made his name as a literary figure and enjoyed a popular reputation that neither Gladstone nor his scholarly Conservative counterparts could hope to rival. Valuing books highly, Disraeli not only inherited approximately 4000 titles from his father's library but also collected himself, specializing, like Gladstone, in history, theology, and the classics, and harbouring a particular enthusiasm for early Italian volumes. Disraeli's library at Hughenden, in which Stafford Northcote described him as 'always at his best', was a large, richly furnished, south-facing chamber overlooking the terrace and gardens, well used by both Disraeli and his house guests.[33]

Nonetheless, despite the existence of this well-established literary political culture, Gladstone both perceived himself, and was regarded by others, as operating well beyond its acceptable confines. According to Algernon West, Gladstone definitely made a distinction between his work and that of Lord Derby, whom he criticized for having passed over a passage of religious significance in Homer 'as utterly unimportant', adding, in a backhanded compliment, that Derby had 'trusted to his great genius and natural gifts more than to hard work'! West further recorded that Gladstone also slighted Goschen who 'had never shown any trace of high literary cultivation or classical knowledge'.[34] Early evidence of such one-upmanship comes from Gladstone's 1844 review of Lord John Russell's translations from Dante published in the *Literary Souvenir*.[35] Gladstone delivered a harsh review asserting that Russell had not accorded enough time to his scholarship, alleging that 'it appears to us he has at ten minutes' notice sat down to translate Dante' whereas, to be successful:

> The translator of Dante must imbue and saturate himself with the spirit of Dante. Unless his intellectual being be in great part absorbed in that of his original, he must, we believe, fail in his task, whatever be his native powers.

Dante, Gladstone pronounced, 'is not an after-dinner relaxation' for the busy statesman. Significantly, Gladstone praised Russell's endeavour as evidence that 'the man is not absorbed in the party-man, or even in the statesman; and that a taste may remain for what is beautiful and incorrupt, even after a long immersion in public affairs'.[36] Gladstone plainly believed at this stage that, if one were first and foremost either a partyman or a statesman, one's capacity to operate in the higher realm of thought would be forever inhibited; a certain separateness had to be maintained.

Part of the difference between Gladstone's approach to scholarship and that of other literary politicians, was, according to A. J. Butler, 'the seriousness which he brought to his handling of it'.

> It was no mere reminiscence of youth, or elegant exercise, no diversion to be taken up in the intervals of business or in hours of relaxation from the sterner duties of life. On the contrary, it was always with him.

Unlike Disraeli, who was careful to distinguish between the 'little room' or 'cabinet' in which he worked, and his library where he liked to 'saunter' and 'watch the sunbeams on the bindings of the books',[37] Gladstone's serious addiction to scholarship let commentators such as Butler to be *'tempted to wonder whether it did not hold the first place in his interests'*.[38] Butler's nervous tone speaks volumes about the negativity implicit in such an order of priorities. As Jeff Hearn has theorized, for a man in the public eye, activity in a private domain should essentially be defined and controlled by his public role, not vice versa.[39]

Gladstone's relationship with the painter George Frederic Watts (1813–1904) demonstrates a continuation of these problematic attitudes and tensions up to and beyond 1860. A central characteristic of this relationship was its intellectuality, which directly influenced the process of painting and the images themselves. Gladstone first sat to Watts, whom he found 'very agreeable' on 14 June 1859. Watts painted two canvases from the five 1859 sittings,[40] the first for Hawarden (cover image) and the second for the National Portrait Gallery. Over the next 20 years Gladstone recorded another 11 sittings to Watts, which varied in both congeniality and artistic production. Watts was a slow, deliberate painter, who sometimes exasperated Gladstone,[41] but the statesman found compensation in Watts' conversation;[42] they shared interests in religion and the classics, and had great respect for the other's learning and insights.[43] Both of Watts' surviving portraits are intense, intimate and emphasize the head: Gladstone's dark eyes are accentuated, exaggerating the pallor and skeletal rendering of the face. In 1898 Claude Phillips acknowledged that Watts' 'interpretative portraiture sums up with the higher truth the noblest qualities of mankind', but regretted it represented only 'the intellectual, the emotional personality', an observation which again draws our attention to a continuing unease with overt representation of intellectuality in the public man.[44]

Other evidence supports the conclusion that bad opinion of Gladstone's scholarship also continued to influence assessments of his political, as well as literary, potential. In 1860 his identity and his future in politics were certainly in doubt. Bagehot wrote:

> Who can calculate his future course? Who can tell whether he will be the greatest orator of a great administration ... whether he will be, as his gifts at first sight mark him out to be, our greatest statesman? Or whether, below the gangway, he will utter unintelligible discourses; will aid in destroying many ministries and share in none; will pour forth during many hopeless years a bitter, a splendid, and a vituperative eloquence?[45]

As well as attacking his intellectual proclivities and verbose literary style, Bagehot drew attention to weaknesses in Gladstone's physical presence. Challenging the very constitution of his manliness on the basis of visual evidence, he wrote: 'Mr. Gladstone's energy seems to be strictly intellectual. Nothing in his outward appearance indicates the iron physique that often carries inferior men through heavy tasks.' 'We are all of us in doubt about him', he added: 'if the country have not a true conception of a great statesman, his popularity will be capricious, his power irregular, and his usefulness insecure'.[46] Just as Carlyle's man of letters was required to transmit the fruits of his knowledge to society and so combat its 'disorganised condition',[47] so Bagehot's ideal politician should be able to communicate effectively with and influence the voters in a safe and controlling way: 'In a free country we must use the sort of argument which plain men understand – and plain men certainly do not appreciate or apprehend scholastic refinements'. In 1860, Gladstone appeared to be falling well short of this ideal and seemed 'the last man to obtain' success in parliamentary life.[48] At the time Gladstone would have probably agreed. He had not yet emerged from the political doldrums of the mid-1850s when 'for a while he had the impression of being the most unpopular man in Britain'.[49] However, contrary to Bagehot's predictions and Gladstone's expectations he did succeed in politics and succeeded so far with the general public as to be elevated to the status of icon in his own lifetime.

The 'People's William'

Numerous commentators have discussed the growth of Gladstone's popular image during the years c. 1860–80,[50] with most – in varying degrees – accounting for the genesis of the 'People's William' in terms of three factors: the development of a new brand of mass politics characterized by large crowds and popular speechmaking, the influential role of the press, and Gladstone's personal agency.[51] What has not yet been clarified is the place Gladstone's intellectuality had in either aiding or limiting the success of this particular representation. There is no doubt that, while Gladstone's 'scholastic intellect and ... laborious official training' proved confusing and unpopular in a traditional political context, in the context of mass oratory his scholarly mannerisms were more easily accommodated.[52] In popular oratory Gladstone found a vehicle by which his vaporous style could be used to his own political advantage, a fact he clearly recognized. Discussing the role of the politician in his *Studies on Homer and the Homeric Age* (Oxford, 1858), Gladstone wrote:

> The ... orator['s] ... work ... is inextricably mixed up with practice. It is cast in the mould offered to him by the mind of his hearers. It is an influence principally received from his audience (so to speak) in vapour, which he pours back upon them in a flood. The sympathy and concurrence of his time is with his own mind joint parent of his work. He cannot follow nor frame ideals; his choice is, to be what his age will have him, what it requires in order to be moved by him, or else not to be at all.[53]

This analysis is very different from the abstruse and theoretical thinker represented in Bradley's 1839 portrait. Here Gladstone recognized the need for the orator to be closely attuned to the world in which he operates and to engage symbiotically with his audience. He further learned the political value of being able, in Rosebery's words, 'to say very cautious things in a very bold manner' and to turn the apparent shortcoming of his exuberant verbosity to his political advantage.[54]

Nonetheless, the short-term popular successes of the 'People's William' persona, as Matthew notes, 'had not led to real warmth or popular affection', and were to be checked dramatically during the resignation and retirement crisis of 1874–5.[55] It is argued here that the reasons for this lay largely with the persistence of negative attitudes towards Gladstone's scholarliness in the public sphere, a problem bolstered by Gladstone's continued tendency to retreat into this unpopular persona rather than to develop a more palatable alternative.

Following his attainment of the premiership, Gladstone once again did not appear unusual in his intellectuality when compared to close colleagues.[56] Surely his determination to read into cataract-hampered old age was no greater feat than that achieved by his first chancellor of the exchequer, Robert Lowe, whose albinism meant that reading was impossible in all but the brightest light, conditions which he willingly endured despite excruciating pain?[57] Yet serious doubts about Gladstone's future continued to be voiced – John Bright stated baldly in 1868, 'I do not see him among our public men'.[58] Moreover, Gladstone's public prioritization of his intellectual preoccupations continued to set him apart from his colleagues. Scholarly disagreements were nothing new. For example, A. J. Butler, who had praised Lowe's abilities as a classical scholar, nonetheless observed that his 'manners had not exactly been softened by the cultivation of the literature of antiquity', noting his politically motivated decision not to fund Stanhope's Troy expedition, reproducing as evidence *Punch*'s representation of Lowe and Gladstone at odds over whether or not they should allow their attitudes to Greek literature to influence their policies:

> *Sairey Gamp.* 'Quite right to refuge the money, my precious Bobsey, but I was sorry to read your languidge to that dear Lord Stanhope about Troy, and Achilles, and 'Omer, which it's well beknown I studies 'im day and night.'
>
> *Bobsey Prig.* 'Bother your 'Omers, and your Achilleses, and your Troys! I don't believe as there was ever no such persons!'[59]

Gladstone's perceived difference from his colleagues continued to be visualized in caricature throughout his first ministry. The *Penny Illustrated Paper*, representing the various 'holiday occupations of the Gladstone Ministry' in 1873 (Figure 7.5) contrasted Gladstone – shown

Figure 7.5 'Holiday Occupations of the Gladstone Ministry', *Penny Illustrated Paper*, 9 August 1873, GG MSS. C. A. Gladstone.

at his desk studying classical texts – with colleagues engaged in vigorous outdoor activities.

Moreover, there were signs, particularly in the early 1870s, that Gladstone was not only talking about, but also literally withdrawing from a popular, public stage.[60] Matthew argues that he 'to some considerable extent set aside' the 'People's William' persona, preferring once more to retreat to Hawarden to concentrate on scholarship.[61] We saw in Chapter 2 how Gladstone found it increasingly difficult to find opportunities for such concentrated work even at Penmaenmawr, and Shannon also presents evidence of Gladstone's frustration when politics interfered with his Homeric work just prior to his retirement.[62]

The hermit of Hawarden, 1874–6

Gladstone finally ended his first ministry in January 1874, and formally announced his retirement from the Liberal leadership the following year,[63] having complained in the meantime that his status as an MP ensured 'his activities were necessarily subject to persistent scrutiny', hampering his 'life of "mental repose"'.[64] His withdrawal from public life was, as we saw in Chapter 1, marked by his relinquishment of 11 Carlton House Terrace, the auction of a sizeable portion of his art collection, and the sale of substantial section of his library. This period of retirement was, officially at least, to last until April 1880 when, despite not being official Liberal leader, he was once again asked to form a government.

Shortly after his resignation as Liberal leader, the Tory magazine *Judy* published a cartoon entitled 'Far From the Madding Crowd' (Figure 7.6) which pictured Gladstone in a monastic cell surrounded by theology books.

That *Judy* judged the bookish Gladstone would become both irrelevant and weak as a political force is obvious from the caricature's tag line: 'The recluse of Hawarden, withdrawing from political strife, devoted himself to questions of theology and to pamphleteering. He did not do much harm at this time.'[65] *Punch*'s commentary on the retirement, by John Tenniel, was less vitriolic but equally dismissive, showing Disraeli bidding Gladstone a patronizing goodbye with the words, 'Sorry to lose you! I *began* with books; you're ending with them. Perhaps you're the wiser of the two.'[66]

These negative reactions were in part provoked by Gladstone's immediate arguments for resignation. These were to some extent political – the lack of a 'present public *cause*', and the fact that his 'views on the question of Education in particular' seemed 'irreconcilable with ... a

Figure 7.6 'Far from the Madding Crowd', *Judy*, 27 January 1875. St Deiniol's Library Collection.

considerable portion' of his party, riven as it was by 'serious & contentious divisions of opinion'[67] – but they were also intellectual. 'The main point is this', Gladstone wrote to his wife in March 1875:

> My prospective work is not Parliamentary. My tie will be slight to an Assembly with whose tendencies I am little in harmony at the present time: nor can I flatter myself that what is called the public, out of doors, is more sympathetic. But there is much to be done with the pen, all bearing much on high & sacred ends, for even Homeric study ... is in this very sense of high importance: and what lies beyond this is concerned directly with the great subject of belief. By thought good or evil on these matters the destinies of mankind are at this time affected infinitely more than by the work of any man in Parliament.[68]

In many respects, this pessimism was justified. Catherine Gladstone, well known for her tolerance and supportiveness towards her husband, made no secret of the fact that she found his decision to retire and his intellectualized explanations of it baffling. Colleagues too were flummoxed; Harcourt, for one, regarded Gladstone as simply being in 'the sulks'.[69] Unsurprisingly, Gladstone thought the prospect of a term in opposition under such circumstances, even with the chance of a following government, was 'not consistent with my views for the close of my life'.[70]

Moreover, the sale of Gladstone's 'historical and political library' – the principal source of his political knowledge and decision-making – can be interpreted as an outright rejection of public life, and the attempt to establish an entirely new and separate existence.[71] Gladstone's politics and speech-making were always rooted as much in textual reference and historical analogy as in immediate observation of political situations, and, in 1874, the results of this deductive and scholarly process had proved unacceptable to the electorate. Gladstone's text-sources, especially *Hansard*, physically represented the sum of his political life, learning, and its recent failure. Thus, early in 1874, when facing up to the reality of electoral defeat and resignation, Gladstone was reading about those subjects on which he felt at odds with the world. For example, on Sunday 22 February 1874, he was reading: 'To Rome & Back – Greg's Creed of Christendom – First Principles of Religion – Wilkinson on Education [and] ... Bennett's Defence of Faith', and writing on issues where he felt certain of the integrity of his moral position: Homer and the defence of the Church of England. Gladstone not only read: he tidied his library and also began divesting himself of books. At least three boxes were sent to Oxford's non-collegiate students, which collection formed the basis of St Catherine's College library.[72] This was followed by the transference of his library's politically 'useful' section to Lord Wolverton, who, as a public man, would continually have need of them, while the remaining theological tomes progressed to the sacred space of the Temple of Peace.

The call from Bulgaria

The question now arises: how do we explain, not only Gladstone's *volte face* in the summer of 1876, but also the sustained renewal of his popularity in terms more favourable to his readerly and scholarly persona? There are at least two levels of analysis needed here – one in which we address the question of how Gladstone himself contributed to this rehabilitation of image, and one in which we consider under what circumstances, and as a result of what negotiations, that image became acceptable in the public sphere.

Gladstone's willingness to abandon his theological writing in the summer of 1876, when, even in the midst of preparing a book on future punishment, he 'was called away to write on Bulgaria',[73] has led biographers to doubt the seriousness of, and the religious motivations for, Gladstone's earlier withdrawal.[74] On the contrary, even though Gladstone gave the overwhelming impression of abandoning public life in 1874–5, he did not actually envisage his retirement as a withdrawal from the concerns of the world, but rather as an opportunity to engage with them from a different standpoint. It is true that his explanations were not always easy to understand, but Gladstone's guiding idea was that his withdrawal to Hawarden was done with a specific *public* intention. Moreover, Gladstone's comprehension of his political role was ultimately dictated by the same conviction as his religious vocation: the call of God was a necessary guide to action. His decision to retire in 1874–5 was, as we shall see in a moment, carefully qualified at the time, and his retired status remained importantly contingent upon from whence he discerned such a call: from politics or the church. Thus, when he professed to Manning in 1873, that 'the future of politics hardly exists for me', he added, 'unless some new phase arise and ... a special call ... appear'; in 1874 he described his plan to revitalize Liberal politics as 'a very special responsibility' and told Arthur Peel that he did not see why 'public men who have given their best years to the service of the country' should be 'bound, in the absence of any strong and special cause, to spend ... old age ... in the career of stress and contention';[75] he mentioned to Catherine those 'exceptional circumstances which would have to provide for themselves', and told Speaker Brand: 'I do not mean ... to renounce any opportunity of effecting any great national good which time may bring about and in which it may be open to me to take a share'.[76]

The Turkish massacre of Bulgarian Christians in 1876 proved to be the special political cause that Gladstone had theoretically anticipated: 'My desire for the shade ... has been since August rudely baffled: retirement & recollection seem more remote than ever', he wrote despondently in December. 'But', he added, it 'is in a noble cause, for the curtain rising in the East seems to open events that bear cardinally on our race'. This conception of an opportunity to contribute through public politics to a universal moral cause had strengthened by the end of 1877 when Gladstone wrote: 'tho' I have not been busied as I could have wished and schemed, the part assigned to me in the Eastern Question has been a part great and good far beyond my measure'.[77]

Not only did Gladstone's interest in Bulgaria renew his enthusiasm for his surviving political and historical books as he prepared his 'Bulgarian Horrors' pamphlet,[78] it also associated him with a new constituency, a constituency which had previously been largely indifferent, if not actively hostile, to him. Whereas many intellectuals had been unimpressed by Gladstone's esoteric and apparently sectarian ideas regarding church establishment and anti-Vaticanism, basking in their status as detached and somewhat anti-clerical observers,[79] they were already fully exercised in opposition to Turkish atrocities and in favour of downtrodden nationality, and could appreciate the advantage of recruiting Gladstone as an ally. Gladstone, moreover – although initially somewhat reluctant to be involved – was, for once, willing to defer to the opinion of leading minds (other than his own) on the new topic which preoccupied him.[80] Gladstone's recognition of the role of good fortune in his favourable reception on the public stage was therefore not unwarranted, as this proved a very serendipitous convergence of interests. On one level, Gladstone was not prepared to change his own intellectual position for the sake of politics, but his increasing employment of a universal moralizing rhetoric,[81] as well as his growing use of the language of political independence in his public discourse,[82] seemed to suggest that his abiding hope, that he might be able to persuade others to accept his conception of politics as 'a second-order activity' in comparison with the '"higher" contemplation of religion and scholarship',[83] dashed in 1874–5, had been realized by the end of the 1870s.

This was no permanent change, however. Gladstone's intellectual position and ideological intentions were viewed with continuing uncertainty even after the Bulgarian campaign had begun in earnest. *Punch*, for example, represented Gladstone as an Arcadian woodcutter completely out of step with public opinion.[84] That even Gladstone's woodcutting could be tarred with negative associations shows how firmly assumptions were set against his scholastic character and how successful his renegotiations over Bulgaria had been. Nonetheless, further work was required to perpetuate such an alliance. Fortunately for him, Gladstone managed to carry over a measure of his separateness and withdrawal successfully into his political rebirth, promoting an independent and autonomous political persona to which a variety of audiences readily responded. Matthew observes how Gladstone began his Midlothian campaign 'emphasizing his separateness: "I am come among you as a stranger"', like one of the Judges of the Old Testament who arrive from nowhere when need arises and then disappear back into the wilderness.[85] Thus, in 1881 Gladstone could describe Midlothian to Bright as 'a special and temporary mission', and inform Newman that:

> I have a feeling that mankind is not now principally governed from within the walls of Cabinets and Parliaments – higher issues are broadly revived, and higher interests are in question, than those with which Ministers and Opposition mainly deal; and it is by subtler and less obtrusive instruments that the supreme wisdom acts upon them.[86]

The similarity between this rhetoric and Gladstone's 1874 discourse on the impact a scholarly life in retirement might have on 'the welfare of mankind' is striking. On the eve of his triumphant return to the forefront of political life, Gladstone had written:

> For the last 3 ½ years I have been passing through a political experience which is I believe without example in our Parliamentary history. I ... believe it has been an occasion, when the battle to be fought was a battle of justice humanity freedom law, all in their first element from the very root, and all on a gigantic scale. The word spoken was a word for millions, and for millions who themselves cannot speak. If I really believe this then I should regard my having been morally forced into this work as a great and high election of God. And certainly I cannot but believe that he has given me special gifts of strength, on the late occasion especially in Scotland.[87]

Employing a discourse which mixed Calvinistic assurance, humanitarianism, and political independence, Gladstone articulated his belief that he had once again discerned – in the popular reception he received during the Midlothian campaign – God's call to undertake a public life in politics. There is little recognition here of his own role in such changed circumstances. What part did Gladstone play in shaping and encouraging the reinvigorated personality cult that increasingly enswathed him?

Making the Grand Old Bookman

There has been disagreement among scholars over this issue. For instance, whereas Matthew considers that Gladstone possessed 'an acute and purposeful flair' for publicity,[88] Biagini plays down contemporary reports of Gladstone's self-promotion, suggesting they were blown out of proportion by 'hostile observers', and argues instead that Gladstone 'was quite restive about satisfying his fans' expectations', and often instead deputed public relations to his sons.[89]

Biagini's analysis correctly identifies an underlying ambivalence and tension in Gladstone's attitude to his popularity, but he understates its complexity and shifting nature. Central to the change was the politicization and visualization of Gladstone's private life in the late 1870s, which involved a conscious reinterpretation in Carlylean terms of Gladstone's physical leisure activity.[90] Despite the unpopularity of his scholarliness, Gladstone, as Peter Bailey has argued, epitomized one important characteristic of Victorian masculinity, that of characterizing leisure as a change of work, which was exemplified 'in his retreat from the toils of office to the arduous pleasures of tree felling on his estate at Hawarden'.[91] Gladstone's purposeful identification of leisure with work rather than idleness was lifelong, and was widely recognized by contemporaries.[92] Bailey and Biagini are right to highlight Gladstone's tree felling and its iconic significance as central to understanding later constructions of his masculinity.[93] However, by concentrating on the woodsman in isolation, we have been in danger of ignoring other, apparently subordinate identities.[94] The way in which the power and symbolism of the woodsman impacted on representations of Gladstone's domestic and scholarly life has been less well documented, and the role Gladstone's intellectuality played in his later popular success has been almost entirely ignored.

The hero woodcutter

Woodcutting imagery drew on a long tradition of radical discourse but had also been used specifically by Carlyle.[95] In 'The Hero as Divinity', he wrote:

> Among the Northland sovereigns ... I find some who got the title *Wood-cutter*; Forest-felling Kings. Much lies in that ... I suppose the right good fighter was oftenest also the right good forest-feller, – the right good improver, discerner, doer and worker in every kind; for true valour, different enough from ferocity, is the basis of all.[96]

It is no surprise that Gladstone 'noticed' this passage in his copy of Carlyle's lectures.[97] By choosing tree felling as the form of recreational labour in which to engage, Gladstone was directly associating himself with the Carlylean idealization of the worker. Crucially, he was also involved in visualizing this representation.

On 4 August 1877, a party of 1400 Bolton trippers visited Hawarden, an occasion Gladstone described as follows: 'We were nearly killed with kindness. I began with W[illy]. the cutting of a tree; and had to speak to them, but not on politics.'[98] The *Times* reported 'the very splinters which flew from his axe were picked up and treasured as relics'.[99] This was no exaggerated claim. William Houghton of 2, Gladstone Place, Farnworth, near Bolton wrote to Gladstone on 3 October 1877 to tell him how he and his family treated the wood chip that they had secured:

> I carried it home as a treasure. I have decorated it and put it under a glass shade, and put a card in front of it to commemorate the work of that day. Scores of people come to my home to look at it, bothe

[sic] Liberals and Tories, and I must say their [sic] is not one that has not praised it to the greatest extent. I shall keep it as an heir loom during my life time, and I hope my children will do the same.[100]

Two days after Houghton's visit, Gladstone and Willy once again 'were photographed' cutting wood. The resulting images explicitly reveal the often tense negotiations which took place between Gladstone and the image makers.[101] One of these photographs (1877; NPG) was definitely taken by Bolton photographer William Currey, who may have been connected with the trippers. The other two photographs (1877; Flintshire Record Office) were clearly taken on the same occasion. One (Figure 7.7) shows Gladstone and Willy on either side of a huge tree.

Figure 7.7 William Currey, *William Ewart Gladstone and William Henry Gladstone* (1877). Flintshire Record Office Photographic Collection.

This shot has been hurriedly posed: Willy's head is out of focus, Gladstone obviously displays the stump of his left index finger which was invariably concealed,[102] and both stare suspiciously at the camera. The locus of power clearly lies with the photographer. However, despite this, Gladstone permitted the photographer at least two more exposures, for which he sat down among the woodchips and posed more carefully (Figure 7.8).

Thus, he displayed the axe prominently, hid his mutilation, and averted his gaze. By such a negotiated compromise, Gladstone succeeded in wresting to himself a significant element of control over these

Figure 7.8 William Currey, *William Ewart Gladstone* (1877). Flintshire Record Office Photographic Collection.

images: an important realignment considering how such representations, as Jeff Hearn has observed, take 'power from the photograph to the image,' on commencing 'circulation in the public domain'.[103] These and similar images ensured working-class readers and viewers 'found a great statesman and popular leader in the plain clothes of the labourer: a most suggestive vision for democratic fantasy, pregnant with precise moral and political values and as eloquent as a long speech'.[104] Houghton indeed noted how 'pleased' he and his wife were 'to see a man in your capacity strip off his clothes down to the waiste [sic]' and 'going to work as a woodman'.[105]

Gladstone's woodcutting became emblematic of myriad political cartoons, but it was also incorporated into other aspects of Gladstone's domestic life. In another photograph (Figure 7.9) Gladstone leans on a felled tree, axe over shoulder but this time fully dressed in jacket and tie and surrounded by his wife and family, photographed against the backdrop of their home. Thus the politicized message of the woodsman invigorates a simple domestic scene.

The propriety of Gladstone's family life, however, needed little boosting, unlike his scholarly identity, which remained associated with those early negative representations discussed above. However, by the time of Gladstone's final retirement in 1894, his literary pursuits were being marketed quite differently, with G. W. E. Russell describing the event as: 'no sooner was this [political] work out of hand than the indefatigable workman turned his attention to graver studies'.[106] Russell's central

Figure 7.9 Gladstone and Family Woodcutting (n.d.) Flintshire Record Office Photographic Collection.

implication – that Gladstone's literary employment was physically exhausting – allied it with nineteenth-century idealizations of manual labour, articulated in texts such as Carlyle's *Past and Present* (1843) and Ford Madox Brown's painting *Work* (1852–65).[107] This directly challenged identifications of Gladstone's scholarship with weakness and effeminacy, interpreting them instead in more positive, useful, and manly ways.

The heroism of brainwork

The woodcutter representation was a crucial catalyst in changing depictions of Gladstone's scholarship; a process which is explicit in the work of Sydney Prior Hall (1842–1922). Two of Hall's paintings depict Gladstone reading. The first, *Gladstone Reading the Lesson in Hawarden Church* (1892; NPG), Figure 7.10, records another of Gladstone's well-publicized activities.[108]

Figure 7.10 Sydney Prior Hall, *Gladstone Reading the Lesson in Hawarden Church* (1892). National Portrait Gallery, London.

Figure 7.11 Sydney Prior Hall, *Gladstone Reading in the Temple of Peace* (n.d.). National Portrait Gallery, London.

There are similarities between Gladstone's pose in this image and the one he habitually adopted in parliament: hands resting on the dispatch box, body rigid and expression combative; there is clearly no tension inherent in this type of 'public' reading. The second, undated image (Figure 7.11) represents Gladstone privately reading in the Temple of Peace.

He is shown reclining on a chaise longue, framed by the tools of scholarship, and completely engrossed in reading. A stray book, momentarily balanced on his legs, completes the outline. Nothing could seem farther from the active woodsman than this reclining figure. However, a fascinating watercolour study for this painting reveals a remarkable linkage between the two personae (Figure 7.12).

The central figure is still Gladstone reclining, but instead of the besuited gentleman, we are presented with the labouring woodcutter in shirtsleeves, displaying a brawny forearm reminiscent of the labourers in Brown's *Work*. Something of this figure's litheness is also present in the finished portrait, especially in the impressionistic brushwork which defines the thighs, but it is the study which is the key to understanding how the changing interpretation of Gladstone the reader depended on a successful blending of two apparently distinct and incompatible iconographies.

Hall's portrait formed one of an increasing number of images (especially after 1879) that presented Gladstone reading in his Hawarden library or

Figure 7.12 Sydney Prior Hall, *Gladstone Reading in the Temple of Peace* (Watercolour Study) (n.d.). National Portrait Gallery, London.

Downing Street study. The proliferation of this category of image was due to a clear alteration in Gladstone's treatment of artists, which built on his re-negotiation of the boundaries of artistic control with photographers like Currey during the 1870s. As I have argued more fully elsewhere, Gladstone was progressively irritated by the controlling conditions imposed on him by artists and, as he had done with photographers,[109] set about deliberately changing the terms under which he allowed artists to paint him.[110] He increasingly only permitted informal sittings invariably located in his library or study.[111] Gladstone was aware of the pioneering and unconventional nature of what he was doing and how his relationship with artists was changing. The novelty of his approach was also fully appreciated by the artists themselves and was especially well attested by John McLure Hamilton (1853–1936).[112]

Gladstone had agreed Hamilton could paint in the Temple of Peace in the mornings if he did not ask for formal sittings. He thus represented Gladstone in natural poses, reading and writing, in a series of drawings and three portraits (1890, Musée d'Orsay; 1892, Pennsylvannia Academy of Fine Arts; c. 1896, Hawarden Castle, Figure 7.13).

Hamilton's series is dominated by the library setting and Gladstone's work within it, and his description of painting such private and

Figure 7.13 John McLure Hamilton, *William Ewart Gladstone sitting at his literary desk in the Temple of Peace* (c. 1896). C.A. Gladstone.

domestic scenes alerts us to the potential impact they may have had on contemporaries. Hamilton described himself 'inspired and invigorated' by the experience and overwhelmed by 'a tumult of ideas' inspired by the sight of Gladstone reading.

> The man I was painting, what he stood for in the Empire, his picturesqueness, his surroundings, the contrast of great power and extreme simplicity, and above all, to me, the ease and comfort of working before one who seemed to be absolutely unconscious of my presence.[113]

Hamilton's iconic interpretation of Gladstone reading affirms the way in which such domestic and scholarly imagery could effectively be politicized. The contrast they offered to mainstream political representation ensured they could both challenge and surprise the viewer. By 1890, Gladstone's reputation was gigantic and yet Hamilton stressed none of his familiar political characteristics. The power of his representations lay in the opportunity they afforded the viewer to gaze on the apparently unconscious, private behaviour of a public man. There was great demand for such visualized access.[114] As the photography pioneer William Fox Talbot observed: 'what a dénouement we should have if we could suppose the secrets of the darkened chamber to be revealed by the testimony of the imprinted paper'?[115] Hamilton himself encouraged this appetite for privileged insight by underlining the fact that Gladstone lived 'in two spheres, a public and a private, the former for and with the people, the other in and for his family'.[116] His representations gained much potency by first constructing and then consciously straddling the boundaries between these spheres and offering a wider public exclusive access to a private, family world. Hamilton's vision was endorsed by Mary Drew, who confirmed his work's naturalness and truth to life.

> For there was the man exactly as we knew him – exactly as day after day we saw him ... Here was no fancy picture, but one of familiar everyday use. Precious for all time, for us and for those that come after us, the man as he actually was – intent – unconscious.[117]

Mary identified the representation of the private family man as the main reason for her approbation. However, her prediction of its relevance to 'all time' and 'for those that come after' confirms that the reading figure was to be understood as a universal and politically engaged image.

But how conscious was Gladstone of the artist? The activities of reading and writing depicted in these representations clearly signal Gladstone's detachment and withdrawal. In all Hamilton's images, as well as those by Hall, A. E. Emslie, and Pierre Troubetskoi, and also in contemporary photographs depicting similar scenes, Gladstone is completely absorbed in his own work, apparently unaware of artist and viewer. However, Hamilton, unlike Mary Drew, suspected Gladstone was 'always conscious of what transpired around him without in the least appearing to be'.[118] In this he was supported by Frank Hill, editor of the *Daily News* who was certain Gladstone's demeanour, 'gestures and changes of his posture and play of countenance, though not addressed to the lookers-on ... are yet shaped, and informed and controlled by the consciousness of hundreds of watchful eyes and commenting tongues'.[119]

A telling example of this consciousness dates from 1896 when Gladstone was photographed for the *Westminster Gazette*'s account of St Deiniol's Library.

> The G.O.M., with face as ruddy from the crisp air as an apple ... with eagle-eyes, taking in everything around ... walks erect, and looks in better health than he has done for some years past.

Has he promised to be specially photographed for the Westminster account of the Library scheme? Very well, then it must be so. Stand here, at the door? Hat off or on? Look at those yellow leaves? And there he stands, hat in hand, motionless; the Octogenarian, to whom to be photographed is anything but a pleasure, but who subjects his own wishes to those of others.

Initially, allusion is clearly made to the popular image of the political Gladstone – eagle-eyed and vigorous, before he distances himself from the implications of the publicity exercise in which he is involved and adopts a passive attitude to the photographer. However, immediately following the shoot, Gladstone unilaterally withdraws into the library where he settles down to read in full view of the journalists outside, who subsequently describe him as having 'an expression of perfect repose and peace about him, [as] he sits quite absorbed'.[120] Gladstone thus successfully withdraws, through an act of reading, from participation in an obviously staged episode into a more ambiguous and powerful position. By observing him supposedly unawares through the library window, the press can claim greater accuracy of representation and privileged access; in turn Gladstone demonstrates non-involvement in publicity while in fact maintaining significant control over his representation.

Further links were made between the work Gladstone did in Downing Street and at Hawarden. Hamilton represented Gladstone similarly in both Hawarden and London, and Troubetskoi represented the scholar in Downing Street. Hulda Friederichs emphasized that the 'brain-work' in which Gladstone engaged was inspired by the same qualities that, when expressed in a public sphere, made him the object of popular veneration. His library was represented as a place of useful work rather than as a symbol of privilege or a scholar's ivory tower. The 'Grand Old Bookman' was continuing the work of popular liberalism albeit from inside a Castle library.

A photograph of Gladstone in the Temple of Peace, *c.* 1885, shows him busily writing at his political desk (Figure 7.14). The cluttered desk and full wastepaper basket testify to the intensity of his work. This concentrated activity contrasts with the stillness of the surrounding space and supplies its dynamic focus. Some photographs of the Temple of Peace included the figure of Gladstone as an imposed drawing, for example, in the photograph by Catherall and Pritchard of Chester reproduced in *Black and White*'s 'Gladstone Memorial Number'.[121] Such simulation was thought necessary because it was important that

Figure 7.14 Gladstone in the Temple of Peace (c. 1885). Flintshire Record Office Photographic Collection.

Gladstone's scholarly activity undertaken in retirement should be represented as active and beneficial to the public interest, an end which would not be served by illustrating the library as an empty and unused room. This above all indicated the importance of the library space itself as a defining environment for later representations of Gladstone, giving it both contemporary relevance and an indomitable individuality. The book as representative image of knowledge was generally recognized throughout society; books, scrolls, and the ephemera of scholarship were the stock-in-trade of the portraitist and studio photographer. However, its sheer universality threatened ultimately to render it meaningless, displaying subjects in thrall to the vagaries of convention and mere fashion. There are many images of Gladstone, which use the book merely as a prop and are little different to equivalent photographs of his contemporaries.[122] There was however a marked difference between these and the photographs and portraits showing Gladstone among his own books. It is true that the texts themselves usually remain unnamed and still function as representations of universal knowledge and scholarship, but these images strongly emphasize Gladstone's individuality and autonomy.[123] The interiors of the Temple of Peace and Downing Street were being used 'as personal expression of the soul, private mirror, and public expression of the owner's personality'. The interior and contents operate 'as the representation of its owner to the outside world'. They were also clearly 'addressed to a public', establishing Gladstone's status as collector, reader and scholar by the utilization of an identifiable environment.[124]

Gladstone's withdrawal into his study and his reading shows him exercising that autonomy which Carlyle and others celebrated in male writers and thinkers in the nineteenth century.[125] Moreover, Gladstone, as well as visually representing such autonomy, called in print for a morally renewed polity to be achieved through the concerted effort of each and every autonomous individual. Thus in his 1887 article on 'The Unity of History', he wrote:

> It seems to me that what we *must* do in the world of action, we at least *may* do in the world of thought; those of us, I mean, whose branch of labour belongs to or includes that world. Take any branch of mental effort, be it ... educative, creative, inquisitive, or materially productive, none should be pursued without a purpose, and all real purpose, though it may be atomic, is permanent and indestructible. All bear upon human relations and the conditions of life, and each ... should have its place in the great design. The farmer, said Mr. Emerson, is man upon the farm. Each writer is bettering (if he be not worsening) the thought, the frame, or the experience of man, upon the subject on which he writes, works, or teaches; he is enlarging the text; he is extending the bounds of the common inheritance.[126]

Gladstone was at last writing, albeit in an explicitly Christian way, like Carlyle had done 40 years before when he had described the function of the man of letters and his interaction with society. Gladstone's reference to Emerson reminds us of the prime importance of autonomy in both his later political and scholarly endeavours. Both had a public, moral agenda, the central aim of which was to advance and communicate human knowledge. Furthermore, his cultivation of a persona of separateness – in both his public rhetoric and private performance – actively encouraged his crucial elevation, in the public mind, to a status above that of an ordinary individual; a status Geoffrey Cubitt adumbrates as one of the key characteristics of the hero.[127] Gladstone was no longer the Oxford stooge nor even a party man. He was an autonomous individual living and working to an extent outside institutions – a fact made explicit by representations of him in his own library.

Rehabilitating the reader

There are, of course, good reasons why such an autonomous, apparently non-partisan, but still intellectually charged representation should have been both welcomed and further promoted by Gladstonian supporters in the later 1880s and 90s. The acrimonious splits engendered by

Gladstone's espousal of Home Rule meant that many straightforwardly political representations of him were no longer going to be as effective. Thus many popular tributes to Gladstone made unprecedented levels of reference to his literary and scholarly life to confirm his Liberal credentials. For instance, a speaker at the Primitive Methodist conference in Derby in 1886 actually cited Gladstone's scholarly contribution 'to the nation and to the cause of humanity at large' before mentioning his (contested) political contribution.[128] Furthermore, persistent representations of Gladstone as reader and scholar visually supported his and his supporters' calls for a universal re-education over the Irish issue. While Gladstone's campaigning on the Eastern Question may have endeared him to the intelligentsia, his Home Rule campaign alienated many of them. For all the academic tone of parliamentary debate on the issue – constitutional lawyers and historians were cited for evidence – Liberal academics, as Collini notes, tended to be overwhelmingly Unionist in their sympathies.[129] The strength of this opposition provided some of the motivation for Gladstone's strong appeal, over the heads of the 'classes', to the judgement of the 'masses'; it also bolstered the survival of that negative strand of commentary which so diametrically opposed Gladstone's political and intellectual concerns.

Criticism of Gladstone was still regularly articulated through visual references to his reading or scholarly retirement on occasions when he appeared reluctant to actively involve himself in matters of public interest. For example, during 1884, an unconcerned Gladstone was repeatedly shown being confronted in his library by pressing political problems, on one occasion personified by the figure of a fearsome Boer.[130] Even within the most favourable commentary, echoes remained of anti-intellectual rhetoric. For instance, despite its favourable comparison of the Temple of Peace with 'the comfortless vastness of foreign *châteaux* and the pretentious splendour of the suburban villa of the *nouveau riche*', The World still referred to Gladstone in his library as the 'scholar-recluse', and as 'the hermit of Hawarden'.[131] Moreover, despite the fact that Gladstone had fully justified his return to politics in 1880 to himself, and met with confidence-boosting acclaim, he found the old tensions persisted between political life and his other intellectual concerns. In 1882 he recorded: 'the sad ungovernable nausea with which I return to the performance of the offices which this life of contention imposes upon me as duties. It is not anything particular in the life, it is the life itself'.[132] Gladstone's confidence in the rightness of both his scholarly and political activities remained fundamentally frail. Whereas the rapid diminution of the popularity of the 'People's William', and its dramatic check during 1874–5, were aggravated by Gladstone's continued tendency to retreat into an unpopular persona, the difference in later years was that such negative representations were increasingly outweighed by new and more positive ones, not only shaped and promoted by Gladstone himself, but also eagerly embraced by beleaguered supporters wishing to focus on Gladstone's abilities divorced from the negative connotations of Home Rule.

Such promotions apparently proved acceptable to many working-class Gladstonians. The belief that Gladstone's actions, both political and scholarly, were motivated by a political desire to benefit the common people was widespread, and continued after his death. As W. T. Stead explained:

> He was a man whose intellect they respected, even if they did not understand. 'He is a capable man, a practical man, a ripe scholar, and an experienced statesman; if it is good enough for him, it is good enough for us.' So reasoned many men more or less logically.[133]

Assertion of working-class affirmation was central to the final representations of Gladstone the reader, made following his death in the early hours of 19 May 1898. This survey of the history of the changing representations of Gladstone's scholarship ends by looking at Gladstone's death and the significant role the library and the politicized image of the scholar played in the theatre surrounding the event.

The body in the library

Following Gladstone's death his body was taken on a lengthy and elaborate progress from deathbed to burial, which included three periods of lying in state and was visually recorded throughout. This imaging spanned the multifarious public and private representational categories that had been established during his life and confirmed Gladstone's library as the ultimate site of his public and private identity.

The first representations of Gladstone after death took the form of three sketches produced by William Blake Richmond, an artist who had painted Gladstone twice in life.[134] His was a private tribute, commissioned by Gladstone's family, which followed well-established conventions in post-mortem representation, concentrating on the head, shoulders, and hands, and featuring no accessories.[135] Richmond did not shy away from representing Gladstone's altered, sunken features, but laid them on a flat plane with minimal background, equivalent to the vignette technique common in post-mortem photography. There are no known photographs of this scene; one was published of the bed in which Gladstone died but after the body had been removed to lie in state.[136] Richmond does not seem to have drawn the body at this second stage; his role, as a trusted friend, was to produce these intimate images in order to capture the truly private and familial Gladstone before his body was displayed to the public.

Several days after death, Gladstone's remains were removed to Hawarden Church and from thence, by train, to Westminster Hall in London. Before either of these displays, Gladstone's body underwent a lying in state in the Temple of Peace, an event which constituted the most elaborate, iconic, and revealing stage of his journey to the grave, and underlines the importance the representation of Gladstone the scholar had attained by 1898.

A series of photographs was taken of Gladstone's body in the Temple of Peace by J. H. Spencer of Chester and show the corpse reposing on a couch-like bier with its head towards the west (Figures 7.15 and 7.16).

These are clearly neither private nor personal images. In contrast with Richmond's drawings, the trappings and background of the scene dominate at least half the available image space, exemplifying an important distinction between post-mortem and lying-in-state portraits, the category into which these images most closely fit. The public display of the body at a lying in state presented the opportunity for political statement. This was usually conveyed by the dress that covered the corpse, the furnishings on and around the bier, and the decoration of the room.[137]

Three important characteristics of this scene stand out. Firstly, these images lack straightforward political or religious iconography. Secondly, the political messages that are present are mediated through the iconography of Gladstone as reader and scholar. Thirdly, this tableau establishes an insistent harmony between the body and its location: for example, the study's name is reflected in the Latin text supporting Gladstone's head: 'REQUIESCAT IN PACE': Rest in (the Temple of) Peace. In contrast to the scene depicted by Richmond, Spencer's subject forcefully exhibited this by then familiar iconography. Gladstone is dressed in his doctoral robes recalling J. E. Millais's powerful images of him in the same dress, which had privileged Gladstone's vital and animalistic qualities and the dominance of his political persona.[138] The reclining figure is also reminiscent of S. P. Hall's painting of Gladstone reading on his chaise longue. Gladstone's continued presence in his own library with all its associations of scholarship, retirement, and serious work bolster the honorary status of his doctorate of civil law, while the robes are a

230 *Reading Gladstone*

Figure 7.15 J. H. Spencer, *Gladstone lying in state in the Temple of Peace* (1898). National Archives, London.

Figure 7.16 J. H. Spencer, *Gladstone lying in state in the Temple of Peace* (1898). National Archives, London.

potent reminder that Gladstone's identity as a scholar has been fully recognized and publicly acclaimed.[139] Gladstone is represented reposing in a room that had become popularly synonymous with his position as autonomous Liberal sage, a point made by the following description of the scene:

> Before his remains were handed over to the authorities to lie in state so near to the scene of his many triumphs, a humbler but perhaps more beautiful lying in state took place at Hawarden, in the room which had been so closely identified with his home-life, and so much written and spoken about as the Temple of Peace, now surely the temple of his peace. There he lay on an extemporized bier, with his scarlet doctoral robes about him, his noble face, spiritualized by suffering nobly borne, so calm and beautiful in the tender spring light, the thin hands clasped upon his breast in token that his work was done: there he lay while the people of the village and the neighbourhood, rich and poor, people who had known and looked up to him so long, entered and gazed and passed reverently out; 'the rough labourer coming in with heavy boots and a stout cudgel in his hand, and going away with a tear trickling down his brown cheek; the bent old man holding his hat in his hands, and tottering up with infirm step; the little children, clinging to their mothers' garments; the lads and lasses, – rosy-cheeked and solemn – they were all there to take a last farewell'.
>
> Nor were these all. Many came long distances, especially from the north, to get a glimpse of the face of him of whom they had heard so much and by whom they had been so greatly benefited. So all day long the crowd surged in and out, silent and awe-struck, until the shades of evening fell, when the last group passed lingeringly away, casting a final farewell look at the white, still face … None who saw that lying in state will ever forget it.[140]

This description indicates the subtle, but insistent political iconography in the arrangement of the library space and the body's place within it. The room was cast as a potent symbol of the people's perceived knowledge of Gladstone the man. It signified the pervasive belief in a personal relationship with Gladstone, fostered by myriad images and descriptions of the place where he spent much of his time.[141] The fact that the mourners had a privileged opportunity to view the body itself, not the closed coffin, is highlighted. Many would not have seen Gladstone at such close range and this again allows the author to underline the statesman's status as ultimate man of the people. 'Everyman' comes to view the body and Liberal progress is represented and endorsed by the procession of ages from the child to the old man. But above all it is the figure of the weeping labourer who both attests Gladstone's support for the working man and asserts the validity of heroic manual labour, paying respectful tribute not only to Gladstone the hero-woodcutter but also to Gladstone the independently minded 'brainworker', the personification accepted and favoured, crucially, by a popular audience. It is testimony to the ultimate success and significance of 'Gladstone as scholar', problematic and unpopular for so many years, that this image was used as the most appropriate summary representation of his identity and his achievements the last time his body was presented to the public.

*

Gladstone's frequently opaque intellectualism and its unpopular associations with outmoded views of church and state had the potential to alienate the masses as well as his own contemporaries and intellectual equals, and yet the above reactions to his death underline how ultimately potent were images of his learning. The body of the active Gladstone, situated within his library, had proved a convenient and effective symbol of his intellectual stature and his heightened political credentials at times when straightforward political representations were being fiercely contested. The image of his dead body in the library served as an equally powerful and self-reflexive image. Gladstone's presence in the place the public had come to associate with him in his last years provided an important continuity with their perceptions of his persona. Their trust in him had been well placed and was now cemented in the changelessness of death. It was a powerful legacy to those who would claim his political mantle.

The library can thus be seen ultimately as the central locus for Gladstone's whole existence, shorthand symbol for his liberal, democratic, and above all autonomous activity in later life and the appropriate resting-place for a period of stasis between the struggle of death and the final leave-taking. Prominent and fashionable men of letters like Bagehot and Macaulay had concentrated their attacks on ridiculing Gladstone's verbose literary style. They had predicted that this, above all, would prevent Gladstone succeeding in politics despite his other obvious accomplishments and might even make him dangerous if his oratory were misinterpreted by the masses. However, Gladstone turned this apparent shortcoming to his political advantage. Furthermore, although he maintained his private devotion to the Oxford ideal to the end of his life, Gladstone, and his Liberal publicists, increasingly saw the political advantage of re-casting his public image in a Carlylean mould of autonomous independence. This involved not only images of Gladstone involved in manual labour and homely pursuits, but also of his scholarly activities. These changes in attitude and representation were clearly spearheaded by Gladstone himself; it was not an official propaganda campaign orchestrated and managed by the Liberal Party *per se*. However, particularly in the face of party splits over Home Rule, his diverse champions increasingly saw the advantages of working with the grain of Gladstone's own self-formation. As a result, by the end of his life, Gladstone's scholarship and his frequent periods of seclusion in the study at Hawarden featured regularly in published material both celebrating his life and career, both actively promoting (and to an extent obscuring) the policies he supported. As we have seen, those who opposed Gladstone continued to try and make capital from his other-worldly intellectualism. However, these attempts proved less and less telling, especially when Gladstone's supporters ceased to be on the defensive about this aspect of his persona and, following his lead, integrated it fully into a representation of a different, 'truer' kind of political figure who transcended ordinary party politics and entered the realm of the heroic.

Thus, after his death, the hallmarks of Gladstone's Oxford education, which had been ridiculed by witty men of letters, were the objects of veneration by respectful Hawardeners who viewed Gladstone's body in the Temple of Peace. There his body remained, soliciting universal recognition for his autonomous and 'manly task of expanding scientific knowledge'.[142] That he could be described after his death as 'eminently a man of practice, always occupied in grappling with the problems of the moment' even though he was 'active-minded and fond of study' represented a remarkable rehabilitation of image.[143]

Conclusion

Gladstone read widely and eclectically, not just because Victorian polymaths like him did, or even because he had the leisure to do so. On the contrary, his contemporaries repeatedly recognized that – although he neither possessed the grandest library nor universally impressed them with his scholarship – Gladstone the reader was in many ways an extraordinary figure; an individual for whom book-reading formed not only the bedrock of his understanding of his own identity, merit, and mission, but also constituted the key delimiter of his daily life.

Gladstone's reading was driven by, in the first place, an open and indefatigable, if not undiscriminating, intellectual curiosity, an attribute sharpened by his upbringing in a disputatious, affectionate, evangelical, and patriarchal home, dominated by book culture. Gladstone remained profoundly influenced by his earliest reading experiences, the advice he received from his parents, and by his own preference for the opinions of others above, as he saw it, his own unformed and unreliable judgements. Throughout his youth, Gladstone had been surrounded by texts and people who portrayed and valued reading, not so much as a tool by which to carve out material success and enhance social status – although neither motive was absent – but rather as the key to a moral, well-balanced, and enlightened understanding of the world and human interaction. As a result he formulated a high ideal of study, which combined private, religious introspection with public duty, accompanied by a desire to share the fruits of education and knowledge with a wider society.

He therefore from the outset dedicated himself to the task of seeking out the best possible knowledge available to him, a position that he aspired to attain by adopting an inclusive approach to reading. On picking up a book, Gladstone may only have read part of it, or concluded it was of inferior quality or of dubious morality, but he would always attempt to engage with it rather than dismiss it out of hand, believing, as he did, that 'good advice is to be remembered come how it may'.[1] This inclusive approach to reading has tremendous ramifications for how we understand and characterize him.

In the first place, Gladstone's inclusive reading method ensured that the practices of collection, reading, and organization were activities with uncertain and widely varying results. While books gave Gladstone ample opportunities to create the order he was determined to achieve in his life; they also frequently proved themselves ungovernable and the generators of the chaos he abhorred. Books were sources of solace, stress relief, and spiritual fulfilment; yet they also could serve as beguiling snares and encouragements to sin. Nonetheless the collecting instinct and the desire to learn – occasionally obsessive and dangerous as they were – remained fundamental to his schemes for self-education and improvement.

The reading methods and rhythms which developed as the outward signs of these inward convictions were also necessary because Gladstone patently neither had, nor allowed himself, unlimited amounts of time for sustained study. Gladstone's practice of concentrated reading on particular topics has long been remarked upon. On matters as diverse as animal husbandry and the question of divorce, Gladstone would regularly cram in order to bolster arguments he wished to make both in and out of parliament. Nonetheless, more fundamental influences – lifelong and profound – were also crucial. Evidence of Gladstone's greatest textual influences, which included the languorously diffuse but memorable phraseology of the English Bible, the mystical visions of Dante, the romantic lyricism and intimations of 'everhanging Doom' pervading Scott,[2] and the creeds of human heroism and nationality delineated by Homer and Tennyson, found their way into Gladstone's prose, both directly, by way of quotation, and also indirectly by way of allusion.[3] Moreover, the way in which he interchanged texts, introduced new matter and mentally compared it to established favourites, and marked passages of equivalence, provided Gladstone with an intertexual understanding which profoundly influenced his appreciation of the ways in which religions and cultures had developed and ought to progress in the future. His conviction that the Homeric epics and the Hebrew scriptures both testified to divine revelation, made sense in a reading world where Homer and the Bible were interchanged on a daily basis. His personal discovery of uncanny echoes of ancient wisdom in modern texts therefore contributed a great deal to shaping his understanding of human history and progress, and helped raise the category of 'humanity' to an exalted place in his understanding.

Reading was for Gladstone not merely a matter of hermeneutics – the interior art of interpretation – it was significantly also the springboard for his exegesis – or expository discourse – to others. Gladstone's preoccupation with the generational transmission of knowledge was a conviction that long-sustained and informed his religion, his politics, and his personal actions. He sought to convey the fruits of what he felt he had learned from books both intimately and directly: through the mutually educative experience of reading aloud, as well as in more mediated and diffuse ways such as the carefully gauged allusion to a well-known and well-loved author in a popular speech. For his contemporaries, there was no getting away from Gladstone as reader. He might accost them directly on a train, divert their attention from pressing political matters to a discussion of books, or encourage them to read rather than visit the public house.[4] When not reading, Gladstone was fond of engaging people in conversation during train journeys, but he was especially pleased when he found 'a *reader* in the train'![5] This behaviour was rooted in Gladstone's conviction that, in order for one generation to gain the knowledge it required to live and work actively, it was essential that it take account of that accrued by those that had gone before.

This quasi-missionary zeal and sense of assurance was, however, only part of the story. Gladstone's reading and his use of his library also illuminate uncertainties and insecurities integral to a sense of self: his political role and vocation; his role as son, husband, and father. As has been argued throughout this book, it is important to recognize Gladstone's uneasy and ambiguous relationship with the world of high politics. In many ways Gladstone was not a 'natural' politician. From his initial, thwarted desire to go into the ministry of the Anglican church, he was dogged with uncertainty about whether politics was really his true vocation, and throughout his life he periodically questioned the extent to which it truly reflected his identity or ideals as either a private or public person. Gladstone's passion, priority, and first source of guidance remained his Christian faith. In many ways his theological reading and writing were produced in response to the religious vocation that he continued to discern, and functioned as mechanisms by which he could distinguish the sacred and secular spheres in his life. Moreover, Gladstone conceived himself not only as a Christian in politics but also as an intellectual in politics. Partly due to the problems he had coping with the stresses of public responsibility, but also due to a sense of intellectual alienation, Gladstone periodically imposed a strict division between his public and private worlds and sought to do work for the public good from within the private context of his library, the most extreme example of which behaviour being his 1874–5 retirement discussed in Chapter 7. It was on occasions such as these that the library operated primarily as a private space.

However, as we saw in Chapter 4, the privacy of the Temple of Peace was in many ways deceptive. In practice the library simultaneously operated as a private space for Gladstone's reading and as a semi-public space for his family, neighbours, and friends to read and borrow. Moreover, its walls did not provide a fail-safe barrier against either the concerns or the temptations of the world; or to the gaze of the public.

As we have seen, Gladstone's library space was made available to the public through increasingly prolific representation in word and image, a circumstance with great import for his contemporary reception. Gladstone's persona as scholar-statesman was central to his public reputation. By presenting himself as a rarefied Oxford scholar at the beginning of his political career, Gladstone adopted a deeply unpopular persona. Fashionable Victorian men of letters and the public at large saw no advantage, attractiveness, or prospects in a politician whose loyalties and priorities seemed suspect, and Gladstone's continued tendency to retreat into his private, library world at moments of stress aggravated the situation.

This is not to say that Gladstone remained impervious to the implications of such unpopularity. As Chapter 7 demonstrated, negative attitudes to his scholarship were at first tempered, before being recast, by the skilful representation of Gladstone's private, scholarly persona in a new, negotiated public sphere – a project he both sponsored and carefully manipulated, and which was increasingly welcomed by supporters desperate to reclaim ground lost as a result of the Home Rule debacle. So successful was this project that the library ultimately served as an important, unifying locus of Gladstone's popular political image, appropriated by various differing British identities, of class and nation, middle and upper as well as lower class; Scottish, Welsh, and Irish as well as English.

The role of the reading in Gladstone's life is crucial in understanding the role he envisaged for his library after his death. Gladstone came to understand theology, not as a defensive and exclusive force for shoring up old dogmas, but as an inclusive and relevant system of knowledge that could make a difference in solving a variety of contemporary problems. This belief was rooted in the complex and ever-developing systematization of Gladstone's religious thought, but was later tempered by his increasing involvement in large-scale humanitarian campaigns in the public sphere – such as the Bulgarian agitation of 1876 – the success of which reinforced his instinct that theology should be practised in, rather than apart from, the secular world. By his reading and reviewing of Seeley's *Ecce Homo*, the literature of faith and doubt, and his engagement with unorthodox belief, Gladstone showed an increasing broadness in his theological outlook and eventually embraced a recognizably liberal catholic position – a result encouraged and fostered by his close intellectual as well as social relationship with the members of the *Lux Mundi* group in Oxford. Gladstone's enthusiasm for liberal catholicism's central aim of fostering a reconciliation between Christianity and the circumstances of modern life was, as Chapter 6 demonstrated, the galvanizing motivation behind his foundation of St Deiniol's Library. Here he founded a non-sectarian institution 'upon the widest basis',[6] with 'inexpensive lodgings together with congenial society',[7] where visiting scholars could 'attempt to put the Catholic faith into its right relation to modern intellectual and moral problems', in the conducive atmosphere of the Welsh countryside.[8] This fraternization was not encouraged with the expectation that faith would be compromised. On the contrary, such broadened knowledge would improve the ability of Anglicans to communicate, with 'positive plainness', and with increased success, the first principles of their faith to a wider society.[9]

When Gladstone spoke or wrote about St Deiniol's, he described the intellectual work that he envisaged going on there as 'divine learning'. As he told a group of Yorkshire Liberals who visited him in 1895: 'stores of Divine learning occupy the first place on these shelves and undoubtedly the maintenance and promotion of it has been in the foundation of this library an object very near my heart'.[10] The definition of this term has proved somewhat fugitive to historians and successive library administrators. It has been suggested that 'divine learning' was Gladstone's way of describing the liberal education he had experienced at Oxford – the classical language, history, and philosophy of *literae humaniores* coupled with divinity.[11] However, on the basis of his memoranda and other writings, it is clear that Gladstone used 'divine learning' as a straightforward synonym for theology. This was theology in its broadest sense. As J. C. Story observed, St Deiniol's was 'a monument of Mr. Gladstone's interest in theology, and an expression of his belief that so far from theology being a declining science, it is one which will make ever increasing demands upon the mind of man'.[12]

As he further made clear to his Yorkshire audience, 'stores of Divine learning ought, in my judgement, to be associated with stores of human learning'. The point of engagement between the two was vital. Theology, as Gladstone had come to realize, could not survive independently, cut off from engagement with other intellectual disciplines or from the circumstances of everyday life. During the autumn of 1889 Gladstone briefly considered renaming the library 'The Monad', which explicitly reflected this understanding of the library as a space in which theological and other types of knowledge were to be unified, and form the basis of a new epistemological consensus.[13]

As we saw in Chapter 6, Gladstone's relationships with liberal catholicism and his St Deiniol's foundation were not without their tensions. St Deiniol's was both a radical, open, and liberal venture, as well as being an intellectually idealistic and overwhelming clerical vision. However, by so holding in tension both liberalism and catholicism, the institution was an authentic outgrowth of the character of Gladstone the reader. Books and reading challenged his preconceptions and his tendencies towards intolerance, broadened his mind, and galvanized his actions. Conversely, and almost paradoxically, Gladstone likewise found in his books – as both texts and as material objects – an unchanging resort and a perennial comfort for a mind constantly preoccupied by the possibilities and perils of change. In this way, 'the books of St Deiniol's tell more of the kind of man William Ewart Gladstone was than could any sculpted marble or storied brass'.[14]

Notes

Prelims

1. W. E. Gladstone, '*Universitas Hominum*: or, the Unity of History', *North American Review*, 373 (1887), pp. 589–602, pp. 601–2.
2. J. C. Story, *The Hawarden Temple of Peace: a description of St Deiniol's Library* (Hawarden, 1905), p. 10.

Introduction

1. 'Mr. Gladstone at Hawarden', *Harper's New Monthly Magazine*, 64:383 (1882), pp. 741–51, p. 751.
2. M. R. D. Foot and H. C. G. Matthew, eds, *The Gladstone Diaries: with prime ministerial correspondence*, 14 vols (Oxford, 1968–96), vol. 14, p. xi. Hereafter *GD* with volume number and/or date.
3. 'The Best Memorial for Mr. Gladstone', *The Library* (1898), p. 261, quoted in F. W. Ratcliffe, 'Mr Gladstone, the Librarian, and St Deiniol's Library, Hawarden', in *Gladstone, Politics and Religion*, ed. P. J. Jagger (London, 1985), p. 49.
4. W. Roberts, 'Bookworms of Yesterday and To-day: The Right Hon. W. E. Gladstone, M.P.', *The Bookworm*, 30 (1890), pp. 161–5.
5. This extended version of an 1894 *Westminster Budget* article was one of the earliest texts written to publicize the Hawarden library and is a key document for understanding the reception of Gladstone's reading and librarianship in a public sphere. See especially, Chapters 5 and 7.
6. A. J. Butler, 'Mr. Gladstone as a Scholar', in *The Life of William Ewart Gladstone*, ed. T. Wemyss Reid (London, 1899), pp. 135–54, p. 135.
7. David Williamson, *Gladstone the Man: a non-political biography* (London, 1898); J. D. Smith, *A Non-Political Treatise of and Tribute to the Late William Ewart Gladstone* (Newport, 1898).
8. J. Gardiner, *The Victorians: an age in retrospect* (London and New York, 2002), p. 182.
9. R. Jenkins, 'Gladstone and Books', in *The Grand Old Man: sermons & speeches in honour of W. E. Gladstone (1809–1898)*, ed. P. B. Francis (Hawarden, 2000), pp. 21–6, pp. 21–2.
10. T. L. Crosby, *The Two Mr Gladstones: a study in psychology and history* (New Haven, CT and London, 1997), p. 11.
11. Bebbington has also published a useful short popular biography, *William Ewart Gladstone: faith and politics in Victorian Britain* (Grand Rapids, MI, 1993), as well as two important chapters on Gladstone's Homerics: 'Gladstone and Grote', in *Gladstone*, ed. P. J. Jagger (London and Rio Grande, 1998), pp. 157–76; and 'Gladstone and Homer', in *Gladstone Centenary Essays*, ed. R. Swift and D. Bebbington (Liverpool, 2000), pp. 57–74.

12. D. Bebbington, *The Mind of Gladstone: religion, Homer, and politics* (Oxford, 2004), p. 11.
13. Bebbington, *Mind*, pp. 2, 5. In its concentration on what were, in many ways, élitist aspects of Gladstone's interior life – something particularly true of its extensive and involved coverage of Victorian Homeric scholarship – the book does not address those key issues of popular reception and representation vital for understanding the practical function of Gladstone's reading and book collection in his relationships with a variety of publics, societies, and individuals. This is also a limitation of J. S. Meisel, *Public Speech and the Culture of Public Life in the Age of Gladstone* (New York, 2001).
14. W. R. McKelvy, *The English Cult of Literature: devoted readers, 1774–1880* (Charlottesville, VA and London, 2007), Chapter 5, pp. 180–220.
15. McKelvy's analysis is also undermined by his almost complete refusal to engage with Bebbington's work. *Mind* is cited in the book's bibliography and endnotes but not referenced in the text, and there is no meaningful discussion of Bebbington's earlier Homeric chapters. See also, W. R. McKelvy, 'William Ewart Gladstone', in *Nineteenth-Century British Book-Collectors and Bibliographers*, ed. W. Baker and K. Womack, *Dictionary of Literary Biography* (Detroit, Washington, DC and London, 1997), pp. 161–72.
16. Ratcliffe, 'Librarian'; P. J. Jagger, *Gladstone, Politics, and Religion: a collection of Founder's Day lectures delivered at St. Deiniol's Library, Hawarden, 1967–83* (New York, 1985); P. J. Jagger, 'Gladstone and His Library', in *Gladstone*, ed. P. J. Jagger (London, 1998), pp. 235–53; T. W. Pritchard, *A History of St Deiniol's Library* (Hawarden, 1999).
17. H. C. G. Matthew, *Gladstone 1809–1898* (Oxford, 1997), p. 553. Jenkins calls the library 'a sort of advance memorial'. R. Jenkins, *Gladstone* (London, 1995), p. 565. See also, M. J. Christensen, 'St Deiniol's Library, Hawarden: the Gladstone National Memorial' (unpublished MA thesis, University of Liverpool, 2000).
18. See, principally, R. Shannon, 'Too busy reading', *Times Literary Supplement* (5 Nov. 2004).
19. Arguing that, while the theme was 'intrinsically interesting', it appeared 'rather lightweight when set beside ... powerful political analyses'. M. Lynch, 'Review of Jagger, *Gladstone, Politics, and Religion*', *Victorian Studies*, 29:3 (Spring 1986) p. 489.
20. E. Biagini, *Gladstone* (London, 2000); M. Partridge, *Gladstone* (London, 2003); R. Shannon, *Gladstone: Peel's inheritor 1809–1865* (London, 1982); R. Shannon, *Gladstone: heroic minister, 1865–1898* (London, 1999). It should be noted that the attention given to ideas in Biagini's more expansive work, see, for example, his recently published *British Democracy and Irish Nationalism 1876–1906* (Cambridge, 2007), constitutes a slightly less traditional approach.
21. S. Collini, 'Review of Shannon, *Gladstone: Heroic minister*', *Guardian* (8 May 1999). An opinion echoed by E. Biagini, 'Review of Shannon, *Gladstone: heroic minister*', *Reviews in History* (Feb. 2000), http://www.history.ac.uk/reviews/paper/gladston.html.
22. P. Magnus, *Gladstone: a biography* (London, 1954), p. 425.
23. See P. Jalland, *Death in the Victorian Family* (Oxford, 1996), p. 144.
24. There are shorter essays which seek to employ this analytical category. See, for example, M. Sinha, '"Chathams, Pitts, and Gladstones in Petticoats": the

politics of gender and race in the Ilbert bill controversy, 1883–1884', in *Western Women and Imperialism: complicity and resistance*, ed. N. Chaudhuri and M. Strobel (Bloomington, IN, 1992), pp. 98–116; R. Clayton Windscheffel, 'Politics, Portraiture and Power: reassessing the public image of William Ewart Gladstone', in *Public Men: masculinity and politics in modern Britain*, ed. M. McCormack (Basingstoke, 2007), pp. 93–122.

25. See, for some recent examples: W. M. Kuhn, *The Politics of Pleasure: a portrait of Benjamin Disraeli* (London, 2006); I. Davidson Kalmar, 'Benjamin Disraeli, Romantic Orientalist', *Comparative Studies in Society and History*, 47:2 (2005), pp. 348–71; B. Glassman, *Benjamin Disraeli: the fabricated Jew in myth and memory* (Lanham, MD, 2003); T. M. Endelman and T. Kushner, eds, *Disraeli's Jewishness* (London, 2002); J. Parry, 'Disraeli and England', *Historical Journal*, 43:3 (2000), pp. 699–728; C. Richmond and P. Smith, eds, *The Self-Fashioning of Disraeli, 1818–1851* (Cambridge, 1998); B. Hilton, 'Disraeli, English Culture, and the Decline of the Industrial Spirit', in *A Union of Multiple Identities: the British Isles, 1750–1850*, eds L. Brockliss and D. Eastwood (Manchester and New York, 1997), pp. 44–59; N. Valman, 'Muscular Jews: Young England, Gender and Jewishness in Disraeli's "Political Trilogy"', *Jewish History*, 10:2 (1996), pp. 57–88; A. Wohl, '"Ben JuJu": representations of Disraeli's Jewishness in the Victorian political cartoon', *Jewish History*, 10:2 (1996), pp. 89–134; A. Wohl, '"Dizzi-Ben-Dizzi": Disraeli as Alien', *Journal of British Studies*, 34 (1995), pp. 375–411.

26. *Punch*, 'Critics', 14 May 1870.

27. For a recent example, see R. Aldous, *The Lion and the Unicorn: Gladstone vs Disraeli* (London, 2006). For a convincing rebuttal, see, R. Quinault, 'Gladstone and Disraeli: a reappraisal of their relationship', *History*, 91:304 (2006), pp. 557–76.

28. See J. S. Meisel, 'The Importance of Being Serious: the unexplored connection between Gladstone and humour', *History*, 84:274 (1999), pp. 278–300.

29. For example, see the recently published A. Isba, *Gladstone and Women* (London, 2006); and J. West, 'Gladstone and Laura Thistlethwayte, 1865–75', *Historical Research*, 80:209 (2007), pp. 368–92.

30. See, H. Lloyd-Jones, *Blood for the Ghosts: classical influences in the nineteenth and twentieth centuries* (London, 1982), Chapter 9; A. Ramm, 'Gladstone's Religion', *Historical Journal*, 28:2 (1985), pp. 327–40. For a more positive account, pre-Bebbington, see F. M. Turner, *The Greek Heritage in Victorian Britain* (New Haven and London, 1981). See also, McKelvy, *English Cult*, p. 203 ff.

31. See, for example, A. Ramm, *Gladstone as Man of Letters. A James Bryce Memorial Lecture* (Oxford, 1981); W. S. Peterson, 'Gladstone's Review of "Robert Elsmere": some unpublished correspondence', *Review of English Studies*, 21:84 (1970), pp. 442–61; G. Joseph, *Tennyson and the Text: the weaver's shuttle* (Cambridge, 1992), pp. 129–40; P. Erb, 'Politics and Theological Liberalism: William Gladstone and Mrs Humphry Ward', *Journal of Religious History*, 25:2 (2001), pp. 158–72; K. Campbell, 'W. E. Gladstone, W. T. Stead, Matthew Arnold and a New Journalism: cultural politics in the 1880s', *Victorian Periodicals Review*, 36:1 (2003), pp. 20–40; P. Waller, *Writers, Readers, and Reputations: literary life in Britain 1870–1918* (Oxford, 2006), *passim*.

32. See D. Beales, *History and Biography: an inaugural lecture* (Cambridge, 1981); R. Clayton, 'Gladstone, Tennyson and History: 1886 and All That', *Tennyson Research Bulletin*, 8:3 (2004), pp. 151–65.
33. As well as Bebbington's work, see J. Gardner, 'William Ewart Gladstone and Christian Apologetics, 1859–1896' (unpublished Ph.D. thesis, University of York, 2005).
34. P. J. Jagger, *Gladstone: the making of a Christian politician* (Allison Park, PA, 1991). Other important studies of this period, as well as of Gladstone's first two books, include A. Vidler, *The Orb and the Cross: a normative study in the relations of church and state with reference to Gladstone's early writings* (London, 1945); R. J. Helmstadter, 'Conscience and Politics: Gladstone's first book', in *The Gladstonian Turn of Mind: essays presented to J. B. Conacher* ed. B. L. Kinzer (Toronto, 1985), pp. 3–42; Ramm, 'Gladstone's Religion'.
35. P. Butler, *Gladstone: Church, State and Tractarianism: a study of his religious ideas and attitudes, 1809–1859* (Oxford, 1982). See also P. Erb, 'Gladstone and German Liberal Catholicism', *Recusant History*, 23:3 (1997), pp. 450–69; J. D. Bastable, ed., *Newman and Gladstone* (Dublin, 1978).
36. B. Hilton, 'Gladstone's Theological Politics', in *High and Low Politics in Modern Britain*, ed. M. Bentley and J. Stevenson (Oxford, 1983), pp. 28–57; B. Hilton, *The Age of Atonement: the influence of evangelicalism on social and economic thought 1785–1865* (Oxford, 1988).
37. J. P. Parry, *Democracy and Religion: Gladstone and the Liberal Party, 1867–1875* (Cambridge, 1986).
38. Butler, *Tractarianism*, pp. 234–5.
39. Magnus, *Gladstone*, p. 429; Shannon, *Gladstone: heroic minister*, p. 477.
40. Boyd Hilton associates Gladstone's admiration for Butler with a continued stress on evangelical tenets, namely sin and atonement. Hilton, *Age of Atonement*, pp. 340–61.
41. W. E. Gladstone, ed., *The Works of Joseph Butler*, 2 vols (Oxford, 1896). See also, W. E. Gladstone, *Studies Subsidiary to the Works of Bishop Butler* (Oxford, 1896).
42. J. Garnett, 'Bishop Butler and the Zeitgeist: Butler and the development of Christian moral philosophy in Victorian Britain', in *Joseph Butler's Moral and Religious Thought: tercentenary essays*, ed. C. Cunliffe (Oxford, 1992), pp. 63–96. In this important article, Garnett identifies Butler's moral philosophy as one of the most crucial resources for the late nineteenth-century liberal apologists determined to revalidate the intellectual warranty of a theological knowledge which had been severely battered by myriad scientific developments. Garnett, 'Butler and the Zeitgeist', pp. 76–9.
43. Garnett, 'Butler and the Zeitgeist', p. 74.
44. Bebbington, *Mind*, p. 307.
45. F. Turner, 'Review of Bebbington, *The Mind of Gladstone* (2004)', *English Historical Review*, 122:495 (2007), pp. 211–13, pp. 212–13.
46. Among the first studies to pioneer such an approach in historical studies were P. Joyce, *Democratic Subjects: the self and the social in nineteenth-century England* (Cambridge, 1994); M. Poovey, *Making a Social Body: British cultural formation, 1830–1864* (Chicago, IL, 1995); J. Vernon, ed., *Re-reading the Constitution: new narratives in the political history of England's long nineteenth century* (Cambridge, 1996); J. Lawrence, *Speaking for the People: party, language*

and popular politics in England, 1867–1914 (Cambridge, 1998); J. A. Epstein, *In Practice: studies in the language and culture of popular politics in modern Britain* (Stanford, CA, 2003). While many have followed in their wake, the linguistic and cultural 'turns' have not been uncontested. See, for instance, M. Bentley, 'Victorian Politics and the Linguistic Turn', *Historical Journal*, 42 (1999), pp. 883–902.

47. M. Nixon, 'Theory and Method in the Work of Samuel Rawson Gardiner' (unpublished Ph.D. thesis, University of Stirling, 2004).

48. R. D. Altick, *The English Common Reader: a social history of the mass reading public, 1800–1900* (Chicago, IL, 1957); R. Hoggart, *The Uses of Literacy: aspects of working-class life* (London, 1957).

49. The ideas of 'reader-response' critics, such as Stanley Fish (*Is There a Text in This Class? The authority of interpretive communities* [Cambridge, MA, 1980]); Wolfgang Iser (*The Act of Reading: a theory of aesthetic response* (Baltimore, MD, 1978) and *The Implied Reader* (Baltimore, MD, 1978)); and Hans Robert Jauss (*Towards an Aesthetic of Reception* (Minneapolis, MN, 1982)) have been particularly influential.

50. See, for example, R. Chartier, *The Cultural Uses of Print in Early Modern France* trans. L. G. Cochrane (Princeton, NJ, 1987); *The Order of Books*, trans. L. G. Cochrane (Cambridge, 1994); *Forms and Meanings* (Philadelphia, PA, 1995); R. Darnton, 'What is the History of Books?' *Daedalus*, 111 (1982), pp. 65–83; and *The Kiss of Lamourette: reflections in cultural history* (New York, 1990).

51. For example, 1991 saw the inauguration of the Society for the History of Authorship, Reading, and Publishing, founded to bring together scholars working on the history of the book who had been largely isolated in other disciplines up to this date. See http://www.sharpweb.org to see the breadth of their remit. An important collection of essays, which was both a product of this burgeoning, and has itself proved influential is J. Raven, H. Small, and N. Tadmor, eds, *The Practice and Representation of Reading in England* (Cambridge, 1996). For some recent publications, see J. Raven, *The Business of Books: booksellers and the English book trade 1450–1850* (New Haven, CT, 2007); and S. Colclough, *Consuming Texts: readers and reading communities, 1695–1870* (Basingstoke, 2007).

52. The central text here is K. Flint, *The Woman Reader, 1837–1914* (Oxford, 1993). There is a particularly strong representation from early modern studies in the history of reading. See, for example, E. Snook, *Women, Reading and the Cultural Politics of Early Modern England* (Aldershot, 2005); and K. Sharpe, *Reading Revolutions: the politics of reading in early modern England* (New Haven and London, 2000).

53. Jonathan Rose's work is of particular importance. His book on the intellectual life of the British working classes has been a considerable influence upon my own work. See J. Rose, 'Rereading the English Common Reader: a preface to the history of audiences', *Journal of the History of Ideas*, 53 (1992), pp. 47–70; and *The Intellectual Life of the British Working Classes* (New Haven and London, 2001).

54. See, for example, L. Smith and J. H. M. Taylor, eds, *Women and the Book: Assessing the Visual Evidence* (London and Toronto, 1997).

55. R. Chartier, 'Texts, Printing, Readings', in *The New Cultural History*, ed. L. Hunt (Berkley, CA, 1989), pp. 154–75, p. 150.

56. J. Powell, 'Small Marks and Instinctual Responses: a study in the uses of Gladstone's marginalia', *Nineteenth Century Prose*, 19:3 (1992), pp. 1–17, p. 2.
57. *GD*, vol. 14, p. v.
58. *GD*, vol. 14, p. v.
59. Powell, 'Gladstone's Marginalia', pp. 2–3. See also D. Beales, 'Gladstone and his Diary: "Myself, the worst of all interlocutors"', *Historical Journal*, 25:2 (1982), pp. 463–9.
60. *GD*, vol. 14, p. v.
61. Heather Jackson, in her book on marginalia, credited much of the success of her research to the existence of a number of important searchable, electronic library catalogues. H. J. Jackson, *Marginalia: readers writing in books* (New Haven and London, 2001), p. 8.
62. See, Jackson, *Marginalia*, p. 6.
63. Powell, 'Gladstone's Marginalia', p. 3.
64. Jackson, *Marginalia*, p. 262. Jackson, the acknowledged expert on the study of marginalia, exhibits only limited interest in Gladstone as a reader. She notes the 'remarkable record of his reading' and the preserved, annotated books at St Deiniol's, but ultimately concludes – on the basis of Powell's article and Colin Matthew's biography – that Gladstone 'does not seem to have been a very forthcoming annotator'. Jackson, *Marginalia*, pp. 73–4. Her lack of interest mainly stems from the fact that Gladstone does not accord with her book's main priorities, which are to study – if possible – 'minor or unknown readers' (p. 9), and 'discursive notes ... as opposed to the minimal and equivocal witness of the question mark or cross' (p. 14). Nonetheless, the methodological underpinning of Jackson's work has had a considerable influence on my reading of Gladstone's marginalia.
65. Powell, 'Gladstone's Marginalia', p. 6.
66. T. Jones, 'Marginal Notes by Mr. Gladstone', *Cylchgrawn Llyfrgell Genedlaethol Cymru / The National Library of Wales Journal*, 4 (1945–6), pp. 50–2, p. 50.
67. Powell, 'Gladstone's Marginalia', p. 13.
68. Jackson, *Marginalia*, p. 87.
69. H. J. Jackson, ed., *A Book I Value: Samuel Taylor Coleridge selected marginalia* (Princeton and Oxford, 2003), p. xx.
70. See Matthew, *Gladstone*, pp. 555–6.
71. H. Friederichs, *In the Evening of his Days: A Study of Mr. Gladstone in Retirement, with Some Account of St. Deiniol's Library and Hostel* (London, 1896), p. 117.
72. Jackson, ed., *A Book I Value*, p. xiv.
73. See R. Clayton, 'W. E. Gladstone: an annotation key', *Notes & Queries*, 246:2 (2001), pp. 140–3.
74. Powell, 'Gladstone's Marginalia', p. 4.

1 *Sacred Dramas*: The History of a Collection, 1815–96

1. *GD* 25, 29/6/92; 2/7/92.
2. *GD* 4–8/7/92. Composition was first encouraged by the American philanthropist Andrew Carnegie (1835–1919) and then by one of Gladstone's most significant friends and confidents, John Emerich Edward Dalberg Acton, first Baron Acton (1834–1902), historian, philosopher, and bibliophile.

Potentially extremely lucrative, Gladstone worked sporadically on the autobiography until 1897 but it was never published. See Matthew, *Gladstone*, pp. 621–2. See also, Gladstone's draft memoranda in J. Brooke and M. Sorensen, eds, *The Prime Minister's Papers: W. E. Gladstone*, 4 vols (London, 1971), vol. 1.

3. BL GP, Add MS 44790 fols 5–25, 8 Jul. 1892, in Brooke and Sorensen, eds, *PMP*, vol. 1, pp. 13–15.
4. Brooke and Sorensen, eds, *PMP*, vol. 1, p. 15.
5. Gladstone's correspondence with Bernard Quaritch (1819–95), the prominent London bookseller, is preserved at BL.
6. *Times*, 24 Dec. 1896, p. 4.
7. T. F. Dibdin, *The Library Companion; or, the Young Man's Guide, and the Old Man's Comfort, in the Choice of a Library* (London, 1824).
8. GD 3/9/25, 17/10/25.
9. GD 17/1/26, 23/8/26, 28–9/4/28. See also, for example, GD 29/5/26, 30/4/28, 29–30/5/28, 7–8/10/29, 27–8/10/29.
10. T. Wemyss Reid, ed., *The Life of William Ewart Gladstone* (London, 1899), p. 35.
11. GD 29/1/39, 11/7/37.
12. GD 8/1/39.
13. GD 29/5/79. T. Sykes, 'Dialogues between a Minister of the Church and His Parishioner' (1823), discussed in W. E. Gladstone, *Gleanings of Past Years*, 7 vols (London, 1879), vol. 7, p. 216.
14. G. Angus, 'Mr. Gladstone's Heraldry', *Notes & Queries* (1898), p. 466.
15. These catalogues had an afterlife as Gladstonian relics. G. W. Smalley, 'Mr. Gladstone. Reminiscences, Anecdotes, and an Estimate', *Harper's New Monthly Magazine*, 97:577 (1898), pp. 476–88; 647–55; 796–802, p. 651.
16. E. W. Hamilton, *Mr. Gladstone: a monograph*, 3rd edn (London, 1899), pp. 67–8. Note Heather Jackson's observation that annotators are, by nature, 'self-conscious readers'. Jackson, *Marginalia*, p. 81.
17. W. E. Gladstone, 'On Books and the Housing of Them', *Nineteenth Century*, 27 (1890), pp. 384–96, p. 388.
18. See, for example, GD 28/11/50.
19. GD 26/1/88.
20. Hawarden FRO, Glynne-Gladstone MSS 1560, Rough Draft of Book Order.
21. Attested by: 'Mr. Gladstone as a Bookman', *The Sketch*, 25 May 1898, p. 6; M. Drew, 'Mr. Gladstone's Library at "St. Deiniol's Hawarden"', *Nineteenth Century and After*, 59:352 (1906), pp. 944–54, p. 947; W. A. Woodward, 'The Personal Interests of Mr. Gladstone', *Pearson's Magazine* (1898), pp. 306–12, p. 312.
22. *Times*, 24 Dec. 1896.
23. Gladstone, 'On Books', pp. 384–5.
24. Gladstone, 'On Books', p. 385. See also, p. 389.
25. Thus we read him imploring his father in 1823 to be allowed to bid at a library sale: 'There are some wh[ic]h w[oul]d be very useful to me & will in a little time be absolutely <u>necessary</u>. These I sh[oul]d get ... very cheap most likely. I write therefore to say, that with your permission, my Dearest Father, I intend to buy some of those which will be necessary to me in the 6th form.' FRO GG 222, 5 Oct. 1823, WEG to JG. His request was given 'ready acquiescence'. FRO GG 394, WEG to ARG, 18 Oct. 1823.

26. Gladstone did not take all his books to Eton with him. In 1820, he wrote to his mother: 'Please be so good as to thank my father for his kind promise concerning my books. I shall not take them to Eton with me.' FRO GG 394, WEG to ARG, Jun. 1820.
27. For instance, his father reassured his son about his Fell prize of '£40 per ann[um]: I wish you to keep it & dispose of it otherwize in Books, or as you like'. FRO GG 637, JG to WEG, 8 Dec. 1829.
28. S. G. Checkland, *The Gladstones: a family biography 1764–1851* (Cambridge, 1971), p. 215.
29. See *GD* 27/11/27–1/12/27. Several of Gladstone's leaving books survive in or have been returned to SDL. English literature was clearly a popular choice: Samuel White's gift was C. Symmons, *The Life of John Milton*, 3rd edn (London, 1822). The presentation from E. L. Robertson, Gladstone's cousin, was a volume of Alexander Pope's poetical works with a 'Life', and engraved portrait of the author. This book is testimony to the mobility that to some degree affected Gladstone's collection, for the volumes now contain the later bookplate of Frederick, Baron Wolverton, brother and heir to the Lord Wolverton to whom Gladstone sold a portion of his library in 1875 (see below). Both volumes are handsomely bound and neatly inscribed with the date and donor's name. On receipt, Gladstone further established his ownership of the books by adding his armorial bookplate (although this statement was somewhat undermined by his pasting one of them in upside down)!
30. *Times*, 24 Dec. 1896.
31. For example, he read and annotated White's gift of Symmons's Milton two decades after receiving it, with particular reference to two of his absorbing passions at the time: the divorce question and Homer. See *GD* 12/6/57 ff and *GD* 22/6/57 ff.
32. The earliest diary entry dates from 1825, when Gladstone ordered 'another book-case' for his Eton lodgings, *GD* 10/10/25. When at Christ Church he explained to his mother: 'My books are some of them put up' but 'I have new bookcases to get (& making bookcases is a work of time)', FRO GG 394, WEG to ARG, 23 Jan. 1830.
33. See Gladstone, 'On Books', p. 388.
34. *GD* 24/12/50.
35. *GD* 3, 6/3/52. See also, *GD* 28/2/52.
36. Gladstone does not seem regularly to have kept supplementary material, taken from other sources such as journals and newspapers, either loosely preserved, or pasted in, at the front of his books. See, for analysis of this practice, Jackson, *Marginalia*, p. 25. As can be seen from the Glynne-Gladstone manuscript collection, and the speeches and pamphlets collection in St Deiniol's, Gladstone preserved such material separately. He did, however, often keep letters, sent to accompany gift books, inside the volumes concerned, and would use visiting cards, envelopes, and other scraps of paper as temporary bookmarks.
37. A griffin, clutching a dagger in its claw, rises from a wreath. The family motto, 'Fide et virtute', by faith and valour, is written on a banner above.
38. As such, it was very similar to the Fasque house library bookplate, and to that of Tom Gladstone, also, until recently, preserved in books at Fasque. This tradition continued among Gladstone's children. For example,

Gladstone's son Henry copied his father's bookplate almost exactly, while the youngest son, Herbert, used a bookplate which represented his father reading in old age at his literary desk in the Temple of Peace. This elaborate *ex-libris*, which is preserved in, among other books, Herbert's set of Charles Dickens's works at SDL R 36 D/2, testifies to the importance, not only of the role of reading relationships within families, but also to Gladstone's considerable influence on his children.

39. One result of the public promotion and celebration of Gladstone's identity as a reader was the presentation, made to Gladstone by his friend and colleague Lord Northbourne in 1889, of a new bookplate. Specifically intended to celebrate the Gladstones' golden wedding, the bookplate nonetheless represents a somewhat ostentatious affirmation of Gladstone's status as a public, gentleman reader and seems to have been rarely, if ever, used. Another 'public' Gladstone bookplate was that designed for the Gladstone Library in the National Liberal Club, *c*. 1890. Circular in design, it featured the Gladstone griffin bordered by an ecclesiastical surround.
40. SDL I 43/17b. For other examples of annotators commenting on previous owners of their books, see, Jackson, *Marginalia*, pp. 90–1.
41. R. Shannon, *Gladstone*, p. 10.
42. See S. M. Pearce, *On Collecting: an investigation into collecting in the European tradition* (London and New York, 1995), pp. 50–1, 269.
43. Gladstone, 'On Books', pp. 388–90.
44. BL GP, Add MS 44727, 'Of Keeping Books and Papers', fol. 256.
45. BL GP Add MS 44727, fol. 256 verso.
46. GD 22/12/25.
47. GD 19/12/27.
48. See, for example, GD 10–11/6/28.
49. Matthew, *Gladstone*, p. 53.
50. GD 28/4/40, my emphasis.
51. Thus, in 1847, he noted: 'Worked much upon the No 6 [Carlton House Gardens] arrangements & made [a] memorandum with the particulars of the bookcases for Henderson'. GD 3/6/47.
52. Catherine Jessy, d. 1850.
53. GD 26–7/7/45.
54. GD 28/7/45 ff.
55. The catalogue remains, with 1865 *addenda*, at Hawarden Castle. I am grateful to Sir William Gladstone for its loan during the writing of this study. Currently only a photocopy of the 1865 section is in FRO GG.
56. GD 1, 4, 14, 16/8/45.
57. GD 7/3/49 ff.
58. FRO GG MS 1252, Correspondence and papers (mainly of Thomas Gladstone and W. E. Gladstone) concerning the division of the estate of Sir John Gladstone, 1845–51. See also, Bebbington, *Gladstone: faith and politics*, pp. 75–6; Shannon, *Gladstone: Peel's inheritor*, pp. 158–9.
59. See, for example, GD 31/5/52, 1/6/52.
60. Wemyss Reid, ed., *Gladstone*, p. 591.
61. GD 3/10/54. See also, C. Morley and H. Friederichs, 'In Mr. Gladstone's Village', *Strand Magazine*, 16 (1898), p. 504.
62. GD 26, 28/12/54.

63. GD 29/12/54, my emphasis.
64. Wemyss Reid, ed., *Gladstone*, p. 591. The earliest diary reference is at *GD* 27/10/60.
65. S. B. Platner and T. Ashby, *A Topographical Dictionary of Ancient Rome* (London, 1929), pp. 386–8. Gladstone recorded visiting 'The Tempio della Pace' in Rome in April 1832. *GD* 3/4/32.
66. GD 3/8/64; 17/10/64.
67. GD 22, 24/10/64. See also, *GD* 25/10/64; 3, 5/11/64.
68. GD 18/8/65.
69. GD 22/8/65. The longest of these, entitled 'Catalogi Στοιχεια quaedam' – 'Certain Elementary Principles/Basics of a/the Catalogue' – survives. A photocopy can be seen at FRO GG 1471.
70. GD 23/8/65.
71. GD 24/8/65.
72. GD 18/10/70. This separate pamphlet survives in the Temple of Peace.
73. GD 28/7/66, 10/8/72.
74. GD 18/5/69. This gothic scheme was never realized.
75. GD 17/4/74.
76. The first diary reference to the decision to sell 11 Carlton House Terrace, which had been the family's London home since July 1856, is at *GD* 13/12/73. The family eventually settled at the comparatively humble 73 Harley Street after a complicated and protracted move. For further coverage, see J. Morley, *The Life of William Ewart Gladstone*, New edn, 2 vols (London, 1905), vol. 2, pp. 130–1; R. Jenkins, *Gladstone* (London, 1995), pp. 388–9; R. Shannon, *Gladstone: heroic minister, 1865–1898* (London, 1999), p. 155; Matthew, *Gladstone*, pp. 313–14. The sale of Gladstone's art collection was handled by Christie, Manson & Woods. It commenced 23 June 1875 and continued over the following three days. See FRO GG 1477; and M. Pointon, 'W. E. Gladstone as Art Patron and Collector', *Victorian Studies* (1975), pp. 73–98.
77. FRO GG, Memorandum, 1 Jun. 1874, printed in *GD* at this date.
78. GD 12/3/75 ff.
79. BL GP Add MS 44773, 'Memorandum Prepared for Mr. Carnegie', 9 Jun. 1890, printed in *GD* at this date. See also, FRO GG 1479, Sotheby, Wilkinson & Hodge to Gladstone, 24 Mar. 1875. Another receipt stated the full valuation of the Library was £820. FRO GG 1479, WEG to Sotheby, Wilkinson & Hodge, 24 Mar. 1875, Receipt for Valuation.
80. Matthew, *Gladstone*, p. 237. See L. C. Sanders, 'Glyn, George Grenfell, second Baron Wolverton (1824–1887)', rev. H. C. G. Matthew, *ODNB* (Oxford, 2004).
81. GD 10/10/67.
82. GD 4/3/73 ff; 14/2/74; 11/3/74.
83. GD 18/9/77. For example, during a stay at Hawarden in 1874, the two men engaged in 'harmonious conversation' despite the turbulent and stressful circumstances, *GD* 4/9/74. Wolverton continued to appear at moments of crisis, including those relating to the Liberal leadership and retirement. See, for discussion of the leadership question: *GD* 13/12/79, 10/4/80; BL GP Add MS 44349, fol. 132, WEG to Lord Wolverton, 13 Apr. 1880. For discussion of retirement: *GD* 30/5/85, 16–17/6/85; BL GP Add MS 44548, fol. 96, WEG to Lord Wolverton, 7 Jun. 1886.

84. *GD* 24/3/75.
85. FRO GG 1479, Lord Wolverton to WEG, 12 Apr. 1875. Matthew notes only that 'part of the library appears to have been sold to ... Lord Wolverton'. Matthew, *Gladstone*, p. 314.
86. Gladstone, 'On Books', p. 395.
87. FRO GG 1479, 'Rough Note', 18 Apr. 1875.
88. Jenkins, *Gladstone*, p. 392. The stowage of books in Hawarden was also going on in 1874, see *GD* 9/6/74 ff.
89. This adjoining lobby was henceforth known as the 'Chapel of Ease'. Wemyss Reid, ed., *Gladstone*, p. 591.
90. *GD* 18, 21/5/75.
91. See 'Mr. Gladstone at Hawarden', *Harper's New Monthly Magazine* 64:383 (1882), 741–51, p. 751; J. E. Ritchie, *The Real Gladstone: an anecdotal biography* (London, 1898), p. 276; Wemyss Reid, ed., *Gladstone*, p. 591.
92. See 'Mr. Gladstone at Hawarden', p. 751. See also, Wemyss Reid, ed., *Gladstone*, p. 591.
93. Gladstone, 'On Books', p. 392. The simple idea of a projecting bookcase was not new. For instance, Leslie Stephen referred to a projecting bookcase 'with books on each side' in his study at 16 Onslow Gardens, London. Leslie Stephen to Oliver Wendell Holmes, 3 Jan. 1869, in Leslie Stephen, *Selected Letters*, ed. J. W. Bicknell (Basingstoke, 1996), vol. 1, pp. 66–7, quoted in T. L. Broughton, 'Studying the Study: gender and the scene of authorship in the writings of Leslie Stephen, Margaret Oliphant and Anne Thackeray Ritchie', in *Mapping the Self*, ed. F. Regard (Saint-Etienne, 2003), pp. 247–68, p. 252.
94. 'Mr. Gladstone as a Bookman', p. 6.
95. Williamson, *Gladstone the Man*, pp. 60–1.
96. *The Young Man*, p. 16.
97. Quoted in Ritchie, *Real Gladstone*, p. 284.
98. Hamilton, *Mr. Gladstone*, p. 83. On Gladstone's lively correspondence with spiritualist correspondents, see R. Clayton Windscheffel, 'Politics, Religion and Text: W. E. Gladstone and Spiritualism', *Journal of Victorian Culture*, 11:1 (2006), pp. 1–29.
99. See, for example, *GD* 1/3/34 and 2/2/36, as well as BL GP Add MS 44727, 'Of Keeping Books and Papers', fols 256–7.
100. Cosmos means 'order'. *GD* 24, 28/2/74.
101. *GD* 15/4/68, 12/8/75.
102. See *GD* 15, 30/8/87; 1, 6, 29/10/87; 8, 21/11/87; 16/12/87; 24/5/88; 1, 4/6/88; 7, 10–11/8/88; 17–18/9/88; 1/5/89; 15/8/89; 9/11/89; 6, 10, 12, 15–16/9/90. Also, Williamson, *Gladstone the Man*, p. 87; Morley, *Life of Gladstone*, vol. 2, pp. 134–6; Checkland, *The Gladstones*, p. 97.
103. *GD* 13/8/88, 23/10/93.
104. Drew, 'Gladstone's Library', p. 947.
105. Acton suffered increasing financial problems during his later years – the result of natural ineptitude conspiring with the depressed circumstances of the 1870s. As well as selling and leasing property, Acton had further burdened himself with large loans, and, by 1890, he was faced with the distressing prospect of having to sell the 60,000 volume historical library he had built up at his ancestral home of Aldenham in Shropshire. Thanks

to Gladstone's intervention, Andrew Carnegie bought the library for £9000, placed the books in trust while allowing Acton to use them until his death, after which Carnegie gave the books to John Morley, who in turn gifted them to Cambridge University Library. See *GD* 9/6/90; BL GP Add MS 44773, fol. 182, 'Memorandum Prepared for Mr. Carnegie'; and W. O. Chadwick, *Acton and Gladstone* (London, 1976), p. 25 ff.
106. Drew, 'Gladstone's Library', p. 947.
107. FRO GG 896, SEG to HNG, 4 Aug. 1886, quoted in Pritchard, *History*, p. 9. As this letter suggests, for the first two years discussion appears to have been restricted to the family circle, and then perhaps only to the male side. For instance, in October 1888 Gladstone was holding 'close talk' on St Deiniol's, *GD* 1/10/88. Gladstone did not fully explain his plans to his wife until 1888, when he 'explained all to C. in the subject of the meditated Institute', *GD* 15/8/88.
108. See *GD* 15/9/87; 15/8/88 ff; 7/9/88 ff; Pritchard, *History*, p. 16.
109. See *GD* 26/11/83 ff; 4/4/88 ff; and E. W. B. Nicholson, *Mr. Gladstone and the Bodleian* (Oxford, 1898). This sketch can be seen in the Bodleian, Library Records, d. 186 fol. 26.
110. BL GP Add MS 44773, fol. 75, printed in *GD* 12/11/88. For discussion, see Chapter 6.
111. See *GD* 8/8/89; 19/8/89; 11/9/89.
112. On 13 September, he confided to his diary: 'I am rather turning to a temporary scheme'.
113. See *GD* 23/8/89 ff, 13/9/89 ff; Drew, 'Gladstone's Library', p. 947.
114. See *GD* 20/8/89 ff, 18/9/89, 1/10/89, 9/11/89, 18/11/89, 22/11/89. For a detailed description, see Drew, 'Gladstone's Library', p. 949. Mary based this on her father's memoranda (now at SDL) and his, 'On Books' article.
115. *GD* 21/12/89. The words 'sent off' rather undermine Roy Jenkins' contention that Gladstone personally wheel-barrowed all the books from the Castle to St Deiniol's. He is further discredited by Mary Drew's description of the move. She stated that, although Gladstone packed and unpacked at each end, 'no vehicle was ever allowed to leave the Castle without its consignment of book bundles'. Jenkins, *Gladstone*, p. 178; Drew, 'Gladstone's Library', p. 948.
116. Wemyss Reid, ed., *Gladstone*, pp. 592, 596.
117. *GD* 28/1/90; 8/8/90 ff; 19/9/90.
118. *GD* 23/9/90 ff; 6/10/90. (The three dots in the latter quotation are present in *GD*.)
119. *GD* 14/11/90; 20/11/90.
120. Friederichs, *Evening of his Days*, pp. 111–12.
121. The memorandum is inscribed on 'Dalmeny Park' headed paper, and the same words are reused in a memorandum written by Gladstone in September 1894: SDL, St Deiniol's Uncatalogued MSS, 'The library of St. Deiniols'.
122. Gladstone, 'On Books', p. 390.
123. See, for example, *GD* 11–12/8/91.
124. Morley and Friederichs, 'Mr. Gladstone's Village', p. 503. See also C. Ribblesdale, 'A Visit to Hawarden', *Nineteenth Century and After*, 55:326 (1904), pp. 637–50, p. 644–5.

125. Ribblesdale, 'Visit to Hawarden', pp. 644–5. Lady Charlotte's negative experience was mirrored by that of Wilfred Blunt who, seeing St Deiniol's under construction, described it 'a terrible building of corrugated iron overlooking the Sands of Dee'. Philip Waller suggests Blunt had both political and poetic reasons for disgruntlement. He was a supporter of Home Rule but not of the annexation of Egypt, and 'on perusing the shelves of Gladstone's own library, Blunt came across a copy of *Sonnets of Proteus* which Blunt had given him in 1884, with the leaves still uncut'. W. S. Blunt, *My Diaries, Being a Personal Narrative of Events 1888–1914* (New York, 1980), vol. 1, p. 73 (2 Sept 1892), quoted in P. Waller, *Writers, Readers, and Reputations: literary life in Britain 1870–1918* (Oxford, 2006), p. 49. SDL still has Blunt's *Esther* (R 37 Bl/4) and *In Vinculis* (R 37 Bl/3).
126. *Hawarden Parish Magazine* (Feb. 1894).
127. See *GD* 20/5/93; T. W. Pritchard, 'The Revd. S. E. Gladstone (1844–1920)', *Flintshire Historical Society Journal*, 35 (1999), pp. 191–241, pp. 227–8.
128. *GD* 11/1/91: Wrote a few notes on the [St. Deiniol's] Trust.' See also, *GD* 16/9/91, 20/5/93; FRO GG 840, fol. 6. Gladstone had written memoranda regarding the trust in September 1889, *GD* 14/9/89. This may refer to the memorandum kept with the Keble memorandum and which Colin Matthew judged from the handwriting to have been written much earlier than 1895. See *GD* 12/11/88.
129. *GD* 14/10/95.
130. This is the equivalent of about two million pounds. *GD* 6/11/95 ff.
131. Pritchard, *History*, p. 30. In March 1896 Gladstone recorded he had 'sent to the *Guardian* a fishing Circular for a Warden of St Deiniol's', *GD* vol. 13, p. 423 ff. [The dating is so sporadic at this point that it is easier to give a page reference.]
132. See also, Pritchard, 'S. E. Gladstone', which, through a careful study of family correspondence, presents a convincing picture of the tensions present within the Hawarden family group and the difficulties this posed for the library's future prospects.
133. *GD* 29/12/96.
134. SDL, Uncatalogued MSS, 'The library of St. Deiniols' (September 1894). Friederichs made specific reference to a collection of theology books, indisputably the most important books to Gladstone, which were earmarked for inclusion in the St Deiniol's collection following his death. Friederichs, *Evening of his Days*, p. 121. There was a substantial deposit of books from the Temple of Peace following Gladstone's death, beginning on 13 August 1898 and continuing spasmodically until the turn of the century, but the total number transferred – approximately 3205 volumes – accounted for less than half of Friederichs' most conservative estimate of the deposit as it had been originally envisaged. This deposit, marked 'Rt Hon W. E. Gladstone Bequest', constitutes numbers 28,214–32,866 recorded in the earliest St Deiniol's accession register (30 Aug. 1897 to 29 Mar. 1900).
135. *GD* 8/7/92.
136. Pritchard, *History*, p. 30. G. S. Joyce had been sub-warden of St Michael's Theological College, Aberdare. In 1897, he became the first warden and chief librarian instituted under the trust deed.
137. *Times*, 24 Dec. 1896.

2 Rhythms of Reading

1. *GD* 3, 6, 7/7/32.
2. G. W. Smalley, 'Mr. Gladstone. Reminiscences, anecdotes, and an estimate', *Harper's New Monthly Magazine*, 97:577 (1898), pp. 476–88; 647–55; 796–802, p. 650.
3. Quoted in Williamson, *Gladstone the Man*, p. 144.
4. 'The Home Life of Mr Gladstone', *The Young Man* (1892), p. 16.
5. E. W. Hamilton, *Mr. Gladstone: a monograph*, 3rd edn (London, 1899), p. 64.
6. T. Wemyss Reid, ed., *The Life of William Ewart Gladstone* (London, 1899), p. 12. Gladstone allegedly regarded himself as a slow reader, although this was largely because he felt he had to undertake much of his reading in 'unconsidered intervals'. F. E. Hamer, ed., *The Personal Papers of Lord Rendel containing his Unpublished Conversations with Mr. Gladstone 1888 to 1898* (London, 1931), p. 80.
7. T. Archer and A. T. Story, *William Ewart Gladstone and his Contemporaries: seventy years of social and political progress*, Revd edn, 4 vols (1899), vol. 4, p. 453.
8. Hamilton, *Mr. Gladstone*, p. 64.
9. Wemyss Reid, ed., *Gladstone*, p. 12.
10. 'Home Life of Mr Gladstone', p. 16. There are numerous volumes in SDL containing annotations over the first few pages while the remainder are uncut.
11. Archer and Story, *Gladstone and his Contemporaries*, p. 453.
12. Quoted in J. E. Ritchie, *The Real Gladstone: an anecdotal biography* (London, 1898), p. 194.
13. W. Roberts, 'Bookworms of Yesterday and To-day: the Right Hon. W. E. Gladstone, M.P.' *The Bookworm*, 30 (1890), pp. 161–5, p. 164. A small collection of books on poultry survives in SDL!
14. W. A. Woodward, 'The Personal Interests of Mr. Gladstone', *Pearson's Magazine* (1898), pp. 306–12, p. 311.
15. *GD* 2/12/33.
16. At one point Gladstone declared: 'This page is <u>fabulous</u> WEG'. J. Brinsley-Richards, 'Mr Gladstone's Oxford Days', *Temple Bar* (May 1883), p. 33. Gladstone's annotated copy is at SDL GX/D/14.
17. Brinsley-Richards, 'Oxford Days', p. 41.
18. 'Do not go well together'. *GD* 8/8/64.
19. *GD* 14/10/59.
20. *GD* 17/12/94.
21. *GD* 20/1/67.
22. W. T. Stead, *Gladstone 1809–1898: a character sketch with portraits and other illustrations*. (London, n.d.), pp. 53–4.
23. Jackson, *Marginalia*, pp. 5–6, 18, 15; Jackson, ed., *A Book I Value*, pp. xvii–xix.
24. Jackson, *Marginalia*, p. 73. See also, p. 7.
25. Jackson, *Marginalia*, pp. 28–9. She writes: 'There may be annotators with private codes that they used over and over again, but I have not come across them.' Jackson, *Marginalia*, p. 29.
26. J. Locke, *Works*, New edn, 10 vols (London, 1823), SDL D 30 Lo/1. The set was purchased by Gladstone from Ingalton's of Eton; it contains his bookplates and characteristic markings.

27. Listed under 'Signs used by the diarist' in the diary volumes edited by Matthew.
28. I am grateful to Mark Llewellyn for this suggestion.
29. BL GP Add MS 44727, fol. 258, 'Of Keeping Books and Papers', 25 Nov. 1837. See *GD* at this date.
30. BL GP Add MS 44727, fol. 258.
31. Locke, *Works*, vol. 2, p. 321. 'There shall be seen what now by faith we scan, / not proved, but primal truth self-evident / and by direct cognition held by man. D. Alighieri, *The Divine Comedy*, trans. M. B. Anderson, 3 vols (Oxford, 1929), vol. 3, p. 15.
32. See *GD* 13, 27/5/27; 1/7/27.
33. *GD* 17/12/34. See BL GP Add MS 44723 fols 327–58 for Gladstone's notes and observations on Locke's *Essay*.
34. BL GP Add MS 44723, fols 328, 342. Gladstone notes his resumption of the text at Book II, Chapter 8.
35. R. Shannon, *Gladstone: Peel's inheritor 1809–1865* (London, 1982), p. 63.
36. *GD* 25/2/36.
37. Gladstone also increasingly used his 'NB' mark in his notes and observations. See, for example, BL GP Add MS 44723 fol. 352.
38. Hamilton, *Mr. Gladstone*, pp. 69–70.
39. Jackson, *Marginalia*, pp. 26, 37.
40. W. Carlisle, *An Essay on Evil Spirits* (London, 1827), SDL K 41/33. See, especially, pp. 174–5.
41. W. Cobbett, *A History of the Protestant Reformation in England and Ireland*, 2 vols (London, 1829), SDL I 52/78. I am grateful to Michael Wheeler for bringing this reference to my attention.
42. Gladstone read Cobbett in November 1887, see *GD* 27/11/87 ff. Over the next two years he produced three reformation articles: 'The Elizabethan Settlement of Religion', *Nineteenth Century*, 24 (1888), pp. 1–13; 'Queen Elizabeth and the Church of England', *Nineteenth Century*, 24 (1888), pp. 764–84; 'The English Church under Henry the Eighth', *Nineteenth Century*, 26 (1889), pp. 882–96.
43. In this section Cobbett had attacked nepotism in the Church of England.
44. Matthew, *Gladstone*, p. 238.
45. Jackson, *Marginalia*, p. 38.
46. His practice of writing a 'line of dates down the left-hand side' of book abstracts, to 'further aid the eye and the mind likewise', parallels his indexing style. See BL GP Add MS 44727, fol. 258.
47. WEG to John Murray, 24 Dec. 1884, quoted in Matthew, *Gladstone*, pp. 528–9.
48. See, for example, his annotations in the front and back of each volume of his *Opere di Dante* (Padova, 1822), reproduced in A. Isba, *Gladstone and Dante: Victorian statesman, medieval poet* (Woodbridge, 2006), pp. 141–3.
49. Jackson, *Marginalia*, p. 38.
50. See, for example, the long list of politician's names at the end of A. P. Stanley's *The Athanasian Creed* (London, 1871), E 10.7/17, which Gladstone listed as reading on 18 August 1872. The names appear to have little to do with the book's theological subject matter, being perhaps more suggestive of Gladstone gauging support over the question of the Irish Universities

Bill brought before the House the following year. I am grateful to Mark Llewellyn for both bringing this reference to my attention, and for discussing his ideas about such endpapers with me.
51. Stead, *Character Sketch*, pp. 53–4.
52. Williamson, *Gladstone the Man*, pp. 57, 59. Gladstone read large numbers of contemporary novels soon after they appeared. In the 1840s and 50s he read the Brontës, Dickens, Harriet Beecher Stowe, as well as the now minor Tractarian novels. In the 1860s he read George Eliot, Anthony Trollope, Harrison Ainsworth and Disraeli. In the 1870s, he tended to alternate between two main books – one religious and one secular – supplemented by selections from the eclectic material sent to him by writers and publishers. The 1880s saw equally prolific reading of novelists of the day including J. H. Shorthouse, Henry James, and Olive Schreiner, a diet supplemented with re-readings of established classics by Defoe, Dickens, Eliot, Scott and Disraeli. The late 1880s saw his consumption of novels dealing with Christian faith and doubt, particularly Shorthouse's *John Inglesant* and Mary Augusta Ward's *Robert Elsmere*. Gladstone kept up his phenomenal pace into the early 1890s, before it was checked by an unsuccessful cataract operation in May 1894. He also maintained his mixture of the old and the new. In 1892, for instance he read William Godwin's *Mandeville* (1817; GD 12/12/92) whilst also keeping up with new styles of best-seller. He both read and met Marie Corelli and Hall Caine, and, although some alleged Gladstone deplored the amoral tone of the work of Zola and Hardy, others registered his admiration. Woodward, for example, claimed that: 'Among living writers of fiction he gives the first place, not to an Englishman, but to a Frenchman – Emile Zola.' (Woodward, 'Personal Interests', p. 312). He certainly included some Zola in the St Deiniol's collection. (Friederichs, *Evening of his Days*, p. 117). Lighter literature, including that aimed at children by authors such as F. E. Hodgson Burnett and R. L. Stevenson, increasingly featured in the reading of Gladstone's later years. See Matthew, *Gladstone*, p. 317, and Waller, *Writers, Readers, and Reputations*, pp. 292, 549, 663, 670, 743–4, 800, 876, 896, 1034–5, 1036.
53. Smalley, 'Mr. Gladstone', p. 650.
54. Jackson, ed., *A Book I Value*, pp. xvi, xviii.
55. Wilhelmine von Hillern, *The Vulture Maiden* [*Die Geier-Wally*], trans. C. Bell and E.F. Poynter (Leipzig and London, 1876). See L. Masterman, ed., *Mary Gladstone (Mrs. Drew) Her Diaries and Letters* (London, 1930), p. 168.
56. Significant items remain, such as Gladstone's copies of Charlotte Brontë's *Shirley* and Ward's *Robert Elsmere*, but there are many books which we know he read, such as *Jane Eyre*, *Middlemarch*, Walter Pater's *Marius the Epicurean*, which are neither preserved at St Deiniol's nor in the Temple of Peace.
57. R. Clayton Windscheffel, 'Gladstone and Scott: family, identity, and nation', *Scottish Historical Review*, 86:221 (2007), pp. 69–95, pp. 71–2.
58. This was sometimes seen as part of a more general practice of occupying spare minutes, which could be used to explain Gladstone's productivity. See 'Home Life of Mr Gladstone', p. 15. Stuart Rendel testified in particular detail to this practice. See Hamer, ed., *Rendel*, pp. 97–8.
59. M. Drew, *Catherine Gladstone* (London, 1919), p. 32.

60. Quoted in F. Birrell, *Gladstone* (London, 1933), p. 140.
61. 'Home Life of Mr Gladstone', p. 17. Joseph Langen, *Geschichte der Römischen Kirche*, 3 vols (1881–92), SDL I 31/29.
62. Wemyss Reid, ed., *Gladstone*, pp. 601–2.
63. 'Mr. Gladstone at Hawarden', *Harper's New Monthly Magazine*, 64:383 (1882), pp. 741–51, p. 747.
64. Stead, *Character Sketch*, p. 67.
65. Schlüter Diary 12/1/88. A. Schlüter, *A Lady's Maid in Downing Street*, ed. M. Duncan (London, 1922), p. 150.
66. Although the *Pall Mall Budget* asserted that Gladstone 'breakfasts lightly about seven o'clock in the morning'. 'The Daily Life of the Grand Old Man. With views of Hawarden and Birmingham', *Pall Mall Budget* (8 Nov. 1888), p. 5.
67. G. Potter, *The People's Life of the Rt. Honourable William Ewart Gladstone* (London, 1884), p. 36.
68. Friederichs, *Evening of his Days*, p. 42. See also, Hamer, ed., *Rendel*, p. 97.
69. 'Home Life of Mr Gladstone', p. 15.
70. Quoted in G. B. Smith, *The Life of the Right Honourable William Ewart Gladstone*, 6th edn (London, Paris and New York, n.d.), p. 575.
71. 'Home Life of Mr Gladstone', p. 16.
72. L. Apjohn, *William Ewart Gladstone: his life and times*, New edn (London, 1898), p. 358.
73. FRO GG 222, WEG to JG, 31 Oct. 1823. Rendel recalled him favouring 'a good candle lamp with reflector at night', noting that he 'carries one with him at all times'. Hamer, ed., *Rendel*, p. 97.
74. Quoted in Smith, *Life of William Ewart Gladstone*, p. 574.
75. 'Home Life of Mr Gladstone', p. 16.
76. West Diary 9/1/91. H. G. Hutchinson, ed., *Private Diaries of the Rt. Hon. Sir Algernon West, G.C.B.* (London, 1922), p. 13.
77. Stead, *Character Sketch*, p. 67.
78. Wemyss Reid, ed., *Gladstone*, p. 598.
79. For example, when at Naples in 1838, Gladstone lamented not having received a letter from home. In consequence he was driven to: 'A long draught at the papers, a sorry substitute'. GD 19/11/38.
80. GD 11/6/57. See also C. R. L. F[letcher], *Mr. Gladstone at Oxford, 1890* (London, 1908), p. 19.
81. GD 9/3/32.
82. GD 25/5/32. *Galignani's Messenger*, an English paper published in Paris. See also, GD 6, 11/2/32; 20/3/32; 26, 28, 31/6/32; 2/7/32.
83. Matthew, *Gladstone*, pp. 1, 130–9, 296–301, 397–8, 554.
84. Stead, *Character Sketch*, p. 65.
85. 'Mr. Gladstone at Hawarden', pp. 748–9.
86. This was a weekly paper associated with the daily *Pall Mall Gazette*.
87. 'Daily Life of the Grand Old Man', p. 8.
88. H. W. Lucy, 'From Behind the Speaker's Chair. XLVII', *Strand Magazine* (1898), pp. 297–303, p. 300.
89. Wemyss Reid, ed., *Gladstone*, p. 603.
90. GD 13/1/73. See also, GD 15/11/27.

91. GD 3/1/83. See also, FRO GG, WEG to CG, 2 Jan. 1885, printed in GD at this date, which describes psalm-reading to combat insomnia.
92. GD 23/8/49. See also, Williamson, *Gladstone the Man*, p. 56.
93. He recorded every deterioration. See, for example, GD 6/9/93.
94. BL GP Add MS 44549 fol. 70, WEG to B. W. Currie, 4 Mar. 1893, printed in GD at this date.
95. GD 15/9/93.
96. See, for example, GD 14/12/93, 4/1/94, 27/1/94.
97. 'The bad eye'. GD 24/12/94.
98. W. E. Gladstone, 'Arthur Henry Hallam', *The Youth's Companion*, 72:1 (1898), pp. 1–3, p. 2.
99. This awakening, as Anne Isba persuasively argues, occurred much earlier than scholars have hitherto recognized, and before Gladstone's first reading of the *Commedia* in 1834. Isba, *Gladstone and Dante*, pp. 14–19.
100. Gladstone, 'Hallam', p.1.
101. H. Hallam, ed., *Remains in Verse and Prose of Arthur Henry Hallam with a Preface and Memoir*, New edn (London, 1869), pp. xliv, xlv.
102. W. G. F. Phillimore, 'Mr. Gladstone (Part II)', *Fortnightly Review*, 69 (1898), pp. 1020–8, p. 1021.
103. Panizzi had known of Gladstone's family since a visit to Liverpool in 1823, but his acquaintance with Catherine Gladstone's great uncle, the bibliophile Thomas Greville, provided the initial introduction to Gladstone himself. Edward Miller judges that 'mutual liking for the great Italian authors', rather than any theological interest, explains why 'two very similar men remained warmly attached to each other' until Panizzi's death. They also shared an interest in modern Italian politics, and Panizzi regularly lobbied Gladstone on this issue, and on matters relating to the British Museum. Gladstone in turn called on Panizzi to check his literary and political work relating to Italy. For example, Gladstone wrote to Panizzi asking for assistance with an article he was writing on Leopardi, see BL GP Add MS 44274. fol. 12, and W. E. Gladstone, 'Giacomo Leopardi', *Quarterly Review*, 86 (1850), pp. 295–336. Gladstone also asked Panizzi to read the proofs of his letter to Lord Aberdeen, see BL GP Add MS 36716. fol. 177. E. Miller, *Prince of Librarians: the life and times of Antonio Panizzi of the British Museum* (London, 1988), pp. 57, 157, 227, 238, 243, 264n, 326.
104. Acton's usefulness to and influence on Gladstone was profound. Acton's fluency in European languages – especially his natal German – and his continental contacts established him as Gladstone's key link with the worlds of scholarly German theology and church history, and Roman Catholic politics in Italy and beyond. It was his position as Döllinger's protégée and prominent fellow campaigner on behalf of Europe's liberal Roman Catholics – who welcomed scholarly approaches to Christianity and virulently opposed the declaration of papal infallibility in 1870 – which made him especially valuable. Acton's reports to Gladstone from the First Vatican Council were, for instance, a significant influence on Gladstone's own *Vatican Decrees* of 1874. Moreover, the impact of Acton's own historical ideas on his friend, particularly those concerning the unifying progress of liberty in modern history, and the promotion of rigorous scientific

methodology and high moral standards in historical scholarship, was also marked in articles such as W. E. Gladstone, '*Universitas Hominum*: or, the Unity of History', *North American Review*, 373 (1887), pp. 589–602. For more on their relationship, see W. O. Chadwick, *Acton and Gladstone* (London, 1976).

105. Ignaz von Döllinger (1799–1890), Munich-based church historian, liberal theologian, and leading opponent of ultramontainism. Excommunicated in 1871 for his role in opposing papal infallibility, he was a significant inspiration for (although did not join) the breakaway *Altkatholiken* or 'old Catholics'. He and Gladstone first met in Munich in 1845. As well as their shared interest in theology and ecclesiastical history, Döllinger also admired Scott and Dante, as well as being an ardent Anglophile. Gladstone was heavily influenced by Döllinger's religious ideas and writings (although he was less admiring of some of his pronouncements on Homer) particularly those which related to religious nationalism, ecumenism, and the idea of Christianity's cultural mission in the world. D. Bebbington, *The Mind of Gladstone: religion, Homer, and politics* (Oxford, 2004), pp. 124–6, 170, 223–7, 278, 310. See also, P. Erb, 'Gladstone and German Liberal Catholicism', *Recusant History*, 23:3 (1997), pp. 450–69.
106. Ritchie, *Real Gladstone*, p. 193. Robertson's book remains in SDL I 39.2/8.
107. Stead, *Character Sketch*, p. 54.
108. Wemyss Reid, ed., *Gladstone*, p. 12.
109. WEG to Laura Thistlethwayte, 25 Oct. 1869, printed in *GD*, vol. 8, p. 570.
110. A. Isba, *Gladstone and Women* (London, 2006); J. West, 'Gladstone and Laura Thistlethwayte, 1865–75', *Historical Research*, 80:209 (2007), pp. 368–92.
111. S. M. Pearce, *On Collecting: an investigation into collecting in the European tradition* (London and New York, 1995), p. 228.
112. R. Jenkins, *Gladstone* (London, 1995), p. 54. The Gladstones' daughter Mary took a similar line. Drew, *Catherine Gladstone*, pp. 7–8.
113. E. A. Pratt, *Catherine Gladstone: life, good works, and political efforts* (London, 1898), pp. 30–1.
114. My emphasis. Pratt, *Catherine Gladstone*, pp. 37–8.
115. Discussion of this is central to M. A. Danahay, *A Community of One: masculine autobiography and autonomy in nineteenth-century Britain* (Albany, 1993). See, for example, pp. 2–3.
116. Drew, *Catherine Gladstone*, p. 32.
117. *GD* 18, 25, 26, 31/7/39.
118. *GD* 17, 27/6/40 ff.
119. *GD* 26/7/39.
120. For example, *GD* 2/1/70.
121. *GD* 9/9/39.
122. For example, *GD* 30/7/92, 10/10/92, 19/11/93.
123. Holograph, 25 Jul. 1894, quoted in *GD* at this date. It is notable that, in general, the only occasions when Gladstone would permit others to read to him were at times of illness or incapacity.
124. 'Home Life of Mr Gladstone', p. 16.
125. *GD* 23/6/33. I am grateful to Christiane d'Haussy, Professor Emerita, Université de Paris XII, for lending me her unpublished paper on 'William Gladstone's Sundays', which significantly influences the following discussion.

126. He also taught in Sunday Schools as a young man.
127. See, for example, *GD* 20/10/33.
128. W. E. Gladstone, *A Manual of Prayers from the Liturgy. Arranged for family use* (London, 1845). The preface to the 4th edition (1899) contains reminiscences from children Stephen and Helen about their father reading the lesson and leading the prayers.
129. BL GP Add MSS 44779–81. See, for the first scholarly discussion of these sermons, Bebbington, *Mind*, p. 85.
130. Bebbington, *Mind*, p. 6.
131. W. E. Gladstone, 'The Lord's Day', in *later Gleanings*, ed. W. E. Gladstone (London, 1897), pp. 338–51, p. 351.
132. Gladstone, 'The Lord's Day', pp. 348–9, 347.
133. Jenkins, *Gladstone*, p. 182. Other holy days, such as Good Friday and Easter Sunday, would also be reserved for exclusive, devotional reading.
134. See *GD* 15/12/38, and 'Opening of the St. Martin's Free Public Library', *The Library*, 3 (1891), pp. 109–15, p. 110.
135. 'Home Life of Mr Gladstone', p. 16.
136. See Bebbington, *Mind*, pp. 86, 89, 92.
137. Wemyss Reid, ed., *Gladstone*, p. 602.
138. For details of this reading, see R. Clayton Windscheffel, 'Politics, Religion and Text: W.E. Gladstone and Spiritualism', *Journal of Victorian Culture*, 11:1 (2006), pp. 1–29.
139. Schlüter Diary 5/6/80; 2, 30/7/80. Schlüter, *Lady's Maid*, pp. 81, 83–4.
140. J. Rose, *The Intellectual Life of the British Working Classes* (New Haven and London, 2001), p. 84.
141. See, for example, *GD* 30/7/59, 28/7/66, 20/11/79.
142. Ritchie, *Real Gladstone*, p. 210.
143. See J. Raven et al., eds, *The Practice and Representation of Reading in England* (Cambridge, 1996), p. 12.
144. 'There is no expression of Christian sympathy that I value more than that of the ancient University of Oxford, the God-fearing and God-sustaining University of Oxford. I served her perhaps mistakenly, but to the best of my ability. My most earnest prayers are hers to the uttermost and to the last.' Quoted in Matthew, *Gladstone*, p. 633.
145. Following his introduction to *Tracts for the Times* by Oxford friend Benjamin Harrison in 1833, he returned the city early in 1834 to undertake three week's residence to qualify for his MA degree (*GD* 17/1/34). As well as engaging in follow-up reading of Tractarian material and the responses to it, he saw not only Harrison, but also Newman and Pusey. (*GD* 20, 23, 29, 30/1/34; 2, 3/2/34). See also, *GD* 8, 10/2/34; 19, 21/5/34;12–15/4/41, and Bebbington, *Mind*, pp. 48–50.
146. See, for example, BL GP Add MS 44517 fol. 232, WEG to Revd W. A. Whitworth, 3 Sept 1893, in *GD* at this date: 'I was myself little more than an occasional visitant [to All Saints', Margaret Street, the leading high Anglican church in London], and external observer'.
147. See, for example, *GD* 25, 27/10/47; 1, 2, 4/11/47; 26, 27, 29, 31/1/49; 16–17/2/49; 20–23/1/52.
148. *GD* 22/10/52.
149. *GD* 21/1/52; see also, 8–9/6/57; 6–7/5/59.

150. *GD* 26/1/57 ff.
151. *GD* 11–13/5/59. 11th: 'Read … P Arentino Putt. Err.' and 12th: 'Read P. Arentino – Tableau de l'Amour – Elegantiae – all Library Books.' Matthew rather coyly remarks: 'The Codrington library at All Souls held (now missing) P. Arentino, *Ragionamenti* (1660) with the pseudo-Arentino *Puttana errante* bound in.'
152. Pusey initially wanted H. P. Liddon as the new warden but, on his refusal and at his suggestion, in 1869 Edward Talbot was appointed instead. W. T. Warren, ed., *Kebleland* (Winchester and London, 1906), p. 68. The Talbot brothers Johnny and Edward were drawn into the Hawarden-Hagley circle by virtue of their mother's friendship with the Lytteltons. Edward and Lavinia were also mainstays of the Lyttelton–Gladstone family Christmases at Hawarden and Hagley, which afforded much opportunity for conversation between the two men and for Edward to use the Temple of Peace.
153. *GD* 1–27/10/60.
154. *GD* 9/4/57.
155. *GD* 9–30/10/57.
156. *GD*. See also 28/9/60 and 21/9/64.
157. *GD* 10/8/67. My emphasis.
158. *GD* 3/9/59: 'Off at 2 ½ for Penmaenmawr with C: where we are again in Mr Harrison's house. Established myself with books & papers in a corner of the dining room.' See also, 10/8/67: 'Unpacked & set my little room in order. Read.'
159. See *GD* 4/9/55, 6/9/59, 12/9/60.
160. *GD* 10/9/60.
161. *GD* 16, 28/8/61.
162. *GD* 27/9/55.
163. *GD* 13/9/59.
164. *GD* 2/9/68.
165. Lucy, 'Speaker's Chair', p. 303.
166. *GD* 6–7/9/60 ff.
167. *GD* 30/9/64.
168. *GD* 28/9/68.
169. *GD* 6/8/74.
170. *GD* 27/8/74 and 26/8/68. 1874 was also the year of Stephen Glynne's death, which may have affected the family's holiday routine.
171. *GD* 28/8/74.
172. *GD* 3/10/82.
173. *GD* 20/8/68.
174. *GD* 19–21/2/87.
175. Stuart Rendel (1834–1913), industrialist, politician, and philanthropist, was Liberal MP for Montgomeryshire 1880–94. He was influential in matters of Welsh politics – especially regarding religion and education. His friendship with Gladstone was strengthened by his daughter Maud Ernestine's marriage to Henry Neville Gladstone in 1890. John Grigg, 'Rendel, Stuart, Baron Rendel (1834–1913)', rev., *ODNB* (Oxford, 2004). George Armitstead (1824–1915) was Liberal MP for Dundee, 1868–73, managing

director of his family's Baltic trading firm, and lifelong bachelor. Matthew describes both men as Gladstone's 'old shoes' in late life. Matthew, *Gladstone*, pp. 610–12.

176. The earliest travel journals recorded in *GD* are tours of Gloucestershire and Worcestershire in July 1825 and of Monmouthshire in September 1825. Both untraced.
177. BL GP Add MS 44818.
178. *GD* 28/7/32.
179. For instance, part of Gladstone's description of his ascent of Etna was reproduced in Murray's *Sicily* 1864 edn, pp. 442–7. See *GD* 29/10/38.
180. For example, Gladstone and his brother took out a month's subscription (thanks to a Miss Mackenzie) to a reading room in Rome in March 1832, *GD* 30/3/32. In 1838 at Messina, Gladstone recorded: 'The Borsa [exchange] reading room appears to be courteously opened to strangers: so at least we found it.' *GD* 2/11/38.
181. *GD* 12/4/32.
182. Marginal note: 'i.e. in the carriage'. Gladstone's susceptibility to travel sickness cannot have helped matters. It does seem that he later found train travel more conducive to reading. See, for example, *GD* 14/10/59 and 27/7/92.
183. Gladstone's exceptional levels of reading did have a detrimental (albeit intermittent) effect on his eyesight. For example, in October 1838 he consulted an Italian oculist who recommended the use of green glasses, which prescription Gladstone followed, but the fact that he translated some Dante on the same day suggests he found it very difficult to abstain from reading, *GD* 9/10/38. See also, *GD* 23/12/38.
184. *GD* 25/2/32.
185. He was fluent in French and Italian, with a reading knowledge of German. Hamilton described him as 'decidedly good'. Hamilton, *Mr. Gladstone*, p. 71. See also, Phillimore, 'Mr. Gladstone', p. 1021.
186. *GD* 1/2/32. See also, *GD* 14, 25/2/32.
187. *GD* 3, 5, 20/3/32.
188. *GD* 23/6/32.
189. *GD* 27/6/32. Further attempts at German were made in July, *GD* 16/7/32.
190. *GD* 28/9/38. French art historian and Roman Catholic thinker, Alexandre François Rio (1797–1874). On Gladstone's relationship with Rio, see J. Conlin, 'Gladstone and Christian art, 1832–1854', *Historical Journal*, 46:2 (2003), pp. 341–74.
191. *GD* 3/3/32.
192. *GD* 10/3/32. The process was repeated for Bologna on 12 June.
193. *GD* 4/7/32.
194. See, for instance, his paraphrasing of Murray's *Hand-book for Travellers ... along the Rhine* (London, 1836), p. 207, at *GD* 15/8/38.
195. See Elizabeth Baigent, 'Starke, Mariana (1761/2–1838)', *ODNB* (Oxford, 2004).
196. *GD* 4/7/32 and 9/5/32. For one other complement, see *GD* 17/5/32.
197. *GD* 10, 28/7/32.
198. *GD* 14/6/32.

199. *GD* 4/7/32. Starke, *Information for Travellers*, pp. 480–2 and Marianna Starke, *The Beauties of Carlo-Maria Maggi ... to which are added Sonnets* (1811).
200. *GD* 6/6/32.
201. *GD* 14/7/32.
202. *GD* 13, 16/7/32.
203. *GD* 19/4/32.
204. *GD* 21, 24/9/38.
205. *GD* 19/9/38.
206. *GD* 4/10/38. R. C. Trench, 'Lines written at the village of Passignano on the Lake of Thrasymene' in *The Story of Justin Martyr and Other Poems* (1835).
207. There is an extensive literature exploring receptions of and allusions to the classical world in the nineteenth century. See, in particular, D. Newsome, *Two Classes of Men: Platonism and English romantic thought* (London, 1974); R. Jenkyns, *The Victorians and Ancient Greece* (Oxford, 1980) and *Dignity and Decadence: Victorian art and the classical inheritance* (Glasgow, 1991); F. M. Turner, *The Greek Heritage in Victorian Britain* (New Haven and London, 1981) and *Contesting Cultural Authority: essays in Victorian intellectual life* (Cambridge, 1993); N. Vance, *The Victorians and Ancient Rome* (Oxford and Cambridge, MA, 1997).
208. 'the black whortle-berries are picked'. *GD* 17/10/38.
209. See, for example, *GD* 26/10/38.
210. *GD* 1/5/32.
211. *GD* 18/10/38.
212. See, for instance, *GD* 30/10/38; 5/11/38.
213. *Histories* 6 and 7 deal with the Sicilian expedition and the siege of Syracuse. See also Gladstone's comment at Agnone: 'I longed for the description of Thucydides to compare with the ground'. *GD* 26–7/10/38.
214. In *Adonais* (1821), his lament for Keats.
215. *GD* 7/4/32.

3 The Gentleman's Inheritance, 1809–36

1. S. Redgrave, ed., *Catalogue of the Special Exhibition of Portrait Miniatures on Loan at the South Kensington Museum* (London, 1865). On Hargreaves, see V. Remington, 'Hargreaves, Thomas (1774–1847)', *ODNB* (Oxford, 2004).
2. The portrait dates from *c.* 1816 and is still in family hands. See FRO GG 1476.
3. For detailed information on Gladstone's ancestry and family, see S. G. Checkland, *The Gladstones: a family biography 1764–1851* (Cambridge, 1971) and 'Mr Gladstone, his Parents and his Siblings', in *Gladstone: politics and religion*, ed. P. J. Jagger (London, 1985), pp. 40–8; P. Gladstone, *Portrait of a Family: the Gladstones 1839–1889* (Kendal, 1989).
4. M. Sanderson, *Education, Economic Change, and Society in England, 1780–1870*, 2nd edn (Basingstoke, 1991); A. Digby and P. Searby, *Children, School and Society in Nineteenth-Century England* (London, 1981).
5. K. D. M. Snell, 'The Sunday-School Movement in England and Wales: child labour, denominational control and working-class culture', *Past & Present*,

164 (1999), pp. 122–68; P. B. Cliff, *The Rise and Development of the Sunday School Movement in England 1780–1980* (Redhill, 1986); T. W. Laqueur, *Religion and Respectability: Sunday schools and working class culture* (New Haven, CN, 1976).
6. L. Dacome, 'Noting the Mind: commonplace books and the pursuit of the self in eighteenth-century Britain', *Journal of the History of Ideas*, 65:4 (2004), pp. 603–25; W. St Clair, *The Reading Nation in the Romantic Period* (Cambridge, 2004); A. O'Malley, *The Making of the Modern Child: children's literature in the late eighteenth century* (New York, 2003); C. Leach, 'Advice for Parents and Books for Children: Quaker women and educational texts for the home, 1798–1850', *History of Education Society Bulletin*, 69 (2002), pp. 49–58; A. Richardson, *Literature, Education, and Romanticism: reading as social practice, 1780–1832* (Cambridge, 1994).
7. J. Marshall, 'John Locke's Religious, Educational and Moral Thought', *Historical Journal*, 33:4 (1990), pp. 993–1001.
8. G. Mandelbrote and K. Manley, eds, *The Cambridge History of Libraries in Britain and Ireland: vol. 2: 1640–1850* (Cambridge, 2006); A. Black and P. Hoare, eds, *The Cambridge History of Libraries in Britain and Ireland: vol. 3: 1850–2000* (Cambridge, 2006); P. H. Reid, 'The Decline and Fall of the British Country House Library', *Libraries & Culture*, 36:2 (2001), pp. 345–66; J. Raven et al., eds, *The Practice and Representation of Reading in England* (Cambridge, 1996); J. Ciro, 'Country house libraries in the nineteenth century', *Library History*, 18:2 (2002), pp. 89–98; P. S. Morrish, 'Domestic Libraries: Victorian and Edwardian Ideas and Practice', *Library History*, 10 (1994), pp. 27–44; R. Myers and M. Harris, eds, *Property of a Gentleman: the formation, organisation and dispersal of the private library 1620–1920* (Winchester, 1991).
9. J. Raven, 'From Promotion to Proscription: arrangements for reading and eighteenth-century libraries', in *The Practice and Representation of Reading in England*, ed. J. Raven, et al. (Cambridge, 1996), pp. 175–201, p. 175. See also, M. K. Flavell, 'The Enlightenment Reader and the New Industrial Towns: a study of the Liverpool library 1758–1790', *British Journal for Eighteenth-Century Studies*, 8 (1985), pp. 17–35. By 1797, this library was deemed insufficient for the needs of Liverpool's wealthy professional middle classes, and 1800 saw the opening of the Athenaeum library. N. Carrick and E. L. Ashton, *The Athenaeum, Liverpool, 1797–1997* (Liverpool, 1997).
10. Raven, 'From Promotion to Proscription', pp. 176, 178, 188, 191, 254.
11. See, for example, J. Whiston et al, *Directions for a Proper Choice of Authors to form a Library* (London, 1766).
12. See, for example, T. F. Dibdin, *The Bibliomania: or, Book-Madness* (London, 1809). See also, P. Connell, 'Bibliomania: book collecting, cultural politics, and the rise of literary heritage in Romantic Britain', *Representations*, 71 (2000), pp. 24–47.
13. I. D'Israeli, *Curiosities of Literature*, First Series, 6 vols (London, 1791–1823).
14. M. Girouard, *The Victorian Country House*, Revd edn (New Haven and London, 1979), p. 6.
15. Checkland, *The Gladstones*, pp. 33, 54, 80.

16. J. Brooke and M. Sorensen, eds, *The PMP: W. E. Gladstone*, 4 vols (London, 1971), vol. 1, p. 13. See also, C. R. Fay, *Huskisson and his Age* (London, 1951), pp. 369–70.
17. After travelling via Birmingham on the coach, William usually took an hour to reach Seaforth from the centre of Liverpool by gig, or longer if he walked. See *GD* 2/8/25, 19/7/26, 6/12/26, 3/4/27, 31/7/27, 6/12/27, 10/6/28, 13/12/28, 22/9/29, 21/12/31.
18. W. H. Ireland, *The Confessions of William Ireland* (London, 1805), SDL R 23.5/2; G. Tomline, *Memoirs of the Life of … William Pitt*, 2nd edn (London, 1821), SDL M 33.9 Pi/1.
19. FRO GG, AMG to TG, 7 Oct. 1818, quoted in Checkland, *The Gladstones*, p. 95. Contrary to Checkland's suggestion that he did not hold it long, Gladstone was prosecuting his duties more than a year after being appointed.
20. As Gladstone wrote to his mother: 'Helen deserves great commendation for her vigilance in the affairs of the Library', FRO GG 394, WEG to ARG, 24 Feb. 1824.
21. *GD* 29/9/29, 10/10/29.
22. In 1825 Gladstone was researching both at Ingalton's and in Gale's catalogue: 'About a Bible for you [ARG]'. FRO GG 394, WEG to ARG, 2 Oct. 1825. Later he unsuccessfully for 'Bibliotheca Gloucesteriensis' at a sale *GD* 17/10/25, writing subsequently to his mother: 'I think you would have liked to have had it, but I was not sure.' FRO GG 394, WEG to ARG, 23 Oct. 1825.
23. John Gladstone's uncertainty in the world he strove to inhabit is also underlined by his calling on William to help him in understanding the unfamiliar social niceties of public-school life. Regarding the amounts suggested for William's 'leaving money', he asked: 'Are these right?' FRO GG 637, JG to WEG, 17 Nov. 1827.
24. FRO GG 394, WEG to ARG, 24 Feb. 1824.
25. FRO GG 222, WEG to JG, 3 Nov. 1824.
26. *GD* 7/10/29.
27. See Checkland, *The Gladstones*, pp. 92–3, and *passim*.
28. FRO GG MS 1359, TG to WEG, 28 Sept. 1819.
29. On domestic ideology and the patriarchal family model in this period, see L. Davidoff and C. Hall, *Family Fortunes: men and women of the English middle class, 1780–1850* (London, 1987); J. Tosh, *A Man's Place: masculinity and the middle-class home in Victorian England* (New Haven and London, 1999).
30. See, for example, Bebbington, *Faith and Politics*, Chapter 2; and *Mind*, p. 44; Checkland, *The Gladstones*, Chapter 1; Jagger, *Christian Politician*, pp. 5–15; Matthew, *Gladstone*, pp. 6–8.
31. FRO GG JG to RG, 20 Feb. 1831; ARG to RG, 2 Mar. 1831, quoted in Checkland, *The Gladstones*, p. 230. See also, Clayton Windscheffel, 'Gladstone and Scott', pp. 73–7.
32. Brooke and Sorensen, eds, *PMP*, p. 15.
33. H. More, *Strictures on the Modern System of Female Education*, 6th ed., 2 vols (London, 1799), vol. 1, p. 64. See also, S. Pederson, 'Hannah More meets Simple Simon: tracts, chapbooks and popular culture in late eighteenth-century England', *Journal of British Studies*, 25 (1986), pp. 84–113.

34. *'Tis all for the best* (1820); *An Essay on the Character and Practical Writings of Saint Paul* (1815); *An Estimate of the Religion of the Fashionable World* (1791); *Hints towards forming the Character of a Young Princess* (1840); *Practical Piety* (1811); *Sacred Dramas: chiefly intended for young persons* (1782); *Strictures* (1799); *Tales* (1819); *The Spirit of Prayer* (1825).
35. FRO GG MS 1286, ARG's spiritual diary (1812–17), 28 Mar. 1816, quoted in Jagger, *Christian Politician*, p. 13.
36. Jagger, *Christian Politician*, p. 14. See also, Rose, *Intellectual Life*, p. 34; Richardson, *Reading as Social Practice*, p. 136.
37. See, for example, Jagger, *Christian Politician*, pp. 33–45; R. Shannon, *Gladstone: Peel's inheritor 1809–1865* (London, 1982), p. 7; Isba, *Gladstone and Women*, pp. 5, 32, 214n.
38. Checkland, *The Gladstones*, pp. 166, 164, 90.
39. FRO GG, AMG to WEG, 4 Dec. 1824, quoted in Checkland, *The Gladstones*, p. 164.
40. GD 22, 27/2/29.
41. Checkland, *The Gladstones*, pp. 165, 221. See also, for example, GD 23/8/33.
42. Jagger, *Christian Politician*, p. 51.
43. For a brief treatment of Helen, see J. Gilliland, 'Helen Jane Gladstone (1814–1880) Sister of William', *Flintshire Historical Society Journal*, 35 (1999), pp. 177–89. For later, more in-depth assessments, see A. Isba, 'Trouble with Helen: the Gladstone family crisis, 1846–1848', *History*, 88:290 (2003), pp. 249–61; and her *Gladstone and Women*, pp. 49–69.
44. See GD 24/11/48, and P. Magnus, *Gladstone: a biography* (London, 1954), p. 84.
45. See, for example, GD 17/10/45, when Gladstone read Burns's ballads to a sick Helen.
46. Gladstone noticed that his sister's Roman Catholic devotional works were all pre-1870, save a few unused or unopened volumes, which suggested to him that she sympathized with the old Catholics who – like him – opposed the declaration of papal infallibility. See Brooke and Sorensen, eds, *PMP*, vol. 4, p. 41.
47. See GD 10, 17/8/28; 26/7/29 ff; 30/8/29 ff; 11/7/30, 12/9/30, 31/7/31, 4/12/31. See also, Brooke and Sorensen, eds, *PMP*, pp. 21–2.
48. For a discussion of such male discourse, see M. Cohen, '"Manners" Make the Man: politeness, chivalry, and the construction of masculinity, 1750–1830', *Journal of British Studies*, 44 (2005), pp. 312–29, pp. 324–5.
49. Quoted in Richardson, *Reading as Social Practice*, p. 55. See also Cohen, 'Construction of Masculinity', p. 313.
50. M. McCormack, *The Independent Man: citizenship and gender politics in Georgian England* (Manchester, 2005), p. 22. For a recent discussion of public school masculinities, see F. Neddam, 'Constructing Masculinities under Thomas Arnold of Rugby (1828–1842): gender, educational policy and school life in an early-Victorian public school', *Gender & Education*, 16:3 (2004), pp. 303–26.
51. Brooke and Sorensen, eds, *PMP*, p. 20.
52. FRO GG 637, JG to WEG, 17, 18 Nov. 1827, 29 Oct. 1830.
53. FRO GG 637, JG to WEG, 29 Mar. 1828.

54. FRO GG 222, WEG to JG, 9 Feb. 1823.
55. FRO GG 222, WEG to JG, 8 Jun. 1823. Progress through the school was competitive, with one's place in the year ranked.
56. Checkland, *The Gladstones*, p. xii.
57. Tosh, *A Man's Place*, p. 116.
58. FRO GG, JG to TG, 21 Apr. 1820, 5 May 1820, and 9 Oct. 1822. Quoted in Checkland, *The Gladstones*, pp. 410–12. Equivalent letters, sent by JG to WEG, have not survived.
59. Checkland, *The Gladstones*, p. 130.
60. M. Wollstonecraft, *Mary, A Fiction* and *The Wrongs of Women*, ed. G. Kelly (Oxford, 1976), p. 4.
61. W. Scott, *Waverley*, 3rd edn, *Novels and Tales of the Author of Waverley in twenty-five volumes* (Edinburgh and London, 1821), vol. 1, pp. 31–2.
62. Checkland, *The Gladstones*, Chapter 15, and *passim*. Tom held several other seats subsequently, but his later life was mainly taken up by the management of Fasque.
63. Matthew, *Gladstone*, p. 5; Checkland, *The Gladstones*, pp. 138, 336.
64. Checkland, *The Gladstones*, pp. 138–40.
65. FRO GG, JG to RG, 29 Jan. 1823, quoted in Checkland, *The Gladstones*, p. 139.
66. FRO GG 394, WEG to ARG, 19 Jan. 1831.
67. Checkland, *The Gladstones*, pp. 135–6, 375–6.
68. Shannon, *Gladstone: Peel's inheritor*, p. 6; Checkland, *The Gladstones*, pp. 240, 254.
69. *GD* 11/10/25.
70. He regularly complained about the poor quality of preaching and religious worship. See, for example, *GD* 16/10/25.
71. For instance, in 1826, Gladstone wrote to his father praising his friend Gaskell's political knowledge and 'intimate acquaintance with English History'. FRO GG 222, WEG to JG, 7 Jul. 1826.
72. FRO GG 222, WEG to JG, 2 Nov. 1830. Gladstone's commentary was clearly not exaggerated. See C. Hollis, *Eton: a history* (London, 1960), pp. 197, 199.
73. Matthew, *Gladstone*, p. 15.
74. Both Matthew and Bebbington use evidence of Gladstone's religious reading at Eton to point up his later departure from the strict limits of his family's evangelicalism, although the connection should not be over-stressed at this stage. See Matthew, *Gladstone*, p. 16; Bebbington, *Faith and Politics*, p. 29; Bebbington, *Mind*, p. 44.
75. See Jackson, *Marginalia*, pp. 19–23.
76. FRO GG 394, WEG to ARG, 26 Sept. 1822.
77. GG 394, WEG to ARG, 3 Feb. 1823.
78. Gladstone himself was more than aware of the dangers of identifying too closely with such heroes. For instance, he regularly measured himself against the erratic reading and unsystematic learning techniques displayed by Walter Scott's first hero, Edward Waverley. See Clayton Windscheffel, 'Gladstone and Scott', pp. 80–1. See also, M. Goode, 'Dryasdust Antiquarianism and Soppy Masculinity: the Waverley novels and the gender of history', *Representations*, 82 (2003), pp. 52–86, esp. pp. 55–66, 78–80.

79. FRO GG 394, WEG to ARG, 2 Oct. 1825. See also, for example, FRO GG 394, WEG to ARG, 23 Jan. 1830.
80. This leads to Anne Isba's contention that Anne was a 'remote figure' to whom Gladstone 'hardly ever wrote ... nor she to him'. A. Isba, *Gladstone and Dante: Victorian statesman, medieval poet* (Woodbridge, 2006), pp. 71, 73.
81. See Richardson, *Reading as Social Practice*, p. 78.
82. FRO GG, WEG to TG, 5 Mar. 1828, quoted in Checkland, *The Gladstones*, p. 216.
83. FRO GG 222, WEG to JG, 12 Nov. 1830.
84. FRO GG 222, WEG to JG, 4 Aug. 1830. On the feminization of the notion of 'sensibility', and its role in the Georgian home, see McCormack, *The Independent Man*, pp. 21–2.
85. In his letters to his son, John Gladstone was far more acquiescent and sympathetic than his son's rhetoric alone implies. He was, for instance, constantly warning William against overwork, 'which of all things is to be guarded against': FRO GG 637, JG to WEG, 22 Dec. 1829, whereas Gladstone constantly asserted his laziness and his father's right to be disappointed in him. See also FRO GG 637, JG to WEG, 2 Feb. 27 May, 24 Jun. 10 Jul. 1830; 23 Apr. 1 Nov. 1831.
86. FRO GG 637, JG to WEG, 10 Aug. 1830; 8 Nov. 1830; 2 Feb. 1831. The latter contains an interesting discussion of Gladstone's cousin John, who his uncle describes as 'so occupied with preparing himself for the next world, that his is disposed to abandon the concerns of this'.
87. FRO GG 637, JG [ARG] to WEG, 18 Aug. 1830.
88. This explains why the letter is wrongly catalogued under letters from JG to WEG in FRO GG 637.
89. FRO GG 223, WEG to JG, 7 Jan. 1832.
90. FRO GG 637, JG [ARG] to WEG, 1 Oct. 1832.
91. FRO GG 637, JG to WEG, 24 Dec. 1832.
92. Gladstone's biographers have generally asserted the importance of this period for his later intellectual development. See, for example, Matthew, *Gladstone*, p. 20.
93. See Checkland, *The Gladstones*, pp. 389–90.
94. Checkland, *The Gladstones*, pp. 162, 281.
95. It involved a journey of 660 miles from London. See *GD* 13/8/34.
96. See, for example, *GD* 10/9/36, 8/11/37, 15/8/46, and 19/12/51.
97. Gladstone maintained the family tradition of education at Fasque with his own children. Thus on 22 December 1851, he: 'Worked on Latin &c. with Willy', who 'brought me his first original Latin verses', which showed 'promise'.
98. Checkland, *The Gladstones*, p. 282. See also *GD* 2/12/33, 21/1/49, 8/9/50.
99. Matthew, *Gladstone*, p. 31.
100. *GD* 1, 3/10/35, 23/11/35, 2/2/36. See also, Bebbington, *Faith and Politics*, p. 46.
101. *GD* 20/11/35.
102. *GD* 24/3/36.
103. See Munro's correspondence with TG at FRO GG 450.
104. Until the building of St Andrew's, it is possible family prayers would have taken place in the library.

4 A Place of Deceptive Tranquillity: Gladstone's Temple of Peace

1. R. Runcie, 'God's Politician', in *The Grand Old Man: sermons & speeches in honour of W. E. Gladstone (1809–1898)*, ed. P. B. Francis (Hawarden, 2000), pp. 27–31, p. 27.
2. See, for example, Matthew, *Gladstone*, chs 3 & 4.
3. See, for example, 'Mr. Gladstone at Hawarden', *Harper's New Monthly Magazine*, 64:383 (1882), pp. 741–51, p. 746.
4. Busts were tremendously popular and were consistently recommended by library manuals. See P. S. Morrish, 'Domestic Libraries: Victorian and Edwardian Ideas and Practice', *Library History*, 10 (1994), pp. 27–44; D. Piper, *The English Face* (London, 1978), p. 187.
5. The earliest surviving document relating to the classification scheme and layout of a library at Hawarden Castle is an undated manuscript in the Glynne-Gladstone Collection. Its title and copperplate hand suggest it refers to the Castle's main library at a time antedating Gladstone's residence, although the lettering used for the bookcase designations, which is the same as Gladstone used in his book catalogues, and the predominance of divinity, mean that his involvement and ownership cannot be ruled out. See FRO GG 2206, 'Notes on the Arrangement of Books in the Library at Hawarden Castle', n.d., [early 19th c.].
6. See *GD* 23–4/8/65.
7. 'Mr. Gladstone at Hawarden', p. 746. See also *GD* 18/10/70.
8. W. E. Gladstone, 'On Books and the Housing of Them', *Nineteenth Century*, 27 (1890), pp. 384–96, pp. 390–1.
9. J. Raven, 'From Promotion to Proscription: arrangements for reading and eighteenth-century libraries', in *The Practice and Representation of Reading in England*, ed. J. Raven, *et al.* (Cambridge, 1996), pp. 175–201, p. 188.
10. See Gladstone, 'On Books', p. 393.
11. Gladstone, 'On Books', p. 391. The seriousness of this tradition was undermined by the family's practice of carving the heights of its members into the wood of the bookcases. 'It was (and long remained) the practice to mark the heights of family members on Gladstone's bookshelves. Among them was "W.E.G., 5 10 ¾, without shoes"'. 'Mr. Gladstone at Hawarden', p. 751. See also, W. A. Woodward, 'The Personal Interests of Mr. Gladstone', *Pearson's Magazine* (1898), pp. 306–12, p. 311.
12. Gladstone, 'On Books', pp. 391, 392.
13. I am grateful to Scott Traynor for this family anecdote.
14. See Morrish, 'Domestic Libraries', pp. 29–30, 35, 37, 40–1.
15. They included Pitt, Fox, Pope, Dryden, King Alfred, Burke, Newton, Locke, Johnson, Molière, Homer, and Virgil.
16. For a contemporary description, see 'Mr. Gladstone at Hawarden', p. 747.
17. For further information on these busts, see B. Keith-Lucas and H. N. Gladstone, *The Gladstone-Glynne Collection: a catalogue of the oil-paintings, water-colours, sculptures and miniatures and a supplementary list of prints and drawings at Hawarden Castle* (Hawarden, 1934).
18. There were no female figures in the Fasque bust collection.

19. T. Wemyss Reid, ed., *The Life of William Ewart Gladstone* (London, 1899), p. 591. The Glynne Library is now part of the SDL collection.
20. Raven, 'From promotion to proscription', p. 176.
21. See, for example: 'A snug evening ... in the Temple of Peace', *GD* 30/8/76; 'Worked on my room to bring it into order, which was tranquillising', *GD* 29/12/79.
22. 'Arranged the remainder of my theology 4toes, to prevent sleep after the ill-omened early dinner!' *GD* 16/9/77.
23. 'Three good hours ... finished in the main the business of arranging my library wh[ich] is now in better order than for many years'. *GD* 17/9/77.
24. *GD* 29/8/78. Such complacency did not last. In 1887 Gladstone exclaimed: 'my chaos is beyond all precedent', and, two years later, the library had to be '*sventrato* as they say at Naples' – cleaned out or, literally, disembowelled. *GD* 10/8/87, 30/12/89.
25. M. Drew, 'Mr. Gladstone's Library at "St. Deiniol's Hawarden"', *Nineteenth Century and After*, 59:352 (1906), pp. 944–54, p. 946.
26. Wemyss Reid, ed., *Gladstone*, p. 592. See also, D. Williamson, *Gladstone the Man: a non-political biography*, 2nd edn (London, 1898), pp. 70–1.
27. C. Morley and H. Friederichs, 'In Mr. Gladstone's Village', *Strand Magazine*, 16 (1898), p. 503.
28. For further discussion, see Chapter 7.
29. *GD* 27/10/60. This is the first recorded use of the name, and note, in a public context.
30. *GD* 28/9/61. James Lacaita, who befriended Gladstone in Naples in 1850, was to serve as another useful source of information for Gladstone on Italian politics and Dante, as well as being engaging company. See, H. R. Tedder, 'Lacaita, Sir James Philip (1813–1895)', rev. H. C. G. Matthew, *ODNB* (Oxford, 2004).
31. *GD* 8/12/74. Note his need to make the room *publicly* presentable.
32. Wemyss Reid, ed., *Gladstone*, p. 592. See also, 'Mr. Gladstone at Hawarden', p. 746; 'The Daily Life of the Grand Old Man. With Views of Hawarden and Birmingham', *Pall Mall Budget*, 8 Nov. 1888; J. E. Ritchie, *The Real Gladstone: an anecdotal biography* (London, 1898), p. 276.
33. Morrish, 'Domestic Libraries', p. 29.
34. While every effort has been made to eliminate duplicate names and decipher illegible entries, these figures remain approximate.
35. Of the other children Agnes made 80 entries, William 89, Helen 138, Henry 36, Herbert 76, Stephen 25, which, with Mary's total, accounts for 35 per cent of the total.
36. Williamson, *Gladstone the Man*, p. 24. See S. K. Harris, *The Cultural Work of the Late Nineteenth-Century Hostess: Annie Adams Fields and Mary Gladstone Drew* (Basingstoke, 2002), esp. Chapter 4.
37. L. Masterman, ed., *Mary Gladstone (Mrs. Drew) Her Diaries and Letters* (London, 1930), p. 361.
38. Register 1, 18 Sept. 1860. This figure does not include books she borrowed on others' behalf.
39. R. Kerr, *The Gentleman's House; or how to plan English residences, from the parsonage to the palace*, 3rd edn (London, 1871), p. 116, quoted in K. Flint, *The Woman Reader, 1837–1914* (Oxford, 1993), p. 103.

40. Quoted in Flint, *The Woman Reader*, p. 103.
41. M. Girouard, *The Victorian Country House*, Revd edn (New Haven and London, 1979), pp. 28–9. See also Morrish, 'Domestic Libraries', pp. 40–1.
42. I. M. Gordon, marchioness of Aberdeen and Temair, *Memories of a Sacred and Inspiring Friendship. An address on Founder's Day, June 28th, 1935 at St. Deiniol's Library, Hawarden* (Chester, [1935]), p. 11. Ishbel Gordon, née Marjoribanks, (1857–1939) was the widow of John Campbell Gordon, 1st marquess of Aberdeen and Temair (1847–1934), whom she had married in 1877. See F. Barbour and M. U. Baird, 'Gordon, John Campbell, First Marquess of Aberdeen and Temair (1847–1934)', rev. H. C. G. Matthew, *ODNB* (Oxford, 2004).
43. Girouard, *Victorian Country House*, p. 35. See Ciro's evidence for extensive female use of country house libraries in the nineteenth century, J. Ciro, 'Country House Libraries in the Nineteenth Century', *Library History*, 18:2 (2002), pp. 89–98, p. 91 ff.
44. M. A. Danahay, *A Community of One: masculine autobiography and autonomy in nineteenth-century Britain* (Albany, 1993).
45. T. L. Broughton, 'Studying the Study: gender and the scene of authorship in the writings of Leslie Stephen, Margaret Oliphant and Anne Thackeray Ritchie', in *Mapping the Self: space, identity, discourse in British auto/biography*, ed. F. Regard (Saint-Etienne, 2003), pp. 247–68, pp. 248–51. See P. Tristram, *Living Space in Fact and Fiction* (London and New York, 1989). For a highly nuanced recent reading of domestic space, see J. A. Hamlett, 'Materialising Gender: identity and middle-class domestic interiors, 1850–1910' (Unpublished Ph.D. thesis, University of London, 2005).
46. In only one category (friends/colleagues) do men outnumber women (26:14 with 2 unknown). Considering that almost all Gladstone's colleagues were men, this is not surprising.
47. These were her personal borrowings; those she took out for the schoolroom are listed under that designation.
48. On women's educational opportunities in this period, see, for example: K. Hughes, *The Victorian Governess* (London, 1993); J. Martin, *Women and the Politics of Schooling in Victorian and Edwardian England* (Leicester, 1999); R. O'Day, 'Women and Education in Nineteenth-Century England', in *Women, Scholarship and Criticism: gender and knowledge, c.1790–1900*, ed. J. Bellamy, et al. (Manchester, 2000), pp. 91–109; C. de Bellaigue, 'Behind the School Walls: the school community in French and English boarding schools for girls, 1810–1867', *Paedagogica Historica*, 40:1/2 (2004), pp. 107–21.
49. W. H. Davenport Adams, *Woman's Work and Worth in Girlhood, Maidenhood, and Wifehood* (London, 1880), pp. 140–1; K. Flint, 'Women, Men and the Reading of *Vanity Fair*', in *The Practice and Representation of Reading in England*, ed. J. Raven, et al. (Cambridge, 1996), pp. 246–62, pp. 247, 251, 253.
50. Masterman, ed., *Mary Gladstone*, p. 12.
51. A. Isba, *Gladstone and Women* (London, 2006), pp. 135–42. Isba persuasively contests earlier readings which suggested Helen's parents' attitude was actively obstructive. See, for example, P. Jalland, 'Mr Gladstone's Daughters: The Domestic Price of Victorian Politics', in *The Gladstonian Turn of Mind: essays presented to J. B. Conacher* ed. B. L. Kinzer (Toronto, 1985), pp. 97–122.

52. It is likely all were Anglicans. Four bishops borrowed.
53. See Chapter 6.
54. The Revd J. Drew Roberts, 'Gladstone and His Curates: Young Preachers' Terrifying Ordeals', *T. P.'s & Cassell's Weekly* (n.d. [post 1923]), p. 474. Copy in FRO GG 1561.
55. *GD* 24/4/40, 23/5/40. A small collection of travel books – marked with a number and the words: 'For the use of Mr W. E. Gladstone's servants 1840' inside the front cover – survive in the Temple of Peace, having been brought there from 10 Downing Street. For comparison, see F. Stimpson, 'Servants' Reading: An Examination of the Servants' Library at Cragside', *Library History*, 19:1 (2003), pp. 3–11.
56. See, for example, *GD* 17/4/40, 3/5/40, 28/2/41.
57. *GD* 14, 17/2/40, 28/3/43. See, regarding premarital sex, *GD* 31/8/47.
58. *GD* 14/11/57. See, on employers' attempts to control servants' reading, Rose, *Intellectual Life*, p. 25.
59. *GD* 7/11/34 ff.
60. A. Schlüter, *A Lady's Maid in Downing Street*, ed. M. Duncan (London, 1922).
61. K. D. Reynolds, 'Schlüter, Auguste (1849–1917)', *ODNB* (Oxford, 2004).
62. Schlüter Diary, 7/7/78; 26/1/79. Schlüter, *Lady's Maid*, pp. 28, 36.
63. Schlüter Diary, 18/6/80. Schlüter, *Lady's Maid*, p. 82.
64. Schlüter Diary, 21/10/77. Schlüter, *Lady's Maid*, p. 17.
65. In one diary entry she gave an extensive review (on the basis of her notes) of a sermon by William Boyd Carpenter (1841–1918), concluding with the observation that 'Mr. Gladstone was another Listener.' Schlüter Diary, 18/3/81. Schlüter, *Lady's Maid*, p. 66. Gladstone appointed Boyd Carpenter to the See of Ripon in 1884. H. D. A. Major, 'Carpenter, William Boyd (1841–1918)', rev. H. C. G. Matthew, *ODNB* (Oxford, 2004).
66. Schlüter Diary, 20/8/78. Schlüter, *Lady's Maid*, p. 29. The book is preserved in the St Deiniol's collection, SDL R 37 Ja/2.
67. Schlüter Diary, 12/1/88; 9/1/89. Schlüter, *Lady's Maid*, p. 150, 162.
68. Schlüter Diary, 8/8/80; 13–14/3/81. Schlüter, *Lady's Maid*, pp. 59, 65–6.
69. Schlüter Diary, 3/3/79. Schlüter, *Lady's Maid*, p. 37.
70. Schlüter Diary, 26/11/79. Schlüter, *Lady's Maid*, p. 45.
71. Schlüter Diary, 18/6/80. Schlüter, *Lady's Maid*, p. 82. Mary Gladstone's Diary 17/8/80. Masterman, ed., *Mary Gladstone*, p. 207.
72. Schlüter Diary, 11/9/83. Schlüter, *Lady's Maid*, p. 107.
73. Schlüter Diary, 16/3/86. Schlüter, *Lady's Maid*, p. 139.
74. Schlüter Diary, 20/11/90. Schlüter, *Lady's Maid*, p. 176.
75. In 1888, for example, despite her sister and her family lying ill in New York, Auguste was obliged to accompany the Gladstones to Naples. When she did finally make the transatlantic journey, they had died. Schlüter, *Lady's Maid*, pp. 156–7.
76. P. Gladstone, *Portrait of a Family: the Gladstones 1839–1889* (Kendal, 1989), p. 102.
77. See M. Pointon, 'W. E. Gladstone as Art Patron and Collector', *Victorian Studies*, (1975), pp. 73–98, p. 85.
78. FRO GG 1475, Alexander Munro to WEG, 4 May 1852. See also, A. Isba, *Gladstone and Dante: Victorian Statesman, Medieval Poet* (Woodbridge, 2006), pp. 36–8.

79. John Gladstone's London house into which Gladstone first moved in 1849 and inherited on the former's death in 1851. R. Shannon, *Gladstone: Peel's Inheritor 1809–1865* (London, 1982), pp. 216, 246.
80. 'That day we read no more'. See Pointon, 'Art Patron', p. 90; Isba, *Gladstone and Dante*, p. 38.
81. J. A. Gere, 'Alexander Munro's "Paolo and Francesca"', *Burlington Magazine*, 105:728 (1963), p. 468, pp. 508–510, pp. 509–510.
82. Matthew, *Gladstone*, p. 158.
83. *GD* 5–6/8/28. See *GD*, vol. 14 for the indexed list of encounters.
84. See *GD* 22/4/49. Gladstone was quoting Matt. v. 28.
85. *GD* 22/4/49.
86. A convoluted libel case, won by H. Gladstone against C. P. Wright, which was brought by the latter after the Gladstones retaliated to Wright's assertion – published in his *Portraits and Criticisms* (1925) – that their father had 'set the tradition in public to speak the language of highest and strictest principle, and in private to pursue and possess every sort of woman'. See, J. P. Gardiner 'Gladstone, Gossip and the Post-War Generation', *Historical Research*, 74:186 (2001), pp. 409–24; Isba, *Gladstone and Women*, pp. xi–xv, 227n; R. Pearsall, *The Worm in the Bud: the world of Victorian sexuality* (London, 1971), pp. 308–9.
87. S. Marcus, *The Other Victorians: a study of sexuality and pornography in mid-nineteenth-century England* (London, 1966) and Pearsall, *Worm*. The topic has been most recently discussed in Isba, *Gladstone and Women*, pp. 99–121. For up-to-date discussions of Victorian prostitution and sexuality, see M. Mason, *The Making of Victorian Sexuality* (Oxford, 1994); F. Mort and L. Nead, 'Sexuality, Modernity and the Victorians', *Journal of Victorian Culture*, 1 (1996), pp. 118–30; L. Nead, *Victorian Babylon: people, streets and images in nineteenth-century London* (New Haven, CT, 2000); J. R. Walkowitz, *City of Dreadful Delight: narratives of sexual danger in late Victorian London* (London, 1992) and *Prostitution and Victorian Society: women, class and the state* (Cambridge, 1980).
88. See Matthew, *Gladstone*, pp. 543, 629–30.
89. See S. G. Checkland, *The Gladstones: a family biography 1764–1851* (Cambridge, 1971), pp. 246, 296.
90. J. G. Smith, *A Non-Political Treatise of and Tribute to the Late William Ewart Gladstone* (Newport, 1898), p. 32.
91. *GD* 29/6/52, 12/10/52.
92. *GD* 27/4/56.
93. *GD* 21/10/52. Harriet Beecher Stowe's *Uncle Tom's Cabin* (1852). On 15 Oct., Gladstone had recorded in his diary: 'Read ... Uncle Tom – which I finished: it is a *great* book, but scarcely denies exaggeration which under the circumstances wd. be a serious error.'
94. *GD* 29/6/58.
95. *GD* 6/10/73, 6/8/87.
96. *GD* 16/2/76, 13/5/76.
97. *GD* 16/10/29.
98. *GD* 13/8/59. See also *GD* 19, 24/7/59. Such was Gladstone's affection for the *Idylls*, that he carried round the 1859 edition in his pocket. See R. B. Martin,

Tennyson: the unquiet heart (Oxford, 1980), p. 423; G. Joseph, *Tennyson and the Text: the weaver's shuttle* (Cambridge, 1992), p. 133.

99. GD 13/8/59; W. E. Gladstone, 'Tennyson', *Quarterly Review*, 106:454 (1859), pp. 454–85.; WEG to Mr Elwin, 16 Aug. 1859, quoted in GD 14/7/59.
100. Bebbington, *Faith and Politics*, p. 131.
101. GD 17, 18, 19, 24/7/59.
102. William Dyce (1806–64), an artist who was a significant influence on the Pre-Raphaelite movement, was commissioned to paint the portrait. Marcia Pointon speculated and Colin Matthew confirmed the model's identity. Pointon, 'Art Patron', p. 92; Matthew, *Gladstone*, p. 158. See also Isba, *Gladstone and Dante*, pp. 78–9.
103. GD 1, 13/9/59.
104. On 14 and 15 September, Gladstone: 'Wrote on Tennyson'. But he also wrote to Marion again.
105. GD 16, 17/9/59.
106. GD 16/3/65, 10/5/76, 25/9/77.
107. J. West, 'Gladstone and Laura Thistlethwayte, 1865–75', *Historical Research*, 80:209 (2007), pp. 368–92, p. 375. Although Gladstone had to be prompted to send Laura a copy of his *Juventus Mundi*, which, having expecting her to be 'repelled by it', he had sent only to 'bookworm friends'; she received a second edition. WEG to Laura Thistlethwayte, 25 Aug. 1869, printed in GD, vol. 8, p. 557. Interestingly, Gladstone's relationship with another infamous woman, Russian 'spy' Olga Novikov, also began following her sending her pamphlet to him. Isba, *Gladstone and Women*, p. 171. On Novikov, see also, H. C. G. Matthew, 'Novikov, Olga (1840–1925)', *ODNB* (Oxford, 2004); R. Harrison, 'Marx, Gladstone and Olga Novikov', *Bulletin of the Society for the Study of Labour History*, 33 (1976), pp. 26–34; W. T. Stead, ed., *The M. P. for Russia: reminiscences & correspondence of Madame Olga Novikoff* (London, 1909).
108. Laura's history, kept for years by Gladstone in a locked case with her letters, is now untraced. It is surmised that he burnt it, along with her earlier letters in 1893. West, 'Gladstone and Laura Thistlethwayte', pp. 376, 379.
109. West, 'Gladstone and Laura Thistlethwayte', p. 382. Such activities were mirrored during Gladstone's visit to Earl Bathurst's Oakley Park in October 1875. This meeting, West persuasively argues, was on a similar emotional level to that at Boveridge in 1869.
110. West, 'Gladstone and Laura Thistlethwayte', pp. 384, 392.
111. Matthew, *Gladstone*, p. 617.
112. There is certainly no extant collection either at SDL or Hawarden Castle.
113. For example, GD 12/5/59.
114. GD 15/4/30.
115. GD 26/10/45.
116. GD 15/1/47, 23/7/50.
117. GD 13/5/48, translated by Matthew. *Fabliaux et contes des poetes francois des XI–XVe siecles, publiés par Barbazon*, 4 vols (1808) was regarded by Victorians as pornographic.
118. GD 22/2/49 saw further reading of *Fabliaux*: '(which I should have let alone)'.

274   Notes

119. *GD* 19/7/48.
120. See *GD* 5/9/50; 13/5/52; 15/9/58; 11/5/59; 18–21/9/61; 25–6/11/61; 21, 24/8/66; 8/9/66; 25/3/69; 5/9/71; 6/7/83; 2/5/84. 'X's indicate disapprobated reading of pornography.
121. *GD* 13–14/4/52. *Satyra sotadica de arcanis amoris et Veneris* (1680) by N. Chorier, passed off as J. Meursius, Dutch philologist and theologian.

5   Humanity: Libraries, Literature, and Liberalism

1. WEG to SEG, 30 Oct. 1889, *Hawarden Parish Magazine* (Dec. 1889). This story was also given wider currency: in 1890, H. W. Lucy described St Deiniol's to *Scottish Leader* readers as 'a kind of annexe to the castle'. H. W. Lucy, 'Mr Gladstone's Home Life', *Scottish Leader* "Special": 'Mr Gladstone in Scotland' 1890, pp. 17–19.
2. H. Friederichs, *In the Evening of his Days: a study of Mr. Gladstone in retirement, with some account of St. Deiniol's Library and Hostel* (London, 1896), pp. 98–9.
3. C. Ribblesdale, 'A Visit to Hawarden', *Nineteenth Century and After* 55:326 (1904), pp. 637–50, pp. 644–5.
4. *Times*, 16 Apr. 1895.
5. L. March-Phillipps and B. Christian, eds, *Some Hawarden Letters 1878–1913: written to Mrs. Drew (Miss Mary Gladstone) before and after her marriage* (London, 1917), pp. 322–3.
6. Friederichs, *Evening of his Days*, pp. 137–8.
7. Friederichs, *Evening of his Days*, pp. ix, 128, 109–10, 37, 124.
8. M. Drew, 'Mr. Gladstone's Library at "St. Deiniol's Hawarden"', *Nineteenth Century and After*, 59:352 (1906), pp. 944–54, p. 947; J. C. Story, *The Hawarden Temple of Peace: a description of St. Deiniol's Library* (Hawarden, 1905), pp. 8, 18, 17.
9. Drew, 'Gladstone's Library', p. 947.
10. See, for example, H. J. Jackson, *Marginalia: readers writing in books* (New Haven and London, 2001), pp. 84–5.
11. W. E. Gladstone, 'On Books and the Housing of them', *Nineteenth Century*, 27 (1890), pp. 384–96, p. 386.
12. *Times*, 24 Dec. 1896.
13. On this, see Clayton, 'Annotation Key', pp. 140–3.
14. *GD* 2/11/50.
15. *GD* 13/6/32.
16. For example: the Vatican Library (*GD* 4/4/32, 16/10/66, 26/11/66); the 'wonderful treasures' of the *Bibliothèque Nationale* (*GD* 15/10/79); the University, Pepys, and Fitzwilliam Museum libraries, Cambridge (*GD* 27/11/41, 3/11/59); Corpus Christi College, Oxford (*GD* 24/4/78).
17. For example, Audley End (*GD* 24/9/54); Chatsworth House (*GD* 31/5/73, 3–4/6/73, 19/11/75, 20/12/80); and Lord Acton's library (*GD* 14/5/90, 9/6/90, 17/6/90).
18. For example, Pusey House, Oxford (*GD* 5/7/85) and the lexicographer James Murray's 'scriptorium' (*GD* 7/2/90).
19. He was a committee member and bought books for the Carlton Club (*GD* 30/5/37, 14/6/37, 9/2/39, 12/2/39, 20/2/40, 16/5/40, 1 & 3/2/41); and was

instrumental in establishing the National Liberal Club library (*GD* 2/5/88, 17/11/88; *Times*, 3 May 1888; D. Williamson, *Gladstone: the Man: a non-political biography*, 2nd edn [London, 1898], p. 54.)
20. For example, in 1865 he received an official deputation to discuss government policy to Scottish libraries (*GD* 23/3/65); In 1869 he made plans for a Civil Service library (*GD* 5/6/69); in 1887 he opened Swansea town library (*GD* 6/6/87; R. Shannon, *Mr Gladstone and Swansea 1887* [Swansea, 1982]); and spoke on free libraries at the Free Public Library in St Martin's Lane, London in 1891 (*GD* 12/2/91; *Times*, 13 Feb. 1891, 'Opening of the St. Martin's Free Public Library', *The Library*, 3 (1891), pp. 109–15.)
21. He donated books to what would become St Catherine's College, Oxford, in 1874 (*GD* 9/2/74); and to Mold town library, Flintshire, in 1891 (*GD* 15/11/91).
22. *GD* 18/9/26.
23. See *GD* 4/10/28, 15/5/29. Gladstone maintained links with the Bodleian throughout his life, for example, through his membership of the Radcliffe Trust, see *GD* 20/11/61 and the *Guardian*, 27 Nov. 1861. He paid several visits to Bodley in the 1880s and 90s. See *GD* 28/11/83, 5/4/88, 25/10/92.
24. In 1831 he noted 'the Dean entrusted to me the keys of the library for the Vacation', *GD* 11/7/31. He also recorded working there, *GD* 12/7/31, 15/7/31.
25. For example, *GD* 15/6/88.
26. For example, *GD* 8/4/53.
27. *GD* 7/1/41, 20/2/41, 6/5/57, 22/2/58, 27/10/65, 20/2/75, 2/7/79, 14/8/82, 31/3/87, 22/6/87, 18/2/88. Many other visits are listed referring to trustees' meetings. See also, W. Baker, *The Early History of the London Library* (Lewiston, 1992), pp. 60–5.
28. *GD* 13, 27/2/32; 9, 22/3/32; 4, 13/4/32; 13–14, 19-20/6/32.
29. *GD* 13, 20/6/32, 7, 9/7/32.
30. *GD* 3/3/32.
31. *GD* 4/4/32.
32. Archbishop Martini's Italian translation of the Bible (1769–77).
33. *GD* 9/7/32. Having said that, Gladstone found plenty of evidence indicating that practices of censorship and prohibition were actively and easily subverted, see, for example, *GD* 16/11/38.
34. *GD* 15/2/32. Travel journal from BL GP Add MS 44818.
35. *GD* 6/11/46.
36. 'I do not regret anything ... yet I would wish that the rest of my life were as worthy as my public life.' *GD* 29/12/74.
37. He had begun it on 17 Dec. 1874.
38. R. Shannon, *Gladstone: heroic minister, 1865–1898* (London, 1999), pp. 118, 151. See also Matthew, *Gladstone*, p. 250; R. Jenkins, *Gladstone* (London, 1995), p. 387.
39. G. Eliot, *Middlemarch* (Ware, 1994), p. 67. See, M. Wheeler, *The Art of Allusion in Victorian Fiction* (London, 1979), p. 14.
40. W. E. Gladstone, 'Robert Elsmere and the Battle of Belief', *Nineteenth Century*, 23 (1888), pp. 766–88.
41. Quoted in J. Morley, *The Life of William Ewart Gladstone*, New edn, 2 vols (London, 1905), vol. 2, p. 596.

42. S. Collini, *Public Moralists: political thought and intellectual life in Britain, 1850–1930* (Oxford, 1991), pp. 81–3.
43. M. A. Ward, *Robert Elsmere*, 3 vols (London, 1888), vol. 2, pp. 9, 10, 14, 15. SDL R 37W/1.
44. See, for example, Ward, *Elsmere*, vol. 1, pp. 15–16.
45. Ward, *Elsmere*, vol. 2, p.136.
46. Gladstone, 'Robert Elsmere', pp. 771, 769.
47. *GD* 29/12/74.
48. Gladstone, 'On Books', p. 386.
49. J. L. Madden, 'Gladstone's Reading of Thomas Love Peacock', *Notes & Queries* (1967), p. 384. See, T. L. Peacock, *Works*, 3 vols (London, 1875), SDL R 34 P/1.
50. See R. Clayton Windscheffel, 'Gladstone and Scott: family, identity, and nation', *Scottish Historical Review*, 86 (2007), pp. 69–95.
51. Drew, 'Gladstone's Library', p. 950.
52. *Chester Courant*, 3 Feb. 1868.
53. Quoted in J. E. Ritchie, *The Real Gladstone: an anecdotal biography* (London, 1898), p. 275.
54. Gladstone, 'On Books', pp. 390–1.
55. *Chester Courant*, 3 Feb. 1868. See also, A. Briggs, ed., *Gladstone's Boswell: late Victorian conversations by Lionel A. Tollemache and other documents* (Sussex and New York, 1984), p. 44.
56. 'Speech at the Cross of Edinburgh', *Daily News*, 24 Nov. 1885.
57. W. E. Gladstone, 'Tennyson', *Quarterly Review*, 106:454 (1859), pp. 454–85, p. 474.
58. Gladstone, 'Tennyson', pp. 460–4. Gladstone qualified his attack when the article was republished in *Gleanings* in 1879, indicating he should have concentrated more on the qualities of the poetry rather than on the views enunciated by the protagonist. See, W. E. Gladstone, 'Tennyson', in *Gleanings of Past Years, 1845–76*, ed. W. E. Gladstone (London, 1879), pp. 131–79, p. 141 ff.
59. Gladstone, 'Tennyson', p. 464.
60. Gladstone, 'Tennyson', pp. 468, 484–5.
61. See R. Shannon, 'Tennyson and Gladstone: From Courtship to Mutual Disenchantment', *Times Literary Supplement*, 2 Oct. 1992, pp. 4–6.
62. W. E. Gladstone, '"Locksley Hall" and the Jubilee', *Nineteenth Century*, 21 (1887), pp. 1–18, pp. 7, 16.
63. Gladstone, 'Locksley', p. 6.
64. Printed in *GD* 8/7/86.
65. Gladstone, 'Locksley', p. 4.
66. Gladstone, 'Locksley', p. 17.
67. BL, GP, Add MS 44548 fol. 111, WEG to Barry O'Brien, 7 Jul. 1886.
68. WEG to QV, 4 Nov. 1872 and Queen Victoria to WEG, 18 Nov. 1872, printed in P. Guedalla, *The Queen and Mr. Gladstone, 1845–1879* (London, 1933), pp. 383–4, 385.
69. 'Mr. Gladstone at the National Liberal Club', *Times*, 3 May 1888.
70. *Times*, 3 May 1888. Gladstone's mounting concern with the selfishness and greed which he felt characterized the younger generation was articulated in such writings as W. E. Gladstone, 'Mr. Carnegie's "Gospel of

Wealth": a review and a recommendation', *Nineteenth Century*, 28:677 (1890), pp. 677–93.
71. *Times*, 3 May 1888.
72. *Times*, 3 May 1888.
73. 'Rectorial Address at Glasgow University', W. E. Gladstone, *Political Speeches in Scotland, November and December 1879* (Edinburgh, 1879), p. 250.
74. *Times*, 3 May 1888.
75. *Times*, 3 May 1888.
76. 'Opening of the St. Martin's Library', p. 111.
77. 'Speech in Liverpool', 28 Jun. 1886, W. E. Gladstone, *Speeches on the Irish Question in 1886* (Edinburgh, 1886), p. 292.
78. 'Speech at Buckley Institute', 11 Nov. 1878, quoted in G. Barnett Smith, ed., *Thoughts from the Writings and Speeches of William Ewart Gladstone* (London, 1894), pp. 365–6.
79. Matthew, *Gladstone*, pp. 113–4.
80. This in turn led Morley to attribute the Lords' 'rejection of the Paper Duties bill' as 'having had no inconsiderable share in propelling him [Gladstone] along the paths of liberalism', as well as helping 'make him more than ever the centre of popular hopes'. Morley, *Life of Gladstone*, vol. 1, p. 699.
81. 'Speech at Saltney Institute', 26 Oct. 1889, W. E. Gladstone, *The Workman and His Opportunities: a discourse delivered at the Saltney Literary Institute* (London, 1889), p. 19.
82. 'Upstairs in the library are to be seen volumes with characteristic inscriptions by Mr. Gladstone.' Ritchie, *Real Gladstone*, p. 275. See also, A. G. Veysey, *The History of Hawarden Institute* (Hawarden, 1993).
83. GD 28/8/84, 8/10/84; BL GP Add MS 44547, fol. 123 and *Daily News*, 3 Sept. 1884.
84. See 'Opening of the St. Martin's Library', p. 112: 'If you want a man healthily developed you must develop him as a creature of body, soul and spirit.'
85. 'Speech at Buckley Institute', 11 Nov. 1878, *Times*, 13 Nov. 1878.
86. 'Speech at Hawarden Institute', 22 May 1893, *Times*, 23 May 1893.
87. For examples of this, see Williamson, *Gladstone the Man*, p. 89.
88. Gladstone, 'On Books', p. 388.
89. *Times*, 24 Dec. 1896.
90. J. Rose, *The Intellectual Life of the British Working Classes* (New Haven and London, 2001), p. 20.
91. My emphasis. M. Arnold, *Culture and Anarchy: an essay in political and social criticism* (London, 1869), p. 49. Arnold sent Gladstone a copy of the book in March 1869 following their discussion of it (see GD 21/3/69; BL GP Add MS 44419, fol. 281; SDL R 36 A/7). Gladstone wrote to Arnold saying: 'If the body of it is as interesting as the Preface, I shall read it with much avidity. The questions which you handle ... are of a constantly growing importance'. BL GP Add MS 44536, fol. 137, WEG to M. Arnold, 30 Mar. 1869.
92. Arnold, *Culture and Anarchy*, p. viii.
93. 'Speech at Chester', 27 Dec. 1862, W. E. Gladstone, *An Address delivered at the Saturday Evening Assembly of the Working Men of Chester, December 27, 1862* (Chester, 1863), pp. 14–15. Despite this concordance, Gladstone apparently read no further in *Culture and Anarchy* and made no comment on Arnold's call for an unrestricted interplay between class and culture.

94. This was a challenge which many took up. As Colin Matthew demonstrates, popular veneration of Gladstone as a leader was significantly supported by, and existed side by side with, serious study of his speeches. *GD*, vol. 9, p. lxix. See also, E. F. Biagini, *Liberty, Retrenchment and Reform: popular liberalism in the age of Gladstone, 1860–1880* (Cambridge, 1992), p. 393.
95. One came up at a Bonhams' sale in July 1987, lot 137, 'A rare "Gladstone" Bookmark, the stamped-out silver figure engraved with the likeness of Gladstone delivering a speech, engraved to reverse with W. E. Gladstone, M. P., London 1889'. NPG, Heinz Archive, *Bonhams Sale Catalogue*, 1987.
96. Ritchie, *Real Gladstone*, p. 276.
97. Gladstone, *Workman*, p. 13. See also Gladstone's speech at Buckley where he indicated that he expected members only to be interested in texts of a certain type. *Times*, 13 Nov. 1878.
98. My emphasis. Gladstone, *Workman*, pp. 13–14, 15, 18.
99. *Times*, 13 Nov. 1878.
100. Quoted in Barnett Smith, ed., *Thoughts*, p. 366.
101. W. E. Gladstone, '*Universitas Hominum*: or, the unity of history', *North American Review*, 373 (1887), pp. 589–602, p. 602.
102. 'Opening of the St. Martin's Library', p. 113.
103. As he had declared in parliament in May 1864: 'I venture to say that every man who is not presumably incapacitated by some consideration of personal unfitness or of political danger, is morally entitled to come within the pale of the constitution.' 'Speech of 11 May 1864', *Hansard*, cols. 312–27, at col. 324, and quoted in Morley, *Life of Gladstone*, vol. 1, p. 760.
104. 'Speech at Chester', 27 Dec. 1862, Gladstone, *Working Men of Chester*, p. 9.
105. M.-L. Legg, *Newspapers and Nationalism: the Irish provincial press, 1850–1892* (Dublin, 1999), pp. 110, 109, 116. See also, pp. 114, 115, 117.
106. W. E. Gladstone, 'The County Franchise and Mr. Lowe thereon', *Nineteenth Century*, 2 (1877), pp. 537–60, reprinted in W. E. Gladstone, *Gleanings of Past Years*, 7 vols (London, 1879), vol. 1, pp. 132, 158; Legg, *Newspapers and Nationalism*, pp. 109–10.
107. 'Speech at Hawarden Institute', 22 May 1893, *Times*, 23 May 1893.
108. My emphasis. Gladstone, *Workman*, p. 19.
109. Gladstone, *Workman*, p. 3; Matthew, *Gladstone*, p. 258.
110. Friederichs, *Evening of his Days*, pp. 98–9.
111. Ritchie, *Real Gladstone*, p. 275.
112. Drew, 'Gladstone's Library', p. 947. See also Friederichs, *Evening of his Days*, p. 109 ff.
113. Friederichs, *Evening of his Days*, pp. 134, 104, 132.
114. See S. M. Pearce, *On Collecting: an investigation into collecting in the European tradition* (London and New York, 1995), p. 248 ff.
115. See Jenkins, *Gladstone*, p. 565; Christensen, 'St Deiniol's Library, Hawarden: the Gladstone national memorial' (unpublished MA thesis, University of Liverpool, 2000), p. 83.
116. See T. Wemyss Reid, ed., *The Life of William Ewart Gladstone* (London, 1899), p. 592.
117. Drew, 'Gladstone's Library', p. 946. See also, H. Friederichs, 'Mr Gladstone's Library & Hostel at Hawarden', *Westminster Budget* (supplement), 23 Nov. 1894, p. 4.

6 Divinity: Gladstone, Oxford, and *Lux Mundi*

1. H. G. Hutchinson, ed., *Private Diaries of the Rt. Hon. Sir Algernon West, G.C.B.* (London, 1922), pp. 11–12. Gladstone took West to 'his Institute' on the succeeding day, when he 'was full of hopes for its future usefulness'. Hutchinson, ed., *Diaries of Algernon West*, p. 14.
2. W. T. Warren, ed., *Kebleland* (Winchester and London, 1906), pp. 63–4.
3. Quoted in S. Fletcher, *Victorian Girls: Lord Lyttelton's daughters* (London, 1997), p. 154. The effective end of university religious tests in 1871, one of the measures instituted by Gladstone's first government, meant that the responsibility for preserving an Anglican ethos in Oxford lay substantially with colleges, like Keble, which were still permitted to insist on a measure of Anglican conformity amongst their members. See J. P. Parry, *Democracy and Religion: Gladstone and the Liberal Party, 1867–1875* (Cambridge, 1986), pp. 297–301, 307–9.
4. Gladstone nominated Frederick Temple to the bishopric of Exeter in 1869, which provoked a rancorous controversy as Temple had contributed to the notorious *Essays and Reviews* (London, 1860). While his own essay on education was uncontroversial, fellow contributors, such as Benjamin Jowett, were accused of heresy. Lord Shaftesbury and E. B. Pusey led strong opposition to Temple's consecration, but both this and his enthronement went ahead in December 1869. Temple subsequently withdrew his *Essays and Reviews* piece from later reprint editions. He was nominated by Gladstone to the see of London in 1885 and to that of Canterbury by Lord Salisbury in 1896. See P. Hinchliff, *Frederick Temple, Archbishop of Canterbury: a life* (Oxford, 1998), pp. 119–29; H. M. Spooner, 'Temple, Frederick (1821–1902)', rev. Mark D. Chapman, *ODNB* (Oxford, 2004). Gladstone first read Temple's essay on 10 May 1860, and re-read it nine years later. At which point he judged: 'On re-perusal it seems to me crude and unbalanced, but neither heretical nor sceptical.' *GD* 21/11/69. His annotation of the essay, made at his second reading, reveals both agreement and disagreement with Temple's arguments. F. Temple, 'The Education of the World', in *Essays and Reviews*, 5th edn (London, 1861), pp. 1–49, SDL E39/17. *GD* shows he also read many other works by Temple.
5. *GD* 7/11/74.
6. Hagley MSS, L. Talbot to C. S. Talbot, 9 Nov. 1874, quoted in *GD* at this date. The series did not materialize.
7. W. Whyte, *Oxford Jackson: architecture, education, status, and style 1835–1924* (Oxford, 2006), p. 112.
8. Warren, ed., *Kebleland*, p. 67.
9. Rather than at the earlier dedication of Butterfield's imposing chapel, which Gladstone thought 'noble'. *GD* 31/1/78.
10. See *GD* 23/4/78 ff, and 'Keble College. Opening of the Library and Hall', *Guardian*, 26 Apr. 1878.
11. *GD* 25/4/78.
12. *Guardian*, 26 Apr. 1878.
13. D. Bebbington, *The Mind of Gladstone: religion, Homer, and politics* (Oxford, 2004), pp. 71, 75.

14. *Guardian*, 26 Apr. 1878. See also, S. Gilley, *Newman and His Age* (London, 1990), pp. 221–2, 371–9; J. D. Bastable, ed., *Newman and Gladstone* (Dublin, 1978), pp. 287–304.
15. Note, for example, 1874 condemnation of the Roman Catholic church for demanding that converts renounce 'moral and mental freedom', and for repudiating both 'modern thought and ancient history'. W. E. Gladstone, 'Ritualism and Ritual', *Contemporary Review*, 24 (1874), pp. 663–81, p. 674.
16. W. E. Gladstone, *Address delivered at the distribution of prizes in the Liverpool College, December 21, 1872*, 5th edn (London, 1873).
17. *Guardian*, 26 Apr. 1878.
18. See M. Poovey, *The History of the Modern Fact: problems of knowledge in the sciences of wealth and society* (Chicago and London, 1998), pp. 14, 198–204, 230–1.
19. The theory in moral theology that, in cases of doubt over whether or not laws should be binding or acts permissible, a person should follow the most probable of the available opinions, or the preponderating evidence. This opposed the Roman Catholic theory, principally associated with the Jesuits, of probablism, which taught that any action or edict can be regarded as permissible when it is supported by a probable opinion supported by a recognized doctor of the Church, even though another solution may be more probable. For a summary of Gladstone's views, see W. E. Gladstone, 'Probability as the Guide of Conduct', *Nineteenth Century*, 5 (1879), pp. 908–34.
20. *Guardian*, 26 Apr. 1878. Gladstone had thus counselled his Liverpool audience: 'Be slow to stir inquiries, which you do not mean patiently to pursue to their proper end. Be not afraid oftentimes to suspend your judgement; or to feel and admit to yourselves how narrow are the bounds of knowledge. Do not too readily assume that to us have been opened royal roads to truth.' Gladstone, *Liverpool College*, p. 29.
21. *Guardian*, 26 Apr. 1878.
22. C. Gore, ed., *Lux Mundi: a series of studies in the religion of the incarnation* (London, 1889). The collection went through ten British and several American editions within a year. J. Garnett, 'Lux Mundi essayists (*act.* 1889)', *ODNB* (Oxford, 2007). See also, P. Hinchliff, *God and History: aspects of British theology 1875–1914* (Oxford, 1992), Chapter 5.
23. See, G. L. Prestige, *The Life of Charles Gore: a great Englishman* (London: 1935); J. Carpenter, *Gore: a study in liberal catholic thought* (London, 1960); P. Avis, *Gore: construction and conflict* (Worthing, 1988).
24. Illingworth paid a visit of some days to Hawarden in 1879, *GD* 16/1/79 ff.
25. Henry Scott Holland (1847–1918), a canon of Christ Church, was a regular visitor to Hawarden and correspondent of Mary Drew. See *GD* 9/8/76, 13/10/81, 27/9/83 ff, 28/10/91.
26. Gladstone stayed with Francis Paget, dean of Christ Church in the run up to his Romanes Lecture, *GD* 24/10/92. There are several references in *GD* before the 1890s which the editors tentatively suggest as meetings with Paget.
27. Furthermore, Ottley's brother, Edward Bickersteth Ottley (1853–1910) – also a Keble product – was curate at Hawarden during the period 1876–80 and a borrower from the Temple of Peace. See *GD* 20/5/77. A collection of letters, collected by Ottley and his wife Maude, relating to Gladstone and

his circle, is preserved at Princeton University Library, Manuscripts Division, C0916.
28. See, for example, *GD* 12/4/77, 27/11/83. Lyttelton became principal of Selwyn, Keble's sister Cambridge college, where Gladstone stayed in 1887, *GD* 1/2/87.
29. *GD* 12/1/85.
30. BL GP Add MS 44093, fol. 254, WEG to Lord Acton, 27 Jan. 1885, printed in *GD* at this date.
31. *GD* 19/9/81; 30/9/84.
32. G. Stephenson, *Edward Stuart Talbot 1844–1934* (London, 1936), p. 20.
33. WEG to CG, 29 Jul. 1881, in *GD* at this date.
34. In 1876 they discussed 'E[dward]. W[ickham].s view of Prayer: on which we agreed.' *GD* 17/1/76.
35. *GD* 14/1/77, WEG to G. V. Wellesley, 20 September 1881 in *GD* at this date.
36. Quoted in Stephenson, *Talbot*, p. 33.
37. *GD* 2/12/83. A. Moore, *Evolution in its Relation to the Christian Faith: a paper read at the Reading Church Congress, October, 1883* (London, 1883). Gladstone's annotated copy survives (SDL 51/E/9), inscribed 'W. E. Gladstone with E. S. Talbot's affn. respect'. See also *GD* 10/12/85; 22, 26/2/88. Moore made quite an impression on Gladstone. Excluding *Lux Mundi*, St Deiniol's contains nine items by him. Moreover, at the Glenalmond College Jubilee in 1891, Gladstone named Moore as living proof that it was still possible to be a scholar and a clergyman. 'He was a man to whom all persons ... looked with the greatest admiration and the greatest interest, because they knew the powerful contribution he would make to the thinking power of the clergy and of the country'. 'Glenalmond College Jubilee', *Times*, 2 Oct. 1891.
38. Fletcher, *Victorian Girls*, p. 111.
39. Stephenson, *Talbot*, pp. 13, 52.
40. See Garnett, '*Lux Mundi* essayists', *ODNB*, G. L. Prestige, *Life of Charles Gore*, pp. 105, 118–9; Hinchliff, *God and History*, pp. 104–5.
41. This broadly signifies a theology which privileges the belief that the eternal word of God (*logos*) was present in the human Jesus of Nazareth, and that this union of divinity and humanity is freighted with redemptive power.
42. Contemporaries compared *Lux Mundi* to *Essays and Reviews*, and it influenced numerous succeeding works such as: B. H. Streeter, *Foundations: a statement of Christian belief in terms of modern thought by seven Oxford men* (London, 1912), including a contribution from Moberly's son Walter; E. G. Selwyn, ed., *Essays Catholic & Critical* (London, 1926), a Cambridge publication. Later publications include: R. Morgan, ed., *The Religion of the Incarnation: Anglican essays in commemoration of* Lux Mundi (Bristol, 1989); G. Wainwright, ed., *Keeping the Faith: essays to mark the centenary of Lux mundi* (London, 1989).
43. C. Gore, 'Preface', in *Lux Mundi* (London, 1889), pp. vii–x, p. vii.
44. Hinchliff, *God and History*, p. 51.
45. M. Ramsey, *From Gore to Temple: the development of Anglican theology between* Lux Mundi *and the Second World War, 1889–1939* (London, 1960), pp. vii, 2. See also, Prestige, *Gore*, p. 124.

46. BL GP Add MS 44249, fol. 116, WEG to H. E. Manning, 16 Nov. 1869, in *GD* at this date.
47. Gladstone, *Liverpool College*, pp. 27–8.
48. H. S. Holland, *Personal Studies* (London, 1905), p. 44.
49. The catholicity embraced by the later Gladstone incorporated all Christians professing belief in the incarnation – including Nonconformists and Presbyterians – into 'the catholic church' alongside Orthodox and Catholics. See W. E. Gladstone, 'The Place of Heresy and Schism in the Modern Christian Church', *Nineteenth Century*, 36 (1894), pp. 157–74. This was recognized by contemporaries. Soon after Gladstone's death, T. H. S. Escott wrote, 'Catholicity to Mr. Gladstone was an extraordinary comprehensive word'. T. H. S. Escott, 'Mr. Gladstone's Conception of a National Church', *New Century Review* (n.d.), pp. 74–9, p. 79.
50. He read Gore's 'Preface', probably that expanded for the 10th edition, in September 1890. *GD* 14/9/90.
51. Prestige, *Gore*, p. 102.
52. H. P. Liddon, *The Worth of the Old Testament: a sermon preached in St Paul's Cathedral ... December 8, 1889* (1890), *GD* 9/2/90.
53. *GD* 2/2/90 ff. See also, Bebbington, *Mind*, pp. 242–3.
54. W. E. Gladstone, *The Impregnable Rock of Holy Scripture*, Revd edn (London, 1892), pp. 267–8.
55. *GD* 12/3/93. On the 19th he called it 'remarkable & admirable'.
56. BL GP Add MS 44549, fol. 73, WEG to SEG, 20 Mar. 1893, printed in *GD* at this date. On 29 Mar. 1893, Gladstone asked Murray, the publisher, for 20 copies to distribute. See *GD* 12/3/93n; BL GP Add MS 44549 fol. 76.
57. It should be noted that Gore would not have understood this to be incompatible with his stance on scriptural inspiration. C. Gore, *The Mission of the Church: four lectures* (1892), p. 26 ff.
58. W. E. Gladstone, 'Robert Elsmere and the Battle of Belief', *Nineteenth Century*, 23 (1888), pp. 766–88, p. 781.
59. Quoted in M. Drew, 'Mr. Gladstone's Library at "St. Deiniol's Hawarden"', *Nineteenth Century and After*, 59:352 (1906), pp. 944–54, p. 953.
60. W. E. Gladstone, 'True and False Conceptions of the Atonement', *Nineteenth Century*, 36:211 (1894), pp. 317–331, p. 330. For more detailed discussion of Gladstone's relationship with esoteric beliefs, see R. Clayton Windscheffel, 'Politics, Religion and Text: W. E. Gladstone and Spiritualism', *Journal of Victorian Culture*, 11:1 (2006), pp. 1–29, pp. 16–20.
61. Gladstone, *Liverpool College*, p. 28.
62. Gore, *Mission*, pp. 6, 52–3, 77, 69, 80 ff, 112, vii–viii, 40–1.
63. Gore, *Mission*, p. 77.
64. Gladstone's annotated *Lux Mundi* is preserved at SDL E 11/47.
65. See E. S. Talbot, 'The Preparation in History for Christ', in *Lux Mundi*, ed. C. Gore (London, 1889), pp. 129–78, pp. 141, 159.
66. Talbot, 'Preparation', p. 165.
67. W. E. Gladstone, '*Universitas Hominum*: or, the Unity of History', *North American Review*, 373 (1887), pp. 589–602, p. 598.
68. Talbot, 'Preparation', p. 144.
69. Kenosis, from the Greek *kenōsis* (an emptying) refers to the belief that Christ deliberately renounced, or limited, the powers of the divine nature

in the incarnation. See Paul's letter to the Philippians 2:5–7: 'Christ Jesus, who, though he was in the form of God, did not regard equality with God as something to be exploited, but emptied himself, [*heauton ekenōse*] taking the form of a slave, being born in human likeness'. *NRSV* (Oxford, 1998). Although it is scarcely more than an inference in Gore's essay, a kenotic understanding of incarnation undergirds the whole of *Lux Mundi*, and would prove to be influential in twentieth-century theology. See M. Grimley, *Citizenship, Community, and the Church of England: liberal Anglican theories of the state between the wars* (Oxford, 2004), pp. 37–42.

70. Talbot, 'Preparation', p. 170.
71. On 5 July 1885, his reading included W. M. Statham, *The Abiding Christ and Other Sermons* (1885), referred to in the diary as 'Statham on Incarnation'. *GD* 5/7/85.
72. Bebbington, *Mind*, pp. 134, 132–5, 141.
73. W. E. Gladstone, *Ecce Homo* (London, 1868). The book was denounced by among others Pusey, and Lord Shaftesbury – who called it 'the most pestilential book ever vomited from the jaws of hell'. See Bebbington, *Mind*, p. 138.
74. L. Masterman, ed., *Mary Gladstone (Mrs. Drew) Her Diaries and Letters* (London, 1930), p. 25; Gladstone, *Ecce Homo*, p. 3.
75. For instance, Alfred and Emily Tennyson were also careful readers of *Ecce Homo* – their copy was so much used and marked that a new cover was required – but their reading of the text exhibited very different priorities than those shown by Gladstone. For further discussion of this, see R. Clayton, 'Gladstone, Tennyson and History: 1886 and All That', *Tennyson Research Bulletin*, 8:3 (2004), pp. 151–65.
76. J. Seeley, *Ecce Homo: a survey of the life and work of Jesus Christ* (London and Cambridge, 1866), pp. 47, 186. Gladstone's annotated copy is preserved in the Temple of Peace, Hawarden Castle.
77. Seeley, *Ecce Homo*, p. 6.
78. W. E. Gladstone, 'Tennyson', *Quarterly Review*, 106:454 (1859), pp. 454–85, p. 474.
79. T. W. Pritchard, *A History of St Deiniol's Library* (Hawarden, 1999), p. 9.
80. H. P. Liddon, *The Life of Edward Bouverie Pusey*, 2nd edn, 4 vols (London, 1897), vol. 4, pp. 391, 394.
81. SDL, Uncatalogued MSS, W. Phillimore to WEG, 25 Oct., 27 Nov. 1895.
82. SDL, Uncatalogued MSS, G. W. E. Russell, 'Memorandum on The Rev. R. L. Page's suggestions about St. Deiniol's', 20 Aug. 1895.
83. *GD* 3/7/85 ff.
84. BL GP Add MS 44549, fol. 73, WEG to SEG, 20 Mar. 1893, printed in *GD* 20/3/93.
85. Shannon, *Gladstone: heroic minister, 1865–1898* (London, 1999), p. 477.
86. See *GD* 5–9/4/88. Also, A. Tilney Bassett, ed., *Gladstone to his Wife* (London, 1936), pp. 252–3.
87. BL GP, Add MS 44503 fol. 152 ff, M. A. Ward to WEG, 12 Apr. 1888; fol. 170, M. A. Ward to WEG, 15 Apr. 1888; fol. 184, M. A. Ward to WEG, 17 Apr. 1888.
88. See, in particular, P. C. Erb, 'Politics and Theological Liberalism: William Gladstone and Mrs Humphry Ward', *Journal of Religious History*, 25:2 (2001), pp. 158–72. Erb argues, largely on the basis of Ward's testimony,

that Gladstone's engagement with *Robert Elsmere* demonstrated his conservatism in religion.
89. Special Collections, Honnold/Mudd Library, Claremont, CA, Mrs Humphry Ward Papers, M. A. Ward to Humphry Ward, 9 Apr. 1888.
90. Gladstone lamented to his wife: 'She has got her Catechism of half-research cut and dry, and does not appear to have read history outside the *negative* literature about the Scriptures.' Quoted in Tilney Bassett, ed., *Gladstone to his wife*, p. 253.
91. Gladstone, 'Robert Elsmere', pp. 769, 770–1.
92. Gladstone, 'Robert Elsmere', p. 778. It is true that the only reference made by name to an Anglican apologist is to that of Brooke Foss Westcott, and his work is criticized for isolating Christianity before studying it. M. A. Ward, *Robert Elsmere*, 3 vols (London, 1888), vol. 2, p. 314.
93. BL GP Add MS 44503 fol. 197, M. A. Ward to WEG, 30 Apr. 1888.
94. BL GP Add MS 44503 fol. 241, M. A. Ward to WEG, 12 May 1888. Gladstone in turn thanked her for 'the beautiful copy of Robert Elsmere', adding: 'It will form a very pleasant recollection of what I trust has been a "tearless battle".' Special Collections, Honnold/Mudd Library, Claremont, CA, Mrs Humphry Ward Papers, WEG to M. A. Ward, 14 May 1888.
95. Special Collections, Honnold/Mudd Library, Claremont, CA, Mrs Humphry Ward Papers, WEG to M. A. Ward, 10 Apr. 1888; BL GP Add MS 44503 fol. 184, M. A. Ward to WEG, 17 Apr. 1888.
96. He would be further reminded the following February when Ward sent him a preview of her article 'The New Reformation', published in *Nineteenth Century* in March 1889. BL GP Add MS 44506 fol. 83, M. A. Ward to WEG, 27 Feb. 1889. Their correspondence continued sporadically thereafter until 1895. See BL GP Add MS 44521 fol. 47, M. A. Ward to WEG, 16 Sept. 1895.
97. GD 10/11/88: 'We reached Keble Coll. soon after six. Long conversation with Mr Gore on meditated Hawarden foundation & other matters.'
98. Prestige, *Gore*, p. 79.
99. GD 11/11/88. Gore was not alone in marvelling at Gladstone's subordination of other responsibilities to planning St Deiniol's. See C. Ribblesdale, 'A Visit to Hawarden', *Nineteenth Century and After*, 55:326 (1904), pp. 637–50, pp. 644–5.
100. GD 12/11/88.
101. BL GP Add MS 44773, fol. 75, printed in *GD* 12/11/88.
102. BL GP Add MS 44505 fol. 148, Charles Gore to WEG, 22 Nov. 1888.
103. BL GP Add MS 44505 fol. 156, EST to WEG, 23 Nov. 1888.
104. Prestige, *Gore*, p. 173.
105. FRO GG MS 896, SEG to HNG, 4 Aug. 1886. See Pritchard, *History*, p. 9. Contemporary commentators also publicized this motivation. See, for example, T. Wemyss Reid, ed., *The Life of William Ewart Gladstone* (London, 1899), p. 592.
106. See Drew, 'Gladstone's Library', p. 947. However, it is unwise to assume Gladstone was completely resigned to a future move. In 1896 Friederichs noted 'it is Mr. Gladstone's wish that the permanent building should be in the same place where, in the present iron structure, the scheme came first into operation'. H. Friederichs, *In the Evening of his Days: a study of*

Mr. Gladstone in retirement, with some account of St. Deiniol's Library and Hostel (London, 1896), p. 127.
107. Ribblesdale, 'Visit to Hawarden', p. 639.
108. Undated document preserved with BL GP Add MS 44773, fol. 75.
109. BL GP Add MS 44773, fol. 75, Keble Memorandum.
110. On Gladstone's relationship with and standing in Liverpool, see P. Waller, *Democracy and Sectarianism: a political and social history of Liverpool 1868–1939* (Liverpool, 1981), pp. 74–6, 123, 132, 384, 401.
111. See A. Wilkinson, *Christian Socialism: Scott Holland to Tony Blair* (London, 1998); J. Garnett, *'Lux Mundi* essayists', *ODNB*.
112. Wilkinson, *Christian Socialism*, p. 133.
113. BL GP Add MS 44773, fol. 75, Keble Memorandum.
114. 'Glenalmond College Jubilee', *Times*, 2 Oct. 1891. He also called for the establishment of rural libraries in 'Opening of the St. Martin's Free Public Library', *The Library*, 3 (1891), pp. 109–115, p. 111. See also, J. C. Crawford, 'The Library and the Rural Community', in *Continuity and Innovation in the Public Library: the development of a social institution*, ed. M. Kinnell and P. Sturges (London, 1996), pp. 104–23.
115. Friederichs, *Evening of his Days*, pp. 97-8. See also, J. C. Story, *The Hawarden Temple of Peace: a description of St. Deiniol's Library* (Hawarden, 1905), p. 7.
116. BL GP Add MS 44773, fol. 75, Keble Memorandum.
117. L. March-Phillipps and B. Christian, eds, *Some Hawarden Letters 1878–1913: written to Mrs. Drew (Miss Mary Gladstone) before and after her marriage* (London, 1917), pp. 322–3.
118. SDL, Uncatalogued MSS, W. E. Gladstone, '1893 St. Deiniol's'.
119. SDL, Uncatalogued MSS, W. E. Gladstone, '1893 St. Deiniol's'. See also Drew, 'Gladstone's Library', p. 944.
120. Gore, 'Preface', p. vii.
121. In an intellectual rather than a denominational sense: both Gore and Gladstone retained an understandable sense of denominational hierarchy that privileged the Anglican church in practical terms.
122. Gore, *Mission*, p. 97.
123. 'Mr. Gladstone', *Times*, 16 Apr. 1895.
124. Gore, *Mission*, p. 68.
125. SDL, Uncatalogued MSS, W. E. Gladstone, 'St Deiniol's library', n.d., [Dalmeny Memorandum 8/7/92].
126. D. Williamson, *Gladstone the Man: a non-political biography*, 2nd edn (London, 1898), p. 62. See also, J. E. Ritchie, *The Real Gladstone: an anecdotal biography* (London, 1898), p. 275.
127. Story, *Hawarden Temple*, p. 18. See also Revd E. T. Slater, *A Temple of Peace: for the advancement of divine learning* (1903), p. 742.
128. For a study of the revival of religious communities in the Anglican church, see A. M. Allchin, *The Silent Rebellion: Anglican religious communities 1845–1900* (London, 1958).
129. Allchin, *Silent Rebellion*, pp. 238–43. See also, S. Koven, *Slumming: sexual and social politics in Victorian London* (Princeton and Oxford, 2004), pp. 236–48, on the settlement house movement.
130. SDL, Uncatalogued MSS, W. E. Gladstone, '1893 St. Deiniol's'.

286 Notes

131. Note, for example, his recorded reservations about the religious life made in Naples in 1838: 'Some other functions than those of prayer and study will commonly be needed in order to absorb the active energies and prevent them from harassing and spoiling the contemplative', further noting that 'Oxford ... surpassed all monasteries'! *GD* 12/11/38. Gladstone had expressed his approval, in a memorandum earlier that year, of orders which did not aim at 'egotistical separation from the world' but engaged in positive works such as the 'pursuit of divine learning'. Printed in D. C. Lathbury, ed., *Correspondence on Church and Religion of William Ewart Gladstone*, 2 vols (London, 1910), vol. 2, pp. 433–7. He himself became a member of such an order, 'The Engagement', in the 1840s, see H. C. G. Matthew, 'Gladstone, Evangelicalism and "The Engagement"', in *Revival and Religion since 1700: essays for John Walsh* ed. J. Garnett and H. C. G. Matthew (London, 1993), pp. 111–26.
132. The SSJE, or Cowley Fathers, was founded in the 1860s in Oxford by Richard Meux Benson. See Allchin, *Silent Rebellion*, Chapter 11.
133. SDL, Uncatalogued MSS, R. L. Page, 'Notes on the proposal of the Rt. Hon. W. E. Gladstone, to found at Hawarden, an Institution for the Cultivation of Divine learning' (1895).
134. SDL, Uncatalogued MSS, R. L. Page to WEG, 24 Apr. 1895. Gladstone had further discussions with a Father Puller of Cowley in 1896 with reference to the wardenship. See *ibid*, WEG to A. C. Headlam, 1 Jul. 1896.
135. SDL, Uncatalogued MSS, R. L. Page, 'Notes', (1895), fol. 6.
136. SDL, Uncatalogued MSS, G. W. E. Russell, 'Memorandum on ... Page's suggestions', 20 Aug. 1895.
137. SDL, Uncatalogued MSS, G. W. E. Russell to WEG, 29 Aug. 1895. In fact the library of SSJE, numbering some 10,000 books, came to St Deiniol's in 1980 following the closure of the Oxford house. Pritchard, *History*, p. 29.
138. He particularly felt that it might not be welcome to Gladstone's children. BL GP Add MS 44505 fol.156, EST to WEG, 23 Nov. 1888.
139. SDL, Uncatalogued MSS, H. S. Holland to WEG, 4 Dec. 1895. Francis Paget also wrote to Gladstone suggesting candidates. See SDL, Uncatalogued MSS, Francis Paget to WEG, 30? Mar. and 29 Jun. 1896.
140. Holland suggested the idea to Gore, whose initial response was that he would not wish Rackham to move to Hawarden without one or two other members of the fraternity. SDL, Uncatalogued MSS, H. S. Holland to H. Drew, 5 Dec. 1895; Charles Gore to WEG, 10 and 19 Dec. 1895.
141. See SDL, Uncatalogued MSS, EST to WEG, 7 Apr. 1896; Charles Gore to WEG, 10 Apr. 1896; EST to H. Drew, 1 May 1896.
142. SDL, Uncatalogued MSS, SEG to WEG, 12 May 1896.
143. This was made clear in Gladstone's original advert for the wardenship. Gladstone elaborated to A. C. Headlam in 1896: 'there is however great advantage, for this juncture at any rate, in having an unmarried man'. SDL, Uncatalogued MSS, WEG to A. C. Headlam (copy), 1 Jul. 1896.
144. Delahay was engaged, hence Gladstone put 'NB. marriage' after his name on his list of candidates and did not seriously consider him. SDL, Uncatalogued MSS, 'List of possible Wardens: names, current employment and proposers', n.d.

145. See M. Grimley, 'Headlam, Arthur Cayley (1862–1947), *ODNB* (Oxford, 2004).
146. SDL, Uncatalogued MSS, W. Saceday to WEG, 17 Jul. 1896. Gladstone and the Drews also received testimonials from Talbot and C. S. Laing for Headlam. See *ibid*.
147. SDL, Uncatalogued MSS, A. C. Headlam to WEG, 31 Jul. 1896.
148. SDL, Uncatalogued MSS, WEG to A. C. Headlam (copy), 1 Jul. 1896.
149. Uncatalogued MSS, A. C. Headlam to WEG, 2 Jul. 1896. Gladstone was unperturbed and invited Headlam to visit Hawarden.
150. BL GP Add MS 44773, fol. 75, Keble Memorandum.
151. Joyce was sub warden of St Michael's Theological College, Aberdare, before his appointment, and afterwards became bishop of Monmouth (1928–40). See A. Edwards, *The Seven Bishops of Monmouth* (Newport, 1996), pp. 14–20; Pritchard, *History*, pp. 30–1. Gladstone's offer to Joyce was very business-like and concentrated on the practicalities of organizing the library. See SDL, Uncatalogued MSS, WEG to G. C. Joyce (copy), 16 Oct. 1896; G. C. Joyce to WEG (copy), 17 Oct. 1896. With Headlam, Gladstone had discussed devotional life and practice, the relationship between parish church and library, marriage and simplicity of living. SDL, Uncatalogued MSS 'Memorandum', 16 Jul. 1896.
152. Drew, 'Gladstone's Library', pp. 944, 947, 952–3, 954.
153. H. Friederichs, 'Mr Gladstone's Library & Hostel at Hawarden', *Westminster Budget (supplement)*, 23 Nov. 1894, p. 5.
154. S. Liberty, *In the Cause of Divine Learning* (London, 1906), p. 3.
155. Liberty, *Divine Learning*, pp. 4–5. See also, Story, *Hawarden Temple*, foreword, and G. C. Joyce's 1903 report to the library's trustees, in which he stated: 'I believe that the chief object ... should be the encouragement of theological study among the parochial clergy', printed in Lathbury, ed., *Church and Religion*, vol. 2, p. 451 ff.
156. This aim, with the exception of an undated holograph preserved with the Keble Memorandum where it follows 'devotion', was always put first by Gladstone and expressed unequivocally by him. Stephen Gladstone also maintained that 'my Father's one great aim: [was] the establishment of this Foundation ... for the promotion of Divine learning', SDL, Uncatalogued MSS, SEG to Duke of Westminster, 24 Mar. 1899.
157. R. M. Benson, *The Religious Vocation*, p. 82 ff, quoted in Allchin, *Silent Rebellion*, p. 199.
158. Allchin, *Silent Rebellion*, p. 202.
159. *GD*, vol. 10, pp. clxxxix–cxc.
160. *William Ewart Gladstone* [Illustrated Memorial Pamphlet] (Bristol, 1898), SDL GX/Y/12.
161. 'Mr. Gladstone', *Times*, 16 Apr. 1895.
162. See Slater, *A Temple of Peace*, pp. 736–7, 742.
163. My emphasis. Friederichs, *Evening of his Days*, pp. 100, 103.
164. SDL, Uncatalogued MSS, 'Opening of St Deiniol's library', 1902.
165. Quoted in Wilkinson, *Christian Socialism*, p. 80.
166. Liberty, *Divine Learning*, title page.
167. Gladstone, 'Unity', pp. 601–2.

7 Political Lotus-Eater to Grand Old Bookman: Re-presenting Gladstone the Reader

1. Quoted in J. Morley, *The Life of William Ewart Gladstone*, New edn, 2 vols (London, 1905), vol. 2, p. 134.
2. GD 29/12/96.
3. F. A., 'William Ewart Gladstone: a study of character', *London Society*, 15:86 (1869), pp. 98–9.
4. H. C. G. Matthew, *Gladstone 1809–1898* (Oxford, 1997), p. 45; W. E. Gladstone, *The State in its Relations with the Church*, 4th, Revd edn, 2 vols (London, 1841), vol. 1, p. 25.
5. Books and reading, long associated with representations of femininity, continued, as Kate Flint and Lene Østermark-Johansen have shown, to define nineteenth-century iconographies of femininity. See, K. Flint, *The Woman Reader, 1837–1914* (Oxford, 1993); L. Østermark-Johansen, 'The Matchless Beauty of Widowhood: Vittoria Colonna's Reputation in Nineteenth-Century England', *Art History*, 22:2 (1999), pp. 270–94. Gendered poses were minutely described, as this example from a later photographic magazine illustrates: 'The pose of a lady should not have that boldness of action which you would give a man, but be modest and retiring, the arms describing gentle curves, and the feet never apart.' *Photographic News*, 5, 8 Mar. 1861, p. 110, quoted in A. Linkman, *The Victorians: photographic portraits* (London and New York, 1993), p. 46.
6. M. Roper and J. Tosh, ed., *Manful Assertions: masculinities in Britain since 1800* (London, 1991), p. 2.
7. Although 'an increasingly problematic term', this signified a professional intellectual who earned both living and status by what he had to say in speech and writing. S. Collini, *Public Moralists: political thought and intellectual life in Britain* (Oxford, 1991), p. 17.
8. See N. Clarke, 'Strenuous Idleness: Thomas Carlyle and the man of letters as hero', in *Manful Assertions*, ed. M. Roper and J. Tosh (London, 1991), pp. 25–43. See also, C. T. Christ, 'The Hero as Man of Letters: masculinity and Victorian nonfiction prose', in *Victorian Sages and Cultural Discourse: renegotiating gender and power* ed. T. Morgan (New Brunswick, 1990), pp. 19–31; M. Butler, *Romantics, Rebels and Reactionaries: English literature and its background, 1760–1830* (Oxford, 1981), pp. 69–93.
9. T. Carlyle, *On Heroes, Hero-Worship and the Heroic in History* (London, 1841), p. 249. All quotations are taken from Gladstone's annotated copy, which is preserved at SDL R 35C/4.
10. Carlyle, *Heroes*, p. 263.
11. See Clarke, 'Strenuous Idleness', pp. 40–1.
12. Matthew, *Gladstone*, p. 32.
13. Quoted in T. W. Heyck, *The Transformation of Intellectual Life in Victorian England* (London, 1982), p. 74. For a recent treatment of the Victorian academic, see H. S. Jones, *Intellect and Character in Victorian England: Mark Pattison and the invention of the don* (Cambridge, 2007).
14. T. Carlyle, *Past and Present* (London, 1843), p. 214.
15. J. R. Robertson, 'Gladstone: a study', *The Free Review* (n.d.), p. 92.
16. W. E. Gladstone, *The State in its Relations with the Church* (London, 1838), p. v.

17. For further discussion, see A. R. Vidler, *The Orb and the Cross: a normative study in the relations of church and state with reference to Gladston's early writings* (London, 1945); P. Butler, *Church, State and Tractarianism: a study of his religious ideas and attitudes, 1809–1859* (Oxford, 1982); R. J. Helmstadter, 'Conscience and Politics: Gladstone's first book', in *The Gladstonian Turn of Mind: essays presented to J. B. Conacher*, ed. B. L. Kinzer (Toronto, 1985), pp. 3–42.
18. T. B. Macaulay, 'Church and State by W. E. Gladstone', *Edinburgh Review*, 69 (1839), pp. 231–80.
19. W. Bagehot, *Biographical Studies* (London, 1914), p. 106.
20. Matthew, *Gladstone*, pp. 41, 38.
21. See D. Wahrman, *Imagining the Middle Class: the political representation of class in Britain, c. 1780–1840* (Cambridge, 1995), p. 342.
22. GD 30/3/39. On the role of withdrawal in Gladstone's psychological response to stress, see T. L. Crosby, *The Two Mr Gladstones: a study in psychology and history* (New Haven and London, 1997), Chapter 4.
23. GD 31/8/41.
24. GD 31/8/41. See also GD 29/12/43: 'Of public life I ... must say every year shows me ... that the idea of Christian politics can not be realised in the State according to its present conditions of existence'.
25. BL GP Add MS 44819 fol. 69 v, Memorandum, 31 Aug. 1841, printed in GD at this date. The prospect of retirement on such grounds again arose in 1844 over Irish education. Gladstone told Peel that he 'could not be an *author* of such a measure, & ... expect to be taken for an honest man' and proposed the following Easter as a date 'to retire'. GD 8/7/44 and BL GP Add MS 44777 fol. 199, Memorandum, 16 Jul. 1844.
26. Peel built a 'Statesmen's Gallery' at Drayton Manor to house his portraits of colleagues and eminent contemporaries. See H. C. G. Matthew, 'Portraits of Men: Millais and Victorian Public Life', in *Millais: portraits*, ed. P. Funnell and M. Warner (London, 1999), pp. 137–61, p. 143.
27. BL, Add. MS 40536, fol. 138, Sir Robert Peel to John Lucas, 18 Nov. 1843.
28. *The Athenaeum*, 1 Jun. 1844.
29. J. E. Adams, *Dandies and Desert Saints: styles of Victorian masculinity* (Ithaca and London, 1995), p. 14.
30. FRO, GG MS 339, W. Walker to JG, 15 Jul. 1842.
31. 'The Royal Academy', *Times*, 7 May 1877.
32. A. J. Butler, 'Mr. Gladstone as a Scholar', in T. Wemyss Reid, ed., *The Life of William Ewart Gladstone* (London, 1899), pp. 135–54, at pp. 135–6, 148. Sir G. C. Lewis, Gladstone's rival as chancellor of the exchequer in the late 1850s, was also a distinguished scholar of ancient Greece. See D. A. Smith, 'Lewis, Sir George Cornewall, second baronet (1806–1863)', *ODNB* (Oxford, 2004).
33. O. Garnett, *Hughenden Manor*, Revd ed. (London, 2002), pp. 11–13. See also R. Blake, *Disraeli* (London, 1966), pp. 110, 558.
34. Hutchinson, *West Diaries*, p. 15.
35. W. E. Gladstone, 'Lord John Russell's translation of Dante's Francesca da Rimini', *English Review* (1844), pp. 1–16. See A. Isba, *Gladstone and Dante: Victorian statesman, medieval poet* (Woodbridge, 2006), pp. 110–11.
36. Gladstone, 'Russell', pp. 3, 15–16, 2.

37. W. F. Monypenny and G. E. Buckle, *The Life of Benjamin Disraeli, Earl of Beaconsfield*, 6 vols (London, 1910–20), vol. 4, pp. 404–5; vol. 3, pp. 157–8.
38. Butler, 'Gladstone as a Scholar', in Wemyss Reid, ed., *Gladstone*, pp. 135–54, p. 146. My emphasis.
39. See J. Hearn, *Men in the Public Eye: the construction and deconstruction of public men and public patriarchies* (London, 1992), p. 6.
40. *GD* 14, 16, 23/6/59; 15, 17/8/59.
41. *GD* 1/6/78 and 20/7/74.
42. *GD* 16/5/76.
43. FRO, GG MS 3018, G. F. Watts to WEG, 15 Jul. 1865.
44. C. Phillips, 'Millais's Works at Burlington House', *Nineteenth Century*, 43:253 (1898), pp. 378, 385. The reception of Watts' early Gladstone portraits was muted, largely because they were exhibited 20 years after production. See the *Guardian*, 14 May 1879 and 11 Jan. 1882.
45. Bagehot, *Biographical Studies*, p. 92. Bagehot was not alone in his opinion: see also, R. H. Hutton, 'Mr. Gladstone', *Contemporary Review*, 65 (1894), p. 617.
46. Bagehot, *Biographical Studies*, pp. 116, 124.
47. Carlyle, *Heroes*, p. 256.
48. Bagehot, *Biographical Studies*, pp. 107, 122.
49. E. Biagini, *Gladstone* (London, 2000), p. 37.
50. See, especially, E. Biagini, *Liberty, Retrenchment and Reform: popular liberalism in the age of Gladstone, 1860–1880* (Cambridge, 1992), pp. 379–425; D. A. Hamer, 'Gladstone: the making of a political myth', *Victorian Studies* (1978), pp. 29–50; C. Harvie, 'Gladstonianism, the Provinces and Popular Political Culture, 1860–1906', in *Victorian Liberalism: nineteenth-century political thought and practice*, ed. R. Bellamy (London, 1990), pp. 152–74; J. S. Meisel, *Public Speech and the Culture of Public Life in the Age of Gladstone* (New York, 2001), pp. 264, 272; A. P. Saab, *Reluctant Icon: Gladstone, Bulgaria, and the working classes, 1856–1878* (Cambridge, MA, 1991), pp. 64, 97, 110, 119, 124–5, 154, 179, 199–200.
51. Biagini, *Liberty*, pp. 380–1; Matthew, *Gladstone*, pp. 135–7, 301; Hamer, 'Political Myth'.
52. Hutton, 'Mr. Gladstone', p. 621.
53. W. E. Gladstone, *Studies on Homer and the Homeric age*, 3 vols (Oxford, 1858), vol. 3, p. 107.
54. Quoted in Hutton, 'Mr. Gladstone', p. 619.
55. Matthew, *Gladstone*, pp. 287, 230. See also R. Jenkins, *Gladstone* (London, 1995), p. 377.
56. As J. D. Clayton notes of Gladstone's first ministry, 'intellectual ability was unusually common'. J. D. Clayton, 'Mr. Gladstone's Leadership of the Parliamentary Liberal Party: 1868–1874' (Unpublished D.Phil thesis, University of Oxford, 1961), pp. 47–8.
57. J. Maloney, 'Gladstone's Gladstone? The chancellorship of Robert Lowe, 1868–73', *Historical Research*, 79:205 (2006), pp. 404–28, p. 405.
58. Quoted in R. B. O'Brien, *John Bright: a monograph* (London, 1910), p. 74.
59. Butler, 'Gladstone as a Scholar', in Wemyss Reid, ed., *Gladstone*, pp. 135–54, at pp. 135–6, 148.
60. See *GD* 24/12/72, 13/3/73, and Shannon, *Gladstone: heroic minister, 1865–1898* (London, 1999), pp. 115, 117.

61. Matthew, *Gladstone*, p. 259.
62. Shannon, *Gladstone: heroic minister*, p. 133. See also *GD* 29, 31/12/73.
63. BL GP Add MS 44762, fol. 162, 'Memorandum read to late Colleagues', 14 Jan. 1875.
64. Matthew, *Gladstone*, p. 247.
65. 'Far From the Madding Crowd', *Judy*, 27 Jan. 1875.
66. 'Good-Bye!', *Punch*, 30 Jan. 1875.
67. BL GP Add MS 44762, fol. 37, Holograph, 7 Mar. [1874], printed in *GD* at this date. For an in depth analysis of the religious differences that tore Gladstone's first government apart, see J. Parry, *Democracy and Religion: Gladstone and the Liberal Party, 1867–1875* (Cambridge, 1986), Part 2.
68. Quoted in Matthew, *Gladstone*, p. 259. This reiterated sentiments expressed in an earlier letter, WEG to CG, 6 Apr. 1874, printed in A. Tilney Bassett, ed., *Gladstone to his Wife* (London, 1936), pp. 201–2.
69. Shannon, *Gladstone: heroic minister*, p. 142.
70. BL GP Add MS 44762, Holograph, 7 Mar. [1874], fol. 37 quoted in *GD* at this date.
71. Susan Pearce posits the idea that collected items 'are made to withdraw from everyday life in order to enable another order of life to come about'. S. M. Pearce, *On Collecting: an investigation into collecting in the European tradition* (London and New York, 1995), pp. 24–5. There is no doubt that Gladstone conceptualized his retirement in such terms, describing his state, post-resignation, as 'one who has passed through a death, but emerged into a better life', and taking leave of Carlton House Terrace as 'a *little* death'. *GD* 16/1/75, 15/4/75.
72. *GD* 9-10/2/74. No indication of subject is given.
73. *GD* 13/8/76 n.
74. See, for example, Crosby, *The Two Mr Gladstones*, pp. 152–3. A. Ramm, 'Review of *Gladstone Diaries*, vol. 9, 1875–1880', *English Historical Review*, (1987), pp. 439–42, p. 440.
75. BL GP Add MS 44762 fol. 4, Memorandum, 19 Jan. 1874, quoted in *GD* at this date; BL GP Add MS 44762. fol. 29, WEG to A. W. Peel, 19 Feb. 1874, quoted in *GD* at this date.
76. Shannon, *Gladstone: heroic minister*, p. 125; Matthew, *Gladstone*, p. 259. BL GP Add MS 44543, WEG to H. B. W. Brand, 23 Feb. 1874, fol. 75, quoted in *GD* at this date.
77. *GD* 29/12/76, 31/12/77.
78. W. E. Gladstone, *Bulgarian Horrors and the Question of the East* (London, 1876).
79. As both Stefan Collini and Julia Stapleton observe, British intellectuals were loath to associate themselves with anything that smacked of party. Collini, *Public Moralists*, pp. 57–8; *Political Intellectuals and Public Identities in Britain since 1850* (Manchester and New York, 2001), p. 13. Stapleton furthermore notes their anti-clericalism, Stapleton, *Political Intellectuals*, pp. 13–14.
80. Collini, *Public Moralists*, pp. 230–1. See, R. Shannon, *Gladstone and the Bulgarian Agitation 1876*, 2nd edn (Hassocks, 1975), for Gladstone's initial reluctance; Saab, *Reluctant Icon*, for intellectuals spearheading the movement.

81. Stefan Collini, rather unkindly, describes Gladstone's later career as 'conspicuously parasitic upon' increasing moral freighting of public issues! Collini, *Public Moralists*, p. 84.
82. Even at the beginning of his retirement, Gladstone had mapped out for himself a sphere of 'individual action' as far as politics was concerned and was clear that in intellectual matters also: 'I must act mainly for myself'. BL GP Add MS 44762, fol. 37, Unsigned holograph, 5 Mar. 1874, quoted in *GD* at this date. See also *GD* 30/10/74.
83. Matthew, *Gladstone*, p. 331.
84. 'Arcades Ambo!', *Punch*, 14 Apr. 1877.
85. Matthew, *Gladstone*, p. 306.
86. BL GP Add MS 43385 fol. 298, WEG to J. Bright, 29 Sept. 1881; BL GP Add MS 44473, fol. 185, WEG to J. H. Newman, 18 Dec. 1881, printed in *GD* at these dates.
87. *GD* 28/12/79. This was reiterated on 31st.
88. Matthew, *Gladstone*, pp. 135–7, 301.
89. Biagini, *Liberty*, p. 398.
90. See H. Sussman, *Victorian Masculinities: manhood and masculine poetics in early Victorian literature and art* (Cambridge, 1995), p. 41.
91. P. Bailey, *Popular Culture and Performance in the Victorian City* (Cambridge, 1998), p. 25.
92. See, for example, J. Bryce, 'Gladstone the Man: written on the occasion of the centenary of his birth', *The Outlook*, 12 Feb. 1910, p. 205.
93. All Gladstone's biographers have explored the symbolic importance of his wood felling. See, for example, Biagini, *Liberty*, p. 397 ff; Crosby, *The Two Mr Gladstones*, pp. 11, 95.
94. Roper and Tosh, *Manful Assertions*, p. 14.
95. Biagini, *Liberty*, p. 397.
96. Carlyle, *Heroes*, pp. 52–3. I am grateful to David Bebbington for this reference.
97. Marked with a single line.
98. *GD* 4/8/77.
99. *Times*, 6 Aug. 1877.
100. FRO, GG MS 702, William Houghton to WEG, 3 Oct. 1877.
101. *GD* 6/8/77.
102. Gladstone had shot off his finger in a shooting accident. *GD* 13/9/42.
103. Hearn, *Men in the Public Eye*, p. 188.
104. Biagini, *Liberty*, p. 397.
105. FRO, GG MS 702, William Houghton to WEG, 3 Oct. 1877.
106. G. W. E. Russell, *William Ewart Gladstone*, 4th edn (1898), p. 270.
107. See C. Trodd, 'The Laboured Vision and the Realm of Value: articulation of identity in Ford Madox Brown's *Work*', in *Re-Framing the Pre-Raphaelites: historical and theoretical essays*, ed. E. Harding (Aldershot, 1996), pp. 61–80, p. 65.
108. Visitors would regularly attend Hawarden Church to hear Gladstone reading.
109. See R. Clayton Windscheffel, 'Politics, Portraiture and Power: reassessing the public image of William Ewart Gladstone', in M. McCormack ed., *Public Men: masculinity and politics in modern Britain*, (Basingstoke, 2007), pp. 93–122.

110. See, for example, *GD* 20/7/74, 17/2/75, 19/1/82.
111. See, for example, *GD* 10/9/77 ff, 6/3/86, and L. Masterman, ed., *Mary Gladstone (Mrs. Drew) Her Diaries and Letters* (London, 1930), p. 401.
112. Joseph Rowley's daughters introduced the American Hamilton to the Gladstones at Hawarden in 1890. J. M. Hamilton, *Men I Have Painted: with a foreword by Mrs Drew* (London, 1921), p. 41.
113. Hamilton, *Men I Have Painted*, pp. 44, 47–8.
114. Note Peter Funnell's reference to the popularity of the '"artist at home literature" of the period'. P. Funnell, 'Millais's Reputation and the Practice of Portraiture', in *Millais: portraits*, eds P. Funnell and M. Warner (London, 1999), pp. 11–35, p. 20.
115. Quoted in J. Green-Lewis, *Framing the Victorians: photography and the culture of realism* (Ithaca and London, 1996), p. 145.
116. Hamilton, *Men I Have Painted*, p. 60.
117. Quoted in Hamilton, *Men I Have Painted*, pp. 7–8.
118. Hamilton, *Men I Have Painted*, p. 47.
119. [Frank Hill], 'Mr. Gladstone – Actor and Orator' in H. Furniss, *Some Victorian Men* (London, 1924), p. 225.
120. H. Friederichs, *In the Evening of his Days: a study of Mr. Gladstone in retirement, with some account of St. Deiniol's Library and Hostel* (London, 1896), pp. 129–30.
121. 'Gladstone Memorial Number', *Black and White*, May 1898, p. 35. The untouched photograph was used in T. Archer and A. T. Story, *William Ewart Gladstone and his Contemporaries: seventy years of social and political progress*, Revd edn, 4 vols (1899), vol. 2, p. 50.
122. This superficiality was noted by *Punch*, 11 May 1889, p. 226. A portrait's subject comments on his book, 'This is a stupid book! There's nothing in it!'
123. Hearn draws an important distinction between 'the *general* category of the "public self" of men in the public domain; and the *particular* "public selves" of particular men'. See Hearn, *Men in the Public Eye*, p. 210.
124. T. Gronberg, 'The Inner Man: interiors and masculinity in early twentieth-century Vienna', *Oxford Art Journal*, 24:1 (2001), pp. 67–88, pp. 78, 87. See also, pp. 85–6.
125. See M. A. Danahay, *A Community of One: masculine autobiography and autonomy in nineteenth-century Britain* (Albany, 1993).
126. W. E. Gladstone, '*Universitas Hominum*: or, the Unity of History', *North American Review*, 373 (1887), pp. 589–602, p. 602.
127. G. Cubitt, 'Introduction', in *Heroic Reputations and Exemplary Lives* eds G. Cubitt and A. Warren (Manchester, 2000), p. 3.
128. *Primitive Methodist*, 8, 24 Jun. 1886, p. 419, quoted in G. D. Goodlad, 'Gladstone and his Rivals: popular Liberal perceptions of the party leadership in the political crisis of 1885–6', in *Currents of Radicalism*, eds E. F. Biagini and A. J. Reid (1991), p. 179.
129. Collini, *Public Moralists*, pp. 233–4. See also, C. Harvie, 'Ideology and Home Rule: James Bryce, A. V. Dicey and Ireland, 1880–1887', *English Historical Review*, 91:359 (1976), pp. 298–314.
130. 'A Terrible Threat!', *Punch*, 11 Oct. 1884. See also *Punch*, 10 Nov. 1884 re. the Navy, and 16 Sept. 1893, showing Gladstone hiding in the hills with Homer.

131. Quoted in J. E. Ritchie, *The Real Gladstone: an anecdotal biography* (London, 1898), pp. 277, 276; G. B. Smith, *The Life of the Right Honourable William Ewart Gladstone*, 6th edn (London, Paris and New York, n.d.), vol. 4, p. 491.
132. GD 6/2/82.
133. W. T. Stead, *Gladstone 1809–1898: a character sketch with portraits and other illustrations* (London, n.d.), pp. 27–8.
134. The most significant of these are the two chalk drawings which remain in the private collection of Hawarden Castle. The third, a pencil sketch, is in NPG.
135. S. Reynolds, *William Blake Richmond: an artist's life 1842–1921* (Norwich, 1995), p. 271. See also, A. Linkman, 'Passing Trade: death and the family album in Britain 1860–1900', *Photohistorian*, 123 (1998), pp. 18–27.
136. See, J. E. Ritchie, *The Life and Times of William Ewart Gladstone*, 5 vols (London, 1898), vol. 5, p. 1436.
137. Linkman, 'Passing Trade', p. 22.
138. The two versions of this portrait plus a studio photograph are reproduced in Funnell, 'Millais's Reputation', pp. 176–7.
139. See J. Wolffe, *Great Deaths: grieving, religion, and nationhood in Victorian and Edwardian Britain* (Oxford, 2000), pp. 186, 288.
140. Archer and Story, *Gladstone and his Contemporaries*, pp. 461–2.
141. Note how David Williamson testified that 'most people know the systematic arrangement of the room, with its well-filled shelves and its tables, devoted either to correspondence, to politics, or to literature'. Williamson, *Gladstone the Man*, p. 81. This was as evident in Welsh as well as English literature. Griffith Ellis wrote: 'Nid oes un ystafell un Nghymru yn fwy adnabyddus na'r ystafell hon'. (There's no room in Wales as well known as this one). G. Ellis, *William Ewart Gladstone: ei fywyd a'i waith* (Gwrecsam, 1898), p. 434. For further comment on British national responses to Gladstone's death, see Wolffe, *Great Deaths*, pp. 6, 113, 121, 176, 284.
142. Sussman, *Masculinities*, p. 41.
143. Bryce, 'Gladstone the Man', p. 202.

Conclusion

1. GD 18/11/84.
2. Part of Gladstone's endpaper annotation of W. Scott, *The Bride of Lammermoor*, 3rd edn, 2 vols, *Novels and Tales of the Author of Waverley (25 volumes)*, vol. 11 (Edinburgh and London, 1822).
3. As Agatha Ramm rightly pointed out, it was Gladstone's usual practice to quote and allude to literary material long after it had been read and internalized. A. Ramm, *Gladstone as Man of Letters. A James Bryce memorial lecture* (Oxford, 1981), pp. 20–1. See also, R. Clayton Windscheffel, 'Gladstone and Scott: family, identity, and nation', *Scottish Historical Review*, 86 (2007), pp. 88–91.
4. For example, on leaving Oxford on 31 Jan. 1857, he 'Saw Mr Lake in the train: resp. Mil[itary]. Ed[ucation]. & Homer.' GD.
5. GD 14/1174. See, GD 20/1/70 and 24/11/70 for discussions with a lady musician and an 'intelligent German' respectively.

6. M. Drew, 'Mr. Gladstone's Library at "St. Deiniol's Hawarden"', *Nineteenth Century and After*, 59 (1906), p. 944.
7. J. C. Story, *The Hawarden Temple of Peace: a description of St. Deiniol's Library, founded by the Right Honourable William Ewart Gladstone* (Hawarden, 1905), p. 11.
8. C. Gore, 'Preface', p. vii.
9. C. Gore, *The Mission of the Church: four lectures* (London, 1892), pp. 3, 85.
10. *Times*, 16 Apr. 1895.
11. T. W. Pritchard, *A History of St Deiniol's Library* (Hawarden, 1999), p. 7; Story, *Hawarden Temple*, p. 10.
12. Story, *Hawarden Temple*, p. 15.
13. Monad, defined by *OED*, is 'An ultimate unit of being', also 'applied to the Deity'. The term is associated with the philosophy of G. W. von Leibnitz. Gladstone knew his work, for instance he recorded reading G. W. von Leibnitz, *A System of Theology*, trans. C. W. Russell (London, 1850). *GD* 31/8/51. See also Matthew, p. 553.
14. Story, *Hawarden Temple*, p. 10.

Bibliography

Primary sources

Manuscripts

Claremont, CA
Honnold/Mudd Library, Special Collections
Mrs Humphry Ward Papers

Hawarden
St Deiniol's Library
Gladstone Book and Pamphlet Collection
Glynne-Gladstone Manuscripts, GG 1-3028
Speeches and Writings by W. E. Gladstone, 12 vols
Speeches and Pamphlets by W. E. Gladstone, 38 vols
Uncatalogued Manuscript Collection

Flintshire Record Office
Bell Jones MSS
St Deiniol's MSS, 1–70

London
British Library
Gladstone Papers, Additional Manuscripts 44086–44835

British Museum, Department of Prints and Drawings
Satirical Print and Cartoon Collections

National Portrait Gallery, Heinz Library and Archive
National Portrait Gallery Collection of Portraits, Prints, Photographs and Cartoons
Reference Material relating to W. E. Gladstone, 5 boxes
Correspondence between W. E. Gladstone and G. F. Watts, 1859–96

Oxford
Bodleian Library
Acland Papers and Photograph Albums, 1840s–90s
John Johnson Collection of Printed Ephemera

Library Records
Proofs with amendments of 'On Books and the Housing of Them', 1889–90
Miscellaneous correspondence

Edited manuscripts, catalogues of manuscripts, and bibliographies

Adcock, L. M., *A Bibliography of Material held at St Deiniol's Library* (Hawarden, 1998).
Bassett, A. T., *Gladstone to his Wife* (London, 1936).
[Bassett, A. T.], *The Gladstone Papers* (London, 1930).
Briggs, A., ed., *Gladstone's Boswell: late Victorian conversations by Lionel A. Tollemache and other documents* (Sussex and New York, 1984).
British Museum Catalogue of Additions to the Manuscripts. The Gladstone Papers. Additional Manuscripts 44086–44835 (London, 1953).
Brooke, J. and M. Sorensen, eds, *The Prime Minister's Papers: W. E. Gladstone*, 4 vols (London, 1971–81).
Foot, M. R. D. (vols 1–2; vols 3–4 with HCGM) and H. C. G. Matthew (vols 5–14), eds, *The Gladstone Diaries: with prime ministerial correspondence*, 14 vols (Oxford, 1968–94).
Guedalla, P., *The Queen and Mr. Gladstone, 1845–1879* (London, 1933).
Hamer, F. E., ed., *The Personal Papers of Lord Rendel containing his Unpublished Conversations with Mr. Gladstone (1888 to 1898) and other Famous Statesmen; Selections from Letters and Papers reflecting the Thought and Manners of the Period; and Intimate Pictures of Parliament, Politics, and Society* (London, 1931).
Holland, H. S., *Memoirs and Letters*, ed. by S. Paget (London, 1921).
Hutchinson, H. G., ed., *Private Diaries of the Rt. Hon. Sir Algernon West, G.C.B.* (London, 1922).
Keith-Lucas, B. and H. N. Gladstone, *The Gladstone-Glynne Collection: a catalogue of the oil-paintings, water-colours, sculptures and miniatures and a supplementary list of prints and drawings at Hawarden Castle* (Cambridge, 1934).
Lathbury, D. C., ed., *Letters on Church and Religion of William Ewart Gladstone*, 2 vols (London, 1910).
Matthew, H. C. G., ed., *The Papers of William Ewart Gladstone* (Reading, 1998). [Microfilm, bibliographies, and catalogue]
March-Phillipps, L. and B. Christian, eds, *Some Hawarden Letters 1878–1913: written to Mrs. Drew (Miss Mary Gladstone) before and after her marriage* (London, 1917).
Masterman, L., ed., *Mary Gladstone (Mrs. Drew) Her Diaries and Letters* (London, 1930).
Schlüter, A., *A Lady's Maid in Downing Street*, ed. M. Duncan (London, 1922).
Williams, C. J., ed., *Handlist of the Glynne-Gladstone MSS in St. Deiniol's Library, Hawarden* (Richmond, 1990).

Contemporary published material

Newspapers, journals, and magazines

Athenaeum
Blackwood's Edinburgh Magazine
Bookworm
British and Foreign Evangelical Review
British Critic and Quarterly
British Quarterly Review
Chambers' Journal
Chester Chronicle
Christian Remembrancer
Church of England Magazine
Contemporary Review
Cornhill Magazine
Daily News
Edinburgh Review
English Illustrated Magazine
English Review
Free Review
Gentleman's Magazine
Graphic
Guardian: the Church Newspaper
Harper's Monthly Magazine
Harper's New Monthly Magazine
Hawarden Parish Magazine
Illustrated London News
Judy
Library
Lloyd's Weekly Newspaper
London Society
Macmillan's Magazine
Magazine of Art
New Century Review
Nineteenth Century
Nineteenth Century and After
North American Review
Notes and Queries
Outlook
Pall Mall Budget
Pall Mall Gazette
Pearson's Magazine
Penny Illustrated Paper
Periodical
Proceedings of the Society for Psychical Research
Punch, or the London Charivari
Quarterly Review
Scottish Leader
Sketch
Speaker
Strand Magazine
Sunday Strand
T.P.'s & Cassell's Weekly
Temple Bar
Theological Review
Times
Weekly Star
Westminster Budget
Young Man
Young Woman
Youth's Companion

W. E. Gladstone

Works by Gladstone

Books and pamphlets

Address by the Rt. Hon. W. E. Gladstone MP at the AGM of Subscribers (Hawarden, 1875).
Address delivered at the Distribution of Prizes in the Liverpool College, December 21, 1872, 5th edn (London, 1873).
An Address delivered at the Saturday Evening Assembly of the Working Men of Chester, December 27, 1862 (Chester, 1863).
Bulgarian Horrors and the Question of the East (London, 1876).
A Chapter of Autobiography (London, 1868).
The Church of England and Ritualism (London, 1875).
Church Principles Considered in their Results (London, 1840).

Ecce Homo (London, 1868).
Gleanings of Past Years 1843–1879, 7 vols (London, 1879).
The Impregnable Rock of Holy Scripture, Revd edn (London, 1892).
Juventus Mundi: the gods and men of the heroic age (London, 1869).
Landmarks of Homeric Study (London, 1890).
Later Gleanings (London, 1897).
A Manual of Prayers from the Liturgy. Arranged for family use (London, 1845).
Political Speeches in Scotland, November and December 1879 (Edinburgh, 1879).
Political Speeches in Scotland, Second Series (Edinburgh, 1880).
The Romanes Lecture 1892: an academic sketch (Oxford, 1892).
Rome and the Newest Fashions in Religion: three tracts: the Vatican decrees – Vaticanism – speeches of the Pope (London, 1875).
Speeches on the Irish Question in 1886, Revd edn (Edinburgh, 1886).
The State in its Relations with the Church (London, 1838).
The State in its Relations with the Church, Revd edn (London, 1841).
Studies on Homer and the Homeric Age, 3 vols (Oxford, 1858).
Studies Subsidiary to the Works of Bishop Butler (Oxford, 1896).
The Vatican Decrees in their Bearing on Civil Allegiance: a political expostulation (London, 1874).
Vaticanism: an answer to replies and reproofs (London, 1875).
The Work of the Universities [Edinburgh Rectorial Address] (London, 1860).
The Workman and His Opportunities: a discourse delivered at the Saltney Literary Institute, on the Opening of the New Reading and Recreation Rooms, October 26th, 1889 (London, 1889).
The Works of Joseph Butler, D.C.L. sometime Lord Bishop of Durham: divided into sections; with sectional headings, an index to each volume; and some occasional notes, also prefatory matter, 2 vols (Oxford, 1896).

Articles and chapters

'Arthur Henry Hallam', *The Youth's Companion*, 72 (1898), pp. 1–3.
'The Bill for Divorce', *Quarterly Review*, 102 (July 1857), pp. 251–88.
'Colonel Ingersoll on Christianity', *North American Review*, 146:378 (May 1888), pp. 481–509.
'The County Franchise and Mr. Lowe thereon', *Nineteenth Century*, 2 (1877), pp. 537–60.
'The Courses of Religious Thought', *Contemporary Review*, 28:168 (June 1876), pp. 1–26.
'The Elizabethan Settlement of Religion', *Nineteenth Century*, 24 (July 1888), pp. 1–13.
'The English Church under Henry VIII', *Nineteenth Century*, 26 (November 1889), pp. 882–96.
'The Evangelical Movement: its parentage, progress and issue', *British Quarterly Review*, 70 (July 1879), pp. 1–26.
'Giacomo Leopardi', *Quarterly Review*, 86 (1850), pp. 295–336.
'Is the Church of England Worth Preserving?' *Contemporary Review*, 26 (July 1875), pp. 193–220.
'"Locksley Hall" and the Jubilee', *Nineteenth Century*, 21 (January 1887), pp. 1–18.
'Lord John Russell's translation of Dante's Francesca da Rimini', *English Review*, (1844), pp. 1–16.

'The Lord's Day', in W. E. Gladstone, ed., *Later Gleanings* (London, 1897), pp. 338–51.
'On Books and the Housing of Them', *Nineteenth Century*, 27 (1890), pp. 384–96.
'On the Place of Homer in Classical Education and in Historical Inquiry', *Oxford Essays for 1857* (London, 1857).
'Mr. Carnegie's "Gospel of Wealth": a review and a recommendation', *Nineteenth Century*, 28 (1890), pp. 677–93.
'The Place of Heresy and Schism in the Modern Christian Church', *Nineteenth Century*, 36 (August 1894), pp. 157–74.
'Probability as the Guide of Conduct', *Nineteenth Century*, 5 (May 1879), pp. 908–34.
'Queen Elizabeth and the Church of England', *Nineteenth Century*, 24 (November 1888), pp. 764–784.
'Ritualism and Ritual', *Contemporary Review*, 24 (October 1874), pp. 663–81.
'*Robert Elsmere* and the Battle of Belief', *Nineteenth Century*, 23 (1888), pp. 766–88.
'Tennyson', *Quarterly Review*, 106 (October 1859), pp. 454–85; reprinted in W. E. Gladstone, ed., *Gleanings of Past Years, 1845–76*, (London, 1879), pp. 131–79.
'True and False Conceptions of the Atonement', *Nineteenth Century*, 36 (1894), pp. 317–31.
'*Universitas Hominum*: or, the Unity of History', *North American Review*, 373 (December 1887), pp. 589–602.

Works about Gladstone, the Gladstone family, and St Deiniol's Library (to 1945)

Books and pamphlets

Apjohn, L., *William Ewart Gladstone: his life and times* (London, 1898).
Archer, T. and A. T. Story, *William Ewart Gladstone and his Contemporaries: seventy years of social and political progress*, Revd and Extended Memorial edn, 4 vols (London, 1899).
Bagehot, W., *Biographical Studies* (London, 1914). [First published (1881)]
Birrell, F., *Gladstone* (London, 1933).
Comyns Carr, J., *Some Eminent Victorians: personal recollections in the world of art and letters* (London, 1908).
Drew, M., *Acton, Gladstone, and Others* (London, 1924).
——, *Catherine Gladstone* (London, 1919).
Ellis, G., *William Ewart Gladstone: ei fywyd a'i waith* [his life and work] (Gwrecsam, 1898).
F[letcher], C. R. L., *Mr. Gladstone at Oxford, 1890* (London, 1908).
Friederichs, H., *In the Evening of his Days: a study of Mr. Gladstone in retirement, with some account of St. Deiniol's Library and Hostel* (London, 1896).
Furniss, H., *Some Victorian Men* (London, 1924).
Garratt, G. T., *The Two Mr. Gladstones* (London, 1936).
Gladstone, H. J., *After Thirty Years* (London, 1928).
Gordon, I. M., marchioness of Aberdeen and Temair, *Memories of a Sacred and Inspiring Friendship. An address on Founder's Day, June 28th, 1935 at St. Deiniol's Library, Hawarden* (Chester, [1935]).
Hamilton, E. W., *Mr. Gladstone: a monograph* (London, 1899).

Hamilton, J. M., *Men I Have Painted: with a foreword by Mrs Drew* (London, 1921).
Hammond, J. L., *Gladstone and the Irish Nation* (London, 1938).
Holland, H. S., *Personal Studies* (London, 1905).
Lathbury, D. C., *Mr Gladstone* (London, 1907).
Liberty, S., *In the Cause of Divine Learning* (London, 1906).
Morley, J., *The Life of William Ewart Gladstone*, New edn, 2 vols (London, 1905). [First published in three volumes (London, 1903)]
Nicholson, E. W. B., *Mr. Gladstone and the Bodleian* (Oxford, 1898).
Potter, G., *The People's Life of the Rt. Honourable William Ewart Gladstone* (London, 1884).
Pratt, E. A., *Catherine Gladstone: life, good works, and political efforts* (London, 1898).
Ritchie, J. E., *The Life and Times of William Ewart Gladstone*, 5 vols (London, 1898).
——, *The Real Gladstone: an anecdotal biography* (London, 1898).
Robbins, A. F., *The Early Public Life of William Ewart Gladstone, Four Times Prime Minister* (London, 1894).
Russell, G. W. E., *Mr Gladstone's Religious Development* (London, 1899).
——, *William Ewart Gladstone*, 4th edn (London, 1898).
Shaw, T., *On Gladstone: a living teacher* (Edinburgh, 1902).
Slater, Revd E. T., *A Temple of Peace: for the advancement of divine learning* (1903).
Smith, G. B., *The Life of the Right Honourable William Ewart Gladstone* (London, Paris & New York, n.d.).
——, ed., *Thoughts from the Writings and Speeches of William Ewart Gladstone* (London, 1894).
Smith, J. G., *A Non-Political Treatise of and Tribute to the Late William Ewart Gladstone (Four times Premier of the United Kingdom); or, An Enquiry into the Factors and Principles of his Noble Life* (Newport, 1898).
Stead, W. T., *Gladstone 1809–1898: a character sketch with portraits and other illustrations* (London, n.d.).
Story, J. C., *The Hawarden Temple of Peace: a description of St. Deiniol's Library, founded by the Right Honourable William Ewart Gladstone* (Hawarden, 1905).
Wemyss Reid, T., ed., *The Life of William Ewart Gladstone* (London, 1899).
Williamson, D., *Gladstone: the Man: a non-political biography*, 2nd edn (London, 1898).
Young, G. M., *Mr Gladstone* (Oxford, 1944).

Articles and chapters

'A Christian Statesman's Memorial', *Sunday Strand*, (1906), pp. 66–71.
A., F., 'William Ewart Gladstone: a study of character', *London Society*, 15 (1869).
Addison, W. G. C., 'Church, State and Mr Gladstone', *Theology*, 39:233 (November 1939), pp. 362–70.
——, 'Mr Gladstone: the churchman', *Theology*, 39:234 (December 1939), pp. 439–46.
Angus, G., 'Mr. Gladstone's Heraldry', *Notes and Queries*, (1898), p. 466.
Brinsley-Richards, J., 'Mr Gladstone's Oxford Days', *Temple Bar*, 68 (May 1883), pp. 29–47.
Drew, M., 'Mr. Gladstone's Library at "St. Deiniol's Hawarden"', *Nineteenth Century and After*, 59 (1906), pp. 944–54.
Escott, T. H. S., 'Mr. Gladstone's Conception of a National Church', *New Century Review* (n.d.), pp. 74–9.

Friederichs, H., 'Mr Gladstone's Library & Hostel at Hawarden', *Westminster Budget* (Supplement) (1894).
Hutton, R. H., 'Mr. Gladstone', *Contemporary Review*, 65 (May 1894), pp. 616–34.
——, 'The Metaphysical Society: a reminiscence', *Nineteenth Century*, 18 (1885), pp. 177–8.
Keble, J., 'The State in its Relations with the Church. By W. E. Gladstone, Esq.', *The British Critic and Quarterly Theological Review*, 52 (1839), pp. 355–97.
Liberty, S., 'Mr Gladstone's Place in Religious Thought', *Nineteenth Century* (1907), pp. 653–64.
Lucy, H. W., 'From Behind the Speaker's Chair. XLVII', *Strand Magazine* (1898), pp. 297–303.
——, 'Mr Gladstone's Home Life', *Scottish Leader* "Special": 'Mr Gladstone in Scotland', (1890).
Macaulay, T. B., '*Church and State* by W. E. Gladstone', *Edinburgh Review*, 69 (1839), pp. 231–80.
Morley, C. and H. Friederichs, 'In Mr. Gladstone's Village', *Strand Magazine*, 16 (1898).
'Mr. Gladstone as a Bookman', *Sketch* (1898), pp. 6–7.
'Mr. Gladstone at Hawarden', *Harper's New Monthly Magazine*, 64 (1882), pp. 741–51.
'Opening of the St. Martin's Free Public Library', *The Library*, 3 (1891), pp. 109–15, p. 110.
Phillimore W. G. F., 'Mr. Gladstone (Part II)', *Fortnightly Review*, 69 (1898), pp. 1020–8, p. 1021.
Ribblesdale, C., 'A Visit to Hawarden', *Nineteenth Century and After*, 55 (1904), pp. 637–50.
Roberts, W., 'Bookworms of Yesterday and To-day: the Right Hon. W. E. Gladstone, M.P.', *Bookworm*, 30 (1890), pp. 161–5.
Robertson, J. R., 'Gladstone: A Study', *Free Review* ([n.d.]).
Russell, G. W. E., 'Mr. Gladstone's Theology', *Contemporary Review*, 73 (June 1898), pp. 778–94.
Smalley, G. W., 'Mr. Gladstone. Reminiscences, anecdotes, and an estimate', *Harper's New Monthly Magazine*, 97 (1898), pp. 476–88; 647–55; 796–802.
'St. Deiniol's Library', *Periodical*, 37 (1906), pp. 74–6.
'The Daily Life of the Grand Old Man. With views of Hawarden and Birmingham', *Pall Mall Budget* (1888) pp. 4–8.
'The Home Life of Mr Gladstone', *The Young Man* (1892), pp. 14–17.
Wemyss Reid, T., 'Mr. Gladstone and His Portraits', *Magazine of Art* (1889), pp. 82–8.
Woodward, W. A., 'The Personal Interests of Mr. Gladstone', *Pearson's Magazine* (1898), pp. 306–12.

Cartoons and illustrations

New Gleanings from Gladstone (Edinburgh, [1880?]).
Punch: the political life of the Right Hon. W. E. Gladstone illustrated from 'Punch' with cartoons and sketches, 3 vols (London, 1898).
The Right Hon. William Ewart Gladstone from Judy's Point of View as Shewn in her Cartoons during the last Ten Years (London, [1878]).
William Ewart Gladstone [Illustrated Memorial Pamphlet] (Bristol, 1898).

General works

(† Denotes a work in the St Deiniol's Collection; ‡ at Hawarden Castle).

Alighieri, D., *The Divine Comedy* (Oxford, 1929).
Arnold, M., *Culture and Anarchy: an essay in political and social criticism* (London, 1869). †
Carlisle, W., *An Essay on Evil Spirits* (London, 1827). †
Carlyle, T., *On Heroes, Hero-Worship and the Heroic in History* (London, 1841). †
——, *Past and Present* (London, 1843). †
Cobbett, W., *A History of the Protestant Reformation in England and Ireland; showing how that event has impoverished the main body of the people in those countries; and containing a list of the abbeys, priories, nunneries, hospitals, and other religious foundations in England, and Wales, and Ireland, confiscated, seized on, or alienated, by the Protestant "Reformation", Sovereign and Parliaments. In a series of letters addressed to all sensible and just Englishmen*, 2 vols (London, 1829) †
D'Israeli, I., *Curiosities of Literature* (London, 1791–1823).
Davenport Adams, W. H., *Woman's Work and Worth in Girlhood, Maidenhood, and Wifehood* (London, 1880).
Dibdin, T. F., *The Bibliomania; or, Book-Madness* (London, 1809).
——, *The Library Companion; or, The Young Man's Guide, and The Old Man's Comfort, in the Choice of a Library* (London, 1824). †
Eastlake, C., *Hints on Household Taste* (London, 1868).
Eliot, G., *Middlemarch* (Ware, 1994).
Essays and Reviews, ed., 5th edn (London, 1861). †
Gore, C., ed., *Lux Mundi: a series of studies in the religion of the incarnation* (London, 1889).†
——, *The Mission of the Church: four lectures* (London, 1892). †
Hallam, H., ed., *Remains in Verse and Prose of Arthur Henry Hallam with a Preface and Memoir* (London, 1869). †
Haweis, M., *The Art of Decoration* (London, 1881).
Huxley, T. H., 'The Keepers of the Herd of Swine', *Nineteenth Century*, 28 (December 1890), pp. 967–79.
Ireland, W. H., *The Confessions of William Ireland* (London, 1805). †
Kerr, R., *The Gentleman's House; or how to plan English residences, from the parsonage to the palace* (London, 1871).
Leibnitz, G. W. von, *A System of Theology*, trans. C. W. Russell (London, 1850). †
Liddon, H. P., *The Life of Edward Bouverie Pusey*, 2nd edn, 4 vols (London, 1897). †
——, *The Worth of the Old Testament: a sermon preached in St Paul's Cathedral ... December 8, 1889* (London, 1890).
Locke, J., *Works*, New edn, 10 vols (London, 1823). †
Lockhart, J., *Memoirs of the Life of Sir Walter Scott*, 7 vols (Edinburgh and London, 1837–8). †
Maurice, F. D., *The Gospel of the Kingdom of Heaven: a course of lectures on the Gospel of St Luke* (London, 1893). †
Millais, J. G., *The Life and Letters of Sir John Everett Millais, President of the Royal Academy*, 2 vols (London, 1899). †
Monypenny, W. F. and G. E. Buckle, *The Life of Benjamin Disraeli, Earl of Beaconsfield* (London, 1910–20).

Moore, A., *Evolution in its Relation to the Christian Faith: a paper read at the Reading Church Congress, October, 1883* (London, 1883). †
More, H., *Sacred Dramas: chiefly intended for young persons* (London, 1782). ‡
More, H., *Strictures on the Modern System of Female Education* (London, 1799).
Newman, J. H., *Loss and Gain* (London, 1848). †
O'Brien, R. B., *John Bright: a monograph* (London, 1910).
Peacock, T. L., *Works* (London, 1875). †
Phillips, C., 'Millais's Works at Burlington House', *Nineteenth Century*, 43 (1898).
Platner, S. B. and T. Ashby, *A Topographical Dictionary of Ancient Rome* (London, 1929).
Prestige, G. L., *The Life of Charles Gore: a great Englishman* (London, 1935). †
Redgrave, S., ed., *Catalogue of the Special Exhibition of Portrait Miniatures on Loan at the South Kensington Museum* (London, 1865).
Scott, Sir W., *Novels and Tales of the Author of Waverley*, 25 vols, 3rd edn (Edinburgh and London, 1821–1824). †
Seeley, J., *Ecce Homo: a survey of the life and work of Jesus Christ* (London and Cambridge, 1866). ‡
Selwyn, E. G., ed., *Essays Catholic & Critical* (London, 1926).
Stephenson, G., *Edward Stuart Talbot 1844–1934* (London, 1936).
Stirling, A. M. W., ed., *The Richmond Papers: from the correspondence and manuscripts of George Richmond, R. A., and his son Sir William Richmond, R. A., K. C. B.* (London, 1926). †
Streeter, B. H., *Foundations: a statement of Christian belief in terms of modern thought by seven Oxford men* (London, 1912).
Symmons, C., *The Life of John Milton*, 3rd edn (London, 1822). †
Tomline, G., *Memoirs of the Life of ... William Pitt* (London, 1821).
Ward, M. A., *Robert Elsmere*, 3 vols (London, 1888). †
Warren, W. T., ed., *Kebleland* (Winchester and London, 1906). †
Watts, M. S., *George Frederic Watts: the annals of an artist's life*, 3 vols (London, 1912). †
Whiston, J., J. Dodsley, and J. Robson, *Directions for a Proper Choice of Authors to form a Library ... intended for those Readers who are only acquainted with the English Language* (London, 1766).
Williamson, G. C., ed., *Bryan's Dictionary of Painters and Engravers*, New revd edn, 5 vols (London, 1920).
Wollstonecraft, M., *Mary, A Fiction* and *The Wrongs of Women* (Oxford, 1976).

Secondary sources

Works about Gladstone, the Gladstone family, and St Deiniol's Library (post 1945)

Books and pamphlets

Aldous, R., *The Lion and the Unicorn: Gladstone vs Disraeli* (London, 2006).
Bastable, J. D., ed., *Newman and Gladstone* (Dublin, 1978).
Battiscombe, G., *Mrs Gladstone: the portrait of a marriage* (London, 1956).
Beales, D., *History and Biography: an inaugural lecture* (Cambridge, 1981).
Bebbington, D., *The Mind of Gladstone: religion, Homer, and politics* (Oxford, 2004).

——, *William Ewart Gladstone: faith and politics in Victorian Britain* (Grand Rapids, MI, 1993).
—— and R. Swift, eds, *Gladstone Centenary Essays* (Liverpool, 2000).
Biagini, E. F., *British Democracy and Irish Nationalism 1876–1906* (Cambridge, 2007).
—— and A. J. Reid, *Currents of Radicalism: popular radicalism, organized labour and party politics in Britian, 1850–1914* (Cambridge, 1991).
——, *Gladstone* (London, 2000).
——, *Liberty, Retrenchment and Reform: popular liberalism in the age of Gladstone, 1860–1880* (Cambridge, 1992).
Butler, P., *Gladstone: Church, State and Tractarianism: a study of his religious ideas and attitudes, 1809–1859* (Oxford, 1982).
Chadwick, W. O., *Acton and Gladstone* (London, 1976).
Checkland, S. G., *The Gladstones: a family biography 1764–1851* (Cambridge, 1971).
Clarke, P., *A Question of Leadership: British rulers – Gladstone to Thatcher* (London, 1991).
Crosby, T. L., *The Two Mr Gladstones: a study in psychology and history* (New Haven and London, 1997).
Deacon, R., *The Private Life of Mr Gladstone* (London, 1965).
Feuchtwanger, E. J., *Gladstone* (London, 1975).
Fletcher, S., *Victorian Girls: Lord Lyttelton's daughters* (London, 1997).
Francis, P. B., ed., *The Gladstone Umbrella: papers delivered at the Gladstone Centenary Conference 1998* (Hawarden, 2001).
——, ed., *The Grand Old Man: sermons & speeches in honour of W. E. Gladstone (1809–1898)* (Hawarden, 2000).
Gilliland, J., *Gladstone's Dear Spirit: Laura Thistlethwayte* (London, 1994).
Gladstone, P., *Portrait of a Family: the Gladstones 1839–1889* (Kendal, 1989).
Hammond, J. L. and M. R. D. Foot, *Gladstone and Liberalism* (London, 1952).
Harris, S. K., *The Cultural Work of the Late Nineteenth-Century Hostess: Annie Adams Fields and Mary Gladstone Drew* (London, 2002).
Isba, A., *Gladstone and Dante: Victorian statesman, medieval poet* (Woodbridge, 2006).
——, *Gladstone and Women* (London, 2006).
Jagger, P. J., *Gladstone: the making of a Christian politician. The personal religious life and development of William Ewart Gladstone 1809–1832* (Allison Park, PA, 1991).
——, ed., *Gladstone* (London, 1998).
——, ed., *Gladstone, Politics, and Religion: a collection of Founder's Day lectures delivered at St Deiniol's Library, Hawarden, 1967–83* (New York, 1985).
Jenkins, R., *Gladstone* (London, 1995).
Kinzer, B. L., ed., *The Gladstonian Turn of Mind* (Toronto, 1985).
Loughlin, J., *Gladstone, Home Rule and the Ulster Question, 1882–93* (Dublin, 1986).
Magnus, P., *Gladstone: a biography* (London, 1954).
Matthew, H. C. G., *Gladstone 1809–1898* (Oxford, 1997). [First published in two volumes: *Gladstone: 1809–1874* (Oxford, 1986) and *Gladstone: 1875–1898* (Oxford, 1995)].
Meisel, J. S., *Public Speech and the Culture of Public Life in the Age of Gladstone* (New York, 2001).
Parry, J. P., *Democracy and Religion: Gladstone and the Liberal Party, 1867–1875* (Cambridge, 1986).
Partridge, M., *Gladstone* (London, 2003).

Pritchard, T. W., *A History of St Deiniol's Library* (Hawarden, 1999).
Ramm, A., *Gladstone as Man of Letters. A James Bryce memorial lecture* (Oxford, 1981).
——, *William Ewart Gladstone* (Cardiff, 1989).
Saab, A. P., *Reluctant Icon: Gladstone, Bulgaria, and the working classes, 1856–1878* (Cambridge, MA, 1991).
Shannon, R., *Gladstone and the Bulgarian Agitation 1876*, 2nd edn (London, 1975).
——, *Gladstone: heroic minister, 1865–1898* (London, 1999).
——, *Gladstone: Peel's inheritor 1809–1865* (London, 1982).
——, *Mr Gladstone and Swansea 1887* (Swansea, 1982).
Stansky, P., *Gladstone: a progress in politics* (New York and London, 1979).
Veysey, A. G., *The History of Hawarden Institute* (Hawarden, 1993).
Vidler, A. R., *The Orb and the Cross: a normative study in the relations of church and state with reference to Gladstone's early writings* (London, 1945).

Articles and chapters

Altholz, J. L., 'The Vatican Decrees Controversy, 1874–5', *Catholic Historical Review*, 57 (1972), pp. 593–605.
—— and J. Powell, 'Gladstone, Lord Ripon and the Vatican Decrees, 1874', *Albion*, 22 (1990), pp. 449–59.
Beales, D., 'Gladstone and his Diary: "Myself, the worst of all interlocutors"', *Historical Journal*, 25 (1982), pp. 463–9.
Bebbington, D., 'Gladstone and the Nonconformists: a religious affinity in politics', in *Church, Society and Politics, Studies in Church History*, 12, ed. by D. Baker (Oxford, 1975), pp. 369–82.
——, 'Gladstone and Grote', in P. J. Jagger ed., *Gladstone* (London and Rio Grande, 1998), pp. 157–76.
——, 'Gladstone and Homer', in R. Swift and D. Bebbington eds, *Gladstone Centenary Essays*, (Liverpool, 2000), pp. 57–74.
——, 'Gladstone and the Baptists', *Baptist Quarterly*, 26 (1976), pp. 224–39.
Blake, R., 'Gladstone and Disraeli', in *Gladstone*, ed. by P. J. Jagger (London, 1998), pp. 51–70.
Blyth, J. A., 'Gladstone and Disraeli: "Images" in Victorian Politics', *Dalhousie Review*, 49 (1969), pp. 388–98.
Briggs, A., 'Victorian Images of Gladstone', in *Gladstone*, ed. by P. J. Jagger (London, 1998), pp. 33–49.
Campbell, K., 'W. E. Gladstone, W. T. Stead, Matthew Arnold and a New Journalism: cultural politics in the 1880s', *Victorian Periodicals Review*, 36 (2003), pp. 20–40.
Checkland, S. G., 'The Making of Mr Gladstone', *Victorian Studies*, 12 (1969), pp. 399–409.
——, 'Mr Gladstone, his Parents and his Siblings', in *Gladstone: politics and religion*, ed. by P. J. Jagger (London, 1985), pp. 40–8.
Clayton, R., 'Gladstone, Tennyson and History: 1886 and All That', *Tennyson Research Bulletin*, 8 (2004), pp. 151–65.
——, 'Masses or Classes? The question of community in the foundation of Gladstone's Library', *Library History* (November 2003), pp. 163–72.
——, 'W. E. Gladstone: an annotation key', *Notes & Queries*, 246 (2001), pp. 140–3.

Clayton Windscheffel, R., 'Gladstone and Scott: family, identity, and nation', *Scottish Historical Review*, 86 (2007), pp. 69–95.

———, 'Politics, Portraiture and Power: reassessing the public image of William Ewart Gladstone', in M. McCormack ed., *Public Men: masculinity and politics in modern Britain*, (Basingstoke, 2007), pp. 93–122.

———, 'Politics, Religion and Text: W.E. Gladstone and spiritualism', *Journal of Victorian Culture*, 11 (2006), pp. 1–29.

Conlin, J., 'Gladstone and Christian Art, 1832–1854', *Historical Journal*, 46 (2003), pp. 341–74.

Erb, P. C, 'Gladstone and German Liberal Catholicism', *Recusant History*, 23 (1997), pp. 450–69.

———, 'Politics and Theological Liberalism: William Gladstone and Mrs Humphry Ward', *Journal of Religious History*, 25 (2001), pp. 158–72.

Fagan, E. F., 'The Religious Life of Mr Gladstone', *Church Quarterly Review*, 155 (1954), pp. 16–21.

Foot, M. R. D., 'Morley's Gladstone: a reappraisal', *Bulletin of the John Rylands Library*, 51 (1969), pp. 368–80.

Gardiner, J. P., 'Gladstone, Gossip and the Post-War Generation', *Historical Research*, 74:186 (2001), pp. 409–24.

Gilliland, J., 'Helen Jane Gladstone (1814–1880) Sister of William', *Flintshire Historical Society Journal*, 35 (1999), pp. 177–189.

Glasgow, E., 'Books and Mr. Gladstone', *Contemporary Review*, 272:1588 (May 1998), p. 258.

———, 'St Deiniol's Library, Hawarden', *Library Review*, 46:2 (May 1997), pp. 113–21.

———, 'Mr Gladstone and Public Libraries', *Library History*, 16 (2000), pp. 57–64.

Goodlad, G. D., 'Gladstone and his Rivals: popular Liberal perceptions of the party leadership in the political crisis of 1885–6', in *Currents of Radicalism: popular radicalism, organised labour and party politics in Britain, 1850–1914*, ed. by E. F. Biagini and A. J. Reid (Cambridge, 1991), pp. 163–83.

Hamer, D. A., 'Gladstone: the making of a political myth', *Victorian Studies* (1978), pp. 29–50.

Harrison, R., 'Marx, Gladstone and Olga Novikov', *Bulletin of the Society for the Study of Labour History*, 33 (1976), pp. 26–34.

Harvie, C., 'Gladstonianism, the Provinces and Popular Political Culture, 1860–1906', in R. Bellamy ed., *Victorian Liberalism: nineteenth-century political thought and practice*, (London, 1990), pp. 152–174.

Hawkins, A., 'Of "Interior Matters": Gladstone's diary, Disraeli's letters and recent biographical studies', *Nineteenth Century Prose*, 22 (1995), pp. 177–188.

Helmstadter, R. J., 'Conscience and Politics: Gladstone's first book', in *The Gladstonian Turn of Mind*, ed. by B. L. Kinzer (Toronto, 1985), pp. 3–42.

Hilton, B., 'Gladstone's Theological Politics', in M. Bentley and J. Stevenson eds, *High and Low Politics in Modern Britain*, (Oxford, 1983), pp. 28–57.

Holmes, D., 'Gladstone and Newman', *Dublin Review*, 241 (1967), pp. 141–53.

Jagger, P. J., 'Gladstone and his Library', in P. J. Jagger ed., *Gladstone* (London, 1998), pp. 235–53.

Jenkins, Roy, 'Gladstone and Books', in *The Grand Old Man*, ed. by P. B. Francis (Hawarden, 2000), pp. 21–6.

Jenkins, R., 'Writing about Gladstone', *Journal of Liberal Democrat History*, 20 (1998), pp. 36–7.
Jones, T., 'Marginal Notes by Mr. Gladstone', *Cylchgrawn Llyfrgell Genedlaethol Cymru / National Library of Wales Journal*, 4 (1945–6), 50–2.
Joseph, G., 'The Homeric Competitions of Tennyson and Gladstone', *Browning Institute Studies*, 10 (1982), pp. 105–15.
Kenyon, J., 'Gladstone and the Anglican High Churchmen, 1845–52', in *The Gladstonian Turn of Mind* ed. by B. L. Kinzer (Toronto, 1985), pp. 43–62.
Knaplund, P., 'William Ewart Gladstone: the Christian statesman', *Church Quarterly Review*, 162 (1961), pp. 467–75.
Lloyd-Jones, H., 'Gladstone on Homer', *Times Literary Supplement*, 3 January 1975, 15–17; reprinted in his *Blood for the Ghosts: classical influences in the nineteenth and twentieth centuries* (London, 1982).
Lynch, M. J., 'Was Gladstone a Tractarian? W. E. Gladstone and the Oxford Movement, 1833–45', *Journal of Religious History*, 8 (1975), pp. 364–89.
Madden, J. L., 'Gladstone's Reading of Thomas Love Peacock', *Notes & Queries* (1967), p. 384.
Malament, B. C., 'W. E. Gladstone: an other Victorian?' *British Studies Monitor*, 8 (1978), pp. 22–38.
Maloney, J., 'Gladstone's Gladstone? The chancellorship of Robert Lowe, 1868–73', *Historical Research*, 79 (2006), pp. 404–28.
Matthew, H. C. G., 'Gladstone's Death and Funeral', *The Historian*, 57 (1998), 20–4; reprinted in *Journal of Liberal Democrat History*, 20 (1998), pp. 38–42.
——, 'Gladstone, Evangelicalism and the Engagement', in *Revival and Religion since 1700: essays for John Walsh*, ed. by J. Garnett and H. C. G. Matthew (London and Rio Grande, 1993), pp. 111–26.
——, 'Gladstone, Vaticanism and the Question of the East', in *Religious Motivation, Studies in Church History*, 15, ed. by D. Baker (Oxford, 1978), pp. 417–42.
McKelvy, W. R., 'William Ewart Gladstone (29 December 1908–19 May 1898)', in W. Baker and K. Womack eds, *Nineteenth-Century British Book-Collectors and Bibliographers*, (Detroit, Washington D.C., London, 1997), pp. 161–72.
Meisel, J. S., 'The Importance of Being Serious: the unexplored connection between Gladstone and humour', *History*, 84:274 (April 1999), pp. 278–300.
Morgan, K. O., 'Gladstone and Wales', *Welsh History Review*, 1 (1960), pp. 65–82.
Murray, G., 'Gladstone: 1898–1948', *Contemporary Review*, 174 (1948), pp. 134–8.
Nolan, D., 'Gladstone and Liverpool', *Journal of Liberal Democrat History*, 20 (1998), pp. 17–22.
Parker, W. M., 'Gladstone as a *Quarterly Review* Contributor', *Quarterly Review*, 293 (1955), pp. 464–76.
Parry, J. P., 'Religion and the Collapse of Gladstone's First Government, 1870–74', *Historical Journal*, 25 (1982), pp. 71–101.
Peterson, W. S., 'Gladstone's Review of *Robert Elsmere*: some unpublished correspondence', *Review of English Studies*, 21 (1970), pp. 442–61.
Pointon, M., 'W. E. Gladstone as Art Patron and Collector', *Victorian Studies* (1975), pp. 73–98.
Powell, J., 'Small Marks and Instinctual Responses: a study in the uses of Gladstone's marginalia', *Nineteenth Century Prose*, 19 (Special Issue) (1992), pp. 1–17.

——, 'Tollemache's Talks with Mr Gladstone', *Nineteenth Century Prose*, 17 (1989), pp. 31–46.
Pritchard, T. W., 'The Revd. S. E. Gladstone (1844–1920)', *Flintshire Historical Society Journal*, 35 (1999), pp. 191–241.
Quinault, R., 'Gladstone and Disraeli: a reappraisal of their relationship', *History*, 91 (2006), pp. 557–76.
Ramm, A., 'Gladstone's Religion', *Historical Journal*, 28 (1985), pp. 327–40.
Ratcliffe, F. W., 'Mr Gladstone, the Librarian, and St Deiniol's Library, Hawarden', in *Gladstone, Politics and Religion*, ed. P. J. Jagger (London, 1985), pp. 49–67.
Robson, A, P., 'A Bird's Eye View of Gladstone', in *The Gladstonian Turn of Mind*, ed. by B. L. Kinzer (Toronto, 1985), pp. 63–96.
Runcie, R., 'God's Politician', in *The Grand Old Man*, ed. by P. B. Francis (Hawarden, 2000), pp. 27–31.
Ruston, A., 'The Unitarian Correspondents of W. E. Gladstone: the British Library MSS', *Transactions of the Unitarian Historical Society*, 18 (1986), pp. 327–40.
Shannon, R., 'Gladstone, the Roman Church and Italy', in *Public and Private Doctrine*, ed. by M. Bentley (Cambridge, 1993), pp. 108–26.
——, 'Tennyson and Gladstone. From courtship to mutual disenchantment', *Times Literary Supplement*, 2 October 1992.
——, 'Too busy reading', *Times Literary Supplement*, 5 November 2004.
Stephen, M. D., '"After Thirty Years": a note on Gladstone scholarship', *Journal of Religious History*, 15 (1989), pp. 488–95.
West, J., 'Gladstone and Laura Thistlethwayte, 1865–75', *Historical Research*, 80 (2007), pp. 368–92.

General works

Adams, J. E., *Dandies and Desert Saints: styles of Victorian masculinity* (Ithaca and London, 1995).
Allchin, A. M., *The Silent Rebellion: Anglican religious communities 1845–1900* (London, 1958).
Allen, J. S., *In the Public Eye: a history of reading in modern France, 1800–1940* (Princeton, NJ, 1991).
Altick, R. D., *The English Common Reader: a social history of the mass reading public, 1800–1900* (Chicago, 1957).
Avis, P., *Gore: construction and conflict* (Worthing, 1988).
Bailey, P., *Popular Culture and Performance in the Victorian City* (Cambridge, 1998).
Baker, W., *The Early History of the London Library* (Lewiston, 1992).
Bashford, A., *Purity and Pollution: gender, embodiment and Victorian medicine* (London, 1998).
Bentley, M., 'Victorian Politics and the Linguistic Turn, *Historical Journal* (1999), pp. 883–902.
Black, A., 'Lost Worlds of Culture: Victorian libraries, library history and prospects for a history of information', *Journal of Victorian Culture*, 2 (1997), 95–112.
——, *A New History of the English Public Library: social and intellectual contexts, 1850–1914* (Leicester, 1996).
—— and P. Hoare, eds, *The Cambridge History of Libraries in Britain and Ireland: vol. 3: 1850–2000* (Cambridge, 2006).
Blake, R., *Disraeli* (London, 1966).

Brake, L., *Subjugated Knowledges: journalism, gender and literature 1837–1907* (Basingstoke, 1994).
Braudy, L., *The Frenzy of Renown: fame & its history* (New York and Oxford, 1986).
Bronfen, E., *Over Her Dead Body: death, femininity and the aesthetic* (Manchester, 1992).
Broughton, T. L. 'Studying the Study: gender and the scene of authorship in the writings of Leslie Stephen, Margaret Oliphant and Anne Thackeray Ritchie', in F. Regard ed., *Mapping the Self: space, identity, discourse in British auto/biography* (Saint-Etienne, 2003), pp. 247–68.
Butler, M., *Romantics, Rebels and Reactionaries: English literature and its background, 1760–1830* (Oxford, 1981).
Carpenter, J., *Gore: a study in liberal catholic thought* (London, 1960).
Carrick, N. and E. L. Ashton, *The Athenaeum, Liverpool, 1797–1997* (Liverpool, 1997).
Casteras, S. P., 'Seeing the Unseen: pictorial problematics and Victorian images of class, poverty, and urban life', in *Victorian Literature and the Victorian Visual Imagination*, ed. by C. T. Christ and J. O. Jordan (Berkley, CA, 1995), pp. 264–88.
—— and C. Denney, eds, *The Grosvenor Gallery: a palace of art in Victorian England* (New Haven and London, 1996).
Chadwick, W. O., *Acton and History* (Cambridge, 1998).
Chartier, R., *The Cultural Uses of Print in Early Modern France* (Princeton, NJ, 1987).
——, *Forms and Meanings* (Philadelphia, 1995).
——, *The Order of Books: readers, authors and libraries in Europe between the fourteenth and eighteenth centuries* (Oxford, 1994).
Christ, C. T., 'The Hero as Man of Letters: masculinity and Victorian nonfiction prose', in T. Morgan ed., *Victorian Sages and Cultural Discourse: renegotiating gender and power* (New Brunswick, 1990), pp. 19–31.
Ciro, J., 'Country House Libraries in the Nineteenth Century', *Library History*, 18 (2002), pp. 89–98.
Clarke, N., 'Strenuous Idleness: Thomas Carlyle and the man of letters as hero', in M. Roper and J. Tosh eds, *Manful Assertions* (London, 1991), pp. 25–43.
Cliff, P. B., *The Rise and Development of the Sunday School Movement in England 1780–1980* (Redhill, 1986).
Cohen, M., '"Manners" Make the Man: Politeness, Chivalry, and the Construction of Masculinity, 1750–1830', *Journal of British Studies*, 44 (2005), pp. 312–29.
Colclough, S., *Consuming Texts: readers and reading communities, 1695–1870* (Basingstoke, 2007).
Collini, S., *Absent Minds: intellectuals in Britain* (Oxford, 2006).
——, *Public Moralists: political thought and intellectual life in Britain, 1850–1930* (Oxford, 1991).
Compton, M., 'William Roscoe and Early Collectors of Italian Primitives', *Liverpool Libraries, Museums and Art Galleries Bulletin*, 9 (1960–1), pp. 27–51.
Connell, P., 'Bibliomania: book collecting, cultural politics, and the rise of literary heritage in Romantic Britain', *Representations*, 71 (2000), pp. 24–47.
Cowling, M., *The Artist as Anthropologist: the representation of type and character in Victorian art* (Cambridge, 1989).

——, *Victorian Figurative Painting: domestic life and the contemporary social scene* (London, 2000).
Craster, E., *History of the Bodleian Library 1845–1945* (Oxford, 1952).
Crawford, J. C., 'The Library and the Rural Community', in M. Kinnell and P. Sturges eds, *Continuity and Innovation in the Public Library: the development of a social institution*, (London, 1996), pp. 104–23.
Cubitt, G. and A. Warren eds, *Heroic Reputations and Exemplary Lives* (Manchester, 2000).
Dacome, L., 'Noting the Mind: commonplace books and the pursuit of the self in eighteenth-century Britain', *Journal of the History of Ideas*, 65 (2004), pp. 603–25.
Danahay, M. A., *A Community of One: masculine autobiography and autonomy in nineteenth-century Britain* (Albany, 1993).
——, *Gender at Work in Victorian Culture: literature, art and masculinity* (Aldershot, 2005).
Darnton, R., *The Kiss of Lamourette: reflections in cultural history* (New York, 1990).
——, 'What is the History of Books?', *Daedalus*, 111 (1982), 65–83.
Davidoff, L. and C. Hall, *Family Fortunes: men and women of the English middle class, 1780–1850* (London, 1987).
Davidson Kalmar, I., 'Benjamin Disraeli, Romantic Orientalist', *Comparative Studies in Society and History*, 47 (2005), pp. 348–71.
de Bellaigue, C., 'Behind the School Walls: the school community in French and English boarding schools for girls, 1810-1867', *Paedagogica Historica*, 40 (2004), pp. 107–21.
Digby, A. and P. Searby, *Children, School and Society in Nineteenth-Century England* (London, 1981).
Edwards, A., *The Seven Bishops of Monmouth* (Newport, 1996).
Endelman, T. M. and T. Kushner, eds, *Disraeli's Jewishness* (London, 2002).
Epstein, J. A., *In Practice: studies in the language and culture of popular politics in modern Britain* (Stanford, CA, 2003).
Fay, C. R., *Huskisson and his Age* (London, 1951).
Fenyo, K., *Contempt, Sympathy and Romance: lowland perceptions of the highlands and the clearances during the famine years, 1845–1855* (East Linton, 2000).
Ferris, I., *The Achievement of Literary Authority: gender, history, and the Waverley novels* (Ithaca and London, 1991).
Fish, S., *Is There a Text in This Class? The authority of interpretive communities* (Cambridge, MA, 1990); [first published (1981)].
Flavell, M. K., 'The Enlightenment Reader and the New Industrial Towns: a study of the Liverpool library 1758–1790', *British Journal for Eighteenth-Century Studies*, 8 (1985), pp. 17–35.
Flint, K., *The Woman Reader, 1837–1914* (Oxford, 1993).
——, 'Portraits of Women: on display', in *Millais: portraits*, ed. by P. Funnell and M. Warner (London, 1999), pp. 181–201.
——, 'Women, Men and the Reading of *Vanity Fair*', in J. Raven, H. Small and N. Tadmor eds, *The Practice and Representation of Reading in England*, (Cambridge, 1996), pp. 246–62.
Funnell, P., 'Millais's Reputation and the Practice of Portraiture', in P. Funnell and M. Warner eds, *Millais: portraits*, (London, 1999), pp. 11–35.
Gardiner, J., *The Victorians: an age in retrospect* (London and New York, 2002).

Garnett, J., 'Bishop Butler and the Zeitgeist: Butler and the development of Christian moral philosophy in Victorian Britain', in C. Cunliffe ed., *Joseph Butler's Moral and Religious Thought: tercentenary essays*, (Oxford, 1992), pp. 63–96.

——, 'Hastings Rashdall and the Renewal of Christian Social Ethics, c. 1890–1920', in *Revival and Religion since 1700*, ed. by J. Garnett and H. C. G. Matthew (London and Rio Grande, 1993), pp. 297–316.

Garnett, O., *Hughenden Manor* (London, 2002).

Gere, J. A., 'Alexander Munro's "Paolo and Francesca"', *Burlington Magazine*, 105 (1963), pp. 468, 508–10.

Gilley, S., *Newman and His Age* (London, 1990).

Girouard, M., *The Victorian Country House*, Revd edn (New Haven and London, 1979).

Glassman, B., *Benjamin Disraeli: the fabricated Jew in myth and memory* (Lanham, MD, 2003).

Goode, M., 'Dryasdust Antiquarianism and Soppy Masculinity: the Waverley novels and the gender of history', *Representations*, 82 (2003), pp. 52–86.

Green-Lewis, J., *Framing the Victorians: photography and the culture of realism* (Ithaca & London, 1996).

Green-Lewis, J., 'At Home in the Nineteenth Century: photography, nostalgia and the will to authenticity', in *Victorian Afterlife: postmodern culture rewrites the nineteenth century*, ed. by J. Kucich and D. F. Sadoff (Minneapolis and London, 2000), pp. 29–48.

Gretton, Tom, 'Difference and Competition: the imitation and reproduction of fine art in a nineteenth-century illustrated weekly news magazine', *Oxford Art Journal*, 23 (2000), pp. 143–62.

Grimley, M., *Citizenship, Community, and the Church of England: liberal Anglican theories of the state between the wars* (Oxford, 2004).

Gronberg, T., 'The Inner Man: interiors and masculinity in early twentieth-century Vienna', *Oxford Art Journal*, 24 (2001), pp. 67–88.

Hall, D. D., *Cultures of Print: essays in the history of the book* (Amherst, 1996).

Harvie, C., 'Ideology and Home Rule: James Bryce, A. V. Dicey and Ireland, 1880–1887', *English Historical Review*, 91 (1976), pp. 298–314.

——, 'Scott and the Image of Scotland', in *Patriotism: the making and unmaking of British national identity*, ed. by R. Samuel (London and New York, 1989), pp. 173–192.

Hastings, A., A. Mason, and H. Pyper, eds, *The Oxford Companion to Christian Thought* (Oxford, 2000).

Hearn, J., *Men in the Public Eye: the construction and deconstruction of public men and public patriarchies* (London, 1992).

Heyck, T. W., *The Transformation of Intellectual Life in Victorian England* (London, 1982).

Hilton, B., *The Age of Atonement: the influence of Evangelicalism on social and economic thought 1785–1865* (Oxford, 1988).

——, 'Disraeli, English culture, and the decline of the industrial spirit', in L. Brockliss and D. Eastwood eds, *A Union of Multiple Identities: the British Isles, 1750–1850*, (Manchester and New York, 1997), pp. 44–59.

Hinchliff, P., *Frederick Temple, Archbishop of Canterbury: a life* (Oxford, 1998).

——, *God and History: aspects of British theology 1875–1914* (Oxford, 1992).

Hoggart, R., *The Uses of Literacy: aspects of working-class life* (London, 1957).

Hollis, C., *Eton: a history* (London, 1960).
Hughes, K., *The Victorian Governess* (London, 1993).
Iser, W., *The Act of Reading: a theory of aesthetic response* (Baltimore, MD, 1978).
——, *The Implied Reader* (Baltimore, MD, 1978).
Jackson, H. J., ed., *A Book I Value: Samuel Taylor Coleridge selected marginalia* (Princeton and Oxford, 2003).
——, *Marginalia: readers writing in books* (New Haven and London, 2001).
——, *Romantic Readers: the evidence of marginalia* (New Haven and London, 2005).
Jalland, P., *Death in the Victorian Family* (Oxford, 1996).
Jauss, H. R., *Towards an Aesthetic of Reception* (Minneapolis, MN, 1982).
Jenkins, K., *Re-thinking History* (London, 1991).
Jenkyns, R., *Dignity and Decadence: Victorian art and the classical inheritance* (Glasgow, 1991).
——, *The Victorians and Ancient Greece* (Oxford, 1980).
Jones, H. S., *Intellect and Character in Victorian England: Mark Pattison and the invention of the don* (Cambridge, 2007).
Joseph, G., *Tennyson and the Text: the weaver's shuttle* (Cambridge, 1992).
Joyce, P., *Democratic Subjects: the self and the social in nineteenth-century England* (Cambridge, 1994).
——, *Visions of the People: industrial England and the question of class 1848–1914* (Cambridge, 1991).
Kerr, J., *Fiction Against History: Scott as storyteller* (Cambridge, 1989).
King, C., 'Made in Her Image: women, portraiture and gender in the sixteenth and seventeenth centuries', in *Gender and Art*, ed. by Gill Perry (London and New Haven, 1999), pp. 32–85.
Koven, S., *Slumming: sexual and social politics in Victorian London* (Princeton and Oxford, 2004).
Kuhn, W. M., *The Politics of Pleasure: a portrait of Benjamin Disraeli* (London, 2006).
Laqueur, T. W., *Religion and Respectability: Sunday schools and working class culture* (New Haven, CN, 1976).
——, 'Fin-de-siecle: once more with feeling', *Journal of Contemporary History*, 31 (1996), pp. 5–47.
Lawrence, J., *Speaking for the People: party, language and popular politics in England, 1867–1914* (Cambridge, 1998).
Leach, C., 'Advice for Parents and Books for Children: Quaker women and educational texts for the home, 1798-1850', *History of Education Society Bulletin*, 69 (2002), pp. 49–58.
Legg, M.-L., *Newspapers and Nationalism: the Irish provincial press, 1850–1892* (Dublin, 1999).
Linkman, A., 'Passing Trade: death and the family album in Britain 1860–1900', *Photohistorian*, 123 (1998), pp. 18–27.
——, *The Victorians: photographic portraits* (London & New York, 1993).
Lloyd-Jones, H., *Blood for the Ghosts: classical influences in the nineteenth and twentieth centuries* (London, 1982).
Mandelbrote, G. and K. Manley, eds, *The Cambridge History of Libraries in Britain and Ireland: vol. 2: 1640–1850* (Cambridge, 2006).
Manguel, A., *A History of Reading* (London, 1996).

Marcus, S., *The Other Victorians: a study of sexuality and pornography in mid-nineteenth-century England* (London, 1966).
Marshall, J., 'John Locke's Religious, Educational and Moral Thought', *Historical Journal*, 33 (1990), pp. 993–1001.
Martin, J., *Women and the Politics of Schooling in Victorian and Edwardian England* (Leicester, 1999).
Martin, R. B., *Tennyson: the unquiet heart* (Oxford, 1980).
Mason, M., *The Making of Victorian Sexuality* (Oxford, 1994).
Matthew, H. C. G., 'Portraits of Men: Millais and Victorian public life', in P. Funnell and M. Warner eds, *Millais: portraits*, (London, 1999), pp. 137–61.
Mauriello, C. E., 'The Strange Death of the Public Intellectual: liberal intellectual identity and the "field of cultural production" in England, 1880–1920', *Journal of Victorian Culture*, 6 (2001), pp. 1–26.
Mavor, C., *Pleasures Taken: performances of sexuality and loss in Victorian photographs* (Durham and London, 1995).
McCormack, M., *The Independent Man: citizenship and gender politics in Georgian England* (Manchester, 2005).
——, ed., *Public Men: masculinity and politics in modern Britain* (Basingstoke, 2007).
McGrath, A. E., *Christian Theology: an introduction* (Oxford, 1994).
McKelvy, W. R., *The English Cult of Literature: devoted readers, 1774–1880* (Charlottesville, VA, and London, 2007).
Miller, E., *Prince of Librarians: the life and times of Antonio Panizzi of the British Museum* (London, 1988).
Moran, M. F., '"Lovely manly mould": Hopkins and the Christian Body', *Journal of Victorian Culture*, 6 (2001), pp. 61–88.
Morgan, R., ed., *The Religion of the Incarnation: Anglican essays in commemoration of* Lux Mundi (Bristol, 1989).
Morrish, P. S., 'Domestic Libraries: Victorian and Edwardian Ideas and Practice', *Library History*, 10 (1994), pp. 27–44.
Mort, F. and L. Nead, 'Sexuality, Modernity and the Victorians', *Journal of Victorian Culture*, 1 (1996), pp. 118–30.
Myers, R. and M. Harris, eds, *Property of a Gentleman: the formation, organisation and dispersal of the private library 1620–1920* (Winchester, 1991).
Nead, L., *Victorian Babylon: people, streets and images in nineteenth-century London* (New Haven, CT, 2000).
Neddam, F., 'Constructing Masculinities under Thomas Arnold of Rugby (1828–1842): gender, educational policy and school life in an early-Victorian public school', *Gender & Education*, 16 (2004), pp. 303–26.
Newlyn, L., *Reading, Writing and Romanticism: the anxiety of reception* (Oxford, 2000).
Newsome, D., *Two Classes of Men: Platonism and English romantic thought* (London, 1974).
Nimmo, D., 'Learning against Religion, Learning as Religion: Mark Pattison and the Victorian crisis of faith', in *Religion and Humanism, Studies in Church History*, 17 (Oxford, 1981), pp. 311–24.
O'Day, R., 'Women and Education in Nineteenth-Century England', in J. Bellamy, A. Laurence and G. Perry eds, *Women, Scholarship and Criticism: gender and knowledge, c.1790–1900*, (Manchester, 2000), pp. 91–109.

O'Malley, A., *The Making of the Modern Child: children's literature in the late eighteenth century* (New York, 2003).
Oppenheim, J., *The Other World: spiritualism and psychical research in England, 1850–1914* (Cambridge, 1985).
Østermark-Johansen, L., 'The Matchless Beauty of Widowhood: Vittoria Colonna's reputation in nineteenth-century England', *Art History*, 22 (1999), pp. 270–94.
Parry, J., 'Disraeli and England', *Historical Journal*, 43 (2000), pp. 699–728.
Pearce, S. M., *On Collecting: an investigation into collecting in the European tradition* (London and New York, 1995).
Pearsall, R., *The Worm in the Bud: the world of Victorian sexuality* (London, 1971) [First published 1969].
Pederson, S., 'Hannah More meets Simple Simon: tracts, chapbooks and popular culture in late eighteenth-century England', *Journal of British Studies*, 25 (1986), pp. 84–113.
Perry, G., ed., *Gender and Art* (New Haven and London, 1999).
Piper, D., *The English Face* (London, 1978).
Poovey, M., *The History of the Modern Fact: problems of knowledge in the sciences of wealth and society* (Chicago and London, 1998).
——, *Making a Social Body: British cultural formation, 1830–1864* (Chicago, IL, 1995).
Ramsey, M., *From Gore to Temple. The development of Anglican theology between Lux Mundi and the Second World War, 1889–1939* (London, 1960).
Raven, J., *The Business of Books: booksellers and the English book trade 1450–1850* (New Haven, CT, 2007).
——, 'From Promotion to Proscription: arrangements for reading and eighteenth-century libraries', in J. Raven, H. Small, and N. Tadmor eds, *The Practice and Representation of Reading in England*, (Cambridge, 1996), pp. 175–201.
——, H. Small and N. Tadmor, eds, *The Practice and Representation of Reading in England* (Cambridge, 1996).
Reardon, B. M. G., *Religious Thought in the Victorian Age: a survey from Coleridge to Gore*, 2nd edn (London, 1995).
Reid, P. H., 'The Decline and Fall of the British Country House Library', *Libraries & Culture*, 36 (2001), pp. 345–66.
Reynolds, S., *William Blake Richmond: an artist's life 1842–1921* (Norwich, 1995).
Richardson, A., *Literature, Education, and Romanticism: reading as social practice, 1780–1832* (Cambridge, 1994).
Richmond, C. and P. Smith, eds, *The Self-fashioning of Disraeli, 1818–1851* (Cambridge, 1998).
Rojek, C., *Celebrity* (London, 2001).
Roper, M. and J. Tosh eds, *Manful Assertions: masculinities in Britain since 1800*, (London, 1991).
Rose, J., 'Rereading the English Common Reader: a preface to the history of audiences', *Journal of the History of Ideas*, 53 (1992), pp. 47–70.
——, *The Intellectual Life of the British Working Classes* (New Haven and London, 2001).
Rowell, G., *Hell and the Victorians: a study of the nineteenth century theological controversies concerning eternal punishment and the future life* (Oxford, 1974).

Sanderson, M., *Education, Economic Change, and Society in England, 1780–1870* (Basingstoke, 1991).

Sell, R. D. and P. Verdonk, eds, *Literature and the New Interdisciplinarity: poetics, linguistics, history* (Amsterdam and Atlanta, GA, 1994).

Sharpe, K., *Reading Revolutions: the politics of reading in early modern England* (New Haven and London, 2000).

Shires, L. M., 'The Author as Spectacle and Commodity: Elizabeth Barrett Browning and Thomas Hardy', in *Victorian Literature and the Victorian Visual Imagination*, ed. by C. T. Christ and J. O. Jordan (Berkley, CA, 1995), pp. 198–212.

Simmel, G., 'Sociology of the Senses: visual interaction', in *Introduction to the Science of Sociology* ed. by R. E. Park and E. W. Burgess (Chicago and London, 1969), pp. 356–61.

Simon, R., *The Portrait in Britain and America: with a biographical dictionary of portrait painters 1680–1914* (Boston, MA, 1987).

Sinha, M., '"Chathams, Pitts, and Gladstones in petticoats": the politics of gender and race in the Ilbert bill controversy, 1883–1884', in N. Chaudhuri and M. Strobel eds, *Western Women and Imperialism: complicity and resistance*, (Bloomington, IN, 1992), pp. 98–116.

Smith, L. and J. H. M. Taylor, eds, *Women and the Book: assessing the visual evidence* (London and Toronto, 1997).

Snell, K. D. M., 'The Sunday-School Movement in England and Wales: child labour, denominational control and working-class culture', *Past & Present*, 164 (1999), pp. 122–68.

Snook, E., *Women, Reading and the Cultural Politics of Early Modern England* (Aldershot, 2005).

St Clair, W., *The Reading Nation in the Romantic Period* (Cambridge, 2004).

Stapleton, J., *Political Intellectuals and Public Identities in Britain since 1850* (Manchester and New York, 2001).

Stimpson, F., 'Servants' reading: an examination of the Servants' Library at Cragside', *Library History*, 19 (2003), pp. 3–11.

Sussman, H., *Victorian Masculinities: manhood and masculine poetics in early Victorian literature and art* (Cambridge, 1995).

Sweet, M., *Inventing the Victorians* (London, 2001).

Taylor, A., ed., *Long Overdue: a library reader* (London, 1993).

Tieken-Boon van Ostade, I., 'Eighteenth-century Letters and Journals as Evidence: studying society through the individual', in *Literature and the New Interdisciplinarity*, ed. by R. D. Sell and P. Verdonk (Amsterdam and Atlanta, GA, 1994), pp. 179–91.

Tosh, J., *A Man's Place: masculinity and the middle-class home in Victorian England* (New Haven and London, 1999).

Tristram, P., *Living Space in Fact and Fiction* (London and New York, 1989).

Trodd, C., 'The Laboured Vision and the Realm of Value: articulation of identity in Ford Madox Brown's *Work*', in E. Harding ed., *Re-Framing the Pre-Raphaelites: historical and theoretical essays*, (Aldershot, 1996), pp. 61–80.

Turner, F. M., *Contesting Cultural Authority: essays in Victorian intellectual life* (Cambridge, 1993).

——, *The Greek Heritage in Victorian Britain* (New Haven and London, 1981).

Valman, N., 'Muscular Jews: Young England, gender and Jewishness in Disraeli's "political trilogy"', *Jewish History*, 10 (1996), pp. 57–88.
Vance, N., *The Victorians and Ancient Rome* (Oxford and Cambridge, MA, 1997).
Vernon, J., ed., *Re-reading the Constitution: new narratives in the political history of England's long nineteenth century* (Cambridge, 1996).
Wahrman, D., *Imagining the Middle Class: the political representation of class in Britain, c. 1780–1840* (Cambridge, 1995).
Wainwright, G., ed., *Keeping the Faith: essays to mark the centenary of* Lux mundi (London, 1989).
Walkowitz, J. R., *City of Dreadful Delight: narratives of sexual danger in late Victorian London* (London, 1992).
—— *Prostitution and Victorian Society: women, class and the state* (Cambridge, 1980).
Waller, P. J., *Democracy and Sectarianism: a political and social history of Liverpool 1868–1939* (Liverpool, 1981).
——, *Writers, Readers, and Reputations: literary life in Britain 1870–1918* (Oxford, 2006).
Ward, W. R., 'Oxford and the Origins of Liberal Catholicism in the Church of England', *Studies in Church History*, 1, ed. by C. W. Dugmore and C. Duggan (London, 1964), pp. 233–52.
Wheeler, M., *The Art of Allusion in Victorian Fiction* (London, 1979).
——, *Death and the Future Life in Victorian Literature and Theology* (Cambridge, 1990).
Whyte, W., *Oxford Jackson: architecture, education, status, and style 1835–1924* (Oxford, 2006).
Wilkinson, A., *Christian Socialism: Scott Holland to Tony Blair. The 1998 Scott Holland Lectures* (London, 1998).
Wilson, A. N., *The Victorians* (London, 2002).
Winter, Alison, *Mesmerized: powers of mind in Victorian Britain* (Chicago and London, 1998).
Wohl, A., '"Ben JuJu": representations of Disraeli's Jewishness in the Victorian political cartoon', *Jewish History*, 10 (1996), pp. 89–134.
——, '"Dizzi-Ben-Dizzi": Disraeli as alien', *Journal of British Studies*, 34 (1995), pp. 375–411.
Wolffe, J., *Great Deaths: grieving, religion, and nationhood in Victorian and Edwardian Britain* (Oxford, 2000).
Wood, C., *Victorian Painters. Dictionary of British Art: volume 4*, 2 vols (Woodbridge, 1995).

Theses and unpublished material

Christensen, M. J., 'St Deiniol's Library, Hawarden: the Gladstone national memorial' (unpublished MA thesis, University of Liverpool, 2000).
Clayton, J. D., 'Mr. Gladstone's Leadership of the Parliamentary Liberal Party: 1868–1874' (unpublished D.Phil thesis, University of Oxford, 1961).
Clayton, R., 'Enlarging the text: a cultural history of W. E. Gladstone's library and reading', (unpublished Ph.D. thesis, University of Liverpool, 2003).
d'Haussy, C., 'William Gladstone's Sundays', unpublished paper lent by the author.

Gardner, J., 'William Ewart Gladstone and Christian apologetics, 1859–1896', (unpublished Ph.D. thesis, University of York, 2005).
Hamlett, J. A., 'Materialising Gender: identity and middle-class domestic interiors, 1850–1910' (unpublished Ph.D. thesis, University of London, 2005).
Linkman, A., 'Not Dead but Sleeping: post-mortem photography in nineteenth century Britain', unpublished paper lent by the author.
Shave, A. M., 'Gladstone's Visit to Ireland: October–November 1877' (unpublished MA thesis, University of Liverpool, 2000).

Index

Aberdeen, Lord, *see* Gordon, George Hamilton-
Acton, John Emerich Edward Dalberg, first baron Acton (1834–1902) (historian and friend), 23, 62, 148, 163, 245–6, 250, 257
  library of, 36, 148, 250–1
Adams, James Eli, 201
All Souls College, Oxford, 69, 182
  Codrington library of, 69, 260
Altick, Richard D., 13
Anglicanism, 161–3, 166–8, 186, 238, 279
  liberal, 164, 168, 174
  revival of religious communities within, 180
Anglo-Catholicism, 160, 164, 180
annotation, 16–17, 48, 52, 93
Apjohn, Lewis (biographer), 58
Armitstead, George (1824–1915) (friend), 73, 260–1
Arnold, Matthew (1822–1888) (author and educationalist), 152, 170, 174, 197
  Culture and Anarchy (1869), 152, 277
Athenaeum library, Liverpool, 135
Austin, Edward (1824–70) (priest at Broughton), 113

Bagehot, Walter (1826–1877) (journalist and writer), 200, 205, 232
Bailey, David (Hawarden carpenter and builder), 31, 33, 38, 104
Bailey, Peter, 214, 215
Balmoral (Crown), 72, 123
Beaconsfield, Lord, *see* Disraeli, Benjamin
Bebbington, David, 5–6, 9, 10, 11, 12, 66, 170, 240–1
Benson, Richard Meux (1824–1915) (founder of SSJE), 185

Besant, Annie (*née* Wood) (1847–1933) (theosophist and political activist), 167
Biagini, Eugenio, 7, 214, 215, 241
Biarritz, 73
bibliomania, 83, 148
Bibliothèque Nationale, Paris, 14
Blunt, Wilfrid Scawen (1840–1922) (poet), 252
Bodleian library, Oxford, 14, 37
book history *see* reading, history of
Bradley, William (1801–57) (Manchester portraitist), 194, **195**, 196, **197**, 198, 202–3, 206
Brand, Henry Bouverie William, first Viscount Hampden (1814–1892) (politician and speaker of House of Commons), 212
Bright, John (1811–1889) (politician), 207, 213
Brighton, 73
Brinsley-Richards, James (biographer), 47, 253
British Museum, 135
  library, 14
Broughton, Flintshire, 113
Broughton, Trev Lynn, 111
Brown, Ford Madox (1821–1893) (Pre-Raphaelite artist), 219, 220
Buckley, Flintshire, 149, 150, 154
Butler, Arthur John (biographer), 2, 203, 204, 207
Butler, Joseph (1692–1752) (bishop of Durham and Anglican apologist), 11, 243
  influence on Gladstone, 11, 165, 243, 280
  probabiliorism, 162, 280
Butler, Perry, 10
Butterfield, William (1814–1900) (architect), 160

Campion, W. J. H. (1851–92), 163
Cannes, 73
Canning, Charles John, Earl Canning (1812–1862) and Charlotte (*née* Stuart) (1817–1861), 106
Canning, George (1770–1827) (prime minister and family friend), 91, 105, 106
Canova, Antonio (1757–1822) (sculptor), 194
Carlyle, Thomas (1795–1881) (author and historian), 45, 52, 197, 198, 200, 205, 214, 226, 233
  on heroes and heroism, 198, 215
  Past and Present (1843), 199, 219
Carnarvon, Lord, *see* Herbert, Henry Howard Molyneux
Carnegie, Andrew (1835–1919) (American philanthropist), 245, 251, 276–7
Cavendish, Lucy Caroline (*née* Lyttelton) (1841–1925) (niece by marriage), 72
Chartier, Roger, 13
Chester, 23, 152, 154
Cheyne, Thomas Kelly (1841–1915) (Biblical scholar), 166
Christ Church, Oxford, 26, 92, 163
  library of, 135
  Lux Mundi connections at, 163
  WEG's career at, 94, 199
Church of England, 172, 189, 200, 211
  clergy, 172, 177, 189, 254
  'crisis of faith' within, 139
  disestablishment and, 163, 177
  attitudes to town and country, 175–6
  see also Anglicanism; Anglo-Catholicism; liberal catholicism
Clinton, Henry Pelham Fiennes Pelham-, fourth duke of Newcastle under Lyme (1785–1851) (politician and sponsor), 96
Clinton, Henry Pelham Fiennes Pelham-, fifth duke of Newcastle under Lyme (1811–1864) (friend), 106

Cobbett, William (1763–1835) (political writer), 52–3, 254
Cobden, Richard (1804–1865) (politician), 71, 121
Coleridge, Samuel Taylor (1772–1834) (poet, thinker, and annotator), 194, 200
collectors and collecting, 64
Collini, Stefan, 7, 139, 227
Community of the Resurrection, 180, 181, 182
Crosby, Travis L., 5
Cubitt, Geoffrey, 226
Cuddesdon, Oxon, 69
Currey, William (Bolton photographer), 216–7, 221

Dalmeny House (Rosebery), 23
Danahay, Martin, 111
Darnton, Robert, 13
Davenport Adams, William, 112
Delahay, E. W., 182
Derby, Lord, *see* Stanley, Edward George Geoffrey Smith
Disraeli, Benjamin, earl of Beaconsfield (1804–1881) (author and politician), 203, 204
  historiography, 8, 242
  images of, 9, 106, 209
  'rivalry' with Gladstone, 8
D'Israeli, Isaac (1766–1848) (writer and bibliophile), 83, 84
Döllinger, Ignaz von (1799–1890) (ecclesiastical historian and opponent of papal infallibility), 56, 62, 160, 168, 258
Doyle, John (1797–1868), (caricaturist known as 'H.B.'), 195
Drew, Harry (1856–1910) (son-in-law), 41, 113
Drew, Mary (*née* Gladstone) (1847–1927), 36, 37, 55, 56, 65, 107–8, 109, 112, 115, 116, 133, 134, 139, 142, 156, 157, 183–4, 185–6, 188, 189, 223
Drew Roberts, J., 113
Driver, Samuel Rolles (1846–1914) (Biblical scholar), 166

Dyce, William (1806–64) (German-inspired painter associated with Pre-Raphaelitism), 121, **122**, 273

Eastlake, Charles Locke (1833–1906) (writer and interior designer), 110
Edgeworth, Maria (1768–1849), (novelist and educator), 87, 89, 90
Edinburgh, 51
Eliot, George [Marian Evans] (1819–1880) (author), 140
  Middlemarch (1871–2), 138–9, 140
Emerson, Ralph Waldo (1803–82) (author and Transcendentalist), 193, 226
Emslie, Alfred Edward (1848–1918) (artist), 223
Eton College, 26–7, 51, 61, 85, 89, 90–1, 92, 196, 198
  tradition of 'leaving books' at, 247
  WEG's studies at, 46–7, 90, 92–3, 94, 246–7
Ewing Ritchie, J. (biographer), 63, 68, 156

Farquhar, Caroline, 51
Fasque House, Kincardineshire (Gladstone), 30, 69, 96–100
  library, 98–9, 104, **105**
  St Andrew's Episcopal church at, 98–100
  WEG's desire to inherit, 31
  WEG's self-education at, 96–7
Flint, Kate, 110, 112
Friederichs, Hulda (1856/7–1927) (journalist), 2, 17, 133, 156, 176, 179, 188, 224

Gardiner, John, 4
Garnett, Jane, 11
Gere, John, 117
Girouard, Mark, 83, 84, 110–111
Gladstone, Agnes (1842–1931) (daughter), 70, 106, 109
Gladstone, Anne Mackenzie (1802–28) (sister), 64, 85, 86, 87, 88

Gladstone, Anne Robertson (1773–1835) (mother), 64, 82, 84–85, 86–7, 89, 90, 97–100, 125
  evangelical Christian influence, 86
  'hidden' letters from, 94
  images of, **98–100**
  influence over WEG's priestly vocation, 94–6
  influence over WEG's reading, 93
  relationship with the Clapham Sect, 24, 86–7, 88
Gladstone, Catherine (*née* Glynne) (1812–1900) (wife and philanthropist), 23, 30, 56, 64–66, 70, 106, 109, 115, 139, 210, 212, **218**
Gladstone, Catherine Jessy (1845–50) (daughter), 70
Gladstone family, 81
Gladstone, Helen (1849–1925) (daughter and educator), 38, 112, 115
Gladstone, Helen Jane (1814–80) (sister), 64, 81, **82**, 84, 85, 86, 87, 88, 265
Gladstone, Henry Neville, Baron Gladstone of Hawarden (1852–1935) (son and businessman), 37, 248
Gladstone, Herbert John, Viscount Gladstone (1854–1930) (son and politician), 164, 248
Gladstone, John, first baronet (1764–1851) (father), 30, 31, 82, 83, 84, 89–90, 96, 98–100, 106, 267
  autodidacticism and attitude to education, 90–1, 246
  bibliographical advice and help from WEG, 26, 85, 264
  images of, **98–100**
  influence on WEG's political vocation, 94–6
  national identity, 90, 96
  as patriarch, 90–2, 94, 98
Gladstone, John (cousin), 267
Gladstone, John Neilson (1807–63) (brother), 44, 73, 85, 92

Gladstone, Mary *see* Drew, Mary
Gladstone, Robertson (1805–75) (brother), 85, 92
Gladstone, Stephen Edward (1844–1920) (son and Anglican clergyman), 31, 37, 41, 113, 119, 166, 182
Gladstone, Thomas (1804–89) (brother), 31, 73, 85–6, 90–2, 98, 105, 266
Gladstone, William Ewart (1809–98)
annotation, 15–17, 46, 48–54, 157, 165, 169, 171, 215, 253; fly-leaf inscriptions, 28, 46, 52, 141; Gladstone's code, 16, 17, 48–51, 97, 152; indexing, 48, 53, 254; of maps, 75; marginalia, 48, 51, 152, 198; miscellaneous jottings, 53–4, 254–5; in school books, 93
art collection, 102–3, 105–6, 117
autobiographica, 17, 23–4, 69, 245–6
autodidacticism, 96–7
books and: binding, 27, 63, 151; borrowing, 124; collecting, 14, 18, 24–27, 128, 134, 135, 137, 148, 149, 151, 246; as friends, 48, 104, 134; as gifts, 24, 27, 34–5, 42, 62, 92, 119–120, 174, 123, 150, 247, 273; marks of ownership, 27–8, 247–8; as moral agents, 146; plans for dispersal of, 36–7; purchasing for others, 92, 93, 264; reflective of owner's mind and development, 88, 103–4; relationships with booksellers, 25–26, 44, 135, 137; rotation of, 54–56, 235; second-hand purchases, 24, 26, 125; travelling library of, 74, 76
conservatism and, 194, 199, 200
as correspondent, 59, 62, 63, 85, 89, 90, 93–4, 246–7, 256, 267
death, 228–232, 294
as diarist, 5, 14–15, 49, 51, 68, 73, 87, 119, 125, 163, 166
Downing Street 'breakfasts', 61, 62, 63–4

education and, 209–210, 211, 226, 227; favours interdisciplinarity, 162, 168, 177–8
empire and, 78, 222
epistemological ideas, 42, 45, 46, 126, 128, 134, 135, 141, 237–9
family life and relationships, 90, 94, 236, 246–7, 267
as historian, 9, 17, 19, 52, 78, 93, 137, 141, 142–3, 144–5, 146–7, 153–4, 169, 211, 226, 236, 254
historiography of, 4, 5–13, 119, 211, 214, 238, 242
holidays and foreign travel, 24–5, 70–8; cruises, 73, 115; grand tour (1832), 44, 59, 73, 74–7, 92, 136–7; as linguist, 74–5; southern Italy and Sicily (1838), 73, 74, 77; travel writing, 73, 75
Homeric study and classical influences, 6, 9, 69, 72, 77–8, 171–2, 200, 205, 207, 209, 210, 211, 235, 262
images of, 9, 81, **82**, 152, 186, **187**, 188, 194, **195, 196, 197**, 201, **202**, 203, 204–5, 207, 209, **210**, 213, **216–222**, 223–4, **225**, 228–9, **230**: issues of gender and, 195, 196, 201, 205, 215, 239; relationships with photographers and artists, 72, 216–7, 221, 223–6
important concepts for: divine learning, 11, 19, 156, 181, 184, 188, 238, 287; divinity, 19, 40, 158, 172; humanity, 11, 19, 40, 117, 131–158, 170–2, 214, 227, 236, 239; independence, 213, 214, 226, 231, 233; unity (monad), 150, 151, 155, 169, 239, 295
intertextuality and, 171–2, 235, 294
liberalism and, 133, 136, 144, 147, 149, 156, 157, 188, 212, 224, 228, 231–2, 233
as librarian, 19, 26, 29, 31, 34, 38, 50, 54, 84, 85, 88, 102, 104, 107, 134, 151, 152–3, 211, 237, 269;

bibliographical advice offered by, 104; bookshelf design, 27, 33, 34, 37 (for Bodleian), 38, 102, 104, 247, 250, 268 (heights recorded on); borrowing registers of, 108 ff; cataloguing, 27–8, 29, 30–1, 33, 103, 248, 249; classification, 28–29, 33, 38, 40 (SDL), 103–4, 142; library design, 104–5

libraries and, 135; estimation of their value and function, 135, 141, 146, 154; public library movement, 148, 150, 151, 154, 157; support of and gifts of books to, 142, 211, 275; visits to and use of, 135–8

literary scholarship, reviewing, and relationships with publishers, 9, 19, 34–5, 46, 53, 63, 73, 120–123, 139, 141, 143–145, 170–1, 173–4, 203–4, 218–9

masculinity and manliness of, 198, 199, 201, 204, 205, 214, 215, 226, 233

memoranda, 50, 117–118, 126, 174, 177, 246, 287

national identity and, 86, 237, 294

publications: *The Bulgarian Horrors and the Question of the East* (1876), 212; *Church Principles* (1840), 161, 200; *Gleanings*, 174; *The Impregnable Rock of Holy Scripture* (1890), 166; 'On Books and the Housing of Them' (1890), 26, 40, 151, *The State in its Relations with the Church* (1838), 64, 69, 199–200; *Studies on Homer and the Homeric Age* (1858), 206; 'Universitas Hominum, or, the Unity of History' (1887), 169, 226

political vocation and career, 51, 54, 57, 59, 69, 71, 72, 95–6, 97, 138, 143–8, 193, 194, 196, 198, 200, 201, 202, 204, 206, 209, 210–211, 212, 213, 214, 227, 233, 236, 292; 'Bulgarian Horrors' campaign, 5, 211–214, 227, 238; Irish Home Rule, 5, 60, 144, 145, 146, 149, 152, 156, 227; Midlothian campaigns, 55, 152, 213, 214; removal of 'taxes on knowledge', 150, 154–5, 277

pornography and, 15, 69, 102, 124–126, 260

the press and, 59

private and political papers, 35–6

public persona and reception, 56, 72, 133, 152, 156, 190, 193–233, 237; 'People's William', 206–9, 227–8

reading: advice about, 63, 145–156; aloud and in company, 55, 61, 68, 120–124, 236; as a bachelor, 64; being read to, 60; by candlelight, 58, 61, 256; with CG, 65–6; critical character of, 51, 53, 152, 203–4; contemporary descriptions of, 1–2, 4, 45–7, 54–60, 62, 66, 67–8, 133, 193, 205, 222–3; of Dante, 50–1, 62, 77, 97, 117, 203–4, 235; effect on family of, 36, 55–6; of Eliot, 138–9; engagement with other readers, 35, 64, 236; 'five-minute', 55–6; health and, 23, 32, 47, 60–1, 66, 71, 97, 109, 126, 207, 255, 258, 261; on holiday, 70–2, 74, 207–8; identification with, 171; on journeys, 44, 64, 76, 236, 261; in other libraries and reading rooms, 74, 261; of literature, 54–55, 58, 72, 115, 120, 124, 138–144, 148, 238, 252, 255; of Locke, 50–1; memory and, 47, 74; methods, practices and rules, 1, 18, 45–54, 82, 125, 234–5; moral purposes of, 97, 99–100, 117, 124–6, 128, 134, 139, 234; newspapers, 58–60; notes and epitomes, 46, 50, 51; of Peacock, 141; philanthropic, 119; importance of 'place' in, 68–78; poetry, 47, 76, 77; reactions to, 3, 8, 193–233;

romanticism of, 202;
relationships forged through,
  45, 61–6, 88, 101, 115, 123–4,
  234; religious and biblical, 65–6,
  67, 93, 119, 165–172, 211, 219,
  235; re-reading, 46, 47–8, 53; as
  research, 46, 235, 253; rhythms,
  18, 54–78, 235; of Scott, 60, 70,
  72, 93, 142–3, 235, 266; self-
  consciousness as 53, 223;
  significance of, 3, 234–9; speed
  of, 45–6, 253; as stress relief, 30,
  68, 87, 88, 237, 239; on
  Sundays, 66–8, 93, 258; of
  Tennyson, 47, 61, 62, 120–123,
  128, 143–145, 235, 272, 276;
  timetables and lists of, 45, 46,
  47, 51, 59, 61, 74, 97; travel
  writing, 75–6; of Ward,
  139–141, 173–4, 284
religion and: 9 ff, 135, 205;
  doctrinal views, 167; ecumenism,
  162, 168, 177, 282; incarnational
  theology and, 165, 170; as a
  liberal catholic, 10–11, 19, 177,
  179, 183, 186, 189, 238;
  Olympian, 169, 235; attitude to
  the religious life, 181, 185, 286;
  providentialism and assurance,
  214, 236; religious practice, 49,
  57, 66–7, 74–5, 115, 136;
  Sabbath observance, 66–7;
  St Deiniol's and, 37, 134,
  159–190; spiritual crisis (1850–1),
  11, 170; attitude to spiritualism
  and unorthodox belief, 35, 68,
  178, 238, 250; theological
  development, 10, 69, 159, 165,
  186, 237–8, 266; theological,
  ecclesiastical, and homiletic
  writings, 11, 66–7, 138, 160,
  199–200, 209, 210, 211, 212,
  236; vocation, 94–6, 198, 210,
  212, 213, 236
rescue work, 14, 102, 117–124; 'the
  declaration', 119; reading with
  rescue cases, 15, 18, 68, 117,
  119–124; the Wright Case (1927),
  119, 272

residences: the Albany, 29; 6 Carlton
  Gardens, 117, 248, 272; 11
  Carlton House Terrace, 33, 209; 13
  Carlton House Terrace, 30, 66
retirement and, 7, 30, 33, 34, 133,
  200–1, 202, 207, 209–212, 214,
  218, 225, 228, 233, 237, 289,
  291; 1875 art and book sale,
  33–4, 189, 209, 249
as scholar-politician, 19, 127, 138,
  139, 141, 193, 194, 196, 203–6,
  236, 237
speeches and speechmaking, 142,
  146, 147, 148–9, 152, 153,
  161–2, 165, 168, 176, 186,
  206–7, 211, 236, 278
as teacher, 71, 81, 89, 112, 114,
  267
women and, 64–66, 117 ff
wood cutting and, 213, 215–221,
  232
working classes and, 132, 149–156,
  227, 228, 231–2, 278: their
  'mental culture', 116, 142,
  148–156; servants, 114, 124, 127,
  271
Gladstone, William Henry (1840–91)
  (son), 31, 37, 71, 106, 144, 215,
  216
Glenalmond College, Perthshire, 176,
  177, 202, 281
Glyn, George Grenfell, 2nd baron
  Wolverton (1824–87), 33–4, 148,
  211, 247, 249–250
Glynne, Catherine *see* Gladstone,
  Catherine
Glynne, Henry (brother-in-law), 113
Glynne, Mary *see* Lyttelton, Mary
Glynne, Stephen (1807–1874)
  (brother-in-law and antiquarian),
  30, 31, 70
Gordon, Arthur Charles Hamilton,
  first Baron Stanmore
  (1829–1912) (politician and
  colonial governor), 132, 177
Gordon, George Hamilton-, fourth
  earl of Aberdeen (1784–1860)
  (prime minister and scholar-
  politician), 97

Gordon, Ishbel Maria (*née* Marjoribanks), marchioness of Aberdeen and Temair (1857–1939), 111
Gore, Charles (1853–1932), 12, 163, 164, 165–8, 174–5, 177–8, 188
  and Community of the Resurrection, 180, 181, 182
  contribution to *Lux Mundi*, 165–6
  kenotic theology, 169–70, 282–3
  publications: *The Ministry of the Christian Church* (1888), 174; *The Mission of the Church* (1892), 166–8, 177
  views on St Deiniol's, 174–5, 176, 182
Gower, Harriet Elizabeth Georgiana Leveson- (*née* Howard), duchess of Sutherland (1806–1868), 106
Great Exhibition (1851), 117
Green, Thomas Hill (1836–1882) (philosopher), 174

Hagley Hall, Worcestershire (Lyttelton), 70
Hall, Sydney Prior (1842–1922) (artist), 219–221, 229
Hallam, Arthur Henry (1811–1833) (school friend and poet), 27, 46, 61–2, 120
Hallam, Henry (1777–1859) (historian), 27, 46–7
Hamilton, Edward Walter (1847–1908) (private secretary and diarist), 45–6, 51
Hamilton, John McClure (1853–1936) (artist), 221–224, **222**, 224
Harcourt, Sir William George Granville Venables Vernon (1827–1904) (politician), 210
Hargreaves, Thomas (artist), 81, 88
Harrison, Frederic (1831–1923) (author), 199
Hawarden, 70, 71, 179, 212, 215, 224
  Castle, 15, 30, 31, 36, 40, 42, 58, 59, 67, 70, 101, 111, 121, 204, 209, **218**, 231, 233; Glynne library, 30, 31, 104, 106–7, **106**, 107, 268; servant readers at, 114–116, 271; visitors to, 132, 215–6, 231, 233, 238
  institute, 116, 142, 150, 151, 155
  parish church of St Deiniol, 57, 131, 156, **219**, 229
  as site of St Deiniol's library, 175–7, 181
  village, 37, 57, 131, 142, 155, 231: readers from, 112, 116, 133; tourists in, 131, 215–6
Haweis, Mary (1848–1898), 110
Headlam, Arthur Cayley (1862–1947) (Anglican clergyman), 182–3
Hearn, Jeff, 204, 218, 293
Herbert, Henry Howard Molyneux, fourth earl of Carnarvon (1831–1890) (scholar-politician), 203
Hill, Frank Harrison (1830–1910) (journalist), 223
Hilton, Boyd, 10
Hoggart, Richard, 13
Holland, Henry Scott (1847–1918) (theologian), 163, 165, 182
Houghton, William (admirer), 215–6, 218
House of Commons (library of), 135
Hughenden Manor, Buckinghamshire (Disraeli), 203
Hume, David (1711–1776) (philosopher), 162
Humphreys, Mr (supplier of 'tin tabernacle'), 38

Illingworth, J. R. (1848–1915), 163
intellectuals and intellectuality, 197–9, 205, 212–3, 227, 291
Ireland
  Home Rule for, 33, 176, 227, 228, 233, 237
  taxes on knowledge and, 155
Isba, Anne, 64, 112

Jackson, H. J., 16, 17, 245
Jacobson, William (1803–1884) (bishop of Chester), 110, 111
Jagger, Peter J., 6, 7, 10
Jenkins, Roy, 5, 6, 64

Jones, Thomas, 16
Jowett, Benjamin (1817–1893) (scholar, theologian, and master of Balliol), 69, 279
Joyce, Gilbert Cunningham (1866–1942) (first warden of SDL; later bishop of Monmouth), 42, 183, 185, 252, 287

Keble College, Oxford, 70, 159–163, 186, 279
  The Light of the World (Holman Hunt, 1853), 186
  WEG's visits to, 160–1, 168, 173–4
Keble, John (1792–1866) (Anglican clergyman and poet), 160, 161
Kerr, Robert (1823–1904) (architect), 110, 111

Lacaita, James (1813–95) (scholar-politician and friend), 108, 269
Legg, Marie-Louise, 154–5
Leibnitz, G. W. von (1646–1716) (philosopher), 295
Lewis, Sir George Cornewall, (1806–1863) (scholar-politician), 289
liberal catholicism, 10–11, 169, 180, 182, 184, 185, 186, 188, 238, 239
Liberty, Stephen (sub-warden of SDL), 184–5, 189
libraries, 14
  fictional, 138, 140
  gender and, 99, 110–113
  history, 82–3, 104–5, 108–9, 110–111, 148
Liddon, Henry Parry (1829–1890) (Anglican clergyman and theologian), 160, 166, 172
Liddon House, 172
Liverpool, 23, 81, 149, 168
  libraries, 83, 135
  1 Rodney Street (Gladstone), 84
  WEG's relationship with and attitude towards, 161–2, 175–6
Lock, Walter (1846–1933) (sub-warden of Keble College), 163, 182
Locke, John (1807–74) (philosopher and educationalist), 82

London, 33, 51, 57, 70, 71, 121–122, 224, 229
  library, 135
Lowe, Robert, Viscount Sherbrooke (1811–1892) (scholar-politician), 207
Lucas, John (1807–1874) (portraitist), 201, **202**
Lucy, Henry (1843–1924) (journalist), 71
Lux Mundi (1889), 163
Lux Mundi group, 12, 19, 163–5, 177, 238
  incarnational theology and, 164
  influence on SDL foundation, 172, 238
Lynch, Michael, 6
Lyttelton, Arthur (1852–1903) (nephew), 163
Lyttelton, George William, fourth Baron Lyttelton and fourth Baron Westcote (1817–1876) (brother-in-law), 56
Lyttelton, Mary (*née* Glynne) (sister-in-law), 56, 70
Lyttelton, Lavinia *see* Talbot, Lavinia
Lyttelton, Meriel (niece), 164

Macaulay, Thomas Babington, Baron Macaulay (1800–1859) (historian, critic, and poet), 146, 200, 232
McKelvy, William R., 6, 241
Magnus, Philip, 7, 11
Manning, Henry Edward (1808–1892) (Roman Catholic convert and cardinal-archibishop of Westminster), 165, 212
marginalia *see* annotation
Matthew, Colin, 5, 6, 14, 15, 33, 49, 59, 97, 117, 125, 155, 186, 194, 199, 200, 207, 209, 213, 214
men of letters, 197, 198–9, 205, 226, 288
Millais, John Everett, first baronet (1829–1896) (Pre-Raphaelite artist and portraitist), 229
Moberley, R. C. (1845–1903), 163
Montaigne, Michel de (1533–92) (writer), 52

Moore, Aubrey Lackington (1848–90) (Anglican clergyman and theologian), 163, 164, 281
More, Hannah (1745–1833) (evangelical writer and family friend), 24, 42, 87
Sacred Dramas (1782), 24, 43, 87
WEG's reading of, 87, 89
Morley, John, Viscount Morley of Blackburn (1838–1923) (liberal politician and official biographer), 2, 40, 193, 251
Munro, Alexander (1825–71), (Pre-Raphaelite sculptor and Gladstone protégé), 98–100, 117, **118**
Murray, James (1837–1915) (founder of the *OED*), 274

National Liberal Club library, 146, 148
National Portrait Gallery, London, 201, 205
Newark-on-Trent, Nottinghamshire, 199
Newcastle under Lyme, 4th duke of, *see* Clinton, Henry Pelham Fiennes Pelham-
Newcastle under Lyme, 5th duke of, *see* Clinton, Henry Pelham Fiennes Pelham-
Newman, John Henry (1801–1890) (theologian, Roman Catholic convert, and cardinal), 161, 213
Nicholson, Edward Williams Byron (1849–1912) (librarian), 37
Nixon, Mark, 12
Northcote, Stafford Henry, first earl of Iddesleigh (1818–1887) (politician), 203
Novikov, Olga (1840–1925) (Russian 'spy' and acquaintance), 273

Ottley, Edward Bickersteth (1853–1910) (Hawarden curate), 113, 280–1
Ottley, R. L. (1856–1933), 163
Oxford, 37, 69–70, 117, 159–190, 199–200, 226, 232–3, 259
influence on foundation of St Deiniol's, 69, 70, 172
libraries of, 135, 211, 275
religious communities in, 180, 181
University museum, 162
WEG's final message to, 259
WEG's reading practices at, 46, 47, 57–8, 59, 96, 165–6, 238
Oxford Movement, *see* Tractarianism

Page, R. L. (SSJE), 181
Paget, Francis (1851–1911), 163
Panizzi, Antonio (1797–1879) (librarian), 62, 257
Parnell, Charles Stewart (1846–1891) (politician and Home Ruler), 38
Parry, J. P., 10
Partridge, Michael, 7
Peacock, Thomas Love (1785–1866) (satirical novelist), 141
Pearce, Susan, 64
Peel, Arthur (1829–1912) (speaker of House of Commons), 212
Peel, Robert, second baronet (1788–1850) (prime minister and political mentor), 51, 195, **196**, 200, 201
portrait collection, 201, 289
Penmaenmawr, Conwy, 69, 70–2, 121–122, 209, 260
Petz (reading companion), 40, 108
Phillimore, Walter George Frank, first Baron Phillimore (1845–1929) (lawyer and friend), 62
Phillips, Claude (1846–1924) (art critic), 205
photography, 107, 195, 216–218, 222, 229
portraiture, 194–6, 201, 204–5, 219–224
Potter, George (biographer), 57
Powell, John, 15, 16
Pratt, Edwin (CG's biographer), 65
Primrose, Archibald Philip, fifth earl of Rosebery and first earl of Midlothian (1847–1929) (prime minster), 23, 38, 45, 207
Prince Albert of Saxe-Coburg and Gotha (1819–1861) (prince consort), 144

Prince Albert Edward of Wales (1841–1910) (later Edward VII), 145–6
Pritchard, T. W., 6, 172
Pusey, Edward Bouverie (1800–1882) (Anglican clergyman and scholar), 160, 161, 166, 172, 184
Pusey House, Oxford, 163, 166, 172, 174, 182

Quaritch, Bernard (1819–95) (bookseller and friend), 24, 43, 151, 246
Queen Victoria (1819–1901), 106, 145–6

Ramsey, Michael, 164
Ratcliffe, Frederick W., 6
Reading
  advice on, 91–2, 104
  bibliomania, 83, 104
  children's, 81, 82, 84, 87, 89, 93
  gender and, 89, 112, 288
  history of, 13, 53, 55, 82, 94, 149–50, 225
  reader-response theory, 4, 244
Rendel, Stuart (1834–1913) (politician and friend), 73, 260–1
Reynolds, K. D., 115
Ribblesdale, Charlotte (née Tennant) (1858–1911), 40–1, 132, 175
Richmond, William Blake (1842–1921) (artist), 228–9, 294
Rio, Alexandre François (1797–1874) (art historian and Roman Catholic thinker), 74, 261
Robertson, J. R. (biographer), 199
Roman Catholicism, 11, 88 (HJG's conversion), 257, 280 (probablism)
romanticism, 194
Rosebery, Lord, *see* Primrose, Archibald Philip
Royal Academy, London, 201, 203
Runcie, Robert, 101
Russell, George William Erskine (1853–1919) (colleague and biographer), 172, 181–2, 218

Russell, John, first Earl Russell (1792–1878) (prime minister), 203–4
Ruskin, John (1819–1900) (artist and critic), 107

St Asaph, Denbighshire, 166, 188
St Deiniol's Library, 1, 2, 37–43, 133, 134, **179**, 223, **239**
  Castle section, 42, 133, 252
  collection, 15, 24, 55, 60, 132, 157, 179, 180, **187**, 252
  Dalmeny memorandum, 38, 42, 251
  donations to, 132, 252
  foundation, 7, 17, 19, 37–43, 63, 103, 131–2, 156, 159, 172, 175–7, 181–3, 251, 284–5
  hostel, 178, 179, **180**
  Keble memorandum, 174, 177, 180, 189, 252, 287
  layout and classification, 178–9
  Lux Mundi group's influence upon, 12, 113, 238
  as memorial to Gladstone, 1, 6, 40, 101, 133, 157, 172–3, 188
  purposes of, 132, 156, 159, 176, 180, 183–6, 188, 287
  religious communities and, 180–3
  'tin tabernacle', 38, **39**, 40–1, 58, 131–2, 158
  Trust arrangements, 41–2, 172
  WEG's search for a warden for, 182–3, 252, 286
Saltney, Flintshire, 153, 155
scholars and scholarship, 197, 199–200, 237
Schlüter, Auguste (1849–1917) (maid-housekeeper and diarist), 57, 68, 112, 114–116, 271
Scotland, 23, 51, 57, 81, 96, 214
Scott, George Gilbert (1811–1878) (architect)
Scott, Walter (1771–1832) (poet and novelist), 55, 92, 93, 142
Seaforth House, Liverpool (Gladstone), 29, 36, 84, 86, 87, 90
  servants' library at, 84–5, 114
  WEG's reading at, 84–6

Seeley, John Robert (1834–1895) (historian and religious writer), WEG's reading and review of *Ecce Homo* (1866), 170–2, 238, 283
servants,
  libraries and reading, 84–5, 114–117, 271
Shannon, Richard, 7, 11, 138, 173, 174, 186, 209
Smalley, George (biographer), 55
Smith, John G. (biographer), 4
Society of St John the Evangelist (SSJE), 181, 185, 286
Spencer, J. H. (Chester photographer), 229
spiritualism, 178
Stanhope, Philip Henry, fifth Earl Stanhope (1805–1875), 207
Stanley, Edward George Geoffrey Smith, fourteenth earl of Derby (1799–1869), (prime minster and classicist), 203
Starke, Marianna (1761/2–1838) (travel writer), 75–6
Stead, W. T. (1849–1912) (journalist and editor), 48, 54, 57, 59, 63, 228
Story, J. C. (biographer), 133, 156, 178, 238
Summerhayes, Marion (rescue case), 121–123, **122**
Sutherland, Harriet, duchess of *see* Gower, Harriet Elizabeth Georgiana Leveson-

Talbot, Edward Stuart (1844–1934) (nephew by marriage, theologian, and warden of Keble), 70, 113, 160, 163–4, 165, 168–70, 174–5, 260
  contribution to *Lux Mundi*, 169–70
  views on St Deiniol's, 174–5, 176, 182
Talbot, Lavinia (*née* Lyttelton) (1849–1939), 70, 109, 160
Talbot, William Henry Fox (1800–1877) (photography pioneer), 222–3

Temple of Peace, 18, 31–33, **32**, 42, 46, 57, 101–104, 119, 211, 227, 233
  CG's use of, 65, 102, 109–110, 111, 116
  'Chapel of Ease', 250
  class and, 114, 152
  clerical use of, 113
  layout of, 102–3, **103**, 105–6
  as lending library, 101–102, 108 ff, 127, 148, 152–3, 189, 237
  named after Vespasian's *Templum Pacis*, 32, 249
  the Octagon, 36
  plan for a crypt, 33
  as public space, 108, 127, 237
  St Deiniol's as successor to, 176
  WEG's lying-in-state in, 43, 228–232, **230**, 237
  WEG reading in, 58, 107–8, **220–222**, 224–6, **225**
  women in, 106, 111–112
Temple, Frederick (1821–1902) (archbishop of Canterbury), 160, 279
Tenniel, John (1820–1914) (caricaturist), 209
Tennyson, Alfred, first Baron Tennyson (1809–1892) (poet), 47, 120, 142, 170, 283
  political activities, 143–4
  publications: *Idylls of the King*, 47, 120–1, 143, 272; *In Memoriam*, 123; *Locksley Hall* and *Locksley Hall Sixty Years After*, 144; *Maud*, 143, 276; *The Princess*, 122
Thistlethwayte, Laura (*née* Bell) (1831?–1894), 68, 123–124, 273
  autobiography, 123, 273
  Woodbine Cottage, 124
Tractarianism, 11, 69, 161, 164, 166, 172, 186
Tristram, Philippa, 111
Troubetskoi, Pierre (artist), 223, 224
Turner, Frank, 12
Turner, J. M. (WEG's pre-Oxford tutor), 94

Waddesdon Manor, Buckinghamshire (Rothschild), 109, 111
Wales, 57, 177, 238, 294
  Anglican church in, 177
Walker, William (engraver), 202–3
Ward, Mary Augusta (*née* Arnold; known as Mrs Humphry Ward) (1851–1920) (author), 139–140, 173–4
  Robert Elsmere (1888), 139–141, 173–4
Watts, George Frederic (1813–1904) (artist), 204–5
West, Algernon Edward (1832–1921) (secretary, biographer and diarist), 58, 159, 203
West, Jenny, 64, 123, 124
Wemyss Reid, Thomas (1842–1905) (biographer), 32, 45, 46, 57, 63, 67, 106–7, 108
Whyte, William, 160
Wickham, Edward Charles (1834–1910) (son-in-law and dean of Lincoln), 113
Wilberforce, William (1759–1833), 86
Williamson, David (biographer), 4, 35, 54, 178
Wolverton, Lord *see* Glyn, George Grenfell
Woodward, Arthur (biographer), 46